Effective
BUSINESS
REPORT
WRITING

Effective

BUSINESS REPORT WRITING

LELAND BROWN
School of Business Administration
Tulane University

Englewood Cliffs, N. J.
PRENTICE-HALL, INC.
1955

Library of Congress
Catalog Card No.: 55–10579

PRINTED IN THE UNITED STATES OF AMERICA

24163

To My Wife

Hilda Lee Heatwole Brown

Preface

Writers of reports today are more than mere recorders and interpreters of information and statistics. They are also originators of significant changes that may affect the operation of a company and the lives of many people. The ability to construct a satisfactory report requires more than a mastery and application of rhetorical principles. The writer must have a clear understanding of the character of the report, its purpose and its relation to the conditions from which it arises.

This is a book on business report writing; the emphasis is on *writing.* Since there is only one way to learn to write – by writing – it is up to the reader to put into practice the principles and techniques discussed here in his own writing of reports.

Report form is a means to an end, not an end in itself. Each report differs from other reports because each has a specific message with a definite business purpose for a particular reader. Therefore *Effective Business Report Writing* reflects current business practice, systematized wherever possible. It also recognizes the wide range of form and usage possible and desirable in establishing effective communication of pertinent material through the medium of business reports.

The book will prove helpful both to the businessman who writes or uses reports in his company and to the reader who is looking for the best method of learning to construct reports. The book has four major divisions – Part I discusses the importance and use of business reports; Part II deals with the preparation of reports; Part III takes up the writing of the report; and Part IV is concerned with application of these principles and practices to the various types of report.

Not every reader will want to make use of the book in the same fashion. It has been organized for flexibility of use, and several suggested outlines for study are included in the appendix. The

Practical Suggestions of Appendix D should serve as a ready guide for report writers; there is also a selective bibliography.

I am grateful to all those who have helped in the preparation of this book. Professor Richard C. Gerfen, Northwestern University; Professor Erwin M. Keithley, University of California; and Professor William P. Boyd, University of Texas, reviewed the manuscript and offered helpful suggestions for revision. Dean Robert W. French of the School of Business Administration at Tulane offered his encouragement and assistance. Charles J. Grayson, Jr., Tulane University Development Office, has written Chapter 20. Mrs. Oran Marcoux, assistant librarian, and Dr. Elsie M. Watters, assistant professor of statistics in the Tulane School of Business Administration, offered suggestions for Chapters 4 and 11, respectively. Mrs. Emily G. Brett, Mrs. Mary Faulk, Miss Elise Gifford, Mrs. Anna P. Robin and Mrs. Mildred Miller typed the manuscript. My wife contributed encouragement, patience and hours of hard work in assisting with the book.

In addition, many people and companies contributed illustrative material and comments. Among them are former students: Wilton Arceneaux, Alfred W. Brown, Jr., Frank C. Buckley, Albert Caproni, Jr., Charles J. Cater, Jr., William D. Evans, James C. Faust, John E. Herman, Leslie C. Laguillon, Louis J. Lanza, L. Marshall LaPoutge, Lee Levy, Thayer T. May, Jr., Benjamin H. McBeth, Arthur J. Naquin, III, Henry Riecke, III, Santos Soto, John W. Wall, Eben T. Watkins, III, S. Conrad Weil, Jr.

Among the businessmen and companies are: Paul L. Smith, Acme Shear Co., Bridgeport, Conn.; Chester R. Anderson, American Business Writing Assn., Urbana, Ill.; C. Stuart Hall, American Can Co., New York; The American Sugar Refining Co., New York; American Wire and Steel Co., Cleveland; The Audiphone Co., New Orleans; Audubon Ice Co., New Orleans; Bankers Trust Co., New York; *Boys' Life,* New York; Brown's Velvet Ice Cream, Inc., New Orleans; Caterpillar Tractor Co., Peoria, Ill.; CBS Television, New York; The Champion Paper and Fibre Co., Hamilton, Ohio; *Collegiate News and Views,* Cincinnati; Continental Can Co., Inc., New York; Dell Publishing Co., Inc., New York; Dixie Drive It Yourself, New Orleans; A. M. Sullivan, Dun & Bradstreet, Inc., New York; Robert E. Curtin, Jr., E. I. duPont De Nemours & Co., Wilmington, Del.; Eastman Kodak Co., Rochester, N. Y.; The Franklin Life Insurance Co., Springfield, Ill.; Goeffry S. Smith, Girard Trust Corn Exchange

Bank, Philadelphia; General Foods Corp., New York; General Motors Corp., New York; *The Indianapolis Star and News,* Indianapolis; J. Kenton Eisenbrey, Insurance Company of North America, Philadelphia; William A. Hanaway, International Paper Co., New York; Jefferson Lake Sulphur Co., New Orleans; Lever Brothers Co., New York; Link-Belt Co., Chicago; Lee McCroklin, Louisiana Power and Light Co., New Orleans; Lykes Brothers Steamship Co., New Orleans; Monsanto Chemical Co., St. Louis; Nash-Kelvinator Corp., Detroit; National Biscuit Co., New York; National Industrial Conference Board, Inc., New York; Hubert Fielder, New Orleans Charga-Plate Association, New Orleans; The Parker Pen Co., Janesville, Wis.; *Printers' Ink,* New York; Republic Steel Corp., Youngstown, Ohio; Charles B. Wade, Jr., R. J. Reynolds Tobacco Co., Winston-Salem; Charles Sparks, Richardson, Bellows, Henry and Co., New Orleans; Royal Supply Co., New Orleans; Scott Paper Co., Chester, Pennsylvania; Sears, Roebuck and Co., Chicago; Shell Oil Co., New York; Southern Bell Telephone and Telegraph Co., Atlanta; Standard Oil Company of California, San Francisco; C. E. Springhorn, Standard Oil Company of New Jersey, New York; Stanolind Oil and Gas Co., Tulsa; State Mutual Life Assurance Co., Worcester, Mass.; D. C. Burkholder, Swift & Co., Chicago; U-Drive It Car Co., New Orleans; Union Oil Company of California, Los Angeles; United States Steel Corp., New York; Wellan's, Alexandria, La.; Westinghouse Electric Corp., Pittsburgh; William D. Carleton, Wyatt-Cornick, Inc., Richmond, Va.

LELAND BROWN

Contents

Part I

EFFECTIVE COMMUNICATION THROUGH BUSINESS REPORTS

CHAPTER *1*

The Need for Effective Business Reports

THE NEED FOR REPORTS IN BUSINESS
DEFINITION AND NATURE OF BUSINESS REPORTS
FUNCTIONS OF REPORTS

WHY THE CURRENT EMPHASIS ON BUSINESS REPORTS? Is it much ado about nothing?

There was a time when one man ran the company all by himself. But no more. Look down the halls of almost any modern office building. The names on the doors will tell you the number of executives it takes to run a business today. When one man ran the company, communication was simple. An associate could walk in to see him, explain his problem and get his "yes" or "no." Things were decided in a hurry. But now that this one man has been replaced by a staff of executives, called top management, a group of men run the business. Decisions are made and influenced at many different levels in the management structure: production, sales, purchasing, personnel. And there is a tremendous volume of activity within each of these subdivisions. It has become impossible for executives to have close personal contact with everyone in their company. This makes effective and regular communication with behind-the-scenes developments through business reports a necessity for all concerned.

THE NEED FOR REPORTS IN BUSINESS

The larger the business, the greater its need for reports. Its efficiency depends on the quantity and quality of information flowing through all its personnel. Information of different kinds is required, and with division of labor and delegation of authority among a large number of employees, reports can be a unifying force which helps build cooperation and knits together the activities of each department.

Reports are used to exchange information, to run accurate checks on events and to record day-by-day operations. Only as an executive receives information from below can he weigh results, make decisions and initiate whatever action is appropriate. A junior executive is often asked to investigate a situation and submit a report. This is his opportunity to sell his conclusions and recommendations. Determining a particular problem and finding its solution is a very satisfying job to most of us.

Reports are also needed to measure performance and costs, to check conformance with policy and to facilitate both long-term and current planning. Without reports as a means of communication it would be very difficult to operate a business.

DEFINITION AND NATURE OF BUSINESS REPORTS

A business report is a factual presentation of data or information directed to a particular reader or audience for a specific business purpose. In essence a good report is a collection of facts to be communicated to someone who will make use of them. It is a highly specialized type of communication, flexible in subject content, organization, form and use.

The facts contained in a business report may be a record of past transactions or accomplishments, a release of new information, an account of conditions past and present, an analysis of conditions for determining future policies or a recommendation of a course of action to be followed. These facts must be accurate, complete and arranged for easy comprehension and reading.

The report writer either has first-hand information which he presents from his experience and knowledge or gathers information from an investigation, using one or several methods of research. He may obtain data from printed sources, interviews, questionnaires, observation, letters of inquiry or experiments. This data may consist of notes, statistics, tables, charts, figures, quoted material, etc. — all the result of research.

The word *report* itself is derived from the Latin, *reporto,* meaning carry or bring back. The report brings back facts from research. Before it is written, the facts must be classified, arranged, examined, evaluated, interpreted and recorded. They are finally arranged according to the plan for presenting them in the report.

In writing, emphasis is on presenting the facts to accomplish a specific purpose. They must, therefore, be clearly stated and practical. Visual aids help, as does the division of material into sections and the use of subject headings. Because the report is directed to the reader and his use, the language for conveying the message and every thing about the report must be marshaled to meet his needs. Reports should always be planned and written for *use*. Every report is different. It varies according to the reader, to the nature of the material, to its purpose and to the writer.

FUNCTIONS OF REPORTS

A sales manager needs to keep in touch with all his salesmen and to have a record of what each one is doing. Particularly if he supervises a large number of men or men scattered over a wide area, he will require them to submit a report periodically giving him such facts as the number of current prospects, the number of calls made and the number and volume of sales.

Management at the policy-making level needs to keep employees informed of company policy. Once a policy is established and known it is the duty of management to publish any changes or new policies that may be put into effect.

Since some of their operations must be integrated the sales department and the advertising department must keep in touch with each other. A problem arising in one may affect the other, so both should know about it and know what action is to be taken.

In each of these instances the report performs one general function: that of informing. Knowledge or data known by the report writer is transmitted through the business report to the reader, who, on receiving it, has the same information known previously to the writer.

When the sales manager has received weekly sales reports from each of his representatives, he consolidates the facts and figures so as to have a composite picture of what is going on. Then if there are large decreases in any one territory or in the sales of one particular salesman, or if total sales are below those of a comparable period during the previous year, he will seek the causes and try to eliminate them in his efforts to improve sales. If there are increases he will try to sustain and surpass them.

The person who receives a copy of a policy statement will analyze it for the way in which it affects his work and his job. He will determine what he should do, perhaps making a mental note or a written record of the statement.

When the sales department receives a report from the advertising department, it uses the information to decide how its work is affected. Then it analyzes and uses the data as a basis for action.

In each of these instances the report performs the general function of analysis. True, it also informs, but the stress is on analysis.

After the sales manager has consolidated and made an analysis of the information in the report, he may decide that the methods he wants to use to improve sales should have the approval of his division manager or of some other superior. He would then cast his analysis, conclusions and recommendations in report form and send them to the man higher up for his consideration and decision.

A reader of the policy statement may find that it does not work out satisfactorily for his department and may try to have it changed. Then he too will send his recommendations in a report to the policy-making group.

After the director of the sales department has read the report from the advertising department and analyzed its effects on the work in his department, he may likewise make a decision requiring higher approval before he proceeds. He too would then send on a report containing his recommendations and the basis for them.

In each of these instances the report is used to present recommendations for someone else to act on. Many additional instances showing the functions of reports could be cited. But from the ones given it is apparent that a report performs one of three general functions: it informs, it analyzes or it recommends. Sometimes it may perform any two or all three of these functions. It may contain and analyze information and reach conclusions forming the basis for a recommendation. In that case its function depends on the emphasis given in the development of its material, but usually its function is to recommend. The other functions would be satisfied, but partly to build up to the recommendation and to obtain favorable reaction toward it.

The situations just mentioned call attention to the internal use of reports. Reports within a company pass between those who supervise and those who carry on the work, between those who are the policy-makers and those who carry out policies — between employees and employers, subordinates and superiors, management and labor. However, reports are necessary to operate a business externally as well as internally. External reports are sent to stockholders, customers, the general public and interested individuals. Both internal and external reports perform one or all of the general functions of reports.

Internal reports move *vertically* through the organizational channels, *horizontally* between departments or individuals on the same level and *radially* inside and outside the company. Many reports in the downward flow of communication are informational. They increase their readers' general knowledge about the organization and work of the company. They may give opinions on various subjects, information about the company's employee benefits or notices about Red Cross and Community Chest drives. Of course much instructional reporting of this nature is of transitory value.

Reports moving downward also transmit policies, procedures and orders. A policy statement furnishes a guiding principle for a specific action to be taken. It is issued at a high level of command to those taking the action. A statement of procedures represents in detail the steps to be followed in carrying out a policy. One cannot always differentiate, however, between a policy statement and a statement of procedures, because a specific policy statement may at times include the detailed steps for its execution.

Many reports in the upward flow of communication contain financial statements or statistics to show the present condition of the business and to be made a part of its permanent records. Reports explaining work done, anticipated problems, progress, increases and decreases and periods or distances over which operated all fall into this same informational category.

The interchange of reports between departments or among men on the same level represents a horizontal flow of communication. The aim here is to coordinate the work of the various departments or divisions. Such reports are especially vital to large companies in which the work is decentralized.

Radially, reports are distributed throughout the company to reach everyone, and frequently are also sent outside the company. A good example of this type of report is the annual report, which is of interest not only to all employees but also to stockholders, the general public and other groups. These reports differ greatly from internal reports sent vertically and horizontally. With most internal reports the reader is already interested in the contents because they affect his work and are of practical value to him in his job. But the writer of a radially transmitted report must present his material to obtain the attention and interest of as many readers as possible.

It is highly important that the flow of communication through business reports be kept open in a company. The informed employee is a happy and productive worker. Facts and their analysis are necessary for all decisions requiring appropriate action. *Effective communication through reports is an integral part of operating any business successfully.*

PROBLEMS

1. Why is it true that the larger the business, the greater the need for business reports?

2. What is the basis of an effective report?

3. Why is each report different from all other reports?

4. Bring a business report to class. Be prepared to point out its general purpose, to indicate how the report accomplishes its purpose, to specify its intended reader and to explain its use in the company from which you obtained it.

5. In one paragraph explain your reasons for enrolling in a course in business report writing and the advantages you expect to gain from it.

6. What would be some of the results if the flow of communication through business reports in a company were stopped?

CHAPTER 2

Communication Through Reports

THE COMMUNICATION PROCESS
RELATION OF WRITER, MESSAGE AND READER
ADAPTATION OF REPORTS
FUNDAMENTAL SKILLS

Communication is a two-way process.
Communication is a continuing process.
Communication is the human interchange
of facts and ideas, opinions and feelings.

ONE EXECUTIVE FUNCTION IS TO DEVELOP AND MAINTAIN A line of communication throughout the entire company. There must be a flow of communication to everyone. Reports are only one kind of communication, but a very important one.

THE COMMUNICATION PROCESS

A report writer has been investigating a particular problem whose solution he wants to present to the management group in his company for its decision. He has gathered the facts and interpreted them. They are very meaningful to him and he has arrived at a solution. In the following diagram, block (1) represents the writer, block (2) the message to be conveyed and block (3) the reader:

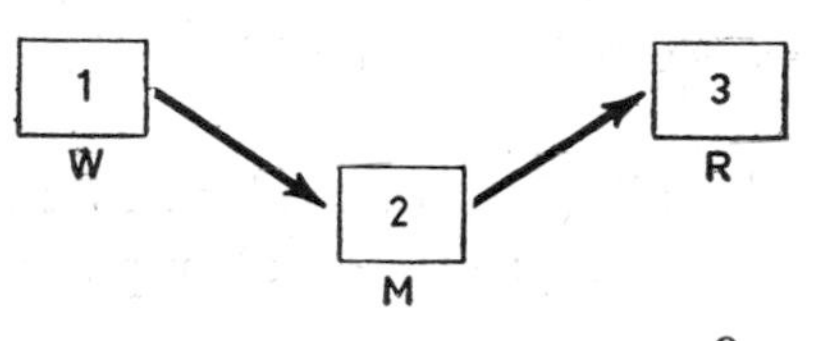

The writer will need to make use of the tools of communication — words and visual aids — to frame his message into a report for transmission to the reader. To the writer this message has meaning; he has a grasp of the facts; he has an insight into the problem. To the reader who receives the report, however, the message will be comprehensible only if the words used have meaning to him.

Communication succeeds only when the reader responds to the message. Whether his action be favorable or unfavorable, he will act if he understands the message. Effective communication depends on the reader's response, making it a two-way process. When he responds, his action in turn will stimulate either the writer or someone else. Thus the communication cycle continues.

Meaning is conveyed by words and illustrations, by interpretations and by insight into situations. But it is conveyed only when it is understandable to the reader. Several underlying principles resulting from this fact are:

Effective communication through reports depends on an understanding of people and their feelings, the interpretation of facts and a recognition of the report's purpose and use.

Words in a report, to have meaning, must refer to something intelligible. The report's message must be within the realm of the reader's experience and knowledge.

A report should be adapted to the reader's needs and to the use he will make of it.

RELATION OF WRITER, MESSAGE, AND READER

When the report is clearly understood the reader should be interested and receptive. Interest and acceptance, however, depend in part on the relationship between the writer and the reader.

The writer should accept the reader as his equal in the total communication process. He must also think of the reader as an individual, since his wants and needs must be met in the report. Often the reader of a business report is in an executive capacity in the company. As an executive he receives reports from the men responsible to him and in turn reports to other executives on his own level or above him. The advertising director, the personnel manager, the public relations director — all receive reports from their assistants and report to executives of equal or higher rank in other departments.

There are of course all kinds of readers. Not all reports are distributed within the company; nor are all reports solutions to problems. The annual report, for example, goes to the general public and must capture the attention and interest of its readers. Each report should be tailored for a particular reader or group of readers according to the information that is available about them. The writer should consider the reader's position in relation to his own. Where is he in the organization's chain of command? Near the top or the bottom? What is his job? What function does he perform in the company? Is he a single reader or a member of a group of readers? How will he use the report?

The answers to these questions will decide the form used, the routing of the report and the manner in which it is transmitted. They will also be helpful in determining what to say and in suggesting what is to be done. The more the writer knows about the reader's age, sex, educational level, occupation, position, interests, feelings and attitudes, the better the rapport he will be able to establish. Individual differences in experience and personality makeup vitally affect the process of assimilating the message.

For a reader who is familiar with the report's subject matter it is not always necessary to begin with explanatory details. The writer can plunge immediately into the results of his investigation and the solution to the problem at hand. The reader who is unacquainted with the situation, on the other hand, has to be given background details at the beginning of the report so he can more easily understand what follows. Emphasis must be given to making the report usable in accomplishing a definite purpose.

In the fast-moving pace of today's business a report must be planned to conserve the reader's time. It should give him exactly what he wants and needs, no more and no less. The use of subject headings guides his reading. Tables and charts save space in the report as well as reading time. Following the principles of good business writing, conciseness, clearness and correctness, also saves space and time.

Every consideration is given the reader because the report's message must reach *him* and must serve *his* purpose. Otherwise the communication process has not been completed nor has the report been effective.

ADAPTATION OF REPORTS

By showing him consideration, the writer is adapting the report to the reader. From the information available about him, the writer adapts the report's message to the reader's interests, knowledge, peculiarities, desires and needs. The subject matter is related to the reader. It is interpreted for his understanding and use. Figures are presented in the easiest and most logical way. Special terms and expressions are made clear. Significant facts of interest and use to the reader are emphasized. The writer must know his subject and how the report is to be used. And he must use this knowledge in adapting his material to the reader, whose major interest lies in the facts and their interpretation. To be effective the report must stimulate the reader to action.

Reports must be adapted to the reader's point of view as well as to his knowledge and experience, his method of thinking and the nature of the subject matter. Adapting to the reader's point of view merely means fulfilling his needs. The reader's method of thinking also may determine the report's organization. If he wants to draw his own conclusions, let him. If he prefers to be told conclusions, tell him. If he thinks data through logically, organize and present them so he can.

The nature of the subject matter and its use determine the form and type of the report. But form is used as the means to an end and not as an end in itself.

The language and style must also be adapted to the reader, the material and its intended use. Material of popular interest directed to the public must be presented in an appealing manner to capture general interest. On the other hand, a report offering an executive the solution to a problem in the company already has his interest. Here the language and style should effect clear, quick comprehension on his part.

Distinctions in style and language are also made in adapting the report to readers with technical, semi-technical or non-technical backgrounds. A report intended for an executive will probably be understood with little difficulty, for he has a college level of comprehension derived from either his experience or formal education. The language and style must still be adapted, however, to saving his time. On the other hand, a report that will be distributed to the firm's semi-skilled labor force must be written on an eighth-grade level of understanding. And its language must also be adapted accordingly.

Adaptation of reports makes for flexibility in report writing. Because of inherent differences in situations and individuals, the report writer has a tremendous responsibility for meeting this demand placed upon him. It means that each report is different from all other reports. The subject matter of a report is developed according to the reader's needs and the particular purpose the report is to accomplish. Only in this way can adaptation fully be made and the report accomplish its purpose.

FUNDAMENTAL SKILLS

The basic skills of all communication — reading, writing, speaking and listening — are utilized in the preparation and writing of business reports. It would be difficult indeed to gather data in an investigation, whether from printed sources, interviews, questionnaires or observation, without using any or all four of the skills. Likewise one can hardly interpret, outline, organize or present information without relying on one or all of them.

Ineffective communication is caused by false observation or inaccurate interpretation and analysis of what is read, seen or heard. Each of the basic communication skills involves human relations and personalities in its application. For that reason an understanding of human behavior is of paramount importance in preparing and writing reports. Human relations are the core of all communication. There must be a response from the reader before the total communication process can take place.

Since business reports are a highly specialized type of communication in which facts drawn from research are presented to a particular individual or group for a specific business purpose, they require a mastery of skills and techniques for their preparation. So few reports are written from information that the writer has at hand that one of the most fundamental skills is fact gathering. A writer needs to understand the procedures and techniques for bibliographic research, questionnaires, interviews, observation and other data-collecting methods. He must know what to look for, where to look and how to use the information he finds. He should develop the ability to understand a problem, see it in its relationship to other problems, recognize what is needed, evaluate possible courses of action and decide on the best solution.

He must be able to plan an investigation and report within a particular time limit. A report which must be completed in an hour will be different from one written in a day, a week or a month. But in the business world, if an hour is all the time there is, the efficient writer will come up with an effective answer.

The ability to organize data and to reach logical conclusions from them is necessary. The thinking process required in preparing and presenting reports is valuable training for anyone, whether used in writing a report or in making decisions. The ability to outline material is another requisite. The ability to use statistics and tables and charts is also important. Being able to achieve exactness and directness in communicating facts and ideas completely, clearly, concisely, correctly and persuasively completes the list of abilities necessary in preparing and writing a report.

The requirements just mentioned for the report writer presuppose his mastery of spelling, punctuation and grammar and his proficiency in the use of the English language. The effective use of English in writing reports consists of its use to convey a factual message for a particular business purpose. This means then that the report writer must have some knowledge of business principles and operations. He must be able also to adapt his material to a particular reader. Familiarity with the many standard types of business reports and their organization and use will help the writer to adjust and develop each report for a particular reader and purpose. He will be able to collect and organize material, to reason intelligently and to write effectively.

Because the facts presented in a business report largely stem from research, the writer should develop the personal attributes which aid in investigation. The power of accurate observation and the willingness to listen make for thorough, unbiased research. The ability to analyze, to exercise methodical judgment and to use common sense is also necessary. Intellectual honesty — giving recognition to every source, acknowledging quoted material, presenting both sides of an issue, showing all the facts and their implications without disguising or coloring them, distinguishing between opinion and fact — simply means being honest in the treatment of the subject and toward the reader. Lead the reader to the truth. Initiative, resourcefulness, persistency, good work habits and dependability are admirable qualities for the report writer to possess. Patience, persuasiveness and ingenuity should also be added to the list.

Report writing is both an art and a science. It is an art because it requires a certain amount of inherent creative ability on the part of the writer. Nevertheless, abilities that are helpful, if not already present, can be developed; and the necessary techniques, procedures and skills can be acquired. It is up to the writer to use all his knowledge, experience, abilities and understanding of human nature to direct his report to a particular reader for a specific purpose and to develop his material accordingly.

PROBLEMS

1. Discuss the principle: Effective communication through reports depends on an understanding of people and their feelings, on facts and their interpretation and on recognition of the report's purpose and use.

2. Bring a sample business report to class. If your instructor wishes it may be the one you brought before; or you may select one of the examples given in Part IV of this book. Discuss the relationship of its writer, message and reader. Explain how it was adapted to its reader and purpose.

3. What effect does conserving the reader's time have upon the report's message and presentation?

4. Analyze yourself. To what degree have you mastered the basic communication skills, reading, writing, speaking and listening? To what extent have you developed your ability to collect material for a report and to organize, interpret, outline and present data? Are you able to achieve exactness, directness and logic in writing? Do you write clearly, concisely, correctly and persuasively? What is your present knowledge of and experience with business principles and operations? Are you familiar with business reports? In other words, where do you stand now? What are your weak points? What must you improve in order to write effective business reports?

Present the results of your analysis in a letter report addressed to your instructor. (A letter report follows the same form as a business letter except that a subject line and subject headings may be used. You will find more detailed information about letter reports in Chapter 15.)

5. Assume that your high school principal has written you for information which he intends to use in counseling students who plan to attend college. He wants information about the college you are attending: choice of curriculum, degrees offered, jobs qualified for upon graduation, scholarships, cost of room and board in dormitories, amount of tuition and fees, cost of books, etc. Write him a letter report giving him as specific information as you can. Wherever possible, draw from experience.

Part II

STEPS IN THE PREPARATION OF BUSINESS REPORTS

CHAPTER 3

Planning the Investigation and the Report

CONFRONTED WITH THE TASK OF PREPARING A REPORT, THE writer works step by step, through several stages of report development, before he submits the finished report. First he plans his investigation. He analyzes the problem to select procedures for collecting data; he determines his purpose and objectives, as well as what is necessary to accomplish them. He then collects data by appropriate methods, such as bibliographical research, interviews, questionnaires, observation and letters. He takes notes; he obtains and tabulates questionnaire results. After he has collected the data he classifies and organizes them. The investigator then analyzes and interprets the data, reaching conclusions and formulating recommendations. He next outlines the material for presentation in the report. Then he writes the report from the outline and finally revises, edits and prepares the final copy.

BASIS AND NATURE OF PLANNING

Planning consists of setting up definite procedures for conducting an investigation, for handling its results and for writing the report. The purpose of planning is to establish policies pertaining to the objectives, scope, cost, time limit and outline of the proposed report.

Planning clarifies the thinking and work of the researcher and provides him with a guide for conducting his investigation and presenting his findings in report form.

An analysis of the situation, problem and reader is the basis for planning. The determination of one point of procedure usually leads to another, as shown by the following example.

The personnel director of a small factory employing about 150 production workers is confronted with the problem of getting his men back to work. It is a non-union firm and the men have walked out. A long-range program which will prevent the recurrence of this problem is also needed. The situation calls for an investigation and a solution to be recommended to top management. Interviewing a few of the employees will give the personnel director some idea of the causes of the walkout. A preliminary survey may reveal that the men are opposed to present methods of figuring the incentive rates, that they dislike the attitude of their supervisors or that there are flaws in the communications program within the company. Each of these aspects would then have to be investigated and analyzed. Planning would be necessary in conducting the research and writing the report.

DETERMINING THE PROBLEM

The problem may be stated in a general way by whoever authorizes the investigation and report. This may be done in a letter of authorization or in a personal conference between the researcher and the authorizer. In these cases the researcher would determine the problem by analyzing the letter or by asking questions during the conference. Problems may also be suggested at committee meetings or at group conferences. Of course an individual may run into a problem in connection with his own job and want to find a solution. A study of the situation giving rise to a problem will help the investigator to see it in proper perspective and to discover its different elements.

Analysis of the Situation

In analyzing a problem or the conditions giving rise to it the researcher begins at its core. In some problems the issues stand out clearly. In other problems the issues may be complex and obscure. A review of all the factors involved will help to point out the basic problem and the approach it requires. Parts of a problem may be isolated and analyzed separately to find their relation to each other and to the central problem. A series of questions to be answered about each element may be listed to insure complete investigation of each and to determine the data required and the means of getting them.

An analysis of the situation will also help determine the purpose and objectives of the report. The writer should understand how the report is to be used in order to decide what he should do and why. He needs to survey all the facts known at the outset and to determine what unknown facts are still to be learned.

Analysis of the Problem

When the writer has sufficient knowledge of the problem he can break it down into its several elements, outlining them wherever possible to provide the framework for his investigation and the later outline of the report. If he is unfamiliar with the subject matter, he will first need to gather some information about it. He will then understand the type and nature of the data needed to arrive at a solution.

The problem is also analyzed in accurately phrasing the title and in determining the scope, limitations and contents of the report. The title naturally designates the subject matter of the report; it indicates the nature of the contents and attracts the reader's attention. Both the problem and the situation giving rise to it help to establish the scope and limitations. From analysis one can also set up a purpose and decide on the type of report to write.

Analysis of the Reader

Consideration must also be given at this point to the reader's present attitude. Is he neutral? Is he antagonistic? Is he biased in his views? Will he be favorable to the solution? Knowing the reader's attitude will help the report writer determine his approach to the subject and decide how he can best get his material across to accomplish the report's purpose.

The present familiarity of the reader with the problem or subject matter must also be considered. Just as the writer's experience with the problem determines the data he must gather, so also the reader's experience determines, in part, what the writer must present in the report. A reader who is familiar with the situation and the need for a solution does not want to wade through those details in a report, nor should he. He is ready to consider a proposed solution. On the other hand, a reader who knows little or nothing about the problem needs to be briefed on the situation and the details giving rise to the problem and to the report.

The investigator should also know whether his reader is to be a single reader or a group of readers, as well as the use that will be made of the report. Is the report, for instance, to be used by the advertising director of a firm to decide whether or not to advertise by direct mail, or is it to be distributed to members of a board of directors to help them set next year's budget? Is it a problem-solution report with recommendations to be carried out, or an informational report for public distribution?

Defining and Limiting the Problem

The problem is generally more or less defined by the person requesting the report. In some cases a description of the situation is given and the investigator is asked to make a statement of the problem. It is then stated in terms of the facts giving rise to it.

The purpose is the long-range goal which the report seeks to accomplish. The objectives are the immediate goals or steps that must be attained in order to reach this final goal. For instance, the purpose of a report may be to show how to reduce the cost of a certain operational process. In such a report the recommendations will present ways in which the cost can be reduced. An objective, however, will be to examine present operations to find out whether changing them would actually reduce costs. This would have to be done before any recommendation could be made. Both the purpose and the objectives would be supplied in defining the problem.

The scope sets the boundaries of the report. It indicates the extent of the material covered, the quantity and nature of the data. A report on the investigation of the annual reports of Swift and Company from 1925 to 1955, for example, sets the boundaries of the study by naming the 30-year period, the company and the type of report. Within those boundaries certain limitations apply. The investigation might deal only with a study of how the reports make for good public relations. This would be a limitation of the subject matter. Often reports are limited to only one or more aspects of a broader subject.

Other limiting factors which often apply are time, cost, procedures available and the qualifications of the researcher. If you are asked for a report in two hours, you certainly will not do the job you would do if you had a whole week for it. Yet you would get the job done and on time. And if you are allotted $10 for an investigation, your course of action would differ from the course followed if you were allotted $100. In either case you would come up with an answer. Likewise, if you are called upon to evaluate something which you are not qualified to pass judgment on, your criticism will be limited by your lack of knowledge or experience.

In addition to a problem's definition in terms of its purpose and objectives, scope and limitations, it must be differentiated from other problems in the same field. A personnel director dealing with a lateness problem among his office workers, who are reporting late for work mornings and who are extending their mid-morning and mid-afternoon coffee breaks, must recognize his problem as part of a larger one — employee morale — and must distinguish between it and other morale problems, still dealing with it as a part of the general morale problem.

The more fully the researcher understands his problem the better able he is to plan and carry out his investigation and present his findings. Determining the problem is merely determining elements of it which will guide the thinking and planning of the investigation and the report. An analysis of the situation, the problem and the reader is a basis for determining such elements as need, purpose, objectives, scope, limitations, divisions of subject matter, etc., which in turn are used as a basis for determining procedures for collecting and organizing the data. After determining and analyzing the problem, the researcher is ready to formulate his working plan, which is simply a plan of what he proposes to do and how he expects to accomplish it.

THE WORKING PLAN

The working plan for the investigation and the report accomplishes two major purposes: it charts the investigation and it clarifies the researcher's thinking. It may also be submitted to seek approval of the project before work is continued. Usually it takes the form of an outline; but sometimes when it is being submitted for approval it is written as a letter. Or, as in some companies, it may entail filling in the blanks of a printed form provided for this purpose.

The working plan will include as many of the following elements as are applicable to a given report problem:

(*1*) Statement of the problem
(*2*) Need and use of the report
(*3*) Purpose and objectives
(*4*) Scope and limitations
(*5*) Divisions of the subject matter
(*6*) Methods and procedures for gathering data
(*7*) Tentative bibliography
(*8*) Methods of organizing data
(*9*) Digest of impressions
(*10*) Tentative general outline of the report
(*11*) Statement of expected results or tentative conclusion
(*12*) Statement of cost and time required
(*13*) Definition of terms (specialized use and technical terms)
(*14*) Work-progress schedule

Determining the sources of data and planning how they will be used are important decisions, and the succeeding chapters in Part II discuss several methods used in collecting data for solving a problem. After one knows the nature of his data and how he is to get them, he can determine how to organize them. Even while he is in the process of collecting material, he can be organizing; and, if he is, he will be saving time by doing two things at once. (This is one reward for careful planning and foresight.) The tentative outline of the report can be formulated as soon as the author has analyzed his problem and broken it down into its basic elements. At this point it may consist of only the major topics arranged in orderly sequence. Or it may break them down further into as many subdivisions as possible, clarifying minor problems for the researcher and simplifying his task of drawing up a final outline later.

Whether or not tentative conclusions can be drawn up will depend on the knowledge of the problem or subject that the author has and how far along he is able to carry his thinking and preliminary work. He should avoid setting up a tentative conclusion if, in directing his effort toward it, he overlooks factors which may prove it false or inadvisable. It should be merely something he is working toward; and all factors and data in the case should be examined, even if in the end he reaches an opposite conclusion to the one he had expected to reach. The work-progress schedule is used as a means of planning work and budgeting time proportionately so the project can be completed in the time allotted it.

In the following working plan notice how the various elements have been planned for making the investigation and outlining the report. It is presented in outline form.

Working Plan for a Report on the Cost of Renting Trucks As Compared to the Cost of Owning Trucks

1. *Statement of problem.* Trucking costs for the Royal Supply Co., a coffee packer in New Orleans, are rising. Some coffee companies in other parts of the country are renting their trucks to reduce costs. Which should the Royal Supply Co. do?

2. *Purpose.* The purpose is to determine whether the Royal Supply Co. should rent its trucks instead of owning them. The results of the report will be used to decide the policy to be followed in the next year.

3. *Objective.* The present cost of operating four jeep trucks now owned by the company will need to be investigated and compared with the cost of renting trucks from available rental agencies in New Orleans.

4. *Scope.* Although cost information is the most important, other factors such as convenience, reliability, advantages, etc. will be considered. The report will cover the over-all desirability of each of the two plans.

5. *Limitations.* The report is limited to cost figures of the rental plans of the two largest truck rental agencies in New Orleans—Dixie Drive It Yourself System and U-Drive-It Car Co., Inc.

6. *Procedure for gathering data.* From the records of the Royal Supply Co. will come the cost figures of operating the presently owned jeep trucks. Personal interviews with men from the two rental agencies will provide the cost figures of the rental plans.

7. *Division of the problem.* Such factors as the original cost of equipment, cost of replacement, insurance, storage, gasoline and servicing under the present setup will be investigated, together with the cost of rental contracts and other expenses under the proposed plan.

8. *Tentative conclusion.* The present plan of operation is less expensive.

9. *Tentative general outline.* First the cost of each item listed in # 7, above, under the present plan is discussed. Then the costs of the Dixie and the U-Drive-It agencies are analyzed and all three compared.

10. *Work-progress schedule.* The investigation and report will be completed and submitted by December 18, according to the following work schedule:

    Working plan finished and submitted for approval, November 11.
    Data to be collected by November 25.
    Data to be organized and interpreted by December 4.
    Report to be outlined by December 7.
    Report written and revised by December 16.
    Final report typed and submitted by December 18.

The following working plan is in business letter form and was submitted to the firm for its final approval of the proposed project. It contains the major elements of a working plan applicable to this particular situation.

BUSINESS RESEARCH CORPORATION OF NEW ORLEANS
712 Canal Bank Building
New Orleans, Louisiana

April 7, 195–

Mr. J. B. Blackwell, President
National Manufacturing Corporation
4031 Tulane Avenue
New Orleans, Louisiana

Dear Mr. Blackwell:

I have just made a preliminary study of your plant and I am enclosing a working plan of the proposed investigation and analysis of your operations.

Purpose and Objectives

The purpose of the report will be to examine your operations for existing and potential high-cost areas and to propose changes that will eliminate or keep them to a minimum. By proper control of costs, prices may then be brought back into line with existing industry prices.

Scope and Divisions of the Problem

The proposed analysis will include a thorough investigation and analysis of the following phases of your business operations.

Personnel Management

We will make a thorough study of your labor policies to determine whether any inefficiency exists and if so, suggest any necessary corrective action.

Advertising Policies

These will also be completely studied to determine:

(*1*) Whether too much or too little advertising is being done.

(*2*) How your advertising policies compare with those of your competitors.

(*3*) Whether your advertising is being carried by the most effective media.

(*4*) Whether it is in fact reaching potential users of your product.

Manufacturing Processes

The entire manufacturing process, from receipt of fabricated materials to completion of the finished product, will be carefully examined for any sources of inefficiency. This examination will include:

(*1*) Sources of raw materials.

(*2*) Plant outlay.

(*3*) A study of each phase of the manufacturing process.

(*4*) An examination of existing machinery, its age, efficiency and suitability to the manufacture of the finished product.

(*5*) A survey of substitute machinery, new inventions and innovations that could possibly be used to improve the quality of the work or decrease time consumed in manufacture.

(*6*) A study of the plant layout, machinery, practices and techniques employed by the industry as a whole, with special emphasis on competitor practices.

Distribution Policies

The present channels of distribution utilized will be examined and compared with industry-wide distribution policies, and alternative methods will be studied.

Sources of Information

The greater part of the information that will be gathered will come from your business files and from interviews. The rest shall come from industry-wide publications and publications of the U.S. Government.

Limitations

The greatest limitation will be in securing competitor information. The main source of this information will come from stockholder reports.

Time and Expenses

We will be able to meet your request and complete the analysis by May 15. Our estimated expenses are somewhat higher than the $1000 you had originally intended. These expenses average $250 per week and include time consumed by special investigators in the fields of labor, marketing and production management. Expenses for the five-week period will therefore be $1250. This figure does not include any incidental expenses incurred during the period. The total charge will therefore vary between $1250 and $1500 but will not exceed this amount.

We plan to begin our study on or around April 10. Is that all right with you?

We are confident that this analysis will reveal the areas where costs are unduly high, and we are certain that we will be able to recommend suitable plans of remedial action. With lower costs, and therefore lower prices, sales should expand and profits increase.

Thank you for consulting us on this problem. Your reputation for quality craftsmanship and woodwork is widespread, and we welcome the opportunity to help you overcome your temporary difficulty.

Very truly yours,

Business Research Corporation of New Orleans
Edwin F. Lacy, President

Because the same elements are included, the working plan can be used as a basis for outlining and writing the introduction to the report. The chief difference is that the plan is *what was proposed* and the introduction is *what was done*. Therefore any changes which took place will naturally be reflected in the finished introduction. The example working plan on the report for the National Manufacturing Corporation is incorporated in the final outline for that report on pages 106 to 108.

PROBLEMS

1. Your college is faced with the problem of planning for increased enrollments in the next five years. A decision must be reached on whether or not to expand present facilities. You have been asked to make an investigation and prepare a report. You already have these figures on United States college and university enrollment in the 20th century:

1900 —	250,000	1945 —	1,025,000
1905 —	251,000	1946 —	2,000,000
1910 —	375,000	1947 —	2,250,000
1915 —	380,000	1948 —	2,350,000
1918 —	400,000	1949 —	2,400,000
1920 —	580,000	1950 —	2,275,000
1925 —	800,000	1951 —	2,175,000
1930 —	1,125,000	1952 —	2,000,000
1935 —	1,150,000	1953 —	2,300,000
1940 —	1,500,000	1954 —	2,388,200
1943 —	750,000		

a. To set your mind to thinking about the problem, first design a graphic presentation of the above figures. Then write an interpretation of it to give yourself a basic understanding of the trend in the United States.

b. What other information would you need for your report and how would you obtain it?

c. Analyze the problem; break it down into its major divisions; determine its elements, such as purpose, scope, limitations.

2. Assume that you have been asked by the leading men's store in your city to investigate the possibility of their opening a branch store in the vicinity of your school campus. Outline a working plan for making your investigation and writing your report. You may present the plan in letter form to the owner of the store and ask his approval before you continue.

3. Read the case study presented in Problem 6 on pages 98 and 99 and analyze the situation, problem and reader. Define the problem, its major divisions and its elements.

4. Select one of the formal, long report subjects listed on pages 414 to 419 in Appendix C. Write out a working plan for making the necessary investigation and report. You and your instructor may decide that this is to be your term project, in which case this will be your first step in getting it under way.

CHAPTER 4

Securing Data Through Bibliographical Research

THE PROCESS OF USING PRINTED MATERIALS AS SOURCES OF information is known as bibliographical research. Printed data may be found in books, periodicals, pamphlets, bulletins, newspapers, reports or company records. Every businessman, whether he owns his own small business or is an executive in a large firm, needs to know current trends and developments in other organizations before he can make decisions on policies or procedures for his company. He will want to find out what others in similar positions have done. He will want to know what authorities in the field have to say. It may be necessary for him to trace the historical development of a problem. If he is not familiar with the subject he will need to build up an extensive background for himself. Or if the reader of his report lacks specific knowledge of the subject he will need to provide it for him. And it may be that the businessman will find that his investigation has already been made and reported upon and that the results are usable as a solution to his own problem.

IMPORTANCE AND USE OF BIBLIOGRAPHICAL RESEARCH

For both businessmen and students bibliographical research is invaluable in each of the following uses:

(*1*) To provide essential data for the solution of a problem or to give information on a particular subject

(*2*) To indicate what others have done and how the investigation fits into the general pattern of knowledge

(*3*) To show findings and opinions of authorities in the field

(*4*) To reveal whether or not the study has been accomplished already, and if so, to indicate any possible need for further investigation

(*5*) To give an understanding of the subject background.

The American Steel and Wire Company, for example, made a survey of the attitude of their employees toward the company magazine, *Wireco Life.* A simple postcard questionnaire was prepared and enclosed with each copy of a current issue of the magazine. To interpret the results the editor needed to draw upon his general knowledge of magazine publishing as well as his knowledge of the company. Moreover, it was necessary for him to have an understanding of what other companies were doing with their employee magazines. With an understanding of how the problem was related to his general knowledge of the field, he could interpret the results significantly. In this instance bibliographical research was helpful to find information on employee magazines.

In another instance a firm was considering the question of whether or not to expand its facilities. The answer to its problem called for an investigation of the expansion possibilities. Naturally, facts about the financial condition of the firm, its policies, the physical plant and equipment, marketing methods and labor conditions had to be obtained. It was also necessary to find out the competitive position of the company within the industry and to determine national and regional trends and the future outlook. Bibliographical research helped supply the necessary information.

COMPILING A BIBLIOGRAPHY

For the investigator using bibliographical research, the first step is to compile a bibliography consisting of a list of printed materials on his subject or dealing with his problem. The list, which includes such facts as the author, title and publication details for each reference item listed, serves as a guide in the investigator's research and is helpful in directing his reading of essential and significant printed material. As a part of the finished report, the bibliography becomes a listing of sources which the investigator used in making his study; and it may serve as a guide for the reader of the report if he desires further information on the subject.

The Process of Compilation

In the beginning the objective in compiling a bibliography is to get a complete list of all available material on the subject being considered. One quick and easy method for doing this is to record the information about each source on $3'' \times 5''$ cards. After the bibliographical items have been recorded, the cards may be arranged according to the subject matter of each. Thus cards on one aspect or phase of the study are grouped together for guidance in reading. After all the data have been collected, the cards listing books are placed in one group, those listing periodicals in another, and so on. Then each group is arranged alphabetically for typing the final bibliography to accompany the report. An example bibliography card for a book follows:

```
Basic Sources                                   000.0

  Coman, Edwin T., Jr.

  Sources of Business Information

  Prentice-Hall, Inc.        good, concise treat-
  New York                 ment; basic works cited;
  1949                     arranged by business sub-
  369 pages                jects such as finance,
                           management, statistics,
                           etc.
```

Bibliography card for a book.

Notice the information included on the card. The number in the upper right-hand corner is the library call number, facilitating immediate location of the book. The designation in the upper left-hand corner is the subject division under which the information, when it is obtained, will best fit. It will also serve as a guide for reading at one time the sources on a given subject division. The author, title, publisher and place and date of publication are needed for making a footnote entry and for making the final bibliographical entry. Knowing the total number of pages makes possible a budgeting of reading time. Sometimes only a part of the book will need to be read, such as pages 142–150, in which case those pages would be designated. The investigator's personal comments are given in the lower right-hand corner. Usually the comments will contain an appraisal or evaluation of the book or indicate the way in which the material may be useful.

A bibliography card for a magazine article differs from the book card only in the publication facts. Compare the illustration on page 31 with the sample magazine card on this page. Cards for any other reference materials likewise differ from a book card only in the publication facts included.

```
Planning                                          000.00

  Blackstone, Earl Glen

  "How to Plan a Research Study"

  National Business Education Quarterly
  Vol. 16, pp. 8-14
  March, 1948              brief treatment of
                      preliminary planning of
                      an investigation
```

Bibliography card for a magazine article.

Another method of recording a bibliography is to use a notebook or sheets of paper instead of the 3″ × 5″ cards. Although the process, in general, is the same as the card system, there is one big disadvantage to the use of a notebook. Alphabetizing and rearranging the list for practical use is difficult and time-consuming.

Bibliographical Sources

In compiling a bibliography the researcher checks available sources in the library for articles, books and other printed material on his subject. Both general and special indexes, as well as prepared bibliographies, are helpful aids.

Prepared Bibliographies. Numerous lists of printed material on a large variety of subjects have been prepared. Some are typewritten, others printed; some are mimeographed or reproduced by some other method. They vary in length from one to twenty or more pages. A number of them may be obtained by writing the United States Library of Congress, Washington, D. C. Many libraries subscribe to services which provide bibliographies. The *Public Affairs Information Service Bulletin* is an example of such a service for libraries. The *Bulletin,* which is issued weekly and is cumulated five times a year and annually, lists books, pamphlets, government publications, reports of public and private agencies and periodical articles related to economic and social conditions, public administration and international relations. Each reference is classified by subject and author. It not only includes materials printed in the United States and in English-speaking countries, but also those printed in English in foreign countries. Started in 1915, it has always been a cooperative clearing house of public affairs information and can be obtained by subscription from its publishers, the H. W. Wilson Company.

Another publication of the H. W. Wilson Company, *The Bibliographic Index,* is a cumulative bibliography of bibliographies sold on a subscription service basis. It is published semiannually with a bound cumulation each December. There are three larger cumulated volumes — Volume I (1937–1942), Volume II (1943–1946) and Volume III (1947–1950). The arrangement is by subject, but under each subject books and pamphlets are listed by author and periodicals by titles. The index includes some foreign periodicals. Complete or comprehensive bibliographies are starred.

Various associations, collegiate schools of business and libraries publish lists. Representative are the Business Information Bureau of the Cleveland Public Library, the Newark (New Jersey) Free Public Library's Business Branch, the Alpha Kappa Psi Fraternity, and the Amos Tuck School of Administration and Finance of Dartmouth College. They select the leading works in each subject field of business.

There are a number of bibliographies in special fields of business. In accounting the American Institute of Accountants publishes lists on all phases of accounting, and the National Association of Cost Accountants lists articles on cost accounting published in the bulletins of the association. A bibliography of the entire subject of finance is the *Selected Bibliography of Money, Credit, Banking and Business Finance* by Roy B. Westerfield, published by Bankers Publishing Company, Cambridge, Mass., 1940. It is a well-rounded list of basic works and is useful to bankers, businessmen and students.

In the field of industrial relations Princeton University has two publications. One is *The Office Library of an Industrial Relations Executive,* Bibliographical Series No. 77, 5th edition, published in 1946 by the Industrial Relations Section of the Department of Economic and Social Institutions. Under broad headings, which are subdivided, it lists basic books and pamphlets. Entries are annotated and suggestions on the use of the information are sometimes given. The other publication is *A Trade Union Library,* Bibliographical Series No. 73, 4th edition, which duplicates some of the references in the preceding bibliography, but places major emphasis on history, organization and operation of labor unions. Both of these are kept current by *Selected References,* which is issued bimonthly and is concerned with an analysis of books, pamphlets and magazine articles.

The National Office Management Association put out the *Bibliography for Office Managers* in 1945, listing material published between 1938 and 1944. Since then yearly supplements have been issued to keep the material current.

In the field of marketing *A Comprehensive Classified Marketing Bibliography* has been compiled by David A. Revzan and published by the University of California Press. Although it is not annotated, carefully selected items prior to 1950 have been listed to present a comprehensive selection of marketing literature. It is divided into three volumes, the first two having come out in 1951 with the third still being compiled. Part I contains books. Part II lists government publications, research monographs and articles in professional journals. Part III will give articles in technical and trade journals. Entries are by 23 subject groups, each one subdivided to list items prior to 1930 and those from 1930 through 1949, alphabetically arranged by authors. Plans include the issuing of annual supplements.

Another bibliography on marketing subjects is *Market Research Sources,* 1940 (Domestic Commerce Series), No. 110, by Rachel Bretherton. It is published by the United States Bureau of Foreign and Domestic Commerce and contains references from 1937 to 1939. Series No. 55 covers the years 1933 to 1937, and a 1936 edition contains references from 1931 to 1935. A very comprehensive bibliography on chainstore marketing was compiled in 1947 by the Institute of Distribution, Inc., New York: *Reference Sources on Chain Stores.*

Most professional magazines print bibliographies in their fields from time to time. *Sales Management,* for example, March 1 and 15, and April 1, 1947, printed "A Current Reading List for Sales Executives and Salesmen."

Not all libraries contain all the printed bibliographies listed here nor is the list a complete one. The ones mentioned, however, are all valuable and may suggest others. The researcher will find most librarians very helpful in suggesting sources for reference.

General Indexes. Indexes to periodicals should always be checked for current articles as well as for older ones. Most libraries of any size will contain several if not all of the following general indexes. *The Industrial Arts Index* is especially helpful; it lists articles pertaining to business, commerce and industry. First published in 1913, it is issued monthly and cumulated quarterly and annually. Over two hundred specialized technical and business magazines are indexed, including publications of a number of technical societies and associations in Great Britain, Canada, France, Germany and the United States, as well as publications of the U. S. Bureau of Foreign and Domestic Commerce. All subject fields are covered; arrangement is by author, title and subject.

In contrast to *The Industrial Arts Index,* which lists articles pertaining to industry, the *Reader's Guide to Periodical Literature* indexes articles of a popular and general nature. Over one hundred magazines are indexed. Monthly supplements are issued and are cumulated semiannually and annually. Entries are alphabetical by title, author and subject. For articles published prior to 1900 consult *Poole's Index to Periodical Literature,* the source for articles written from 1802 to 1916. The arrangement in *Poole's Index* is by subject only. The *International Index to Periodical Literature,* first published in 1907, is similar to the *Reader's Guide* in the type of magazines indexed. It lists, however, a selected number of magazines of the world and is not confined, as is the *Reader's Guide,* to those published in the United States. It issues a monthly bulletin which is cumulated periodically into bound volumes. It is arranged by author and subject and indexes over 150 magazines pertaining to the humanities, social sciences and science.

The only index to newspaper items is the *New York Times Index,* and, although it indexes only those in the *Times,* it gives a complete coverage. It is published semimonthly and is cumulated annually. For news items it provides the most thorough listing available because the *New York Times* regularly provides a comprehensive coverage of the news.

To locate any book in a particular library the investigator simply checks the card catalog of the library, because it lists all the books in the library by author, title and subject. In most instances, if the library is a good one, checking the books it has will give sufficient material for the subject or problem at hand. There are times, however, when the researcher is making as thorough a study as possible and checks not only available material in the library he is using but what is available elsewhere. The *Library of Congress Catalog* indexes all books published in the United States. The *United States Catalog* lists all books printed in the English language in English-speaking countries. Listings are by author, title and subject. Full bibliographical information is given, including the publisher and price of the book. *The Cumulative Book Index,* issued monthly and cumulated semiannually and annually, keeps the *United States Catalog* up to date. At five-year intervals since 1928 a large cumulative volume has superseded the five annual ones preceding it. The *Publishers' Weekly* is a list of American books published each week. It is a book trade journal and gives brief descriptions of each book.

Special Indexes. There are also a number of special indexes in particular fields which should be checked in compiling a bibliography. The names of the following indexes are self-explanatory:

The Accountants' Index
Agriculture Index
Art Index
Education Index
Engineering Index
Index to Legal Periodicals
The Management Index
A World List of Scientific Periodicals

Book lists may also be obtained by sending to publishing houses for them. The *Vertical File Service* catalog, obtained on a subscription basis by libraries from the H. W. Wilson Company, indexes pamphlets, brochures, leaflets and other material falling outside the classification of periodicals and books. The researcher should check with his librarian for material of this nature that is available in the library files. *United States Government Publications: Monthly Catalog,* issued by the Superintendent of Documents, Washington, D. C., contains just what its name suggests, and cumulative volumes are available in most large libraries.

Thus far library sources to be used in compiling a bibliography have been discussed. Consideration should also be given to sources which in themselves can give data and business information. Each source containing information on the subject being investigated would be listed as part of the bibliography.

Handbooks and Yearbooks. Business handbooks present within the boundaries of one volume the condensed picture of an entire business field. They are highly factual and assume some familiarity with the subject on the part of the reader. A few are revised annually, thus keeping their information up to date. The following examples show the nature of the material covered in each handbook. Most business libraries will have most of the following, all of which are good:

Accountants' Handbook
Cost Accountants' Handbook
Handbook of Business Administration
Corporate Secretaries' Manual and Guide
Handbook of Insurance
Handbook of International Organizations in the Americas
Financial Handbook
Handbook of Labor Unions
Management's Handbook
Marketing Handbook
Production Handbook
Sales Manager's Handbook
The Real Estate Handbook
Current Abbreviations
The United States Government Organization Manual
United States Postal Guide
Handbook of Foreign Currencies

Business yearbooks are published annually and give the year's summary of facts and data of a particular nature. The *Statistical Abstract of the United States,* for example, presents summary statistics in industrial, social, political and economic fields in the United States. It covers statistics on topics such as population, education, employment, military affairs, social security, vital statistics, manufacturing and commerce. The *Commerce Yearbook* provides information on commerce, trade and industry. The *Shipping World Yearbook* gives shipping data for the year. Other yearbooks with business information include the *American Labor Yearbook, The Spectator Insurance Yearbook, Social Science Abstracts* and *The Pan-American Yearbook.*

Encyclopedias, Dictionaries and Almanacs. Encyclopedias, dictionaries and almanacs contain general data, statistics and concisely presented authoritative information. Their format makes them easy to use. There are numerous encyclopedias on the market today, both general and special. The three leading general ones are the *Encyclopædia Britannica,* the *Encyclopedia Americana* and the *New International Encyclopædia.* Each is kept up to date by an annual yearbook. The *Encyclopedia Americana* is probably the one best suited to business. The treatment is authoritative and comprehensive. Some of the encyclopedias which furnish pertinent business information of a more specialized nature are the *Encyclopedia of Banking and Finance,* helpful to investors and banking and investment institutions, the *Exporters' Encyclopædia,* giving complete export shipping data about each country in the world, and the *Encyclopædia of Social Sciences,* containing some information on business subjects.

Dictionaries not only supply definitions of terms, but also brief statements of facts, biographical information and so forth. A list of several dictionaries of special interest to businessmen and students includes:

Prentice-Hall's *Encyclopedic Dictionary of Business*

Crowell's *Dictionary of Business and Finance*

The Government Printing Office's *Dictionary of Occupational Titles*

E. L. Kohler's *Dictionary for Accountants*

Frank Henius' *Dictionary of Foreign Trade*

Marquis' *Who's Who in America*

Marquis' *Who's Who in Commerce and Industry*

The various titles indicate the nature of the information included and may suggest other dictionaries that are helpful.

The one-volume reference book with the widest coverage of subjects is the *World Almanac and Book of Facts.* Issued by the World-Telegram Publishing Company annually since 1885, it contains brief information on all phases of human endeavor and is familiar to most people. Almanacs differ from yearbooks in that they give briefer information and treat details in a general way. Of special interest for business information are *The Economic Almanac* and *The Management Almanac.* Both are published by the National Industrial Conference Board, and they are very useful for executives and labor officials.

Directories. A directory provides a ready reference for those seeking specific facts on a particular subject or field. It may present such facts as alphabetized names and addresses, geographic listings and product listings. Directories vary in size; some give general information, others details. City and telephone directories are the most common general directories. Of special use to people engaged in purchasing activities is *Thomas' Register of American Manufacturers,* which is a complete and informative buying guide. It gives the names and addresses of manufacturers, producers and importers. Published annually, it is divided into sections or alphabetically arranged lists of manufacturers, trade names, international trade sections, commercial organizations and trade papers. Another purchasing guide, though not as comprehensive nor as voluminous as *Thomas' Register*, is *MacRae's Blue Book.* Its information is arranged under product headings.

For industrial editors the *Directory of House Organs,* published annually by *Printers' Ink,* is of interest. It lists both internal and external publications as well as employee and sales magazines and gives the name of the publication, editor and company.

Some directories of particular interest to advertisers are listings of current newspapers and periodicals. An example is *Ayer's Directory of Newspapers and Periodicals.* It is published annually and covers Canada, Newfoundland, Bermuda and Cuba as well as the United States and its possessions. It gives facts such as the name of the newspaper or periodical, its editor, publisher and circulation. Another directory important to advertisers is published by Standard Rate and Data Service, Inc. It is issued semimonthly in separate sections devoted to newspapers, radio, television, consumer magazines, transportation, and advertising and business publications. Its information follows an alphabetical arrangement by states, with subdivisions by cities, and includes advertising rates for the media listed and data concerning the area covered.

The corporation directories, which provide a wealth of detailed financial information on corporations, are of unlimited use to investors and to banking and investment institutions. Because of the comprehensive information furnished, *Moody's Manual of Industrials* is the most valuable directory of its kind. Separate annual volumes deal with public utilities, railroads, government and municipals, together with banks, insurance, real estate and investment trusts. The volume on corporations includes over 4,000 American, Canadian and foreign industrial corporations. Information pertaining to company history, organization, operation and financial condition is given. Financial statements, taken largely from the reports submitted to the Securities and Exchange Commission, are included. Company information of this nature is indispensable to sellers of securities and to the banking community generally. It is also extremely useful in market research, sales promotion, credit reference, production, planning, financing and investment analysis work. Supplements issued provide current information; the material is cumulated and issued in annual volumes.

Information similar to Moody's can be found in *Standard's Corporation Manual,* but for corporations only. It is issued monthly and is cumulated so that the last issue supersedes the preceding one; thus current information is always available. Those who have use for Moody's or Standard's manuals will also have use for *Poor's Register of Directors and Executives,* which is the only directory of industrially important people published in this country. About 90,000 names of executives and directors of manufacturing and mining concerns, utilities, railroads, banks and insurance companies, as well as partners of financial and investment institutions and of law firms, are listed. It is divided into six main sections, each alphabetically arranged: product index, classified index, corporation directory, register of directors, obituary and new names. It comes out annually, but cumulative supplements issued each May, August and November keep the information up to date.

The directories mentioned here are those commonly used by businessmen and students. Of course, a number of trade and professional associations have directories of their members. For help in finding directories there is the *Guide to American Business Directories,* published in 1948 by the Public Affairs Press, which gives brief descriptions of American business directories under headings indicating the type of business or industry.

Additional Sources. Several other sources of business information are worthy of inclusion here. They may be found in most libraries.

Dun & Bradstreet Credit Service
Prentice-Hall Services
Rand McNally Services
Real Estate Analyst Reports
Commerce Clearing House Services
Directory of 10,000 Trade Names
Shepherd's Historical Atlas
American Men of Science
Bureau of the Census
Publications of the U. S. Department of Labor
Publications of State Governments

EVALUATION OF THE BIBLIOGRAPHY

After a complete listing of all sources of data has been made on cards, the next step in bibliographical research is to evaluate the bibliography. This is accomplished by considering the authors and the material they have written. By finding out about an author's educational training and experience, business connections and previous publications, the investigator can get an estimate of his qualifications for writing. *Who's Who* is one source of information of this sort. Another is the *Book Review Digest* for the year in which the book appeared. Other published reviews of books also contain information about the author.

An examination of the text itself, including a look into its prefatory matter, will give such facts as the date and place of publication and the purpose of writing the book. A quick perusal of the table of contents and of the book itself will disclose the extent of coverage on the subject, whether or not the author is an accurate observer and reporter, whether or not the material is biased, the basis for the facts presented and the method of presentation.

The author and text may be checked, either as the bibliography is compiled or after it has been completed. In either case an entry for each book should be made on a bibliographical card as illustrated on page 31, if the card system is being used; otherwise the entries may be made in a notebook. Sources which are judged unreliable and not pertinent should be so marked or discarded. The list should be arranged according to subject headings. The next research step, then, is to read all the sources pertaining to each phase of every subject according to the headings on the cards.

RECORDING BIBLIOGRAPHICAL DATA

When reading to secure information for a report the reader will find the following suggestions helpful:

(*1*) Visualize the facts. Connect words to the facts to which they refer.
(*2*) Understand dictionary meanings and connotations of the words.
(*3*) Examine factual statements and figures for their accuracy and logic.
(*4*) Distinguish between vague and definite statements, between hasty generalizations and careful judgments, between opinion and accuracy.
(*5*) Scan material for important points found in topic sentences.

Use of Cards or Notebooks

In reading, notes are taken for later analysis and use in presenting facts and drawing conclusions in the final report. Cards are preferred for recording notes. They may be of any size convenient for the reporter to handle. Each card should contain only one fact. It should be classified under a subject heading indicated in the upper left-hand corner. A specimen note card is at the bottom of this page.

Subject headings are indicated for later use in classifying and

Subject heading
Sub-head

The note itself ______________

____

____

Source: ________ Page reference ______

Note card.

organizing data. While the material is being read, source and page references should be made for footnote entries later in the report. Instead of writing out the source, however, a number may be used, which would then be placed on the corresponding bibliographical card. Sometimes colored cards are used to indicate division of material.

Loose-leaf notebooks, or even half-sheets of paper, may be used for recording notes. Their advantage is more space for recording details. This can also be a disadvantage, however, if the reader has a tendency to record several facts on one sheet. He will later have difficulty in arranging his notes when he outlines and writes the report.

Methods of Taking Notes

There are several methods of taking notes: direct quotation, paraphrase, précis, outline or summary. A direct quotation must be recorded word for word so as not to misinterpret or change the author's meaning. Omissions of words should be indicated by ellipses (. . .). The whole must be enclosed in quotation marks. To paraphrase is to express, interpret or give the meaning in other words. The précis, on the other hand, is an exact, sharply defined statement. However, specific phrasing of expressions and style used by the original author should not be copied, consciously or unconsciously, in the précis. A summary usually indicates the main idea or point of view of the author but is stated in the language of the note taker. An outline also records the main points but shows the relationship of several ideas. In taking notes frequent use of quotations, especially long quotations, should be avoided. It is usually best to record information in the form of brief summaries. After one has read and recorded the data from bibliographical sources, the next step is to classify, organize and interpret the facts. This problem is discussed fully in Chapter 7.

THE FINAL BIBLIOGRAPHY

The final bibliography is a complete listing of the printed materials used in preparing the report. It is placed at the end of the report, sometimes as part of the appendix. The bibliography compiled as a guide for the investigation is a basis for the final bibliography. After the data have been recorded and sifted to determine which should be used in the report and which should be discarded, it is evident which sources should be listed in the final bibliography. From the bibliography cards he has accumulated the researcher selects the ones containing entries for all the sources used in writing the report. These are then classified according to the type of source represented. All cards from books are placed together, as are all those from magazines, encyclopedias, directories, etc. Cards in each group are then arranged alphabetically by the last name of the author. If the author is not known the title of the source is used for alphabetizing. Sometimes instead of being divided according to the type of source, bibliographies are arranged by topics, with alphabetical arrangement by author or source under each topic. This procedure is useful in indicating sources used for each subject. It is not often used, however, because it makes for repetition and is difficult to organize. The forms of entry must be consistent throughout the bibliography. Suggestions and examples are shown in Appendix D, pages 420 and 421.

PROBLEMS

1. Answer the following questions, recording the source of your information in bibliographical form with the appropriate library call number:

a. What was the population of your state per square mile in 1870? In 1950?

b. In what year did the Bulova Watch Co. incorporate? What is the par value of its common stock?

c. What are the names and addresses of two manufacturers of air-conditioning parts?

d. List several government publications on starting a small business.

e. What is the name of the Massachusetts town in which Marshall Field, the Chicago merchant, first entered the dry-goods business as a shopclerk?

f. List five recent articles on the subject of direct mail advertising.

2. Look up the answers to the following questions, making out appropriate note cards and bibliographical cards:

a. Is the auditor's certificate legally required in a corporation's annual report?

b. In the consolidated balance sheet of Oscar Mayer & Co., Inc., for November, 1952, what is the figure for accrued taxes?

c. Is Simplicity Pattern Co., Inc., listed on the American Stock Exchange?

d. On what date were the new communications tax rates of 1954 effective?

3. Identify the following sources and explain their uses:

Industrial Arts Index
Accountants' Handbook
Moody's Manual
Ayer's Directory
Statistical Abstract
Public Affairs Information Service
New York Times Index
U. S. Catalog
Poole's Index
Reader's Guide

4. Assume that you have been asked to investigate the possibility of starting a credit union in your company. Prepare a tentative bibliography that would be useful in giving you the information you would need.

5. Prepare a bibliography on a subject in your major field of interest such as direct mail advertising, office management, cost accounting or labor-personnel.

6. Select one of the subjects listed in Appendix C for a formal, long report and prepare the bibliography you would use in gathering needed information. (You may decide to write a report on this same subject later.)

7. Arrange the following items in correct bibliographical form as they would appear in a final, typed bibliography. (You may check the section on bibliography in the Appendix, p. 420, for correct punctuation and form.)

Shister, Joseph, New York: 1949, Lippincott Co., pp. 305. *Economics of the Labor Market.*

"Professor Slichter Analyzes Taft-Hartley Act," p. 22, *The Commercial and Financial Chronicle,* 1949, March 3.

Robert N. Denham, *Factory Management and Maintenance,* p. 86, May, 1950, "Don't Let NLRB Repeal Taft-Hartley."

Business Week, June 24, 1950, pp. 98–108. Three Years After: the Taft-Hartley Record."

Taylor, George W., Prentice-Hall, Inc., *Government Regulation of Industrial Relations,* New York, pp. 710. 1948.

"Some Effects of the Taft-Hartley Act," University of Illinois *Bulletin,* October, 1949, p. 17.

Interview with Dr. Howard Wissner, Professor, December 6, Tulane University.

New York Times: Section 6, page 10. "Tobin Plans for Labor Peace." November 28, 1948.

June 4, 1948. U. S. News, "Meaning of Taft-Hartley Act—Clarified by NLRB and Courts," pp. 24–25.

John A. Hogan. "The Meaning of the Union Shop Election" Industrial and Labor Relations Review, page 321. April 1949.

Labor Management Relations, Act 1947, with Explanation. 1947 New York: Prentice-Hall, Inc., pp. 3–15.

8. Your firm is interested in starting a company library and has a limited amount of money to spend. Submit a report on the professional magazines in your field, recommending those which you think should be included in the new library and explaining your choices.

9. Write a report evaluating and recommending basic sources that an advertising agency should buy for its company library or those that a public accounting office should have.

CHAPTER 5

Securing Data Through Questionnaires

A LARGE BAKERY LAST YEAR, EXPANDING INTO A NEW modern plant, wanted to determine whether or not it should change its wax paper bread wrapper to one of either cellophane or plastic material. As a part of the investigation, it made a survey to find out the housewife's reaction to the three kinds of wrappers under consideration. This entailed the use of a questionnaire for interviewing homemakers. To insure reaching women of different income groups, stores were selected in different sections of the city and customers were interviewed while shopping. The results of the questionnaire showed the homemakers preferred the wax paper already in use and revealed the reasons for their choice.

A wholesale distributor mailed a questionnaire to all RCA dealers in his territory to determine what they considered the most effective form of advertising for RCA products. Results showed that both large and small dealers in cities chose the newspaper as the most effective advertising medium. Dealers in towns, however, considered television more effective and newspapers were second choice.

At any time a person may be called to the telephone and asked what program he is listening to on the radio and several other questions about a particular program. In such instances a survey is being made to measure the listening habits of the radio audience.

In each of these three cases a predetermined list of questions was used to obtain information from a group of individuals. After all the answers were reviewed they were tabulated and analyzed to find out the general pattern of response, which in turn was used to formulate a conclusion as a basis for a course of action. A questionnaire survey can thus be defined as any study which uses a prepared list of queries to obtain replies from people on a list or in a survey sample.

PURPOSE AND USE OF QUESTIONNAIRES

Questionnaires are used to secure information on behavior characteristics, to gather opinions or attitudes or to obtain facts. Knowing what a person does and why, how he reacts as part of a group and what the general characteristics of the group are is important in understanding an individual person or a group of people, as well as any business problem connected with them. Finding out what a person or group of people thinks or feels, and why, also gives a necessary basis for making decisions pertaining to them. There are also occasions on which questionnaires are used to obtain facts known by only a few, because of their special experience or knowledge.

Take a look at the following five questions taken from an opinion survey of employees in Standard Oil Company of California and certain subsidiaries. A total of 37 questions, plus a space for writing in additional comments, made up the questionnaire, which was distributed at group meetings on company time. It was felt by management that an employee opinion poll was an important step toward improving efforts toward effective two-way communication between the company and its employees. Thirteen questions, of which five are given here, were asked concerning communications:

12. How well do you feel your Company keeps you informed about the Company's activities?

- ☐ (1) *Always keeps me informed*
- ☐ (2) *Usually keeps me informed*
- ☐ (3) *Sometimes keeps me informed*
- ☐ (4) *Seldom keeps me informed*

13. I get MOST of my information about our Company from: (Please check ONE only.)

- ☐ (1) *Notices on bulletin boards*
- ☐ (2) *Articles in the STANDARD OILER*
- ☐ (3) *Letters to me at home*
- ☐ (4) *Talks with my supervisor*
- ☐ (5) *Employee handbook ("You and Your Company")*
- ☐ (6) *Group meetings*
- ☐ (7) *Newspapers*
- ☐ (8) *Fellow employees*
- ☐ (9) *Other (Please specify)* ____________

14. I would PREFER to get most of my information about our Company from: (Please check ONE only.)

- ☐ (1) *Notices on bulletin boards*
- ☐ (2) *Articles in the STANDARD OILER*
- ☐ (3) *Letters to me at home*
- ☐ (4) *Talks with my supervisor*
- ☐ (5) *Employee handbook ("You and Your Company")*
- ☐ (6) *Group meetings*
- ☐ (7) *Newspapers*
- ☐ (8) *Fellow employees*
- ☐ (9) *Other (Please specify)* ____________

15. Your Company is interested in knowing how you feel about your opportunities for expressing your ideas and obtaining answers to your questions. Do you feel free to go to your immediate supervisor and discuss: (Please check ONE answer to EACH part.)

	Always	*Usually*	*Sometimes*	*Seldom*
a. Questions about your job	☐ (1)	☐ (2)	☐ (3)	☐ (4)
b. Ideas and suggestions	☐ (1)	☐ (2)	☐ (3)	☐ (4)
c. Personnel practices	☐ (1)	☐ (2)	☐ (3)	☐ (4)
d. Complaints	☐ (1)	☐ (2)	☐ (3)	☐ (4)
e. Personal problems	☐ (1)	☐ (2)	☐ (3)	☐ (4)

16. How do you feel about the amount of information your Company gives you on: (Please check ONE answer to EACH part.)

	Not Enough	*About Right*	*Too Much*	*No Opinion*
a. Company's expansion plans	☐ (1)	☐ (2)	☐ (3)	☐ (4)
b. Company's financial problems—income, expenses, and profit	☐ (1)	☐ (2)	☐ (3)	☐ (4)

. . . .

k. Information on employee benefit plans	☐ (1)	☐ (2)	☐ (3)	☐ (4)
l. The American business system in general—how it operates.	☐ (1)	☐ (2)	☐ (3)	☐ (4)

The questions ask for facts, opinions and preferences. The answers would be of definite concern to management and directors of personnel or industrial relations. Over 42% answered "always" and over 41% "usually" to Question 12, which shows that there is need for improvement. The response to Question 13 indicated that a large majority get their information from *The Standard Oiler,* bulletin boards and fellow employees. In answering Question 14, however, they indicated they prefer, in addition to *The Standard Oiler* and bulletin boards, meetings, talks with supervisors and letters at home. From a survey of this type it can readily be seen that questionnaires can be a very useful management tool. They are also used in dealing with marketing problems and in public relations work.

A Tool of Management

The information obtained from questionnaires helps management in making decisions and establishing policies necessary for the running of the business. Answers to some of the questions used in the Standard Oil survey, for instance, provided an objective measure of personnel administration at the supervisory level; others showed places where the communications program needed improvement and suggested possible changes. Although the bakery's survey for finding consumer acceptance is a type of marketing problem, its results would also help management in making the final decision to retain the wrapper of wax paper. Information from questionnaires is also of benefit to management in building mutual understanding among departments and groups and in coordinating and integrating the work of all.

An Aid in Marketing Research

Much of the research in market and marketing analysis falls into general categories concerning products and markets or advertising and selling. Questionnaires may be used to gather information concerning the uses of a product, consumer approval of changes, brand preferences, brand purchases, potential market and the testing of a product — all useful in putting products on the market, appraising attitudes toward products, improving products and distributing them. Surveys of buying habits and motives and of the readership of advertisements and advertising media contribute to the evaluation of advertising and help in selling a product.

The more information available on why people buy certain items, what they like or dislike and what they want and use, the better the job that advertising and selling can do. Knowing that housewives prefer to buy bread wrapped in wax paper is certainly an important factor for consideration in deciding what type of packaging to use. The consumer will buy what he wants.

A Basis and Measure of Public Relations

Finding out the attitudes of various publics toward the company, product or individuals and educating them in the direction of favorable opinion or approval is an important aspect of public relations work. There are six general publics of a company: the general public, consumers, employees, stockholders, management and the government. The attitudes of each and the interrelation of the different groups can be determined by questionnaires. After this knowledge is obtained it can be used as a basis for mutual understanding and harmony among the various publics and for educational campaigns.

Even in a well-developed public relations department public opinion polls and employee-attitude surveys can be used from time to time to measure and improve effectiveness. They measure public confidence in the business, labor unions and advertising; they determine opinion toward a specific problem such as a labor dispute, toward a person such as John L. Lewis or toward a specific industry; they find out the stockholders' attitudes toward management and corporation policies; they provide knowledge of what the worker thinks about his job and his company; and they measure job-security attitudes.

KINDS OF QUESTIONNAIRES

The method of distributing questionnaires is the basis for classifying them as mail, personal interview or telephone interview questionnaires. The discussion this far has pertained to all three types. The next chapter, however, takes up both types of interview questionnaires at length; thus the emphasis in the remainder of this chapter is on the mail questionnaire. It should be noted, however, that principles of phrasing and organizing questions and of selecting the sample apply to all types of questionnaires and not merely to those sent through the mail.

The mail questionnaire is the most widely used of survey techniques, for it can reach a large number of people scattered over a large area — in most cases people who could not be reached in any other way. Although it does take time to plan and execute, the time the respondent takes to fill it out is less than he would spend if he were being interviewed, and the questioner's time is also saved. Other advantages are:

(*1*) Questions can be answered at the convenience of the respondent.
(*2*) The respondent has a chance to deliberate and look up information.
(*3*) People generally will take care in filling out written information.
(*4*) The bias of an interviewer is eliminated.
(*5*) Specific segments of the population can be reached.
(*6*) The respondent need not be identified.
(*7*) Questions can be standardized.

Generally the mail questionnaire is less costly than interviewing. Time and labor are spent in preparing, mailing and handling the questionnaires, but that is all. The cost per mailing is low, but the cost per return may be high. If fewer than 10% reply, the cost of mailing has been increased ten times over what it would be if there were 100% returns. Percentage replies usually range from 2% to 30%; however, it is not uncommon to obtain 75% or better returns if there is a selected, interested mailing list and the questionnaire itself has been perfected.

The disadvantages of the mail questionnaire lie in the difficulty in securing replies and in the nature of the answers. If the response is too small, the data will not furnish a true picture. It is also difficult to obtain a representative sample. The sample sent may be representative, but the returns may not necessarily include all elements of the population. Often questions are inadequately answered. The answers to some questions may be meaningless, and some questions may remain unanswered. Complex or confidential information is not readily given on mail questionnaires. Most of these disadvantages can be corrected by using a carefully planned, well-prepared questionnaire and by proper selection of the sample or mailing list.

At any rate the advantages of the mail questionnaire far outweigh its disadvantages.

PREPARATION OF THE QUESTIONNAIRE

Construction of Questions

First of all it is necessary in preparing a questionnaire to understand the subject matter in the light of the purpose of the investigation. Because questions are drafted to seek the desired information, the data necessary and how they will be used should be determined. The list of basic elements of the problem or main issues involved can be used as a basis for making an itemized list of data to be requested. Questions are then worded so that they will best obtain the information needed.

Phrasing of Questions. Questions must be absolutely clear. They should allow for only one interpretation and should mean the same thing to everybody. Phrasing them in concrete, specific terms helps. Technical and unfamiliar words should not be used. The question should indicate the form the answer is to take, such as: "What make car do you own? ________________" Questions should not be ambiguous. Using words with only one meaning or possible interpretation keeps them clear. Likewise negative phrasing should be avoided; state the question in positive terms. Each question should include only a single subject. General opinions should be avoided; specific facts should be sought — information the respondent will have readily available.

If an opinion or attitude survey is being made, ask for opinions on specific points or attitudes about particular things. Ask for reasons for preferences, seeking to find out "why?" in each case in order to understand better the response given.

Questions that begin with *what, when, where, why, who* or *how* force thought and generally make for definite answers. Leading questions should be eliminated. They are usually worded to suggest an answer which, if given, may not be representative. A question similar to "Did you see this advertisement?" for instance, will be answered "yes" by 50% to 75% of the respondents regardless of whether they did or not.

Questions that call for "yes" or "no" answers should provide for a "don't know" possibility. Conditional answers should also be provided for, as: "If __________, would you __________?" All questions that are short and to the point will save the reader's time. He will also be more likely to understand the question and to respond to it. Questions dealing with behavior should be kept objective and stated as unemotionally and as impersonally as possible.

If a great deal of time and effort are required for the respondent to get the facts, few people will respond. Whenever possible, questions should ask for facts that are either quickly recalled or are readily available. This will prevent guesswork. Objectionable questions should be avoided. The questionnaire is not the best way to get confidential or inside information. The respondent when asked for confidential information should be assured that it will be handled confidentially. His name and any identification may be omitted from the questionnaire.

Form of Questions. In deciding on the types of questions to be used, one must consider not only the nature of the information and the respondent's time, but also how the answers can be tabulated. Check lists are very popular because they are easily and quickly checked. A statement or question is given and a list of possible answers or items follow to be checked:

Check the items you had for dinner today:
Soup
Salad
Vegetables
Etc.

Useful in measuring attitudes or preferences is the question calling for a ranking of items:

Indicate in order of preference the qualities you consider necessary in a secretary by placing 1, 2, 3, etc. before the quality:
Neat appearance
Punctuality
Good English
Speed in typing
Neat work
Etc.

Of course, closely related to a check list is the multiple-choice question:

As a group to work with, my fellow employees are:
As fine a group as I could want
A good group
Fair
Unsatisfactory

This particular example also allows for intensity of reply, as does also:

Do you make use of your charga-plate when shopping in stores where this service is offered?
Always_____
Frequently_____
Seldom_____
Never_____

Another form of question is the one calling for a simple "yes" or "no" response:

Does the use of a charga-plate save you time in shopping?
Yes_____ No_____

This is naturally the easiest type of question to ask, to answer and to tabulate.

A question may also ask for a single fact:

About how much money did you spend on groceries last week?

or:

What is your favorite method of preparing tuna?

or:

Who sponsors the Hopalong Cassidy show?

Unless a question calls for a specific fact, it is sometimes difficult to tabulate the answers:

Please list your objections to__________.

or:

What do you think of __________?

Sequence of Questions. Questions should be arranged in proper sequence so that the flow of thought will be continuous from the beginning to the end of the questionnaire. This will make answering easy for the reader, which means a better response to the questionnaire.

Either a logical or a psychological arrangement may be followed. A logical sequence gives full consideration to the subject matter of the questions, which must be covered thoroughly, and the chain of thought moves unbroken from one question to the next. The psychological order, on the other hand, gives full consideration to the respondent. The first questions are easy, the reader then proceeding to the more difficult ones. Some transition is used between questions to keep his interest stimulated.

Personal questions are buried somewhere in the middle of the questionnaire, as are those which may reflect on the respondent's intelligence and those which are likely to be of little interest to him.

In dealing with motives the first questions should call for "surface" replies and lead to the more important underlying points. The "why" should follow the "what" in such a series of questions. The total number of questions should be as low as possible to gather the needed information. Questions of similar nature may be combined or grouped together and superfluous ones rejected. A well-arranged questionnaire, even if long, will not seem so to the respondent if he is interested in the subject matter, if questions can be answered quickly and if the flow of thought is continuous.

Makeup of Questionnaires

Elements of a Questionnaire. Notice the parts of the following questionnaire. The heading, which establishes contact by identifying the source of the questionnaire, is followed by the title, which tells the reader its subject matter. Instructions, simple and clear, are given next. Numbered questions follow with spaces for checking appropriate responses. An open-end question is provided at the end for additional comments. Corollary data are called for last, although sometimes they are called for first. Usually personal facts such as age, sex or income group are called for and are used for two purposes — as a basis for cross-tabulating the answers to analyze the influence of such factors and as a means of checking the representativeness of the returns from the sample taken. In this particular example a check was made to see that various types and sizes of businesses were included in the returns. The questionnaires were also tabulated according to size and type of business, and it was found that neither of these factors had any bearing on the responses.

Sometimes the name and address of the person replying is sought. More often no place is provided for this information, and in some instances the request, "Please do not sign your name," is placed at the bottom of the questionnaire. This assures the respondent that his name will not be used in connection with the answers, and he feels more free to give his answer because of this assurance that the information will be treated confidentially.

Questionnaires should be made as neat and attractive as possible. Care shown in making up the questionnaire calls for equal care in completing it. Charts, diagrams and pictures are sometimes introduced to create attention and interest. These take up considerable space, but if the reader is interested he will not notice the length. In long questionnaires a booklet is sometimes used. Although this makes for an attractive appearance, the processing of the data afterwards can be awkward and time-consuming.

COLLEGE OF COMMERCE AND BUSINESS ADMINISTRATION
TULANE UNIVERSITY
New Orleans 18, Louisiana

APPLICATION LETTER CHECK-LIST

According to your opinion and practice, please place check marks in the appropriate spaces:

	Always	Frequently	Seldom	Never
1. Do you want applicants to submit letters of application?				
2. Do you give consideration to unsolicited letters of application?				
3. Do you give consideration to accompanying letters of recommendation?				
4. Do you require a photograph of the applicant?				
5. Do you want the applicant to include stamped, return envelope for your reply?				
6. Do you consider the follow-up letter when the first application letter has failed to impress you?				
7. Do you like a conventional, straightforward approach better than the clever, out-of-the-ordinary application letter?				
8. Do you want the applicant to address his letter to a specific person within your company?				
9. Do you require the applicant to submit a data sheet?				
10. Do you like the applicant to submit a one-page letter with a data sheet?				
11. Do you like the applicant to submit a two- or three-page letter without a data sheet?				
12. Do you like an elaborate presentation of qualifications which might be three to ten pages in length?				
13. Do you give attention to the letter which merely requests an application blank?				
14. Do you want an applicant to apply for a specific position with your company rather than for just a job?				

Questionnaire mailed by a university to study employment application preferences.

	Always	Frequently	Seldom	Never
15. Do you like for the applicant to state in his letter his reasons for leaving a previous position?				
16. Do you desire that the applicant relate his experience to the work of your company?				
17. Do you desire that the applicant relate his education to the work of your company?				
18. Do you want an applicant to include in his letter his average grades in school?				
19 Do you want an applicant to include information on extracurricular activities?				
20. Do you want an applicant to include information on his participation in community activities?				
21. Do you want the applicant to include information on his family's background?				
22. Are you favorably impressed if the applicant shows a knowledge of your company?				
23. Do you want the applicant to state in his letter an expected salary?				
24. Do you like the application letter to include a request for an interview?				
25. Do you consider an application letter that contains mechanical errors?				

Additional Remarks (List your pet peeves and principal likes. Use back of sheet if necessary.)

Position and company

Type of business

Address

If you wish to receive a summary of this survey, check here: ☐

Questionnaire (second page).

Use of Covering Letter. The application-letter survey form was mailed with the following covering letter:

TULANE UNIVERSITY
School of Business Administration
New Orleans 18, La.

Office of the Dean

April 11, 195–

Dear Sir:

To find out what you and other personnel men want in an application letter, the students of this College, under my direction, have undertaken a survey among employers in this area.

The purpose of this survey is to discover the value of the application letter to your company and what you want it to contain. The results of this investigation should benefit you as an employer, teachers of business letter writing, students who will be writing application letters and advisory personnel in placement offices.

Your cooperation is needed in securing pertinent information. It will be a step toward adequate application letters for both you and the applicant.

Will you have the person in charge of employment in your company check the appropriate answers to the enclosed questions? It will take only a few minutes. A stamped, return envelope is enclosed for your reply.

Receipt of your answer within the next few days will be greatly appreciated. A summary of our findings will be mailed you if you would like to have it.

Very truly yours,

Leland Brown
Assistant Professor of
Business Communications

LB:idp
enclosure

The covering letter should explain the questionnaire and sell the recipient on filling it out and returning it. It should be short and tactful. It should give a reason for the questionnaire and state the purpose of the study. The reader usually likes to know why he has been asked to reply. His cooperation should be sought by stressing the benefit to him or others and by appealing to his sense of pride or self-interest. Sometimes a little sincere flattery will help. A copy of results may be promised or some premium or reward given as a special inducement.

The letter might also include general instructions pertaining to the questions and to returning the form. It is good practice to state a time limit and urge reply at once. Appreciation should also be expressed, and when confidential data are sought the reader must be assured they will be handled confidentially.

The following letter accompanied the questionnaire on pages 88 and 89. Here notice how interest is created in the first paragraph by the use of benefits and appeals to obtain responses.

CHARGA-PLATE SURVEY

April 24, 195–

Dear Charga-Plate Owner:

ARE YOU ENTIRELY SATISFIED WITH THE CHARGA-PLATE SERVICE OFFERED BY A NUMBER OF RETAIL STORES IN NEW ORLEANS?

DO YOU FIND THAT THE USE OF YOUR CHARGA-PLATE SAVES YOU TIME IN SHOPPING?

_____These and many similar questions confronting the management of the New Orleans retailers in an effort to provide you with the maximum in a Charga-Plate Service, can be adequately answered only by you and other Charga-Plate users.

In order to find the answers to such questions I am asking your cooperation to the extent of filling in the blanks on the enclosed form.

I am a graduate student in the School of Business Administration of Tulane University. At present I am writing a thesis on the "Evaluation of the Use of the Charga-Plate Service to the Retailer in New Orleans." This thesis is a requirement for my degree which I will receive in June.

Will you please fill out the enclosed questionnaire as promptly as possible and return it to the New Orleans Charga-Plate Association in the enclosed self-addressed envelope. This will take but a few minutes of your time and will be of real value to me in completing this survey. Please DO NOT SIGN YOUR NAME or identify yourself with the questionnaire.

Thank you for your cooperation in this matter.

Very truly yours,

L. M. LaPoutge

P. S. This survey has been approved by Mr. Hubert Fielder, President of the New Orleans Charga-Plate Association.

Not all questionnaires or covering letters are as long as the ones shown. The following one, for instance, presents the questionnaire on a postcard, and the letter is brief and to the point:

WYATT-CORNICK, INC.
Home Office: RICHMOND 16, VIRGINIA
P. O. Box 2118

Distributors
RCA

Branches:
NORFOLK
ROANOKE

April 28, 195–

Dear Dealer:

Will you take one minute to give us your very candid advice on an important question?

RCA and other manufacturers often ask us, "What do you consider to be the most effective form of advertising for our product: magazines—newspapers—television—or radio?"

No one is in a better position to answer that question than you, on the basis of actual experience.

Will you help us, therefore, by checking and mailing the attached card today.

Thanks very much for your assistance.

Cordially,

William D. Carleton
Advertising Manager

WDC/asd

In terms of its effectiveness in producing sales, I rate the value of product advertising in the different media as follows:

(Please check only one block for each.)	Magazines	Newspapers	Television	Radio
Most Effective------	( )	( )	( )	( )
2nd Best-----------	( )	( )	( )	( )
3rd Best-----------	( )	( )	( )	( )
Least Effective-----	( )	( )	( )	( )

Signed.......................................

Company.......................................

Address.......................................

Postcard questionnaire.

Testing and Revising the Questionnaire. The questions and questionnaire should be checked and tested, revised and finally mailed. The scope and sequence of the questions should be checked for thoroughness and logic. The wording of the questions must be clear. The questionnaire should be as brief as possible. A study of the questions may call for eliminating several or combining and adding others. The instructions should be examined for clarity. The format, spacing, numbering of questions, indentation and other technical features should also be considered.

When the questionnaire is ready it should be tested in a small number of interviews or mailed to a sample group before being mailed for the survey. This gives some idea as to the clearness of the questions and instructions and to the soundness with which the sample was chosen. It also aids in further revision, should weak points still show up in the questionnaire.

Sources for Mailing List

Questionnaires seeking information are usually directed to those whose connection with the subject is known through their position or through their contributions to magazines and discussions. Then a mailing list is obtained and questionnaires are mailed to each name on the list. The following are sources for compiling a mailing list:

Censuses
Telephone Directories
Subscribers to Public Utilities (Other Than the Telephone)
Automobile Registrations
List of Voters
List of Customers
Credit Lists
Subscribers to Magazines
Graduates of Schools and Colleges
Members of Organizations
Professional Directories
Clients of Social Agencies
Clients of Public Agencies
Payroll Lists
City Directories
Tax Assessor's List

PLANNING THE SAMPLE

When a survey of a large group of people is made, questionnaires are not mailed to everyone; only a *part* of the total group is chosen for sampling on the assumption that a representative number of responses is indicative of the whole. Sampling is used extensively in making market surveys, public opinion polls and employee surveys in which it would be almost impossible to reach the entire population. Two major problems are involved in planning the sample—selection of the kind of sample and determination of the size of the sample.

Selecting the Sample

To select the sample the investigator must first study the nature of the population. What groups does it contain? What characteristics do they possess? If the sample is to be a true reflection of the entire population, each individual must be assured an equal and independent chance of inclusion in the sample.

Care must be taken to assure the sample's being representative and unbiased. Sampling may be random, stratified or proportionate — depending on the method of selection. For an employee survey, for instance, the payroll list would contain the entire group under study. For the sample individual names on the list could be selected at equally spaced intervals, such as every tenth or twelfth name. That would be *random* selection. But would every significant element be included? Would the sample contain employees at all the different salary levels? Both men and women? Employees of all age groups? Of every nationality?

Would it not be more representative to divide the employees into categories and select names from each group? Then each group would be assured of being represented in the sample. This would be *stratified* sampling. If the investigator also controls the selection so that characteristics of the whole group are represented proportionately, the sample is also *proportionate*. The proportionate sample is used only if a specific class will affect the responses or conclusions. If age groups would have no bearing on the conclusions, for example, then it is not necessary to have proportionate age group representation. Stratified or random sampling would be sufficient.

Determining the Size

To determine the size of the sample one needs to consider his purpose. If it is to find out whether or not the layout of an advertisement emphasizes certain sales points of a product, a check with a few people who know advertising will give the answer. If it is to learn why the odor of a deodorant offends, a few dozen women can tell. The information would be the same as if several hundred were asked, so why bother with the larger number when a small sample is sufficient? When the purpose is to generalize on the attitudes or opinions of a large group of people, however, the sample will have to be large. An adequate sample is one that is large enough for generalization about certain characteristics.

The size of the sample varies with the problem. A sample should increase with the number and variety of the categories it includes. A sample should also increase as the required accuracy of the results increases. The increased size of the sample reduces the errors of chance.

Testing the Sample

The returns from a stratified sample are tested to see if all categories are included; if they are, the sample is valid. For a proportionate sample each class represented in the returns is represented in proportion to its occurrence in the entire group. Because it shows the characteristics of the respondents the corollary information from the questionnaires is used in checking the validity of both stratified and proportionate samples.

The normal percentage returns on most mail questionnaires is from 10% to 15%. With a carefully selected mailing list, however, and a questionnaire of general interest, returns often will reach 75% or more. When they reach approximately 80%, reliability can be given the findings without further testing, because answers from those not responding would have had little effect on the total responses. The basic principle here is the same as that involved in the cut-off method of measuring the reliability of the sample. A stabilization point is determined for the responses beyond which no more returns need be considered.

In applying the cut-off method, the total number of questionnaires is divided into several sets, which may be equal or unequal in number. The percentage of "yes" answers to a question is computed. As additional sets of questionnaires are added the cumulative percentage is derived. When the questionnaires make very little or no change the responses are said to have been stabilized. A cut-off point has then been established. Probably there would be less than 2% or 3% fluctuation either way, so the sample is reliable.

Another method of measuring the reliability of the sample is to analyze subsamples. The total number of questionnaires is divided into two or three groups of equal size. Standard errors of deviation are computed statistically for each group and differences are analyzed for significance. If there is little difference, the sample is reliable.

There are other statistical measures which may be applied in testing the sample and which investigators without a background in statistics may find in books on the subject.

MACHINE TABULATION

After the returns of questionnaires have been received, they are evaluated and sorted, then tabulated so that generalizations may be formulated. They may be tabulated by hand or by machine. When there is a very large quantity of data (a sample of several thousand or more), when a large number of cross-classifications are needed or when repeated studies are to be made, it is desirable to use machine tabulation.

The process of classifying, evaluating and tabulating data manually is discussed in the chapter on organization and interpretation of data. Machine tabulation is highly technical and requires specially trained personnel for its effective use. Special electrically operated tabulating machines sort cards into groups, count data and print the totals. Powers, Remington Rand, Inc. and International Business Machines all have machines designed to count a large number of items rapidly. It is the coding that requires time. Either a clerk must read the information on the source document and punch the proper code number on a card, or it must be processed through a special machine. The questionnaires must be coded in such a way that the responses can be punched on a card of the appropriate size and weight to be run through the machine. The cost is prohibitive for small counts, but is correspondingly low for large ones. The greatest advantage of machine tabulation is probably the ease and rapidity with which it cross-classifies. Responses can be broken down into as many as eighteen different cross-tabulations. This would of course be unnecessary and confusing for small operations, but efficient for large ones.

Tabulation accuracy is assured by machines. Both the elimination of transcription errors and their pinpointing in enumeration are possible. Other advantages of machine tabulation include making results available early, preparing duplicate files for filing in a different sequence, flexibility of sequence listings, unlimited statistical analyses within the scope of punched data and saving in cost and time.

PROBLEMS

1. Explain the uses of questionnaires in market research, public relations and management.

2. Suggest ways of improving the application letter check-list questionnaire on page 56.

3. How does the covering letter used in the Charga-Plate survey, page 59, sell the recipient on responding to the questionnaire?

4. What are the advantages and disadvantages of machine and manual tabulation of questionnaires?

5. You have been asked to make a marketing survey of tuna fish buying habits in the supermarkets of your city. The results are to be used in your sales and advertising program. Prepare the questionnaire that you would use.

6. Write the covering letter and a return postcard questionnaire that could be used in making a readership survey of the employee magazine in your company; of the company annual report.

7. Your company wants you to make an investigation of employee morale to determine ways in which it can be improved. Construct a questionnaire and make plans for its use in surveying the feelings and attitudes of the employees.

8. Your college wants to launch a program of informing its students. Just as the well-informed employee is an efficient, cooperative producer, so the student informed of the activities, purpose, objectives, organization, etc. of his college is an efficient student.

   a. Prepare a questionnaire to be used in a student survey to determine what the student knows, wants to know, should be told and how he is to be informed.

   b. How could the results be used?

CHAPTER 6

Securing Data Though Interviews and Other Research Methods

COLLECTION OF DATA THROUGH BIBLIOGRAPHICAL RESEARCH and through questionnaires has been discussed. In this chapter let us consider three other important methods of securing data for the solution of a business problem – interviews, observation and letters.

INTERVIEWS

The process of securing information directly through a conversation with an individual is an interview. It involves conversing with a purpose other than personal satisfaction. It allows for a direct exchange of information, and the interviewee's voice, facial expression, gestures and general behavior all contribute to this exchange of information.

Uses of Interviews

Interviews are used to determine objective facts such as events, conditions, practices, policies and techniques. They are also used to gather subjective data such as attitudes, preferences, opinions, tastes or emotional reactions. Sometimes their purpose is to discover why or how an individual responds as he does or has a particular attitude or opinion. In this case they enable the interviewer to have a clear understanding of the facts he obtains from the interview and to analyze his information accordingly.

At the very outset of an investigation an interview might be used to obtain help in defining the problem and in planning the investigation. For this purpose the person who authorized the report might be interviewed, as might those involved in the situation giving rise to the investigation. An interview may also be used to win cooperation from and to establish working relations with persons involved in the problem being investigated. For information to be used in the analysis and solution of a problem the interview is used most frequently for discovering opinions, attitudes or trends of belief. It should be avoided as a method of obtaining general information or of securing facts that are commonly known or can be obtained from other sources, such as company records, committee meeting minutes and other written documents. It is an effective method of determining facts known to a single individual or group of people. It is also very worthwhile when the data that are revealed are the opinions of experts. A consensus of opinion can thus be obtained. The interview is also helpful in determining facts which vary from person to person or from one situation to another.

Saunders and Anderson in their book, *Business Reports,*[1] list the five following special advantages of the personal interview over the mail questionnaire:

1. The interviewer can, to some extent, control the situation.
2. He can interpret questions.
3. He can clear up misunderstandings.
4. He can secure fully and accurately the most representative replies.
5. He will receive first-hand impressions which will throw light on the data procured by his questions.

Directors of industrial relations, personnel specialists, lawyers,

---

[1] Alta Gwinn Saunders and Chester Reed Anderson, *Business Reports,* McGraw-Hill Book Company, Inc., New York, 1940, p. 77.

social workers, psychiatrists, reporters, salesmen, vocational counselors and employment managers all make use of the interview. Interviews are also used in marketing surveys and in the fields of education and guidance. Our concern here is the use of interviews for business purposes. There are three special aspects of business in which interviews are used a great deal: in marketing studies, in personnel work and in industrial relations. Space does not warrant a full treatment of these special uses of the interview; however, each is worthy of some consideration. Special books dealing with research in each of the fields should be consulted for full treatments.

It is necessary to ascertain in market analysis the existing and potential sales possibilities of a product. Consumer preferences, when known, are used as a basis for advertising and sales promotional plans. Salesmen, advertisers, manufacturers and dealers use the data. Surveys provide a consensus of opinion and attitude which can be put to effective use.

Personnel specialists and business executives use interviews as a means of keeping informed of business conditions and relations. Through interviews they learn to know the employees and can establish proper contacts. Interviews are not used as much here to solve a business problem calling for an investigation and a report as they are used to transact a business purpose. Important examples are the employment interview used in hiring men, the vocational guidance interview used to help the employee adjust to his job or to place him properly on another job, or the exit interview used when a person leaves a job to go elsewhere. These situations do not necessarily call for a business report; yet each makes use of the personal interview.

Problems in personnel do arise, however, and call for reports in their solution. Suppose a firm has a rapid turnover of its employees and wants to stabilize its working force. It will need to find out why people leave the company; it will need to know something about the attitudes of the employees toward present working conditions and policies; it will need to investigate the hiring procedures. Interviews can be used as a source of information in each of these situations.

For the industrial relations director the interview reveals the attitudes of his employees. It is a valuable morale builder, because it gives the employee a chance to "get it off his chest" and helps build goodwill. The interview enlightens management by giving it an insight into the human nature of its workers. This insight can be used to train supervisors in educating the workers. Determining the employees' attitudes brings to light certain conditions which need to be corrected and calls attention to the need for improvements.

Kinds of Interviews

There are two kinds of personal interviews — fact-finding interviews and depth interviews. In securing business information both are usually necessary. In the *fact-finding interview* the investigator may seek either objective or subjective information or both. The information he obtains is usually in answer to direct questions which may be general or specific.

For example, suppose an interview is being made to determine the employees' attitudes toward their working conditions. The question might be asked: "Are your working conditions conducive to efficient work?" The answer may be a "yes" or a "no." A survey of a representative number of employees would give a consensus of opinion among the workers in the company. But how beneficial would the concensus be? In the *depth interview,* also known as the open-end or intensive interview, the interviewer would seek to find out why the respondent answered "yes" or "no." He would try to find out what conditions were considered conducive to efficiency and why, what changes the worker would like to have made and why. He might do this not so much through the use of direct questions as by getting the worker to talk about the subject and by drawing him out on the points on which information is desired.

The chief difference between the fact-seeking interview and the depth interview is the degree of intensity to which the interview is carried out. The depth interview begins where the other ends. After a fact or attitude has been determined the depth interview gets behind the fact or attitude to discover motives or causes. The depth interview is thus more time-consuming than the purely fact-seeking one, but is more enlightening.

Recently a survey was made for Stanolind Oil and Gas Company to test the results of the freedom course, "Let's Talk It Over," which was being given their supervisory and hourly employees. Both depth and fact-finding interviews were used. Their aim was to compare the attitudes, beliefs and opinions of the workers before and after the course was conducted. At the close of the program employees met at work in groups of 10 to 25 and filled out questionnaires under the supervision of the staff members. During the months when the course was in operation staff members also conducted depth interviews. This made possible cross-evaluation of the results. Specific questions were used in the depth interviews, but the staff members conducting the interviews drew out the workers, encouraging them to talk on the subject and express the thinking behind their responses.

Sometimes interviews are conducted over the telephone. Such interviews are useful for opinion polls when a limited number of questions can be asked and are certainly more inexpensive than the personal fact-finding interview or the depth interview. The *telephone interview* permits wide coverage of either particular or general groups, and a representative or random sample may be obtained. As a method of research the telephone interview has been widely used in the field of radio audience evaluation. Here the method has been used extensively and developed fully by C. E. Hooper, Inc. A full treatment of the techniques used may be found in *Radio Audience Measurement* by Chappell and Hooper.[2] A number of radio telephone surveys have been made on both the national and local level. Questions on the product being advertised are frequently asked, as are questions as to whether or not the radio is turned on and to which program and station.

The following lists taken from Mildred Parten's *Surveys, Polls and Samples: Practical Procedures* summarize the merits and disadvantages of the telephone interview.[3]

Merits of the Telephone Interview

1. The telephone interview is the quickest of the survey techniques. Interviewers can complete about thirty calls per hour if the calls are brief. It is especially adapted to surveys of radio programs where a great many interviews must be made during a given program.
2. The refusal rate is usually low among people who are reached by phone.
3. The coincidental method can be used, thus eliminating the memory factor.
4. It is easy to train and supervise interviewers since they can work in one room directly beside the supervisor.
5. The approach and questions are easy to standardize from one interviewer to another.

---

[2] Matthew N. Chappell and C. E. Hooper, *Radio Audience Measurement,* Stephen Daye Press, Inc., Brattleboro, Vermont, 1944.

[3] Mildred Parten, *Survey, Polls and Samples: Practical Procedures,* Harper & Brothers, New York, 1950, pp. 91–93.

6. The cost per completed interview is low for the sample covered.

7. The geographic distribution of the sample can be easily controlled. An address listing of numbers is usually available and can be used for drawing the sample.

8. For studies of middle- and high-income groups the telephone interview may be satisfactory because most of them have phones.

9. Interviews may be scattered over a wide area within a city without adding to the cost.

10. As compared with a mail questionnaire, the telephone survey is preferable because it usually costs less per return. Returns are higher on first solicitation, and they can be more effectively controlled from the point of neighborhood distribution.

Disadvantages of the Telephone Interview

1. As a sample of the general population, telephone subscribers are not representative. So unless the telephone interview is supplemented by a method that covers nonsubscribers, it should not be used. Less than half of all homes in towns over 2,500 have telephones.

2. Detailed data cannot be gathered by this method because the informants soon become annoyed or impatient. If the schedule is too lengthy, the informant may either hang up or give unreliable answers.

3. When observation of the situation is an important element, the telephone interview is not useful. If the interviewer is supposed to evaluate the answers as to trustworthiness, he has very little to go on in a short telephone conversation.

4. Information about the respondent must be limited to one or two facts. Such items as age, nationality, income, etc., are difficult to secure by telephone.

5. Attitude scales must be used with caution. Also opinions are less likely to be given freely since the informant cannot be certain of the credentials of the person calling.

6. Since rural telephone ownership is low, the telephone interview is not useful in such areas. Also, because rural rates are higher than urban, the cost of telephone inquiries is greater than in cities.

7. The brevity of the introduction and questions does not give the informant much time to orient himself to the subject matter of the survey. Reactions requiring careful thought—such as criticism of various products, suggestions as to new uses of products, appeals, etc.—should not be obtained by this technique.

8. The telephone situation neither encourages the respondent to amplify his replies nor gives the interviewer much time to jot down the comments. A face-to-face interview is more conducive to a considered response.

9. The task of checking the no-answers, wrong numbers, busy signals, etc., is time-consuming but must be done if the sample is to be representative of telephone subscribers.

10. It is difficult to secure privacy on party lines.

11. The time may come when the telephone technique will be used by so many groups that informants will develop an antagonism to all telephone inquiries.
12. The surveyor must be careful not to antagonize informants by phoning too early or too late in the day. One well-known survey agency makes it a policy never to call before 8:30 a.m. or after 10:30 p.m.
13. Misinformation is hard to detect and check in short inquiries.

No matter which kind of interview is conducted there are a number of general procedures and techniques which should be followed in order to obtain best results.

Procedures in Interviewing

Careful planning in advance of the interview will increase the likelihood of its success. The ways an interview can be organized must be considered and thought out in advance.

Prior to the Interview. It is necessary that the interviewer think through his problem and formulate in his own mind the factors involved so that the interview can contribute to its solution. In doing this he will need to master the subject with which the problem deals and to understand fully the background of the situation giving rise to it. This is done as a part of the preliminary planning of the investigation. Then prior to interviewing, the investigator needs to review these phases of his planning and to understand how the interview will accomplish what he is seeking. Part of the interviewer's knowledge and background in the subject must come from bibliographical research. He must recognize also his own personal bias, feelings and prejudices and eliminate them so that he will have an open mind and can be objective during the interview.

Interviewees should be selected with care. They must be in a position to have the desired information. If a survey of a group is being made by interviews, then enough of a sample must be secured to assure its validity and its representativeness. The procedures outlined in Chapter 5 on using the questionnaire can be applied here in making surveys through interviews.

Likewise the interviewer can apply the principles outlined there in composing a questionnaire, especially the suggestions pertaining to the wording and phrasing of the questions. He needs to list the questions he plans to ask if he is interviewing a group, because he will want to ask the same questions in the same way at each interview. Consideration should be given to both general and specific questions, to questions which may be asked directly and those which may be brought in indirectly or casually. An exact knowledge of the purpose of the interview and what it should accomplish will help. A well-thought-out list of topics and questions is the result of an advance knowledge of the main points to be discussed. Advance planning should also include a consideration of the approach to take in the interview.

In order to plan his approach in the interview, the interviewer should find out information about the person or group of people to be interviewed. He can do this in the case of an individual by checking in *Who's Who* or some other source of biographical information, by finding out something about the individual's position and work and what he may have written or by asking others about him. Any group to be interviewed needs to be analyzed according to its characteristics. Information on the interviewee will also help the interviewer to explain the purpose of the interview in terms of the interviewee's experience and interest, thus getting him interested in the subject of the interview. Such information will enable the interviewer to adapt his questions to his purpose and to the interviewee. In cases of the depth interview he will be able to lead the interviewee into a freer and more nearly complete discussion than would otherwise be possible. Consideration should also be given to controlling the interview, to keeping the conversation on the subject or problem at hand.

In a survey, when a large number of interviews is being conducted, it is sometimes appropriate to secure letters of recommendation or of introduction to show the interviewee, so he will feel that the interview has the proper backing. This procedure is followed also when only a few people are being interviewed, especially when interviews have not been arranged in advance, which is the case in conducting surveys or in taking polls. Whenever only a few people are being interviewed for information, it is customary and courteous to arrange an appointment in advance. This will let the interviewee know what is wanted and will enable him to get ready for the interview. It will also assure the interviewer that time will be allotted to the interview. A busy executive will not be likely to sit down for thirty minutes and give information on the spur of the moment. His time is too valuable for that. He has his day planned and does not always have time for an unscheduled interview to help some one else.

An appointment for an interview may be made by letter, by telephone or by a personal office call. The latter is too expensive and time-consuming to use often. The telephone has the advantage of expediency. The letter is the most costly of the three. With all three, however, it is necessary to let the interviewee know who the interviewer is and what he is doing. Interest should be created so the interviewee will be willing to be interviewed. A selling job must be done. It can be accomplished in much the same way as the covering letter to a mail questionnaire sells its reader on responding. The same points, such as showing how the reader can benefit, letting him realize the importance and need for the interview, and motivating him to action, should be followed. At the end of the letter or telephone conversation specific arrangements should be made, suggesting or designating a specific time and place for the interview.

During the Interview. The logical way to begin is to introduce oneself and to explain the purpose of the interview. This should be done in such a way as to break the ice. In fact, the purpose can be explained in such a way that the interviewee will appreciate it in terms of his own experience and interests and will reveal the desired information. A psychological approach to the interview might be to engage the interviewee in casual conversation, getting him to talk freely and then leading into some main point of interest for discussion. Again, the interviewer might first seek to create a desire on the part of the interviewee, then show how this desire can be fulfilled by the investigation. A frank mutual exchange of ideas and facts on the problem or subject would follow.

During the interview the interviewer should observe the following suggestions:

(*1*) Gain the cooperation of the interviewee.
(*2*) Listen sympathetically to personal opinions.
(*3*) Be frank and sincere.
(*4*) Gain and deserve the interviewee's confidence.
(*5*) Be pleasant and friendly.
(*6*) Keep control of the interview.
(*7*) Keep the center of interest on the interviewee and what he has to contribute.
(*8*) Ask questions, general and specific.
(*9*) Guide the interviewee to discuss facts freely and thoroughly.
(*10*) Introduce topics of conversation which will call for significant facts desired.

(*11*) Get the full meaning of each statement or answer given.
(*12*) Give the interviewee the opportunity to qualify his answers.

Of course, direct questions should not be asked until the interviewee is ready. His cooperation and interest must be obtained first; then his answers may be sought. Nor should he be inhibited in any way. Spontaneous statements are generally more accurate than forced ones.

The conversation might be guided by pertinent statements of the investigator. He might introduce his questions so that they will interest the interviewee. He should also permit the interviewee to tell the story his way. Afterwards he can supplement it by answering questions. As questions are asked the answers should not be implied. The interviewee can be made to realize his responsibility for the facts and the importance of giving accurate ones. Sometimes a casual suggestion that certain statements can be verified will cause him to be accurate. The interviewer should be on the lookout for new leads for information or for additional information. Sometimes this comes toward the end of the interview; sometimes it is in the form of a casual remark.

The information secured from an interview must be recorded at once. It can be done during the interview or immediately afterwards to avoid omissions and inaccuracies in recording data. In recording his facts, the interviewer should observe the following suggestions:

(*1*) Understand all that is said.
(*2*) Discern significant points.
(*3*) Record testimony.
(*4*) Recognize inaccuracies.
(*5*) Record specific answers to questions.
(*6*) Distinguish between observed facts and facts reported by interviewee.
(*7*) Distinguish inferences from facts whether observed or reported.
(*8*) Check percentages, figures, etc.
(*9*) Remember and report facts accurately.
(*10*) Distinguish attitudes and opinions from facts.
(*11*) Record explanations for opinions and attitudes.
(*12*) Get all the necessary facts.

When making a survey the interviewer usually records the answer to each question as it is given. Often a check list will be used for this purpose, making tabulation easy later. On the other hand, in some depth interviews note-taking might hamper the interviewee, in which case all the information would have to be recorded immediately afterwards. The question sheet itself may be used in recording answers to prearranged questions. Note cards should be used to record general information or facts revealed during the interview. The procedure followed in recording interview facts on note cards is the same as that for recording notes from bibliographical research discussed in Chapter 4. Separate facts should be recorded on separate cards, with subject headings indicated on each card.

After the information sought has been obtained, the interview should be brought to a logical close. Care should be taken to complete the interview within the alloted time. The interviewee should be led to feel that he has made a valuable contribution and that his efforts and the information he has given are appreciated and worthwhile.

After the Interview. Although the interviewee has been thanked at the close of the interview, he will still appreciate a thank-you note if his interview is not one of a large number in a survey. This courteous act will build goodwill for future business relations. Just a brief letter, thanking him for his time and effort and letting him know that his contribution was useful, is all that is necessary. This should be done within two weeks after the interview.

If the data were not recorded during the interview, then they should be recorded as soon as possible afterward. Frequently answers to questions are recorded during the interview, but it is still necessary to make notes of observed facts and data after the interview has been completed.

The interviewer should also take stock of himself and the interview. He will want to relate his results to his objectives and problem. He will want to review the interview critically. This will enable him to discover his weaknesses and to improve at the next opportunity. If he decides that he wants to quote the interviewee directly, he should secure permission to do so. He may even want to have the quotation checked or verified by the person he is quoting. After an important interview he may also want to secure a confirmatory statement of significant facts. This will enable him to check figures, statistics, etc., for their accuracy and authenticity.

A list of interviews should be maintained. It will be used in making necessary acknowledgments in the report and will become a part of the final bibliography. Cards are used to record entries similar to those on bibliographical cards. The necessary information includes name, position, company, address, date and place of the interview.

The Role of the Interviewer

Because of the nature and purpose of the interview as a research method, the interviewer must maintain at all times an impartial point of view. His role is a difficult one, for he must be continually on the alert and always tactful. At the same time he must be friendly and pleasant. He should like people, and people should like him. A neatly dressed person who is confident and businesslike in his manner and knows when to smile will be likely to create a favorable appearance at the beginning of the interview. Throughout he must remain calm and collected, never giving opinions or voicing approval or disapproval of the interviewee's ideas.

He should also be accurate and honest in recording data and in filling in answers to a questionnaire. Characteristics of the ideal interviewer are listed by Mildren Parten in *Surveys, Polls and Samples: Practical Procedures.* Some of the most important ones she lists are the ability to size up people and situations quickly and correctly, the ability to talk easily with all types of people, keen powers of observation, a regard for details, persistence and thoroughness, conscientiousness and reliability, a ready wit, a good memory, an inquiring mind and an interest in research and ideas.[4]

Interviewing is an art which can be acquired and developed. When surveys and polls are taken, a number of people are usually selected to do the interviewing. The undertaking is on too large a scale for one person. Interviewers are selected for the characteristics mentioned and then are given some general training and specific instructions. The purpose of the general training is to give some background in survey work. The purpose of the specific instruction is orientation to the survey being undertaken. The instructions usually include a statement of the purpose of the survey; a list of interviews to be made, including how, when and where; instructions for handling the questionnaire; the approach to use; how to identify

[4] *Ibid.*, pp. 138–139.

oneself; etc. These points need to be understood also by the independent researcher who is conducting his own study.

The interviewer is also an observer, but he must keep his observations apart from his interpretations. The findings are recorded, tabulated and analyzed for relative importance and usefulness.

Reliability and Validity of the Interview

Because each interview discloses facts concerning attitudes, preferences and opinions known only to a single individual, it must be recognized that it has its limitations as a research method.

Sources of unreliability inhere in the interviewer, in the person interviewed, and in the relationship between the two.

The interviewer may fail to think through his problem and formulate it in such a way that the interview can contribute helpfully to its solution. He may fail to recognize and eliminate his own predilections or personal bias. He may neglect other vital steps of preparation: mastering of background data; planning the interview so as to adapt it to its special purpose; attending to the sequence of topics, the precise wording of key questions, and similar details of method and technique. Or he may fail in the presence of the interviewee through inability to gain his cooperation, or to understand him, or to select the significant points in his statements, or to record his testimony accurately and interpret fairly what he says. The interviewer then should look to his techniques while conducting the interview, as well as to the planning and organization of his inquiry.[5]

It is important for the interviewer to plan his interview and to follow procedures and techniques that will assure him of reliable data. Information that has been secured from a single individual is recorded on note cards in the same way that bibliographical data are recorded. Then the facts can be examined for their reliability in the same way that bibliographical data are examined: by checking the source and by examining the facts themselves.

Information that has been secured from a number of interviews, however, can be expressed in quantitative terms. Thus its reliability and validity can be tested by statistical methods. The responses to questions are tabulated and examined to formulate generalizations or conclusions. A test of reliability would be a test for adequacy of the sampling. Responses from two sets of interviews under comparable conditions secured by the same interviewer or another inter-

[5] Walter Van Dyke Bingham and Bruce Victor Moore, *How to Interview,* Harper & Brothers, New York, 1934, p. 7.

viewer can be put into quantitative form and coefficients of correlation can be computed statistically as a measure of the data's reliability. The coefficient of correlation between data from one-half of the interviews and data from the other half can also be used. The same statistical tests used for testing the reliability of the results of the mail questionnaire can be applied here; likewise the same tests for the validity of data may be applied. The standard error of deviation is used to test the validity of data secured from both interviews and mail questionnaires. Finally, although it is sometimes impractical to apply statistical measures to facts secured from interviews, data can always be scrutinized for consistency, accuracy and logic.

OBSERVATION

Observation is one of the chief sources of securing firsthand information, and it is often combined with other methods, especially with the personal interview. Just as an interview in its simplest form is conversation with a purpose, so observation in its simplest form is seeing with a purpose. It is recognizing and recording information pertaining to objects and people that are seen. In order to determine the amount and nature of the flow of traffic one can stand on a streetcorner and observe the cars that go by, noting the model and number of automobiles, the licenses, the drivers, etc. In a grocery store one can determine brand preferences by observing the customers as they buy certain brands off the shelves. On the production line in a factory one can observe the procedure being followed in order to find out the steps in the production process. Through observation the investigator gains information firsthand; it is in the realm of his experience. He not only observes but also forms a mental impression of what he has perceived. Information thus secured is recorded and analyzed for drawing conclusions.

Types and Uses

There are two kinds of observation — uncontrolled observation and controlled observation. In *uncontrolled observation* the observer views things as they are. In the case of observing a worker at his job he would watch him under normal working conditions to see how he performed his tasks. The worker's reaction to his job would also be noticed. Impressions and facts would be recorded. In *controlled observation* the observer selects pertinent data for observation and controls the conditions under which he observes. He might standardize all but one of the factors to be observed. He more or less sets the stage and then observes what happens.

Controlled observation is experimental research. It is commonly used in the scientific laboratory. The scientist carries on an experiment and records his findings, which are observations under controlled conditions. For business purposes controlled observation is used in testing. One way to decide whether or not to buy a certain piece of equipment is to install it temporarily and observe it at work. Before proceeding with an advertising campaign an agency will want to test it. A company interested in devising a new package for one of its products will test several possibilities for their results before deciding on which package to use. Mailing lists likewise are tested. So are sales-promotion devices and advertising media, in order to determine which ones to use.

Both controlled and uncontrolled observation make use of memory. Objects or actions are observed and understood through mental impressions that are preserved through memory and recalled for a purpose. The difference lies in the control the observer exercises over the situation and the conditions under which he observes. Both types of observation are used for similar business purposes. In marketing, pertinent facts about consumers, products, competitors and the market are observed, reported and analyzed. In the operation or production phases of a business, processes, problems, procedures and techniques are observed. In personnel or industrial relations an individual's actions and responses are noted and analyzed. The observer can make use of a psychological approach to a problem. Sometimes it is necessary to examine something and describe it. Observation is thus the chief source of information used in examination reports. Sometimes the investigator needs to observe how something is being done in a firm other than his own. He makes a field trip and observes what is done. Observation can also be used in making surveys, particularly those to determine brand preferences. Instead of asking the customers what brands they buy, the observer obtains permission to look in their pantry shelves and see what brands they have on hand.

One of the chief advantages of the observation method is that it makes the observer a reporter of behavior and not an interpreter of it. In this respect it tends to eliminate such elements as the observer's personal prejudices and biases. On the other hand, the method is limited in that it gets at motives only insofar as they are expressed in overt acts of behavior. Another disadvantage is that the observer is likely to be so impressed with an exceptional piece of data that he thinks it occurs frequently. Or he may be at times so concerned with finding what he is looking for that he sees it even when it is not there, while at other times overlooking other pertinent information.

The observation method for surveys is costlier and slower than the interview or questionnaire. It can, however, lend itself to statistical treatment for reaching conclusions in a survey and can be used for considering subjective data objectively.

Procedures in Observing

Careful planning for observation is just as important as it is for an interview. The observer must have a clear and complete understanding of the problem and of what he is to observe. He must not only determine the main points to look for but also the details, and he should know how they are interrelated and fit into his subject. In some instances he will jot down an outline of what to observe. He will also try to foresee people's reactions and their relation to the incidences he will observe, so that he will know what to expect. Prior to the observation the observer must also assume the proper mental attitude and maintain it. It is important that his mind be free of all prejudice and bias. He should cultivate an inquisitive attitude and keep an open mind.

During an observation the observer must concentrate on what he is doing. It is necessary for him to keep his mind on the subject and to be interested in it. If he has thought out things ahead of time and has listed important points to observe, he will have a guide to follow. He should first observe as a whole the object or person, then take in the details. This will help him see things in relation to each other and to the problem at hand, as well as giving the proper perspective to the facts observed. In most instances it is better to observe one thing at a time. The purpose is to get all the essential facts. Irrelevant facts may well be excluded. In making a survey a questionnaire might be used, and the observer will record the answers to the questions, taking down other pertinent data observed. Otherwise he will follow the same procedures for recording notes as outlined in the chapter on bibliographical research, making use of note cards and indicating subject headings on the cards. Notes may be recorded while he is observing or written as soon afterwards as is possible.

The human element must also be considered in observing. The observer feels as well as sees. He should, however, make a clear distinction in his notes as to what was seen and what was felt. He should strive to report behavior as it is rather than as it might be interpreted. Therefore he must observe accurately, impartially and thoroughly, so that his facts will be reliable and applicable. When interpretations are given they should be recorded as such.

Results from observations are either evaluated, edited and incorporated with other facts, if recorded on note cards, or are edited, tabulated, placed in tables and charts and interpreted along with other statistical data, if the purpose has been to observe a number of occurrences as in conducting a survey. They are thus organized along with similar data for analysis and presentation in a report.

LETTERS

Letters are also used as a means of securing information. Sometimes they are combined with a questionnaire; sometimes a simple letter of inquiry or a request for a booklet or available printed material will secure the information one is seeking. A sample letter follows:

Dear Mr. Jones:

In the May 12 issue of *Printers' Ink,* I noticed that you have prepared a booklet for your employees informing them of social security benefits. I am faced with the problem of keeping our employees similarly informed and would like to know what other companies are doing along these lines.

May I have a copy of your booklet please? I shall also appreciate any comments you might make or any further information you may have.

Sincerely yours,

The letter begins by giving the source of information about the booklet which is requested. Then the reason for the request, the request itself and appreciation are presented. An indirect compliment is given which may tend to motivate the reader to grant the request. An appeal is also made for his cooperation. The letter is very brief; yet it asks for information, is to the point and is courteous.

Whenever questions are asked in a letter they should be placed in an itemized list. The letter writer should seek to interest the reader in the questions and to make it easy for him to reply. Emphasis can be placed on the importance of the information, on how it can be used or on how the reader will benefit from its release. The letter then takes on several aspects of the covering letter used to sell the reader on responding to a questionnaire. (This was discussed in Chapter 5.)

Letters are used much in the same way as personal interviews. Their advantage is that the investigator can reach people at a distance and over a widely scattered area. The disadvantage is that they lack the face-to-face contact provided by a personal interview. Information secured from a single letter is organized along with other factual data. If a form letter is sent to a large number of persons and specific questions are asked, the replies can be tabulated and interpreted in much the same way as the replies to a questionnaire.

PROBLEMS

1. What determines whether you should use interviews or mail questionnaires in securing data for a report? What are the advantages and disadvantages of each method?

2. Under what circumstances is it appropriate to use the telephone interview?

3. If you were obtaining data for each of the following report subjects, what use would you make of interviews? Which kinds of interviews would you use? Why?

a. A group purchasing plan for fraternities at your university.
b. Revision of the present bookkeeping methods of the ________ Restaurant.
c. The tuna fish market in ________ City.
d. Consumer attitudes toward ________ Department Store.
e. Readership study of ________ employee magazine.
f. Listening habits of the radio audience of Station ________.

4. If you were securing material for a report on each of the following subjects, what use would you make of observation? Explain.

a. The advisability of purchasing the Shell Pakit machine to reduce the cost of coffee bags for the ________ Coffee Company.
b. The process of selecting trainees for the ________ Company.
c. Increasing production by using industrial music in the ________ Factory.
d. Improving the office layout of ________ Company.
e. The traffic problem at the intersection of ________ Avenue and ________ Street.

5. Arrangements may be made by you or your instructor for your class to

make a visit to one of the companies in your community. It may be the newspaper plant, a large business office, an advertising agency, a manufacturing concern or a distributing company. Before making the visit plan what to observe, how and why. After your return, write up your notes on your observations in the form of a memorandum.

6. Interview a businessman who is successful in the field in which you are most interested and write up the results. Before making the interview, you will want to plan it carefully and decide what information to seek from him. Afterwards send him a thank-you letter.

7. Observe the arrangement of materials on the bulletin boards in your college and write up a report on the results of your observation. The report may point to changes for improving the bulletin boards.

8. Assume that you are making a study of the background of the students in your college. Interview one of your fellow students and write a report on the information you obtain.

9. Go into a store, office or similar place where people are working and write up the results of what you observe taking place. Can you recommend any changes that would make for increased efficiency of operation?

CHAPTER 7

Organizing and Interpreting Data

THE INVESTIGATOR, AFTER HE HAS SECURED HIS DATA, IS confronted with the problem of organizing and interpreting them so that they will be comprehensible and usable in formulating his conclusions and recommendations and in achieving his purpose. The first step in organizing data is that of sorting and arranging them so that like data will be grouped together. This process is usually referred to as classification of data.

CLASSIFICATION OF DATA

Data may be classified as they are secured; or classification may be made after the data have been gathered. There are four kinds of data: qualitative, quantitative, chronological and geographical. In classifying, data are grouped according to type. Data in the form of facts, expressing ideas and thoughts on a subject, are *qualitative.*

They are recorded in the form of notes and may be secured from bibliographical research, interviews, letters, experience, observation or even experimentation. Data expressed in terms of figures and adaptable to statistical treatment are *quantitative*. They are easily recognizable because they refer to quantities or amounts. They are usually the results of questionnaires, although information from interviews, observation, etc. sometimes consists of responses which can be counted. The other two kinds of data — chronological and geographical — are self-explanatory. *Geographical data* are classified according to areas or regions, and *chronological data* are arranged according to a time sequence.

The purpose of classifying data is to get like data together. The investigator can then find out whether he has secured all his data and can discover relationships between groups of information. After classification has taken place he continues the process of organizing and interpreting. The type of data he is working with, however, will determine the procedure to be followed.

ORGANIZING AND INTERPRETING QUALITATIVE DATA

Usually qualitative data are recorded on note cards or in notebooks. The first step in organizing qualitative data is to examine them as a whole, considering them for completeness, for their relationship to the purpose of the investigation and for their total significance to the problem at hand. Then they should be broken down into their component parts. If note cards have been used as suggested in Chapter 4, and subject headings have been placed in the upper left-hand corner of each card, then it is a simple process to group together all note cards having the same subject heading. Each group of notes is then considered as a whole, in part and in relationship to other groups. In analyzing the relationship of each group of data the researcher may well find that he will want to arrange his data to show this relationship, which in some cases will necessitate his forming new groups, perhaps by combining several. In each case he considers a common denominator for each group of data.

Let us consider how this works out. In a study of company practices and policies concerning employee benefits, there is a large number of notes on the following policies: accident, hospitalization, credit union, jury duty, military duty, sickness, pay advances, sick leave, profit sharing, surgical expenses, guaranteed annual wage, maternity leave, stock purchase, terminal leave, life insurance, seniority wage increase, merit rating, dismissal pay, vacation, pension plan and suggestion plan payment. The investigator will first need to group together all his notes on each subject. Then he will need to examine each group of notes for some significant relationship to other topics. In doing this he will find that several of the benefits are closely related. To be exact, seven of them deal with absences or leave from work. This is a fact they have in common, and it becomes the common denominator for combining the seven groups under "leave-type benefits." He would thus have in one group of notes:

> Leave-type Benefits—Jury duty, military duty, sick leave, maternity, terminal leave, dismissal pay, vacation.

Another group of policies pertain to insurance benefits. There are six of these:

> Insurance Benefits—Accident, sickness, surgical expenses, hospitalization, life, pension.

The other common denominator is monetary-type benefits:

> Monetary Benefits—Credit union, pay advances, guaranteed annual wage, profit sharing, stock purchase, seniority wage increase, merit rating, suggestion plan payment.

Qualitative data are thus organized under common subject headings. Considering the data again in relationship to accomplishing the purpose of the investigation is the next step. First there is an examination of the data as a whole, in part, then as a whole again. Qualitative data may then be considered in relation to other types of data.

ORGANIZING QUANTITATIVE DATA

Examining and Editing Data

Quantitative data too must first be examined. They need to be checked for accuracy and pertinency. The question should be asked and answered in the affirmative about each piece of data: "Does this fact help accomplish the purpose of this study?" Quantitative data also should be examined for their reliability. Statistical procedures should be followed in testing for reliability. The data may be checked for proportionality to determine whether or not they are representative, or the standard error of deviation may be used. The purpose in examining the data is to find out whether they are valid and to what degree they are valid. Unreliable and non-pertinent data are then discarded. The next step is to prepare the data for tabulation

Preparation for Tabulation

Work sheets need to be set up for tabulating data. Tabulation enables one to compare, analyze and evaluate responses. For example, answers to each question on a questionnaire must be tabulated. Examine the following questionnaire and the type of responses called for in order to determine how to set up a work sheet for tabulating the results.

CHARGA-PLATE QUESTIONNAIRE

1. Do you make use of your Charga-Plate when shopping in stores where the service is used?

*Always*_______ *Frequently*_______ *Seldom*_______ *Never*_______

2. In your opinion does the use of a Charga-Plate result in a saving of time in your shopping?

*Yes*_______ *No*_______

3. When do you carry your Charga-Plate with you?

*At all times when going to the business district*_______
*Only when going to town particularly to shop*_______
*Seldom carry at all*_______

4. Do you use your Charga-Plate for purposes of identification other than charging purchases in stores offering the Charga-Plate Service?

*Yes*_______ *No*_______

5. How many people other than yourself, living in your household, have a Charga-Plate?

*1*_______ *2*_______ *3*_______ *4*_______ *5*_______ *Over 5*_______

6. Do you take the initiative in handing your Charga-Plate to the salesperson when making credit purchases?

*Always*_______ *Frequently*_______ *Seldom*_______ *Never*_______

7. **If the 6th question was answered "Seldom" or "Never,"** then to what extent does the salesperson ask for your Charga-Plate?

*Always*_______ *Frequently*_______ *Seldom*_______ *Never*_______

8. Do you think there is a tendency for people to charge more freely when using a Charga-Plate?

*Yes*_______ *No*_______ *No idea*_______

9. For how many stores is your Charga-Plate notched; that is, in how many stores can you use your Charga-Plate?

(*Number*) _______

10. Please check the stores in which you **actually use** your Charga-Plate at present.

*Holmes*________ *Godchaux*________ *Keller-Zander*________
*Gus Mayer*________ *Krauss*________ *Labiche's*________
*Maison Blanche*________ *Marks Isaacs*________ *Imperial*________
*Mayer Israel*________ *Kreeger*________

11. Are you inclined to use your Charga-Plate more when purchasing certain kinds of merchandise than other kinds?

*Yes*________ *No*________

12. Do you find that the use of a Charga-Plate Service simplifies your shopping?

*Yes*________ *No*________ *Don't know*________

13. Did you ever encounter any difficulties in having incorrect charges entered on your account before the time you started using your Charga-Plate?

*Yes*________ *No*________

14. **If the 13th question was answered "Yes,"** has this difficulty been reduced or eliminated by the use of your Charga-Plate?

*Yes*________ *No*________

15. Have there been errors of any kind made in your charge account since you have been using the Charga-Plate?

*Yes*________ *No*________

16. Prior to the use of the Charga-Plate Service was merchandise bought by you delivered elsewhere, or merchandise belonging to someone else delivered to your address?

*Yes*________ *No*________

17. **If the 16th question was answered "Yes,"** has the situation been improved since you started using your Charga-Plate?

*Yes*________ *No*________

18. Is there anything that you do not like regarding the use of your Charga-Plate?

*Yes*________ *No*________

If "*Yes,*" please list your objections or criticism:

In order to classify the questionnaires received for the purpose of tabulation would you kindly check your approximate income. Also show whether the questionnaire is being filled out by male or female.

Approximate Annual Income:		*Person Answering Questionnaire:*
Under $1,000	________	Male________
$1,000 to $1,999	________	Female________
$2,000 to $2,999	________	
$3,000 to $4,999	________	
Over $5,000	________	

PLEASE DO NOT SIGN YOUR NAME

Questions numbered 1, 6 and 7 call for an *Always, Frequently, Seldom* or *Never* response and may be tabulated on the same sheet. Questions numbered 2, 4, 8, 11, 12, 13, 14, 15, 16, 17 and 18 ask for a *Yes* or *No* answer and so may be checked together. The other questions have no "common response" and must be handled separately. Thus a work sheet would be set up as on the following page.

MALES

	ALWAYS						FREQUENTLY						SELDOM						NEVER						SUM TOTALS					
	Income Level						Income Level						Income Level						Income Level						Income Level					
QUESTION	1	2	3	4	5	Total	1	2	3	4	5	Total	1	2	3	4	5	Total	1	2	3	4	5	Total	1	2	3	4	5	Total
1																														
6																														
7																														

FEMALES

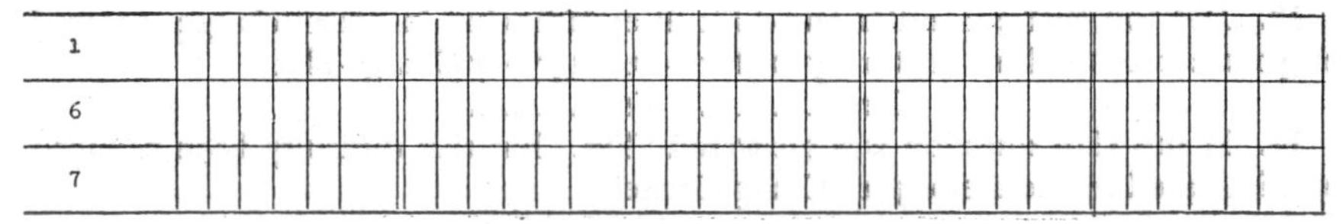

1																														
6																														
7																														

Work sheet for tabulation of **Always, Frequently, Seldom** *and* **Never** *responses.*

The corollary information at the end of the questionnaire must be considered in tabulation to determine whether the income affects the type of response given. For the same reason a work table would need to be set up for *Males* and *Females.*

For the questions calling for *Yes* or *No* answers the work sheet could be arranged as on the opposite page.

The column heading *Other* is used because two questions, 8 and 12, call for responses other than *Yes* or *No.* The total column on the extreme right should be checked with the number of returned questionnaires for a check on accuracy in tabulating.

Separate work sheets need to be set up for each of the other questions. After data have been edited and work sheets set up, tabulation is the next step.

Tabulation of Data

Data may be tabulated by counting and recording the responses in the proper places on the work sheets. To tabulate the charga-plate survey it would be necessary to divide the questionnaires into two groups at the outset — male and female — and to check each group. Then the totals of the two groups may be reached. When the work sheets are completed, a single master or recapitulation sheet is made up from them, showing the number and type of responses for every question.

MALES

	YES						NO						OTHER						SUM TOTAL					
	Income Level						Income Level						Income Level						Income Level					
QUESTION	1	2	3	4	5	Total	1	2	3	4	5	Total	1	2	3	4	5	Total	1	2	3	4	5	Total
2																								
4																								
8																								
11																								
12																								
13																								
14																								
15																								
16																								
17																								
18																								

FEMALES

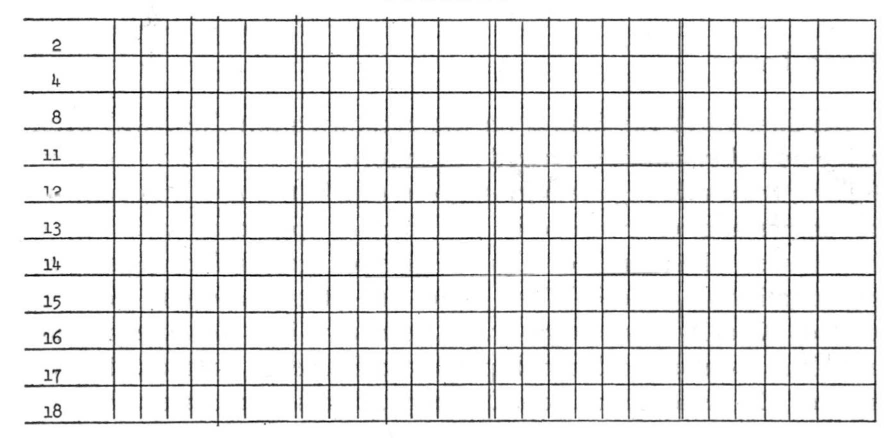

2																								
4																								
8																								
11																								
12																								
13																								
14																								
15																								
16																								
17																								
18																								

Work sheet for tabulation of Yes *and* No *responses.*

Sometimes the recapitulation sheet is arranged with the same headings as the work sheets, the only difference being that the totals would be substituted for the tabulating lines. Sometimes it is necessary to work out different combinations and headings. In the charga-plate survey the same arrangements could be used in the recapitulation and work sheets; however, a provision would need to be made for indicating the combined totals of male and female responses.

After the recapitulation sheet is made up, the data are re-examined for their significance and relationship to the problem. This step is very similar to the corresponding one in organizing qualitative data in which the investigator considers the significance of his data as a whole. This precedes his breaking them down into their component parts or grouping like data together into a broader category. It is partially an interpretative process as well as an organizational one. The chief difference here between handling qualitative and quantitative data is that one must work out a way of presenting quantitative data in the form of tables and also determine what statistical measures can be applied to make the data comprehensible.

INTERPRETING QUANTITATIVE DATA

For practical purposes the processes of organizing and interpreting quantitative data at this stage are the same process. It is necessary to interpret in order to organize, and to organize in order to interpret. The two processes are one.

Using Tables

An analysis of the figures on the recapitulation sheet will determine how they can be arranged in the form of tables. One compares figures, thinks through relationships of one fact to another, evaluates the importance of the material and decides upon the significance of his figures. This enables him to group together like figures for presentation in tables.[1] When tables are set up they must be interpreted. Usually percentages must be determined because percentages bring out the relationship of one figure to another. For example, "50 responses out of 392 replies" does not express the relationship as pointedly as "13% of the responses," which is more comprehensible. Even the 13% expressed in simpler terms could be "about one in eight." Thinking in terms of small, round numbers puts the data into easily understood terms.

Using Statistical Measures

Selecting a central tendency when interpreting tables helps to spot trends. There are three statistical averages which indicate a

[1] See Chapter 11, "Using Visual Aids Effectively," for information on how to present data in tables.

central tendency — the mean, median and mode. The mean is the arithmetical average and is obtained by totaling figures and dividing by number of cases. The median is the mid-point between the upper and lower halves. It indicates the case that is in the middle of a list of figures arranged in rank order. The mode indicates the pattern followed most often. It is the point of highest frequency, where most cases occur. The three averages refer to different ideas. The mean is the true average, but no case may be that realistic. It shows what the situation would be if all things were equal. It is the socialistic average of a group. The median, on the other hand, does indicate a true picture. There are as many cases above it as below it. It is in the middle of the road. The mode is the pattern established by the occurrence of the highest number of cases. In considering the averages it is necessary also to consider the range and the extremes and how they might affect the central figure selected.

The range makes the average more significant. Statisticians use standard deviations to indicate the range, but most report readers will not understand their use. The report writer with an advanced knowledge of statistics may find himself using them for his own interpretation, but he would be likely to use a simple explanation in the final report. In addition to the range, exceptional cases also need to be noted. They add interesting sidelights to the data, although they may not be necessary statistically. Interpreting data in a table calls for considering the totals first and looking at the table as a whole. Then an examination of the appropriate statistical measures — the range, the extremes and the exceptions — should be made. All of this is a basis for drawing statistical conclusions. Before final conclusions can be drawn, however, quantitative data must be considered in its proper relationship to the qualitative data. This is a "fitting in" process, in which the investigator re-examines each type of data in light of the other and organizes each of them accordingly.

REACHING CONCLUSIONS

Conclusions are the result of reasoned judgment. They refer to the generalizations which can be formulated from an interpretation of data. They may be derived from particular detailed facts or inferred from a general principle or premise. The researcher carefully examines the results of his investigation point by point to find a general pattern or a solution to his problem. There are three major steps involved in the process:

(*1*) Considering facts and setting up tentative conclusions.
(*2*) Testing tentative conclusions.
(*3*) Reaching final conclusions.

Considering Facts and Setting Up Tentative Conclusions

The mass of data secured as results of an investigation becomes the heart of a report and gives life to the other elements which depend on it. For this reason the detailed facts must all be considered not only in relationship to each other but also to other elements of the research. A check should first be made to determine whether or not the data are relevant to the purpose and objectives by comparing the results of the investigation with the original working plan. Asking the questions, "Does the information I have obtained fulfill my objectives?" and "Will these facts accomplish my purpose?" helps to explain the relationships of purpose, objectives and data. The purpose is the aim or long-range goal of the report, and the objectives are the obstacles that must be overcome or the short goals which have to be reached in order to accomplish this aim. The analysis the investigator makes at this point should start with the purpose and then move from the objectives to the data. The following diagram should prove helpful in considering these points and the fact that data form the heart of the study:

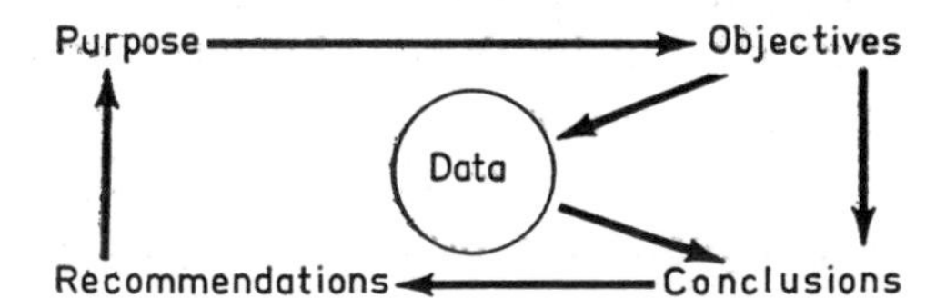

This is a means of squaring the circle. The data are in the center. They are gathered in answer to the objectives, and in turn they serve as a basis for the conclusions. The conclusions in this sense are the fulfillment of the objectives. They are the generalizations formulated from the results of the investigation, and they serve as a basis for the recommendations to which they give rise. The recommendations suggest a program of action indicated by the conclusions. Such a program is dependent on the conclusions, the data and the objectives for support and in turn accomplishes the purpose of the report. In considering the data in relation to these elements, the importance of each fact must be kept in mind. Using logic will provide a means of progressing reasonably from one fact to another and on to a logical conclusion.

Deductive reasoning sometimes will be followed; at other times inductive reasoning will be used. In applying deductive reasoning, the analyst will reason from the general to the specific, from the universal to the individual or from given premises to their necessary conclusions. He might first state his point of view or his proposition, then present his reasons which support it and finally reach a conclusion which will be a restatement of his original premise. Alternative propositions and conditional premises may also be considered, if needed, to give evidence of the original statement. Analogies are sometimes useful for clarification. In any good analogy there are strong similar points; however, there may be points of difference, too, which should not be overlooked. In deductive reasoning, the results or effects can be stated, then the causes or sources examined to reach a conclusion.

The simplest application of inductive logic is to enumerate instances which will serve as evidence to confirm a "pattern," which will become the conclusion. Sometimes causes are listed, then their effects or results are examined, and a conclusion is reached. A series of events observed might serve as a basis for the establishment of a generalization. In reaching conclusions through inductive reasing, the researcher considers his data for points of agreement and differences and seeks an explanation for them. He will also want to find out reasons for the causes and effects. He will be on the alert for recognition of relevant factors to be considered and variations from accepted patterns. Throughout his consideration of facts, he is seeking a conclusion established by the inductive process of reasoning.

Testing Tentative Conclusions and Reaching Final Ones

Conclusions reached through statistical measures, and through deductive and inductive reasoning, are considered tentative until they are tested and proved valid or true. Then they become final conclusions and are used as a basis for making recommendations. The analyst must prove each conclusion before accepting it as final. If he has reached his conclusion by the inductive or deductive reasoning process, he should try to prove it by checking his evidence. If he cannot prove it, then he has a false conclusion, or he has made an error in his reasoning. Here again a check of the evidence should disclose which it is.

Another test of tentative conclusions is simply to apply common sense. A final conclusion must sound practical and must be workable. A real effort must be made to see if all available data have been used and nothing overlooked. All exceptions must be carefully noted too. Sometimes an exception may be such as to make the conclusion impractical, or some detailed fact may be overlooked which would cause the conclusion not to be workable. If the conclusion that has been reached is concerning a solution to a problem, the researcher needs to find out how his proposed solution would work out if it were to be put into effect. This solution would need to be tested before he would be able to decide whether or not to recommend it. In this case he would project his conclusion into the future and, assuming its being put into effect, would test to see how it would work out. If it proved itself workable, then the tentative conclusion would become a final one.

Conclusions that have been reached statistically can be tested by re-checking the statistical processes and techniques which were used and considering their validity in relation to other evidence and data that were secured. In the case of replies from a questionnaire survey, the conclusions are valid only to the extent to which the sample was representative of the population from which it was taken.

The negative test may also be applied in testing tentative conclusions. Here it is assumed that the direct opposite is the conclusion, and the analyst uses the evidence to prove it. If careful consideration of his facts should prove his assumed opposite conclusion, then his original tentative conclusion would not be true. The negative test may also be applied to alternative conclusions which are not opposite conclusions. If the assembled evidence supports the alternative conclusion, then a number of alternative conclusions may have to be examined before arriving at a general conclusion on which the alternatives show agreement. This generalization would then become the final conclusion.

Another method of testing tentative conclusions is to use references. The researcher may make use of bibliographical research to find out whether or not writers agree with him on his findings and conclusions; and if they do not agree, he will seek to find logical explanations as to why they do not. His findings may be referred to others to determine whether or not they can reach the same conclusions that he has reached. He may also consult with others to test the soundness of his reasoning. References might be used further as a check to determine whether or not business practice or policies in general agree with the tentative conclusions set up.

After testing tentative conclusions by applying logic and common sense, by determining whether or not they are workable, by using statistical measures, by applying the negative test and by using references, final conclusions may be reached. The tentative conclusions that have been proved by testing can be re-stated as final conclusions. They are the generalizations derived from the interpreted results of an investigation. They must be clear, concise and definite.

A final check must be made of the relationship of each conclusion to the objectives and purpose of the report. Usually each conclusion will be a fulfillment of an objective and will be necessary in order to achieve the purpose of the report. The original working plan may be used as a basis for this final check on relationships. At this point the analyst should also turn to the statement of his problem or subject and check to determine whether or not his final conclusions are adequate. If his final conclusions are adequate he turns to the next and last step in the process of interpreting data — the formulation of recommendations.

FORMULATING RECOMMENDATIONS

Conclusions are the basis for recommendations suggesting action that should be followed. They are the logical outgrowth of conclusions which support them and which in turn are supported by data. Just as conclusions are the fulfillment of the objectives of a report, so recommendations are the achievement of the purpose of the report. They indicate what is to be done and in a specific way tell how, when, where and by whom. In order to get action recommendations must be practical and definite. The businessman is not interested in a recommendation that is not reasonable and feasible, nor will he take the recommended action unless it is proved to be the best course of action to follow.

Before final recommendations are formulated tentative ones

should be tested. Many of the tests for tentative conclusions are applicable in testing recommendations also. The researcher wants to make sure that his recommendations are logical, workable and sound. He will check to determine whether or not they accomplish his purpose and present a solution to the problem.

When a number of recommendations are listed, each one may be based in a corresponding conclusion. In this case they would appear in the same order as the conclusions. Sometimes general recommendations are given, followed by specific ones. At other times the most important recommendation may be given first or presented last in order to give it special emphasis. Whenever possible recommendations are grouped together according to subject content in order to make them easy to follow.

PROBLEMS

1. Compare the processes of organizing and interpreting qualitative and quantitative data.

2. How does classification of data help in their interpretative analysis?

3. Explain the use of tests with tentative conclusions reached before arriving at final ones.

4. Distinguish between deductive and inductive reasoning.

5. What is the relationship between purpose and objectives? Data and conclusions? Conclusions and recommendations? Purpose and recommendations?

6. Read the following case study and work out the problems presented after it:

The management of the Elliott Oil Company Refinery at Houston, Texas engaged Henderson, Jones, Aton & Co. to investigate the attitudes, beliefs and feelings of the technical men toward their work situation in the refinery and in the Elliott Laboratories. Conferences were held between HJA members and refinery representatives to establish the persons to be included, the techniques to be used and the time schedule to be followed in the investigation. As part of the complete survey, personnel psychologists of HJA held interviews with a sample of eighty technical men in the company.

A basic introductory statement was given at the beginning of each interview: "I would like you to tell me about you and your job situation—what you like about it and would like not to have changed, and what you dislike about it and where you would like to have some action taken." The interviewer then sat back and listened, perhaps asking at times for amplification or clarification of a point, but never asking a direct question. Detailed notes were taken, but the fact that they were was never concealed from the interviewee. Attempt was made to cover areas such as promotion, salary, "how you stand," recycling, utilization of abilities, work load, supervision, recognition, confidence in management and training.

From these interviews several points emerged. Some of them dealt with grievances, some with satisfactions. Without any statistical tabulation the following points are worthy of noting and considering.

Information on changes in company policy was disseminated verbally from supervisors, notices or letters and group meetings. One-third of the group felt that the messages were neither clear nor complete. Group meetings were voted the least effective and verbal discussions the most effective media of communication.

"Recycling" means rewriting correspondence or reports to make their content and language acceptable to superiors. Reportedly, material was passed up the entire chain of command and rewritten to satisfy each man's objections until it finally passed the level responsible for sending it outside. Half of the men reported that they wrote material at least twice and sometimes from three to five times. Common reasons given for rewriting letters and reports were that the men did not always have complete information and supervisors were picayune concerning petty details. Other comments were that the message became obsolete as it went up the line and that there were mechanical errors in the finished report.

Men did not sign their reports and thus felt cheated of credit for them. Sometimes reports were held up until they were out of date.

The over-all attitude of the technical people was favorable. The company's provisions for security of jobs and generous benefit programs were widely appreciated. Pride was taken in being a member of a select group. Office buildings were comfortable and attractive. Apparatus, equipment and materials for work were readily available. The orientation program received praise. The lack of regimentation was liked. The employees were grateful for a certain amount of freedom. They liked to say, "My job is what I make it."

Houston was highly regarded as a desirable place in which to live.

The engineers in the equipment inspection department objected to the lack of adequate locker rooms and shower facilities, which were necessary because of the dirty jobs they performed. Process engineers showed more enthusiasm for their work than did other engineers. Mechanical engineers were stronger than those in other departments in their complaints. They complained of long hours of work and of pushing by their supervisors and were discontented with recent promotions following resignations.

Most of the employees indicated a feeling of unimportance in their jobs. Many jobs were designated for immediate attention. Men said, "Every job I'm given is a rush job." They no longer felt quality of work was important, simply that it be done in a hurry. A few employees found themselves responsible for work which they lacked authority to carry through to completion. Men did not feel a part of management.

Men who had received promotions were more favorable in their attitudes. Men with longer length of service tended to identify themselves with the company. Older men who had not been promoted were critical of the company. They concentrated on criticisms of salary, selection of supervisors and promotion policies.

---

a. What did the technical employees express favorable attitudes toward?

b. Into what general areas may their complaints be classified?

c. Organize the facts under several main divisions of the problem.

d. Interpret the facts you organized and reach conclusions.

e. What possible solutions should be considered to meet the problems presented here?

f. What action do you recommend?

g. What further investigation do you recommend? Why?

7. Assume that you are a member of Henderson, Jones, Aton & Co., a per-

sonnel consulting firm. Write the report that would be submitted to the Elliott Oil Company.

8. Obtain a sample business report. Analyze methods of gathering facts for the report. Tell how they were organized and interpreted and how conclusions were reached. Your instructor may have you write out your analysis or present it orally as part of the class discussion.

CHAPTER 8

Outlining the Report

AN OUTLINE IS A PLAN. CAREFUL PLANNING IN REPORT writing facilitates the achievement of the specific purpose of the report. It is necessary to plan for making the investigation and to plan for writing the results. Thus, just as a preliminary outline or working plan is necessary as a guide in the investigation, as has been discussed in Chapter 3, a logical and well-organized outline is needed as a basis for writing the report. The preliminary outline provides a basic understanding of the problem. It compels the investigator to think through his problem and to understand the relationship of its various aspects. It thus serves him as a guide in collecting data and prevents improper procedure. It also enables him to complete his investigation within a limited time.

NEED AND USES OF THE OUTLINE

The final outline serves as a means of organizing data and as a guide for writing the report. Business practice often calls for the submission for approval of both preliminary and final outlines to the person authorizing the report before the writer continues with his investigation. Some companies demand outlines for this purpose so that their personnel will be guided toward presenting clear, logical reports as results of keen analysis of the problem. An outline forces the organization of thoughts; it is a means of thinking through a problem from its beginning to its end. It divides a report into its major parts and shows the relationship of each subdivision. For this reason it can also serve as a basis for formulating subject headings used in the report and for organizing the table of contents. Consider, for example, the following from a sentence outline:

A. One-floor operation is properly justified for heavy industry, wherein the difficulty of processing heavy materials requires simplification.

Such a main point in an outline may serve as a topic sentence in developing the subject of a section of the report. In that respect it becomes a guide for writing. From the sentence an appropriate subject heading can be selected for a particular part of the report. For instance, "Justification of One-Floor Operation" is a subject heading derived from the example outline heading. In the table of contents the subject heading for the section will be listed with the page number on which it appears:

Justification of One-Floor Operation 10

Another use of the outline is as a basis for writing a summary of the report.[1] A sentence outline, with the addition of transitional words and phrases, becomes a brief, which carries the outline one step further in showing the relationship between ideas. Likewise a sentence outline, with the addition of connectives and presented in paragraph form rather than outline form, becomes an abstract or summary of the report. A part of a report brief in which the connectives have been added to the original outline follows. (The connectives are italicized to indicate the additions.)

II. One type of executive training program is the multiple-management plan.

A. It was inaugurated in 1932 by the McCormick Company of Baltimore.

Under this plan,

B. Three boards supplement the senior board of directors.

1. They are the factory executive board, the sales board and junior executive board.

2. The junior executive board provides management training for its members.

---

[1] See pages 266–267 for discussion of different types of summaries.

C. There are three chief advantages to this plan,

such as the following:

1. Future executives are given the opportunity to tackle significant company problems, to discuss them freely and openly, to exhibit their judgment and originality, and to meet with senior officers on matters of significance to them;

2.

and

3.

Also

D. There are several disadvantages.

1. Development of men comes slowly,

and

2. Company action is a slow process handled in this way.

However,

E. Multiple management develops executive ability at the same time it uses its executive talent.

But

1. Full cooperation is necessary,

and

2. Top authorities must be ready to share authority and responsibilities.

The fact must not be overlooked, however, that the major use of the final outline is as a guide for organizing and writing the report.

TYPES OF OUTLINES

There are several kinds of outlines. In form an outline may be either sentence or topic. With respect to the material presented, it may be general or specific. It is also possible and sometimes practical to mix the two forms or to mix the general with the specific. Main points may be couched in general terms with details stated specifically, or vice versa. Major divisions may all be presented in topical form and all subdivisions and details in sentence form, or the other way around. The guiding principle is to be consistent from the beginning to the end of the outline. For instance, if the first main topic is in sentence form, all main topics must be in sentence form. If the main topic is expressed in general terms, all main topics must be expressed in general terms.

General Outline

A general outline serves as an excellent guide in organizing material. It indicates general divisions and subdivisions for the report.

According to function there are three main divisions in the body of most reports: introduction, presentation and analysis, conclusions and recommendations. The purpose of the introduction is to present the necessary background for the reader to understand the report. It may contain authorization or circumstances under which the report was requested, need for the study and the use to be made of it, history of the problem, purpose and objectives, scope and limitations, method of procedure, definition of terms and a summary of what is to follow. The purpose of the presentation and analysis section is to present facts and their interpretation to the reader. Here the report may be broken down into various factors to be considered, parts of the subject presented, comparisons and evaluations given and relationships shown. Often several aspects of the same problem are presented. The present situation may be analyzed, indicating the need for changes, and the changes and possible results may also be analyzed. The purpose of the conclusions and recommendations section is to secure needed action. Conclusions are reached from the analysis of the facts, and recommendations based upon the conclusions are then presented.

A general outline may indicate the three main divisions of the report with some subdivision. It does not, however, present all the details that are needed for developing the outline points. For that reason it serves as a guide, but does not give information for writing the report proper. Many reports might follow the same general outline. Here are two possibilities for general outlines:

Outline 1

I. A statement of the problem
II. An analysis of the problem
  A. Weak points
  B. Strong points
III. Need for changes in the present situation
  A.
  B.
  C.
IV. Proposed solution to the problem
  A.
  B.
V. Advantages and disadvantages of the solution
  A.
  B.
  C.
VI. Conclusions and recommendations

Outline 2

I. Introduction
- *A.* Authorization and purpose
- *B.* Need for and use of report
- *C.* Scope and limitations
- *D.* Procedures
- *E.* Summary

II. Presentation of facts and their analysis
- *A.*
  - *1.*
  - *2.*
- *B.*
- *C.*

III. Conclusions

IV. Recommendations

These outlines are guides, but they can be applied to reports written on any number of subjects. They are general outlines, and because they are general they do not include details. They are organizational patterns or logical arrangements of report divisions.

A report may also be outlined in the reverse order of Outline 2, in which case the following arrangement would be used:

I. Recommendations
II. Conclusions
III. Explanation of the problem
IV. Results of the investigation
V. Summary

This outline presents the material in the order of the significance of points in accomplishing the purpose of the report. Since recommendations are the fulfillment of the purpose and the most important part of the report, they are placed first. Busy executives interested in results and in quick action prefer this order. It points the reader's attention toward the recommendations at the outset, and the rest of the report supports the recommendations. This is sometimes referred to as the psychological order of arrangement. In recent years it has become more commonly used for business reports than it was earlier.

A general outline for a long report, thesis or book might indicate chapter divisions:

Chapter I. The problem
- A. The problem and its aspects
- B. Need and use of the study
- C. Scope of subject
- D. Definitions
- E. Purpose and objectives

Chapter II. Previous Research
Chapter III. Method of Solution
A. Procedure for collecting data
B. Reliability of data
C. Summary of conclusions
Chapter IV.
Chapter V. } Devoted to separate aspects of the problem or subject
Chapter VI.
Chapter VII. Conclus
A.
B.
Chapter VIII. Recommendations
A.
B.

A general outline, in other words, is a pattern or guide for organizing material for different kinds of reports. Any number of reports might follow the same general outline. For examples of the use of general outlines in various kinds of reports see Part IV.

Specific Outline

A specific outline gives the detailed facts not included in the general outline. Instead of using the term "purpose," the purpose itself is stated, such as "to recommend improvements in the sales promotional practices of the Smith Department Store." The best use of the specific outline is as a guide for further development of topics in writing the report. The following outline contains the details which make it specific. Unlike the general outline it pertains to only one report and thus can be used as a guide for writing only the report for which it is set up.

An Outline on
IMPROVEMENT OF MANUFACTURING AND LABOR POLICIES

I. Introduction
- *A.* Purpose
  - *1.* To improve present manufacturing and labor conditions
  - *2.* To increase profitability
- *B.* Need for the study
  - *1.* To regain competitive position
  - *2.* To increase profits
- *C.* Scope and limitations
  - *1.* Scope
    - *a.* Study of the manufacturing processes
    - *b.* Study of labor policies
  - *2.* Limitations
    - *a.* Exclusion of other policies
      - (*1*) Advertising

(*2*) Distribution
b. Lack of sufficient information about competitors
D. Procedure
1. To secure information from company files
2. To observe processes
3. To secure information from competitors
II. Analysis of manufacturing processes
A. Sources of raw materials
1. Present and potential supplies of raw materials
2. Comparative costs of sources of raw materials
3. Comparisons of quality of raw materials
B. Plant outlay and the manufacturing process
1. Office
a. Personnel
(*1*) Efficiency
(*2*) Costs
(*3*) Requirements
b. Methods of operation
(*1*) Effectiveness
(*2*) Costs
2. Receiving and shipping department
a. Volume of work handled
b. Personnel effectiveness
c. Equipment
d. Costs
3. Machine department
a. Labor
(*1*) Number and classification of workers
(*2*) Wages
(*3*) Efficiency
b. Machinery
(*1*) Effectiveness
(*2*) Cost
4. Assembly department
a. Labor
(*1*) Number and classification of workers
(*2*) Wages
(*3*) Efficiency
b. Operational techniques
(*1*) Assembly line
(*2*) Special techniques
5. Finishing department
a. Labor
(*1*) Number and classification of workers
(*2*) Wages
(*3*) Efficiency
b. Operational methods
(*1*) Machine
(*2*) Hand
(*3*) Cost
(*4*) Effectiveness

- *C.* Analysis of present machinery used in the manufacturing process
    - *1.* Age
    - *2.* Suitability
    - *3.* Effectiveness
    - *4.* Advantages and disadvantages
    - *5.* Need for replacement

III. Analysis of labor policies
- *A.* Wage policies
    - *1.* Payment methods
    - *2.* Job evaluation
    - *3.* Employee satisfaction
- *B.* General wage level
    - *1.* Local labor market
    - *2.* The industry
    - *3.* Unions
- *C.* Promotion policy
    - *1.* Seniority
    - *2.* Ability
    - *3.* Favoritism
    - *4.* Objectivity
    - *5.* Worker morale
- *D.* Layoff policy
    - *1.* Lack of objective standards
    - *2.* Morale

IV. Conclusions
- *A.* Need new machinery
    - *1.* Savings
        - *a.* Time
        - *b.* Costs
    - *2.* Morale
        - *a.* Less worker effort required
        - *b.* Increased unit output needed
- *B.* Need changes in labor policy
    - *1.* Increase earnings of employees
    - *2.* Decrease work week to 40 hours
    - *3.* Unionize

V. Recommendations
- *A.* Buy new machinery at outlay cost $55,000
- *B.* Unionize
    - *1.* Increase hourly wage
    - *2.* Decrease work week

Usually a report writer will begin with a general outline — determined by the nature of his problem, the type of report and the reader — then develop a specific outline. The general outline thus serves as a guide for organizing data. The specific outline will serve for a writing guide. Another example of the specific outline is one set up for a report written to determine equipment and layout in a photography studio for plastic surgery. It shows at a glance the basic information which the report will contain. For more specific detail than is shown this outline would give facts under each of its subdivisions. But it serves its purpose well as it is. This outline also indicates how easily subject headings can be composed and how quickly a table of contents can be made up. The same topics, with very little variation, can be used in each case as subject headings and as a table of contents.

An Outline on
PHOTOGRAPHY SERVES PLASTIC SURGERY

I. Introduction
- *A.* Purpose of investigation
- *B.* Scope of investigation
- *C.* Limitation of investigation

II. General arrangement of facilities to be established
- *A.* Size of suite of offices
- *B.* Arrangement of rooms
- *C.* Specific areas in suite to be used for photography

III. Darkroom layout
- *A.* Arrangement of permanent tables
- *B.* Arrangement and locations of permanent and collapsible shelves

IV. Darkroom equipment
- *A.* Location of safelights in ceiling
- *B.* Type and location of enlarger
- *C.* Wash trough
  - *1.* Size, location and material
  - *2.* Plumbing connections
- *D.* Print trays and portable stand
- *E.* Type and location of print dryer
- *F.* Miscellaneous darkroom equipment

V. Studio layout
- *A.* Dimensions
- *B.* Placing of furnishings and equipment

VI. Studio equipment
- *A.* Still photography
  - *1.* Number and types of cameras
  - *2.* Special camera stand
  - *3.* Background screen
  - *4.* Type of illumination
- *B.* Motion picture photography
  - *1.* Type of camera and supplementary equipment
  - *2.* Tripod
  - *3.* Illumination
  - *4.* Tilting equipment
  - *5.* Splicer

VII. Photographic materials
- *A.* Still photography
  - *1.* Film—black-and-white and color
  - *2.* Photographic printing paper
  - *3.* Color slide mounts
  - *4.* Chemicals

a. For black-and-white film
b. For color film
c. For black-and-white prints
d. For color prints
B. Type of motion picture color film
VIII. Stationery, supplies and files
A. Master daily record journal
B. Envelopes for black-and-white stills
C. Filing cabinet for envelopes
D. Filing cabinet for color slides
IX. Procedures for photographing
A. Envelope data completed by secretary in consultation room
B. Patient returns to waiting room near studio with envelope in hand, to be called according to serial number on envelope
C. Additional data entered on envelope by photographer
D. Envelopes returned to secretary for filing next day
X. Conclusions and recommendations

FORMS OF OUTLINES

Topic Outline

The outline just considered is a topic outline. Main points, divisions and subdivisions have been expressed in words or phrases used as topics which serve as a guide for further development in writing. A topic outline is used when the writer is fully aware of the relationship of each point to the whole problem and to all other points. It enables him to outline his data quickly and easily.

Noun forms are used whenever possible. For both thought and phrasing parallel construction should be followed. Ideas that are parallel in thought must also be parallel in grammatical construction; therefore, corresponding parts of an outline, being of equal significance, must be stated in the same grammatical form. When an infinitive construction is used for expressing an idea in a subdivision under a major division in an outline, the other points of equal significance, and listed under the same division, must also be stated in infinitive form. Likewise when point number "1" is a participial phrase, points "2," "3" and all other points appearing with it under the same subdivision must be expressed in a participial construction. The first word or phrase in an outline point is the key to the construction used.

In a topic outline each point should be a single phrase or idea. Each subhead should support its main head. Points of equal importance should, by their positions in the outline, be given equal rank. Subdivision means division into at *least* two parts. A "1" in an outline calls for a "2," an "A" for a "B," etc.

Sentence Outline

A sentence outline states each point in a complete sentence which may serve as a topic sentence in writing a paragraph in a report. By using a sentence outline, the writer carries his thinking one step further than in a topic outline. He has begun his writing. Sentence outlines are used later as briefs or summaries, whereas a topic outline is later used for subject headings and may be converted into a table of contents. A sentence outline often begins with an unnumbered thesis sentence which states the main idea of the entire report. Norman Shidle in his *Clear Writing for Easy Reading* calls this the "peg" idea and would use it as a starting point for all outlines.[2] The "peg" guides and limits the natural flow of ideas that follows. Often it is a brief statement of the problem; sometimes it states the purpose of the report or the solution to the problem. A portion of a sentence outline on the future expansion of the delivery service of the Mid-City Cleaners follows:

II. The management of Mid-City now feels that there is a possibility of further expanding delivery service.
- *A.* Lakeview route is becoming too large for present driver to handle.
- *B.* New subdivisions on lakefront offer advantage of easily acquiring many new customers.
- *C.* Neighborhood trade is very competitive and delivery service offers best means of expanding.

III. Since management desires to limit delivery expansion to lakefront area, a study of present and proposed developments in that area would be beneficial.
- *A.* Lakeview is rather well developed and serviced.
- *B.* Lakeshore West is only about a year old and is sparsely developed.
- *C.* Lake Vista is rather fully developed and well serviced.
- *D.* Lake Terrace was opened this November and promises to be a very successful and large development.
- *E.* Oak Park is close to lakefront subdivisions and is developing like Lake Vista.
- *F.* With the filling of the former New Basin Canal, area along Pontchartrain Boulevard, from Metairie Cemetery to Lake, should develop fairly well in next year.

IV. Because new route servicing lakefront would be similar to present route serving Lakeview, management intends to use same setup with new route as with present one.

---

[2] Norman Shidle, *Clear Writing for Easy Reading,* McGraw-Hill Book Company, Inc., New York, 1951, pp. 19–26.

A. Three-day service is given: pick-up on Monday, delivery on Thursday.
B. Driver gets 35% commission on all dry cleaning and 10% on laundered shirts.
C. Mid-City pays all gasoline and truck repair bills on its trucks.
D. Prices for delivery are usually 10¢ more per article than shop prices.
E. Expansion of route in area covered depends on driver; new customers who call in are given to driver who services their area.

V. Now that area to be covered and policy to be followed are known, their effects on present shop labor, trucks and other equipment and on management's finances have to be considered.
A. Cleaning and pressing work is done by three employees at present.
B. Of two trucks owned one is used only at night at present.
C. The only expense management feels it will incur is through the addition of more machinery.

OUTLINING SYSTEMS

There are two systems which can be used in outlining: the numeral-letter system and the decimal system. The examples used in this chapter thus far have followed the numeral-letter system.

Numeral-Letter System

In the numeral-letter system Roman numerals are used to designate the major divisions. Capital letters show the breakdown of each main part. Arabic numbers indicate the subdivisions under each capital letter heading, and lower-case letters indicate further subdivisions under each Arabic number heading. For example:

I. First main point
  A. First part in the breakdown of the major division
    1. Subdivision
      a. Subdivision
      b. Subdivision
    2. Subdivision
    3. Subdivision
  B. Second part in the breakdown of the major division
II. Second main point

The numeral-letter system alternately uses numbers and letters. It provides the writer with four degrees of headings at the outset. After the four degrees have been used they may be repeated in parentheses to indicate further subdivision: (*I*) would be the first division under *a.* Then (*A*), (*1*) and (*a*) would be used. For instance:

a.
(I).
(A).
(1).
(a).

This scheme thus permits four additional degrees of headings, making a total of eight. Therefore, the numeral-letter system is used a great deal in short reports and for problems that are simple and uncomplicated. In most cases it is not necessary to carry an outline beyond three or four degrees of subdivision.

Other patterns which are sometimes followed in outlining are:

I.
1.
2.
A.
a.
b.
B.
3.
II.

A.
1.
a.
b.
2.
a.
b.
3.
B.

1.
A.
a.
b.
B.
a.
b.
C.
2.

None of these allows as much flexibility as the pattern suggested earlier. They are, however, practical adaptations which can be used at the outliner's convenience. Regardless of the pattern used, consistency must be maintained.

All headings must stand out conspicuously. Each one begins on a separate line. When it covers more than one line the second line begins directly under the first line. Each subsequent subdivision is indented. All headings of equal rank have the same indention. Relative weights of various points are thus indicated by the system of numbers and letters, as well as by indention. In the numeral-letter system the numbers and letters used to designate the divisions and subdivisions of the outline are followed by a period. However, in keeping with the trend toward using as little punctuation as possible, the period may be omitted. In either case the principle of consistency must be followed. The topics in a topic outline are usually left unpunctuated; however, the writer may use end punctuation if he does so consistently. In a sentence outline each division is punctuated like a sentence.

Although the numeral-letter system is commonly used, it has several disadvantages. When the outliner comes upon a heading numbered *5*, for example, he does not know at once whether it belongs under *A*, *B*, *C* or *D*; and when he looks back to find out he still does not know whether it is under *I*, *II* or *III*. This is a disadvantage both in organizing and in writing the report. Another disadvantage is the limitation in the number of degrees of headings that can be used.

Decimal System

In the decimal system only Arabic numbers and the decimal point are used. The number of degrees may be expanded without limitation. Every item can be immediately identified in its proper relation to the major subject and subtopics with which it is associated. In the book, *Technical Reporting,* for example, Joseph N. Ulman, Jr. effectively used the decimal system for his headings and organization.[3] The points in the outline became his subject headings and table of contents.

Arabic numbers placed to the left of the decimal point indicate major subjects or topics in a report. The Arabic numbers to the right of the decimal point indicate various subdivisions of the topic. The degree of subdivision is indicated by the number of digits to the right of the decimal point. For example:

1. First main topic
- *1.1* First item in first degree of subdivision
  - *1.11* First item in second degree of subdivision
  - *1.12* Second item in second degree of subdivision
  - . . . .
  - *1.1(10)* Tenth item in second degree of subdivision
  - *1.1(11)* Eleventh item in second degree of subdivision
    - *1.1(11)1* First item in third degree of subdivision
    - *1.1(11)2* Second item in third degree of subdivision
      - *1.1(11)21* First item in fourth degree of subdivision
      - *1.1(11)22* Second item in fourth degree of subdivision
        - *1.1(11)221* First item in fifth degree of subdivision
        - *1.1(11)222* Second item in fifth degree of subdivision
- *1.2* Second item in first degree of subdivision

2. Second main topic
- *2.1* First item in first degree of subdivision
  - *2.11* First item in second degree of subdivision

3. Third main topic

The sequence of each subdivision is indicated by the numerical value of the digit. When more than nine items are listed within

[3] Joseph N. Ulman, Jr., *Technical Reporting,* Henry Holt and Company, New York, 1952.

any one subdivision, two or more numerals will be required, and the sequence should be enclosed within parentheses. (However, to avoid the parentheses in the tenth and succeeding items in the second degree of subdivision, you can show the first item in the second degree of subdivision as *1.101* and proceed: *1.102 . . . 1.110,* etc.)

It is rarely, however, that more than nine items would need to be listed under any one sequence, so the use of parentheses will seldom be required. The system can be expanded indefinitely as needed, to any degree of subdivision and to any number of topics within any subdivision. This great a flexibility is not obtainable with the numeral-letter system. Another advantage is that every item is completely identified in its proper relation to the major subject or subdivision with which it is associated. For use in arranging note cards, the outline number may be placed on its corresponding note card. Thus the note cards can readily be arranged to correspond to the outline. This makes for ease and convenience in writing the report. The report can be written in sections according to the wishes of the author and later assembled in proper order as indicated by the numerical identification of each section.

In addition to these advantages, the use of the decimal system forces the author to give careful consideration to the position and proper classification of every detail in his material. An outline showing use of the decimal system follows.

Should Weston & Weston Company Incorporate?

1. Introduction
- *1.1* Statement of problem and background
  - *1.11* Trust and trustee
  - *1.12* Will of John Paul Weston
  - *1.13* Business in financial straits
  - *1.14* Overcoming financial straits
  - *1.15* Expansion of business
    - *1.151* Veneer
    - *1.152* Oil well supplies
- *1.2* Purposes
  - *1.21* Discover means for continuing Weston & Weston Company
  - *1.22* Present evidence of best method of continuing business
- *1.3* Objectives
  - *1.31* To gather pertinent information
  - *1.32* To present evidence in a usable form
- *1.4* Scope and limitations
  - *1.41* Means by which Weston & Weston Company can be continued
  - *1.42* Legal aspects of incorporating
  - *1.43* Costs in taxes
  - *1.44* Views of beneficiaries
  - *1.45* Effect on two minors

- *1.5* Methods of collecting data
    - *1.51* Personal interviews
    - *1.52* Company records
        - *1.521* Annual reports, 1951, 1952
        - *1.522* Last will and testament of John Paul Weston
        - *1.523* Report from Enders and Anders
    - *1.53* Current news items concerning excess profits tax

2. Difficulties of present setup and need for changes
    - *2.1* Expiration of trust
    - *2.2* Two minor beneficiaries
    - *2.3* Liquidation
        - *2.31* The Smithwick Trust Company
            - *2.311* Their attorney
            - *2.312* Their interests
        - *2.32* Financial effect
            - *2.321* On beneficiaries
            - *2.322* On employees
            - *2.323* On momentum of business
        - *2.33* Future of two of the four beneficiaries

3. Proposed changes
    - *3.1* Partnership
        - *3.12* Prohibitive because of minor beneficiaries
            - *3.121* Cannot transact business
            - *3.122* Giving power of attorney to tutrix
            - *3.123* Partnership laws of state
            - *3.124* Results of bankruptcy
            - *3.125* Courts favor minors
            - *3.126* Liability too great for other beneficiaries
    - *3.2* Remain a trust
        - *3.21* Cannot act for minors
        - *3.22* Two beneficiaries not minors
    - *3.3* Corporation
        - *3.31* Definition
        - *3.32* Liability
        - *3.33* Legal move
        - *3.34* Safe for minors
        - *3.35* Beneficiaries' security as well
        - *3.36* Continuation of business
            - *3.361* Position of trustee
            - *3.362* Termination of trust
            - *3.363* Effect on minors
        - *3.37* Taxes
            - *3.371* Comparison with present setup
            - *3.372* Effect of excess profits tax
        - *3.38* Legal aspects
            - *3.381* No laws pertaining
            - *3.382* A legal brief necessary

4. Necessary action to effect change
    - *4.1* Prepare a legal brief
    - *4.2* Take action before trustee ceases to exist

4.3 Get a judgment by the courts
4.4 Apply to the state for corporate license

5. Conclusion
5.1 Necessity to act immediately
5.2 Corporation only possible organization

6. Recommendations
6.1 Change organization now
6.2 Incorporate

PROBLEMS

1. If you did not write the report on the oil company problem at the end of Chapter 7, outline it now; then write the report from your outline. You might first make up a general outline, then a specific one. Use either topics or sentences, as you wish, or as your instructor assigns. Likewise, use either the numeral-letter system or the decimal system.

2. During 1951 a series of communication articles, "Is Anybody Listening?" by William H. Whyte, Jr., appeared in *Fortune* and in 1952 were published in book form by Simon and Schuster, Inc. Read one of the articles or chapters and outline its contents.

3. Select one of the reports used as an example in Part IV of this book and outline it.

4. Organize and outline the following material for a report on reducing the time and cost of loading ice cream trucks at the ________ ________ Ice Cream Company. (Your instructor may have you also write the report.)

Data were obtained from personal interviews with officials and employees of the company, from observation of the loading process and from the experience of the writer in working for the firm. The author had three weeks for preparing the report, was attending summer school and was working 40 hours a week.

The trucks at present are supplied with ice cream at the plant directly from a large freezing room. From the packaging room ice cream is sent to the freezer room and remains in the freezer until properly hardened. A conveyor sends it to the trucks. Only one conveyor is used. One man operates it and checks quantity at the same time. "Cooler-men" or laborers place ice cream on the conveyor. There are three cooler-men, paid $1 per hour and time and a half for overtime beyond a 40-hour week.

The truck drivers are dissatisfied, and there is a threat of their becoming unionized. Excessive costs prevail in the present system. Purpose of report is to reduce costs and ward off motivation for unionization of truck drivers. Dissension is caused partially by long hours of waiting to load trucks.

There must be only one conveyor because of the design of the plant. There are four categories of trucks.

(*1*) City route trucks–14–service retail stores in the city–make deliveries 6 days a week–each truck loaded on each of 6 days–morning and afternoon shifts for loading.

(*2*) Country route trucks–4–service retail stores outside the city–make deliveries 5 days a week–loaded after last evening "city route" truck–6:30 P.M.–loading completed by 11:30 P.M.

(3) Relay route trucks–10–service outside Louisiana and long distances from the city–given double load–but not loaded every day–route men reside in their locale–two in Gulfport, two in Hattiesburg, two in McComb and four in Baton Rouge.

(4) Trailers–3–service substations used for distribution–one each in Lafayette, Natchez, Mobile.

Six of the 14 city trucks are loaded in the morning before route is covered. The first begins loading at 4:00 A.M., the last at 7:30 A.M. Eight of the 14 city trucks are reloaded, after drivers have completed routes, from 1:30 P.M. to 6:00 P.M. Barring interruptions, first of country trucks is loaded at 6:30 P.M. and last one at 11:00 P.M., when cooler-men change shifts. Relay trucks are supplied from plant in New Orleans, but drivers don't come in every day to load. Route men live in the locale of their routes. No definite schedule for loading trucks. Drivers come in at their convenience, day or night.

The substations are only storage stations. All manufacturing is done at the city plant. Trailers are needed to carry large supply to substations. Trailers are loaded at any available time during the day, usually 11:00 A.M. Four hours are required to load one trailer. One hour is required for a truck.

Relay trucks arrive during loading of city trucks. City trucks wait. Drivers are late and off schedule. Cooler-men working until 7:00 A.M are retained to save time, but cost company overtime pay. A trailer starting to be loaded at 11:00 A.M. is completed at 3:00 P.M., and city trucks are returning to be reloaded any time after 1:00 P.M., necessitating a two-hour wait. Drivers are paid on commission basis, not hourly rate. Thus they resent idle waiting time. Cooler-men with quitting time at 3:00 P.M. are held over and extra labor costs ensue.

Management has tried to avoid unionization and employees do not want it, but dissension leaves them open for it. There is need for a schedule for relay trucks and trailers.

Relay trucks most often arrive in the early morning. Can they be scheduled before the morning city trucks or after? Can period for loading morning city trucks be extended? Could trailers be loaded from 11:00 P.M. to 4:00 A.M.?

One Proposed Time Schedule for Loading

Type of Truck	*From*	*To*
City trucks (morning)	4:00 A.M.	7:30 A.M.
Relay route trucks	7:30 A.M.	1:30 P.M.
City trucks (afternoon)	1:30 P.M.	6:30 P.M.
Country trucks	6:30 P.M.	11:00 P.M.
Trailers	11:00 P.M.	4:00 A.M.

All drivers would need to be notified of new schedule. Should loading take place only at specified times for all trucks? Some method of instructing checkers on how to enforce the schedule would be needed.

Part III

EFFECTIVE PRESENTATION IN BUSINESS REPORTS

CHAPTER 9

Characteristics of Factual Writing

TONE
- **Characteristics of Good Tone**
- **Techniques for Developing Good Tone**

STYLE
- **Characteristics of Style**
- **Unity**
- **Coherence**
- **Emphasis**

LANGUAGE

AFTER THE OUTLINE OF A REPORT HAS BEEN PREPARED, THE writer needs to plan the way in which he can best present and interpret his facts. Even before the outline has been composed, he may decide how to present particular figures and statistics in tables or charts, and may even construct them. He has also followed a definite line of reasoning to logical conclusions and has arranged his outline accordingly. Then, when he is ready to write and as he writes, he must be conscious of the techniques of presenting the report's message. The experienced writer, of course, has mastered these techniques to the extent that he applies them out of habit.

It is the purpose of Part III of this book to discuss the principles and practices of good report writing: to consider the over-all characteristics of tone, style and language—how they affect the report writer and his report, what techniques and devices he can use to achieve an effective tone and style; to explain the methods of expressing facts and ideas clearly, interestingly and persuasively, thus achieving the qualities of effective writing; to examine the possibilities of using tables, charts and other graphic illustrations; to discuss making the report readable; and to take up the problems of writing, revising and editing the report.

The results of an investigation form the essential basis of all report writing. Specific facts and data are accurately and objectively presented through the conscious effort of the report writer to eliminate all personal bias, feelings and opinions. Interpretations and ideas growing out of the facts are rationally presented as a basis for sound conclusions and recommendations. Thus an effective report will have an objective and impartial tone; its data will be logically presented and readily understood. Language, style and tone are all used to achieve this end.

TONE

Characteristics of Good Tone

Tone reveals the author's attitude toward his subject and reader, his frame of mind in writing the report, his way of thinking and his method of gathering data. The writer who is thorough in his investigation, attends to details and thinks logically will naturally have a complete report, paying attention to pertinent details and arranging his facts in logical sequence. The unbiased writer presents his message impartially. An effective tone must be objective, impartial, tolerant, sincere, fair and honest. The writer strives to exhibit these characteristics at all times. Emphasis should be on the facts and what they indicate. Tone is adapted to the reader's point of view and to the purpose and type of report. In informal, short reports, when the reader and writer are personal friends, an informal, personal tone may be used. In formal, long reports or in cases when the reader and writer are not close friends, a formal, impersonal tone is followed. At all times the writer must exercise keen judgment in his evaluation and interpretations. He should present a definite, positive, impersonal treatment of facts, making clear distinctions between facts, opinions and assumptions. He must be thorough, accurate and dependable. An inquiring mind, the ability to see a job through to completion, the skill of writing correctly and persuasively and the ability to reason clearly are personal characteristics which contribute to an effective tone.

Techniques for Developing Good Tone

An objective tone is reached by observing facts as a disinterested observer and eliminating personal feelings and prejudices. Further objectivity is achieved by recognizing relationships between facts and ideas and exercising sound judgment in reaching conclusions.

An impartial tone is expressed by weighing and discussing both sides of an issue. Considering advantages and disadvantages of a solution to a problem helps in deciding whether or not to recommend it. Being tolerant of all viewpoints, letting the facts speak for themselves, also indicates impartiality in a report. Inspiring confidence that the material presented is accurate and valid goes a long way toward convincing the reader of the writer's impartiality.

Writing in the third person keeps the writer apart, emphasizes the results and reflects an impersonal tone in the report. Some companies and organizations have adopted a policy requiring use of the third person, which enables the writer to present a detached attitude. In an informal, short report, however, when the reader and writer are personal friends, an informal, personal tone may be adopted and the first person used. For long or formal reports, and especially if the reader and writer are unacquainted, it is best to use the third person consistently. Of course a good principle to follow is to adapt the report to the reader and purpose. Even in some long, rather formal reports, for instance, the reader can relax a little from the conventional third person by a change of pace. Generalizations and results should be stated in the third person. The reader can be advised, though, in the second person, and the writer can bring in his personal observations and views, when appropriate, in the first person. In using all three persons, it is important to strive for naturalness without sounding egotistical, subjective or commanding. When an awkward situation arises from constant use of the words, "author," "writer" or "one," or when a passive construction is weak and vague, then it is better to use "I" than the third person. Any shift in persons should be consistently and judiciously accomplished. In a report such as the company's annual report to stockholders and employees, the second person is very effectively used to bring the reader into everything being said. It is not "the company" and "the dividends" but "your company" and "your dividends," not "we" and "our" but "you" and "yours." But here person is being used to achieve a tone other than an impersonal one and is being adapted to a specific purpose in line with that particular type of report. Most reports based on results of an investigation and used to solve a problem or to make a decision for management should retain a third-person, impartial tone.

Facts and figures are desirable in the present tense. A statement of fact or a result *was* not true merely yesterday but *is* still true today. The present tense indicates this accuracy of statement. The use of exact titles of persons, places and things also helps to convey accuracy in the report and to gain the confidence of the reader. Likewise concrete, vivid illustrations and the active voice of verbs make the data stand out, enlivened and strong as they should be, giving them dignity and sincerity and adding to the general tone of the report.

STYLE

Applied to factual writing, style consists of the techniques the author uses in writing a report. It is the expression of the writer's ideas, his manner of perceiving and thinking. It reflects his sense of humor, the degree of his self-confidence. It should inspire confidence and respect for what he has written. Some of the techniques applicable to achieving good tone are also used to accomplish an effective style. The third person, for example, not only makes for an impartial tone but also for an impersonal, matter-of-fact style, while the first person makes for a personal, intimate style.

Characteristics of Style

A simple, straightforward, direct style is used to present facts. The reader expects to get to the heart of the subject immediately. He usually does not want to waste time on nonessential preliminaries and unimportant data. He is eager to get to the point and find out what the conclusions and recommendations are, so he should not be kept in suspense. A good "rule-of-thumb" principle to follow is: *Have something to say, say it directly and stop.*

A persuasive style convinces and induces action. Accuracy of the investigation and a convincing presentation of its results entail presenting the pros and cons of a point and relating the facts. Tabular and graphical methods of presenting figures, statistics and facts are used rather than verbal exposition alone. Illustrative material, examples, pictures—all emphasize the data and convince the reader as well as make things easily understood. The use of graphic presentation is a stylistic characteristic of most reports and, as one of the methods for presenting data, warrants special treatment in a separate chapter (Chapter 11). Likewise, sufficient techniques for achieving readability are available to warrant special treatment in Chapter 12.

To produce an effective style that will be direct, straightforward, persuasive, convincing, readable and objective requires careful application of the principles of unity, coherence and emphasis, together with the skillful use of language.

Unity

Unity denotes the state of being one. It may be applied to sentences, paragraphs, sections, divisions or an entire report. Unity demands that each simple sentence contain a clearly expressed single idea or meaning and that each complex or compound sentence make a single complete statement in each main clause. Related sentences form a unified paragraph. Each paragraph which presents unity of thought contributes to a unified section, until structurally the entire report becomes a unified whole.

Unity also demands one clearly defined purpose. This means including everything pertinent and eliminating irrelevant material. Consideration should be given to what the reader already knows and to what he still needs or wants to know about the subject. Thus concentration is placed on the problem and its solution. A clearly defined problem with a purpose and objectives to be fulfilled serves as an adequate guide to determining what to include in a report, thus further strengthening its unity. All parts of a report should fit together to accomplish a definite purpose.

Of course, an orderly arrangement of ideas flowing into other ideas and progressing to conclusions helps achieve unity and is a major aid to coherence or relatedness. The relationship between a main idea and a subordinate idea in a sentence is indicated by placing the subordinate or lesser idea or fact in the dependent clause and using a conjunction to point out the relationship, which may be one of space, time, cause, condition, result or concession. In paragraphs and larger thought units the relationship is indicated by some transitional means, which is discussed under coherence. This provides an element of sequence and motion, which makes the report move forward in a definite direction toward accomplishing its purpose.

Coherence

There are two aspects of coherence—relatedness and clearness. To be coherent, a report must be readily understood and must hang together. Like unity, coherence applies to sentences, paragraphs, sections and the report as a whole. Applied to sentences the principle of coherence simply insists that the relationship of all elements in the sentence be immediately apparent and the ideas clearly stated.

By interlinking sentences so that the thought flows smoothly from one to the next, a paragraph is given coherence. This can be implemented by arranging sentences in clear, logical order and by relating them by means of pronouns, transitional words or phrases, the repetition of words or ideas and parallel structure.

Likewise, by interlinking paragraphs so that the thought flows smoothly from one to the next, coherence is given to a section or division of a report. This can be accomplished by: arranging and developing the paragraphs in clear, logical order, linking paragraphs by transitional phrases or sentences, relating paragraphs by repetition of ideas and progression of thought and using topic sentences and topic paragraphs to direct the flow of thought in the section.

Sections of a report are then tied together by using transitional paragraphs and subject headings which directly indicate the relationship of a major topic and its various degrees of subdivision.[1] Careful planning of the outline and following it in writing the report also make for coherence in the report as a whole.

Emphasis

Subject headings indicate points of emphasis by highlighting topics treated and by making their relationship stand out. The more details used, the more illustrations given, the fuller the development of a point, the more emphasis is given to what is being treated. Of course, undue weight should not be given unimportant points, and material must be adapted to the reader's background and to the problem at hand. By eliminating unessential details, superfluous words and hackneyed expressions emphasis is given to the facts and ideas that are presented.

Place the fact to be emphasized in a prominent position. The beginning and the end of a paragraph, a section or a division are emphatic spots. Placed at the beginning main thoughts are given attention and then are further developed. In short reports a major thesis sentence stated at the beginning of the report gives the main idea of the entire report and thus gives it emphasis at the outset. In

[1] See pp. 435–437 in the appendix for use of subject headings of various degrees.

long reports a thesis paragraph or section may serve the same purpose. In some cases it will mean placing conclusions, recommendations or a summary of findings first, which will emphasize those points to accomplish the writer's purpose or to satisfy the reader.

Placed at the end of a paragraph or report, important ideas are given the reader for a final impression. Sometimes the analysis of data will lead into conclusions and the writer will want to achieve a climactic effect, in which case he will place his conclusions at the end of the report.

A number of devices which may be used in the typography of a report will give emphasis to a point by calling attention to it.

Leave a large amount of white space
around the idea or fact to be set off.

USING ALL CAPITAL LETTERS, underscoring the portion to be emphasized, using *italics* or another style of print, using colored ink—all are mechanical means of calling attention to certain words, phrases and sentences and thus emphasizing the thought they express. Indenting material, single spacing or presenting an itemized list also lends the same effect.

Figures, statistics and other data can be emphasized by presentation in graphic form. All sorts of graphs, charts, tables and pictorial forms are used for this purpose. Figures may also be highlighted by spot tables. After they are presented in some graphic form, attention can be called to the significant figures in interpreting the table by pointing out the important ones, drawing relationships and pointing up conclusions from them.

Special techniques that will make the chief idea stand out can be applied also to the structure of sentences. For example, put the main idea in an independent clause in a complex sentence and the subordinate idea in a dependent clause:

> Although total sales volume was down this past year, total profits increased.

Two ideas of equal importance should be stated in main clauses of a compound sentence:

> All representatives are pledged to render every possible assistance to policyholders, and their counsel is given cheerfully from a fund of expert knowledge.

When a number of facts are being given and long sentences are used, putting the most important fact in a short, simple sentence will cause that fact to stand out. The principle of obtaining emphasis by position may also be applied to sentences by putting the emphatic idea at the beginning or the end of the sentence.

Other ways of attaining emphasis include the use of parallelism, repetition and building to a climax. A series or an itemized list calls for parallelism to emphasize the points listed; for instance, if a prepositional phrase is used to state one item, it should be used for all the other items. Facts restated in different ways through repetition of the main idea emphasize that idea. The careful selection and combination of words is also important for emphasis. The precise, specific word will always convey a concrete idea. Vivid words, figures of speech properly used, euphonic words, strong active words—all call attention to ideas and thus give them emphasis. As much use of these words should be made as is consistent with naturalness of style and is appropriate to the material and purpose.

LANGUAGE

Language is the means of communicating thought. Words are its tools, and clear thinking lies at the base of all communication of ideas. Thinking itself requires words. Putting ideas into understandable language eliminates careless, fuzzy thinking. Words are names given to objects and actions. They are symbols used to convey ideas to others. Developing the skill to analyze thoughts and the ability to select the right words for transmitting ideas improves communication.

Words should be selected for their denotations and connotations. The denotation is the idea the word exactly expresses. The connotation is the idea the word suggests. The purpose of the report must be considered to determine whether the words should be used principally to inform or to impress the reader. In most reports words are selected for their denotations. Definite, exact words are used to express clear, exact meanings. This is one major difference in writing business letters and formal business reports. Most business letters are written to impress as well as to inform the reader. Words are then selected chiefly for their connotation or suggestive power.

Simplicity is a dependable guide. Words should be selected that will be clearly and easily understood. Technical and unnecessarily detailed explanations should be avoided. Familiar terms are preferred over unusual words, short rather than long words, concrete rather than abstract terms, precise words over vague ones. Abstract nouns tend to be vague and general. They are less direct and less forceful than concrete nouns. When abstract nouns are used they should be qualified by illustrations pointing out their characteristics.

Unnecessary words should always be eliminated. Superfluous words waste time, obscure meanings and lack force. Roundabout expressions should also be omitted. There is no need to use several words to say what one will say. Indirect expressions such as the following should be omitted: *it was found that, it can be seen that, it is obvious that, it appears that.* Words like *however, it is* and *there are* placed at the beginning of a sentence generally have little value, although sometimes they are used there for transition. Likewise, words that express the imperative, such as *must, ought to, have to* and *demand* are often psychologically bad and, when they are, should be avoided. Other words that waste time and space are *in order to, in regard to, due to the fact that, in connection with* and other hackneyed expressions. Unless jargon is used in a specialized sense and adapted to the reader in an informal, personal report, it should be avoided, because it usually is fuzzy and unintelligible.

Skillful use of a diversified vocabulary will go a long way toward making reports convey their messages clearly and toward getting the desired action. Now that consideration has been given to the over-all characteristics of tone, style and language and to developing them appropriately in writing reports, the methods of expressing facts and ideas clearly, interestingly and persuasively need to be discussed next.

PROBLEMS

1. What factors must be considered in determining the tone of a report?

2. Point out what is wrong with the tone and style in the following paragraph, and rewrite the material for increased effectiveness:

I think that what is wrong is that the base-pay rate is too low. To begin with, I feel that I am not paid enough. Hourly wage employees receive $1.45 per hour, or rather Mr. John Sampson told me that was what he was receiving. And Mr. Henry Penson said he had an offer of $1.50 per hour from Brookington Corporation. Well, I happen to know that Mrs. Emily Smith, an accountant there, told me that their men were paid $1.30 an hour. The employees have complained to me according to our open-door policy that they are not receiving sufficient wages. I believe we pay overtime in some cases. I don't know, however, whether it is in accordance with our over-all personnel policy or not. Since I began work in the personnel department two years ago there have been many changes taking place.

I have checked the base rate of five other companies doing similar work as ours, and we are paying above average.

3. The following paragraph was taken from an employee booklet welcoming and orienting new employees to the company. Rewrite it for effective tone and style:

Let us take this opportunity at this time on behalf of ______ ______ and Company and its employees to welcome you to the organization and let you know that we wish for your success on the job. We have been in business for some time and have seen many men come and go. We are confronted with a variety of problems each day. You will have many responsibilities, and it will be necessary to become accustomed to your work. We want you to feel free to talk to us about your problems and would like to talk to you about ours. To work cooperatively will mean increased production to the ______ ______ Company, and we are desirous at this time to stress cooperation to you. We are all one team here working together for the good of the company. It should be necessary for you to find that out as soon as possible for our good.

4. How do the techniques of emphasis in presenting material in a report differ from those applicable to business letters?

5. How would you characterize the tone and style suitable to a problem-solution report done by an outside research agency and the tone and style suitable to an annual report to employees within a corporation? What determines these differences?

6. Explain *adaptation of language* in the two reports mentioned in Problem 5.

CHAPTER 10

Expressing Facts Clearly, Interestingly and Persuasively

QUALITIES OF EFFECTIVE WRITING
- **Clearness**
- **Completeness**
- **Conciseness**
- **Concreteness**
- **Consistency**
- **Correctness**

TECHNIQUES FOR EXPRESSING FACTS AND THOUGHTS
- **Using Topic Sentences**
- **Developing Thoughts**
  - ***By Details***
  - ***By Comparison and Contrast***
  - ***By Illustration and Example***
  - ***By Logical Reasoning***
- **Arranging Facts and Ideas**

USING STRUCTURAL PARAGRAPHS
- **Introductory**
- **Transitional**
- **Summary**

EXPOSITORY WRITING
- **Analysis**
- **Definition**
- **Description**
- **Narration**
- **Argumentation**

THE MATERIAL IN A REPORT MUST BE PRESENTED CLEARLY, interestingly and persuasively for it to be effective and for it to accomplish its specific purpose. All of the qualities of effective writing—clearness, completeness, conciseness, concreteness, consistency and correctness—when applied are invaluable aids in presenting material in a report. There are also a number of special writing techniques which may be used so that the reader will have a clear understanding of what he is reading as he progresses through the report. Structural paragraphs and the various types of expository writing — analysis, definition, description, narration and argumentation — are employed as needed in getting the report's message across to its reader.

QUALITIES OF EFFECTIVE WRITING

Clearness

Writing clearly simply means writing to be understood rather than misunderstood. At the outset it depends on careful, efficient planning. Planning the investigation, planning the organization of the data, planning the writing of the report — all make for a logical, easy-to-follow arrangement of text material, all the sections of which are connected, and the ideas and thoughts of which flow smoothly from beginning to end. One of the chief ways to achieve clearness is through the arrangement of the material in a report. Writing from a well-planned outline makes this possible.

The use of transition, whether by words and phrases, sentences, paragraphs or a natural flow of ideas, is another important aid to clarity, because it points out relatedness of parts of the report. Using subject headings indicating both main divisions and subdivisions of the material is a mechanical but effective means of ensuring clearness.

Careful attention to layout and display possibilities, such as typing and spacing subject headings, tables, charts and other forms of graphic presentation, makes for clearness as well as interest. Alignment and indentation as used in listings indicate subordination of ideas and facts. Principles of parallelism should be applied in listings and subject headings. If a sentence is used for one item in a list, sentences should be used for all; if a participial phrase is used for one, participial phrases should be used for all items.

Clarity is also secured through the language used. Concrete, simple language can be understood by all readers. When a report is intended for a reader with technical knowledge, special and technical terms may be used; but when it is intended for a layman, terms must be made clear through definition. The definite word to express a single idea should be carefully selected and adapted to the reader.

Inaccuracy of expression should be avoided. Likewise, dangling modifiers and pronouns with antecedents not clearly expressed or not agreeing in number and person should be avoided. If a split infinitive makes for good natural expression it may be used. If it is awkward then it should not be used. Long introductions and descriptive passages and overuse of quotations usually result in a lack of clarity. The same is true of nonessential details. Specific details, however, when pertinent are an aid to clearness.

There is a direct relationship between clearness and completeness, on the one hand, and completeness and conciseness on the other. Completeness makes for clearness and should not be sacrificed for conciseness.

Completeness

Completeness means comprehensive treatment of the subject or problem at hand, and results in clear, persuasive writing. All points and explanations should be sufficiently detailed that no misconception will follow. Evidence must be precisely stated; the significance of the facts in relation to the problem must be shown. The treatment of each section of the report must be complete, so that the reader will have an understanding of that particular section and a basis for understanding what is to follow. For the analysis is a basis for the conclusions, and the conclusions are a basis for the recommendations. All must be used to point toward the accomplishment of the purpose of the report.

In working for completeness the writer must consider his reader. For the reader who is familiar with the problem few details are needed. They may be recognized and their relationship pointed out without being included. For the uninformed reader complete explanations and interpretations are necessary. Treatment should be comprehensive so that the reader will find answered any questions he might have about the material presented.

Completeness must be adhered to in all elements of the report: complete title page, complete table of contents, complete tables, complete bibliography, complete footnote entries, complete index.

Conciseness

Writing concisely requires that every thought be expressed in as few words as are consistent with writing completely and clearly. By culling the insignificant facts and treating the significant points, conciseness can be achieved. It means more than mere brevity, because conciseness involves the omission of unnecessary points. Some awareness of the reader's knowledge of the subject will result in the recognition of unimportant points or ones that are already familiar to him, so that they can be omitted or properly subordinated.

Conciseness is also secured through economy and careful selection of words. As few words as possible should be used to give complete clear meanings. Whenever possible a word should be used instead of a phrase, a phrase instead of a clause, a clause instead of a sentence, a sentence instead of a paragraph. The process of condensing, however, should not be carried so far that the message becomes general and loses its meaning. Words should not be wasted, irrelevant and repetitious details should be omitted, and hackneyed words and phrases should be eliminated. Definite terms should be used rather than general or abstract words. Long parenthetic and digressive remarks should be avoided. The use of the passive voice construction requires more words than the active voice and may obscure the meaning. Long, rambling sentences use words needlessly and should be recast. Sometimes, though, long, well-knit sentences should be used, since variety of sentence length makes for interest.

Conciseness also depends on careful revision. Checking, criticizing and rewriting a report before its final typing make for not only conciseness but also for all the other qualities of effective writing. Writing, revising and editing are treated, however, in Chapter 13.

Concreteness

The purpose of concreteness is to help the reader visualize the subject. Abstract statements must be illustrated with specific, concrete examples. To be specific is not always to be concrete; but when one applies specific details to a concrete idea, object or event, then it becomes specific. The specific application of an idea illustrates it, making for concreteness. The illustration solidifies or strengthens the point to which it is applied so that it can be readily visualized by the reader. The result is vividness and interest.

Consistency

Maintaining report uniformity by conforming to a pre-determined pattern is being consistent. The writer must be consistent in the form and style he uses and in his methods of presenting his message to the reader.

Consistency in form includes uniformity of typing details such as margins, indentation, degrees of subject headings, listings, tabulations, numbering of pages, footnote and bibliography entries, etc. Consistency in mechanics of writing means following a set pattern concerning abbreviations, hyphenation, capitalization, use of numerals, spelling and punctuation. Consistency likewise must be followed in presenting graphic material. If curves are to be compared, the same scale must be used throughout their plotting. Chart "A" must always be referred to as Chart "A" and not "a" or "1." Consistency can be achieved by setting up all tables in the same form and by using the same units of measurement. It must likewise be maintained in making comparisons and in reasoning through to logical conclusions. Each section of factual material must be consistent with other parts of the report so the reader will not be confused. Contradictions must be avoided. Sticking to one trend of thought at a time and following thoughts in agreement with one another result in consistency.

Correctness

Correctness is accuracy; it is the result of competent judgment and conformity to an accepted conventional standard. It involves a careful checking with the standard to find out that there is freedom from error. Accuracy should begin with the first step of report preparation and be carried out to the final stage. There must be accuracy all the way through in:

(1) analysis of the problem
(2) planning the investigation
(3) collecting data
(4) analyzing and interpreting the facts
(5) reaching conclusions
(6) formulating recommendations
(7) outlining the material for presentation in the report
(8) writing, revising and rewriting the final copy

Correctness applies to both subject matter and to the manner in which it is expressed. The data must not only be correct but must be exactly stated and used to show accurate reasoning and reaching of conclusions and recommendations. This also involves careful selection of words and conformity to rules of grammar, spelling and punctuation. Correctness does much in convincing the reader that the report is accurate, that it is based on sound judgment and that its recommended action should be taken.

All of the qualities of effective writing — clearness, completeness, conciseness, concreteness, consistency and correctness — when applied, are invaluable aids in expressing facts clearly, interestingly and persuasively.

TECHNIQUES FOR EXPRESSING FACTS AND THOUGHTS

Using Topic Sentences

By indicating the essential thought that is developed in the whole report, chapter, section or paragraph, the topic sentence clearly, accurately and forcefully guides the writer while he is presenting his data and later enables the reader to understand it. The sentence, "The differences in initial costs of the four trucks are due to several factors," for instance, concisely introduces the ideas that follow. The reader knows to expect an enumeration of the factors and an explanation of them.

The topic sentence of a paragraph may be placed at the beginning, end or middle, or it may be unstated. The reader, however, must be able to understand it. Stated at the beginning it lets the reader know what logical development to expect; stated at the end it serves as a conclusion or summary and leaves the reader with the idea that the topic has been treated completely. For emphasis it may be stated in the beginning and restated at the end. The important point is for ideas to flow from or into the topic sentence.

Used to express the main idea of a report or of a division of it, the topic sentence comes near the beginning and is sometimes referred to as the thesis sentence. A series of topic sentences are then used throughout as thoughts and facts are further developed. Sometimes topic sentences are expanded into topic paragraphs, used for the same purpose.

In addition to indicating the subject matter a topic sentence generally shows how the subject matter is to be developed. The sentence, "Two plans are provided by the lessor for purchasing gasoline and oil," indicates that a number of details or a comparison of the two plans will be made in developing the subject of the topic sentence. Or again, "All services provided by the Dixie System are provided by the U-Drive-It Company," leads the reader to expect a comparison of the services of the two companies.

Developing Thoughts

There are a number of methods of developing thoughts in presenting factual material. Many of the methods of developing paragraphs, such as by details, comparison and contrast, cause and effect, illustration and example and logical reasoning, are of course just as applicable in reports as in other kinds of writing. The logically developed paragraph, which consists of a summarizing topic sentence at its beginning, followed by a series of details, evidence and examples illustrating the main thought and a concluding statement reached from reasoning through the discussion of facts, is well fitted for reports. At times there is a deliberate and intentional violation of paragraph unity for clarity and emphasis. The thoughts are broken up into small units. There may be even one-sentence paragraphs. When this is done extensively a section of the report, rather than a single paragraph, becomes a unit of thought. The principles governing the development of a paragraph and the flow of ideas are merely applied on a larger scale. Thoughts in a report may be developed and expressed by any or all of the following methods.

By Details. A unit of thought may be divided into parts with details given about each part, thus developing the main ideas in logical order. Details may consist of exact numbers, specifications, specific points, definite facts, structural details and details of action. They help the reader to understand an explanation or to visualize what is being said. Details make for complete understanding by providing concrete substantiating evidence, and by being vividly presented add interest to the material. Presented in itemized lists, details add emphasis.

By Comparison and Contrast. Discussing points of likeness and unlikeness of similar ideas or objects is comparison. Discussing dissimilar objects or ideas and emphasizing the points of difference is contrast. The two may be intermingled or used separately. The respective elements might also be listed in a columnar arrangement. In any case, by comparison and contrast the relationship of points is shown.

The treatment of both subjects being compared must be similar, as indicated by the following outlines comparing personnel policies:

I. Personnel policies of White Brothers Store
- *A.* Hiring
- *B.* Absenteeism
- *C.* Conferences, etc.

II. Personnel policies of Smith Brothers Store
- *A.* Hiring
- *B.* Absenteeism
- *C.* Conferences, etc.

I. Hiring Policies
- *A.* White Brothers Store
- *B.* Smith Brothers Store

II. Absenteeism
- *A.* White Brothers Store
- *B.* Smith Brothers Store

III. Conferences
- *A.* White Brothers Store
- *B.* Smith Brothers Store

In using comparison and contrast a good illustrative device is *analogy*. Between two essentially unlike things or ideas several points of similarity are indicated for the sake of illustrating one in terms of the other. Analogy thus adds vividness, clarity and interest. One must select two objects sufficiently alike to be actually comparable and yet different enough to make the comparison meaningful through the contrast. The device is especially useful in description and analysis.

By Illustration and Example. The general idea stated in the topic sentence may be illustrated by a single incident or by a series of examples. Anecdotes, events and everyday occurrences are types of examples which may indicate the application of the general idea, thereby creating an understanding of it. Illustrations in the form of pictures, charts, graphs, etc., as well as word pictures, may be used for the same result. Both illustrations and examples are best used in explanation and argumentation, for they give clear proof of the evidence at hand.

By Logical Reasoning. Logical reasoning is a form of clear thinking which must precede all effective writing. It may be expressed simply by stating reasons in explaining an idea, object or action. One may reason from a cause or source to its result or vice versa, showing the relationship between the two elements. From a series of observed events or a mass of collected data the reader is led from one position to the next until a conclusion is reached — this is *inductive reasoning.* By examining sufficient phenomena until a pattern emerges, a conclusion is formed to explain the pattern. In *deductive reasoning,* the writer begins with a widely accepted generalization or pattern and evaluates particular cases to determine whether they conform to it.

The original premise must be precise and accurate. For reports designed to persuade or to offer recommendations, deductive reasoning can be very appropriately used.

Some form of logical reasoning is used in criticism and evaluation. Here a set of standards might be applied to the procedure or process being evaluated and conclusions reached as to what is good or bad. Advantages and disadvantages may be weighed to determine which course of action should be followed.

The nature of the material and the method used in interpreting it in a report — whether it be by details, comparison and contrast, illustration and example or by logical reasoning — will largely determine the arrangement of thoughts as they are expressed.

Arranging Facts and Ideas

The order of presenting the results of logical thinking, for example, depends on whether it is the result of deductive or inductive reasoning. In arranging facts inductively the details, facts and interpretations are presented first. Next the conclusion is inferred from them and tested; then it is stated at the end. In contrast to material presented in this order is the line of deductive reasoning, which presents first the conclusion and then its application to the situation at hand. In the end the original premise is restated as a final conclusion.

A technique commonly used in analysis and description is to begin with a concept of the whole idea and proceed to the several that compose it. This often involves classification and division and makes for clear, logical development. A topic idea presents the major divisions first; then each in turn is analyzed or described. In the end they may be brought together as a summary.

A similar principle involves presenting familiar facts to the reader first and leading from them into unfamiliar information. The reader is then prepared to understand the new data confronting him. Ideas may also be presented according to their importance. They may be arranged with the least important idea first and the most important one last, or vice versa.

When dealing with events or other facts that involve dates or a step-by-step process, a chronological arrangement of ideas is followed. The material is presented in the order in which it occurred. This method is especially useful in narrating procedures in the history of a problem or subject. In addition to a *time* sequence, a *space* sequence may be used to describe the relative position of parts. It is best suited to describing a machine or structure.

The important principle to follow is to arrange ideas and facts according to some pre-determined method or methods. Doing this will certainly make for effective writing of reports.

USING STRUCTURAL PARAGRAPHS

So that the reader will have a clear understanding of what he is reading as he progresses through the report, structural paragraphs should be used to guide him. They provide the framework around which the facts are presented, thus pointing out relationships of paragraphs and sections.

Introductory

An introductory paragraph gives the reader a clear preliminary view of the subject matter as a whole. In the introduction of a report, for example, a statement of the problem or subject is pertinent. Then in the introductory paragraph of each section of a report the writer presents the subject matter taken up in that particular section. Essential points or generalizations are often summarized as an introduction to save time for the reader and to inform and interest him. Sometimes the introductory paragraph indicates a plan of what is to follow. It may show the division of the material; for instance, $A = a + b + c$. A discussion of each component of A would then be in order. At other times an introductory paragraph may resemble the lead paragraph of a newspaper article. It is easy to read a report rapidly and clearly when lead headlines and paragraphs give the gist of the material at a glance.

Transitional

Transitional paragraphs make clear the relationship of paragraphs or sections to each other and to the report as a whole. Because they look backward and forward, they point out the relationship of the parts of the report and leave the reader not only with an understanding of facts at hand but also with a clear feeling that he has moved forward. Often a pertinent comment or a reference to both previous and subsequent ideas or facts is sufficient. Sometimes there is a logical flow of facts and thoughts so that transitional sections are not necessary. This is more likely to be true in short than in long reports, because of the closer relationship among topics discussed.

Summary

In providing the framework of the report, structural paragraphs let the reader know what is going to be said and why (introductory), relate sections which present the facts (transitional) and finally tell the reader what has been said (summary). A summary paragraph, if presented at the beginning of a report or section, is also introductory; it introduces the reader to what is to follow. If used at the end of a section it sums up what has been said. In setting forth the main points brought out in the analysis of facts the final summary also reasons from them to the conclusions.

Reducing structural paragraphs to a formula basis, the writer may state his problem in an introductory paragraph by breaking it down into its components: *A (the problem)* $= a + b + c$ *(its component parts).* He then proceeds to discuss a in a section of the report. After analyzing $a = 1 + 2$ and discussing the facts pertaining to a he is ready to move on to b. Before he can do this, however, he may want to summarize the main points he made about a and also relate a to b. He would thus use summary and transitional paragraphs. The same procedure would be repeated for b and c. Thus facts and their discussion are presented and a cumulative progression of thoughts is made. Afterwards a final summary would bring all the main facts together: $a + b + c$ *(component parts of the problem)* $= A$ *(its solution).* The final summary then would serve as a basis for the conclusions which would follow.

EXPOSITORY WRITING

Just as structural paragraphs provide the framework for writing a report, expository paragraphs fill in the framework with facts and interpretations, so that the report is solidly built.

Because reports present facts, show relationships and offer interpretations, report writing is a type of expository writing. It aims to inform or enlighten the reader by making clear an idea, fact, process or object. It is concerned with presenting the truth by delving into the meaning and significance of facts in relationship to other facts and interpreting them to reach conclusions. Accordingly, exactness of knowledge, orderly arrangement of data and careful planning of how to present evidence are all necessary if the reader is to understand what has been written. Thus the five major composition forms of expository writing — analysis, definition, description, argumentation and narration — are utilized in expressing facts clearly, interestingly and persuasively.

Analysis

According to *Webster's New Collegiate Dictionary,* 1953, analysis is the "separation of anything into constituent parts or elements; also, an examination of anything to distinguish its component parts or elements, separately or in their relation to the whole"; or "a form of statement . . . exhibiting the results of a process of analysis." In making a preliminary analysis of a problem (prior to the investigation for data), the situation is analyzed by breaking it down into its component parts in order to determine the problem involved. Then the problem is broken down to determine what aspects need investigation and analysis.

In writing up the report, analysis is the result of resolving anything into its elements. A point is broken down into its parts, which in turn are examined or traced to their sources for the purpose of discovering some general principle or truth. The analytical process involves partition and classification. The systematic arrangement of facts into groups or categories based upon some common denominator or relationship is classification. The enumeration of a class into parts of which it is composed is partition. Suppose you are writing a report for the purpose of determining which brand of accounting machines your firm should purchase. You would first analyze each of several brands. The information you obtained would be grouped according to the make of machine it pertained to. That would be classification. You would also want to analyze each machine by its own individual parts or characteristics. This breakdown would be partition. The type of problem you are dealing with will determine whether you use classification or partition, and you may also use both.

Analysis is used in dealing with data resulting from an investigation. It interprets facts and figures by explaining their significance and their relationship, making possible the reaching of a conclusion from phenomena or statistics. In a direct way this is done by classification or partition; indirectly, however, it is done by making effective use of comparison and contrast, illustrations, cause and effect, inductive and deductive reasoning and other concrete techniques for expressing facts and thoughts, which were discussed earlier in this chapter.

Definition

Although analytical paragraphs make up the bulk of a report, other forms of expository writing are important too in presenting material clearly, interestingly and persuasively. Definition is especially helpful for clear understanding of the problem and the report.

The problem, aim, scope, limitations, technical and special terms all need to be defined for the reader to have an adequate background of information for completely understanding the report. Most of the defining is thus done in the introductory section of a report. The definition of a term, however, may be given when it is first used. Technical terms are defined unless the reader already has an understanding of them, and special terms according to the limited sense or particular meaning the author wants to convey.

In the "Introduction" to a report entitled *U. S. Television Ownership by Counties, November 1, 1953,* by the CBS Television Research Department, definitions of special terms are given:

> The following definitions apply in all the tables appearing in this report:
>
> *Total families:* "Sales Management" estimates of total families in each county as of November 1, 1953.
>
> *TV families:* The number of families with television sets (VHF, UHF or both) in each county on November 1, 1953, as determined by this survey. These figures are reported individually by county only if 10 percent or more of all families in a county report having a television set.
>
> *UHF families:* The number of families with television sets equipped to receive a UHF signal. These figures are reported only if 10 percent or more of *all* the families in a county report having a UHF set.
>
> *TV counties:* Counties with at least 10 percent set-owning families.

Each of these definitions consists of three parts:

(1) The *term* to be defined

(2) The *genus* or class or concept to which the term belongs

(3) The *differentiae* or characteristics which distinguish it from other members of its class.

Some pertinent principles helpful in using definitions in a report are:

(*1*) Use clear and direct language. (Words simpler and more familiar than the term being defined should be used.)

(*2*) Express the concept in *terms* other than those involving the one to be defined. ("An annual report is a report issued annually" is mere repetition which should be avoided.)

(*3*) Be sure the *genus* is large enough to include all members of the term. (This will make for exactness and clearness.)

(*4*) Make certain that the *differentiae* completely differentiate. (Essential and secondary characteristics may be given.)

(*5*) Avoid terms such as "is when" and "is where." ("An informational report is where the author informs the reader" is meaningless.)

The sole purpose of definition is to establish a common concept of idea, process or object. This may be accomplished in a single sentence or statement such as the examples earlier cited, or the definition may be expanded into a paragraph by enumerating a number of differentiae, by explaining the differentiae or by discussing the meaning or use of the term. A general statement, for example, may define the aim or object of a report and, by developing an explanation of how the report is to be used to accomplish its purpose, an expanded definition would result. Likewise the report's scope might be stated in a single sentence and the sentence developed into a paragraph by using specific details in discussing the breakdown of the problem into its elements that are later analyzed. The treatment of the subject in a particular report, for instance, must be differentiated from other possible treatments of the same subject matter. The following paragraph illustrates the way in which purpose, scope and limitations of a report may be combined into a single paragraph defining all three:

The purpose of this report is to determine whether the Royal Supply Co. should rent its trucks instead of owning them. The results of this report will decide what policy the company will follow in 1954. The analysis of the present system covers the costs of the four Jeep trucks now owned by the Royal Supply Co. The two largest rental agencies in the New Orleans area were likewise examined for cost of renting and operating Ford, Dodge and Chevrolet trucks. The report is limited to cost figures as they apply to the New Orleans area. Although cost is the most important factor considered, other factors such as convenience, reliability, etc. are given consideration. As a result this report covers the over-all desirability of each of the three possible systems.

In using expanded definition descriptive details may be given, specific examples narrated, comparisons made or explanations of causes and results presented.

Description

Although description is used in literary writing almost entirely for entertaining the reader, explaining feelings and emotions and describing places and objects, in expository writing it is used chiefly in setting forth and explaining phenomena observed, and only secondarily for entertainment – when it is used for enlivening material. In the CBS Television Research report on ownership by counties description is used in explaining the procedures used in the study:

> This is a brief description of the techniques used to determine television set ownership as of November 1, 1953. Additional detail is available on request.
>
> *Background*: In May, 1952, the A. C. Nielsen Company conducted a study (Nielsen Coverage Service, Spring 1952) which measured television set ownership by individual counties with a relatively large population, and by clusters of two or more less populous counties. This study was based on interviews with approximately 100,000 homes located in every county of the United States, and selected by probability sampling techniques developed (and executed) in collaboration with the U. S. Census Bureau. Every effort was made to minimize non-response bias by the use of call-backs on the "not-at-home" and by special mailings to the small percentage of families not reached by personal interviews. No UHF stations were in operation at the time of this study. In May, 1953, the CBS Television Research Department made this study the basis of a report called "U.S. Television Ownership by Counties."
>
> *Present Study:* The present study consists fundamentally of a re-survey of the 100,000-homes panel to determine changes in television set ownership status that have occurred since May, 1952. For this purpose, the sample was divided into three groups:
>
> Group A—72,561 non-owners as of May, 1952. This group was surveyed to measure new television set ownership (VHF or UHF) since that date.
>
> Group B—13,133 owners as of May, 1952, within range of one or more UHF signals by November, 1953. This group was surveyed to measure conversion to, or acquisition of, UHF equipment.
>
> Group C—13,491 owners as of May, 1952, beyond the range of UHF in November, 1953. It was assumed that the set ownership status of this group had remained unchanged, and hence, the group was not re-surveyed.
>
> Groups A and B were reached by a first-class mailing sent on October 15 and 16, 1953. This mailing consisted of a letter asking for cooperation in supplying the requested information, a return reply card, and a letter opener sent as a premium. On October 19 and 20, a follow-up reminder and "thank you" containing a duplicate reply card was mailed to each family. By November 9, the closing date set for mail returns, usable replies had been received from 54,233 of the 85,694 cases in Groups A and B. This represented a return of 63.3%.
>
> The 54,233 families who replied in Groups A and B combined with 13,491 families in Group C brought the total number of cases whose set ownership status

had been determined as of November, 1953, to 67,724, or 68.3% of the over-all panel.

The figures as reported in this booklet represent the information gathered from these 67,724 cases adjusted for two types of bias:

(*1*) non-response bias—i.e. the possibility that the television set ownership of the non-repliers differed from that of the repliers;

(*2*) exaggeration bias—i.e. the possibility that some of the repliers had incorrectly reported acquisition of a television set since May of 1952. Separate studies, described below, were conducted to determine these two factors. . . .

Here specific details have been selected and arranged chronologically so that the reader visualizes the procedures. He also is led from familiar facts of the previous study to new ones in the recent analysis and develops a sense of the importance of the data thus determined. Three principles in using description have thus been applied:

(*1*) Arranging details by a time sequence

(*2*) Leading the reader from the known to the unknown

(*3*) Giving the reader a sense of the importance of the material described.

Other principles of description, more applicable in describing a piece of equipment, device, property or data than a procedure, are:

(*1*) Letting the reader see the whole, then the related parts, then the whole again

(*2*) Anticipating the reader's questions and answering them

(*3*) Making comparisons

(*4*) Using illustrative material such as examples, diagrams and photographs.

In describing a piece of equipment in a report recommending its purchase, the first principle just listed would be applied by creating a general impression of the machine. It would be named, its use or general purpose stated, the general appearance described and perhaps its main working principle explained. This would give the reader a concept of the machine as a whole. Then what the reader wants or needs to know about the machine would be answered in specific detail (second principle). The machine's outward, then inner, appearance and mechanism could be explained and its various parts described. The machine could be compared with other similar machines (third principle) and illustrative material used to picture in detail the machine's parts or function (fourth principle). The writer's feelings and emotions would be left out, for he is using objective description to set forth his facts even though he has enlivened them by applying some descriptive techniques.

Narration

Because it employs many of the same techniques narration is very closely related to description. It is not, however, used so much nor is it so important in report writing as description.

Narration gives pleasure; it appeals to the reader; it creates the illusion of the reader's experiencing the events disclosed. To enliven otherwise dull, uninteresting material and to create a lasting impression on the reader, narration is best used in reports written for the public or for employees, when getting the reader's attention and interest is highly important. It is also used often in sales promotional reports, but rarely in problem-solving reports for management.

To use narration for a practical purpose in a report you may:

(*1*) introduce the subject by a brief narrative incident — humorous or thought-provoking, but related to the idea — leading the reader pleasantly into the main subject of the report,

(*2*) give an account of the procedures used in gathering the data and in organizing it for the report,

(*3*) provide the reader with a history of the problem so he will have a basic understanding of the present situation in view of the past,

(*4*) intersperse relevant narrative incidents throughout to maintain reader interest and to illustrate points, making them understandable and vivid,

(*5*) tell a story and in expanding and interpreting it clarify the points in the report,

(*6*) present plans for carrying out a suggested project or recommended action.

Narrative technique demands the ability to create an illusion of reality. It uses characters, setting and plot. In using narration the writer may make use of personal references, conversation and events. The report moves; the reader is told where he is going and why; active words move him along; a chronological recounting of events helps him to experience them vicariously; he arrives at the same conclusions as the author and agrees with his recommendations.

Occasionally, when all the data lend themselves to arrangement by time sequence, the entire report is narration from beginning to end. This is most likely to be true in giving an account of a process or activity. The report might begin with a summary of the story, letting the reader see the purpose, extent or direction of the narration. Then details would be related for understanding and interest as the story unfolds from one step to the next. In the end a summary would be used to bring together the main points or the conclusions drawn from the narrative.

Argumentation

Used more often than narration in report writing is argumentative exposition, because in almost every report factual and reasoned proof is presented. Especially is argumentation invaluable in recommendation reports.

Argumentation in reports is concerned with the presentation of facts and evidence to prove a point, conclusion or recommendation. A neutral or antagonistic reader must be persuaded by argumentative proof to accept the action which the report recommends. The argument must be calm, reasoned and businesslike. It should not be opinionated, biased, emotional or unfair. Evidence presented must be weighed and evaluated; reasoning followed must lead to sound conclusions. In this manner the reader can be convinced of the validity of the proof and will accept the action suggested in the report.

When argumentation is dominant in the report four steps taken in the argumentative process might be used as a basis for organizing the entire report:

(*1*) Discussion of the problem
(*2*) Explanation of the main issues
(*3*) Submission of the proof
(*4*) Conclusions and recommendations

The discussion of the problem should point to a need for a change or improvement, or should state a proposition or recommendation. The main issues are determined by their importance and use, and often are a breakdown of the proposition into the factors calling for discussion and reasoning. Proof may be factual or reasoned. Factual proof consists of facts, opinions, figures and conclusions. Reasoned proof is the result of the use of logic. Up-to-date, pertinent facts must be given. If opinions are cited they should be those of authorities. Statistics, tables of figures, etc. present concrete evidence. All facts are used to reach conclusions. Reasoned proof consists of inductive and deductive thinking, an examination of causes and effects, comparisons and analogies and treatment of both sides of the question, similarly leading to conclusions.

Accompanying factual and reasoned proof, persuasion attempts to influence action. Here the author needs to indicate an open mind and fairness to appeal to the reader's intellect and emotions. Every consideration is given to winning over the reader. Anticipated objections should be presented and refuted. The justification report is a good example of argumentative report writing, for the entire report marshals its data to convince the reader that he should accept the report's recommendation. An example can be examined in Chapter 18, page 341. Of course the presentation of factual and reasoned proof is common to most reports and expository writing.

PROBLEMS

1. Select a sample business report and evaluate its presentation according to the six qualities essential to effective writing.

2. Develop the thought expressed in each of the following topic sentences. You may use any appropriate method, such as comparison, illustration or use of details.

   a. The form of a business report is a means to an end and not an end in itself.

   b. The content of a business report reveals the nature of the man who prepared it.

   c. Quotations on the stock exchange reflect business conditions.

   d. The NOMA letter form saves time.

   e. The length of a business report is determined by the reader, writer and the message.

   f. The present income tax law should be changed.

3. Define the following:
   a. Fact-finding interview
   b. Depth interview
   c. Decimal system of outlining
   d. Profit
   e. Credit union
   f. Inductive reasoning

4. Describe a process. The following list is suggestive:
   a. How to take notes
   b. How to dictate a letter
   c. How to scan a book or article
   d. How to make (a product you are familiar with)
   e. How to make a sale
   f. How to proofread a report

5. Describe something you have observed. The following list is suggestive:
   a. Noon hour in the cafeteria
   b. A business office

c. An automobile accident
d. An electric typewriter
e. An Addressograph machine
f. A printing press at work

6. Compare and contrast two brands of the same item, such as two typewriters, two cake mixes, two shirts, two accounting machines.

7. Narrate a personal business experience.

8. Select a sample business report (It may be one you have written.) and point out the techniques used to develop its facts and thoughts—structural paragraphs, such features of expository writing as analysis, definition, description, etc.

CHAPTER 11

Using Visual Aids Effectively

VISUAL AIDS ARE ESSENTIAL TO EFFECTIVE COMMUNICATION in business reports. They not only convey exact meanings and specific information which can be readily understood and easily remembered, but also emphasize important facts and figures, improve the physical appearance of the report and add interest to the text material. Visual aids are widely used. Psychologists tell us that about 80% of all we learn comes to us through our eyes, so this vital means of communication needs to be put into effective use.

Visual aids are essential to the analysis of numerical and statistical data and are also helpful in the explanation of business processes and organizational structure. Data too numerous to be interpreted and presented singly can be organized in tables and graphs. Charts and diagrams convey directly and vividly data which otherwise might take many words and paragraphs to explain. The correlation of two variables, for example, or a comparison of two sets of observations may be difficult to explain; but the reader can see a clear picture of the results when put in chart or graph form.

Visual aids include all devices of graphic presentation of information: tables, charts and graphs, and other pictorial illustrations such as photographs, maps and diagrams. Those that are to appear in printed reports may need to be prepared by a draftsman. Often mere sketches, however, will be sufficient for communicating ideas effectively, and many tables and charts can be prepared on a typewriter. It is not necessary to be a professional statistician or a skilled draftsman to use visual aids in reports. It is necessary, however, that the report writer have sufficient knowledge of the different types of visual aids to be able to select and use the best possible ones to convey his data effectively to the reader and to achieve his purpose. The treatment of visual aids in this chapter emphasizes their presentation rather than their construction.

SELECTING VISUAL AIDS

For a visual aid to lift important information out of the main text in a report and emphasize it so that the busy reader will not overlook it, for a visual aid to be useful in analyzing data and in improving the appearance of the report, for it to turn a fact or a figure into interesting information for the reader — it must be carefully selected. The selection of appropriate visual aids depends on:

(*1*) the nature and purpose of the report,
(*2*) the intended reader of the report,
(*3*) the way in which the aid is to be used,
(*4*) the data to be presented in the report.

The nature and the purpose of the report are very important in deciding which visual aids to use and must be considered in relation to the intended reader of the report. Widely distributed reports, like annual reports, and advertising and promotional material intended to boost the company or the product, for instance, should contain charts and tables selected to gain the popular interest and understanding necessary for readership. A report used internally to convince management of the wisdom of taking positive action on a recommendation, on the other hand, must assemble visual aids as proof that the action is necessary.

Consideration must be given to the type of reader — to what he wants in the report and to his ability to comprehend charts and tables. Top management may want logarithmic curves to show rates of change, or curves showing the relationship between two variables, and would have the know-how to understand them. For non-technical readers who would not comprehend ratios, however, the data must be reduced to their simplest terms. For such readers pictorial charts are very suitable. The reader needs to be presented with a chart or table containing information that he can grasp quickly and accurately.

After deciding upon which types of visual aids are necessary to accomplish the purpose of the report and which ones are needed to interest the reader and to aid him in understanding the message, the writer must decide *how* the visual aid is to be used. What special purpose will the visual aid accomplish? What information should it portray? Although visual aids add interest and make the report attractive, their real function is to make the material understandable. They must effectively display facts and figures. The questions, "What significant point do we want the chart to explain?" and "Which chart will best explain this point to this reader for this purpose?" should be answered.

In this connection some consideration should also be given to the nature of the data. Specific types of charts show certain kinds of data to advantage; certain other data are better presented in tabular form. Are the data chronological or geographical in nature? What are their common characteristics? Can the data best be shown pictorially, as a part of the text, or in some other manner to accomplish the purpose of the report? The answers to these questions will reveal the nature of the data and will help determine the type of visual aid to present in the report.

Most visual aids are prepared before the accompanying text material is written, the text later being written around them. The opposite, however, can be done. Prepared before the text, visual aids help the author to understand the material with which he is working. Prepared afterwards, the ones which fit the text and purpose must be selected. In either case the writer gives primary consideration to the reader's requirements and to the conditions set by the report and its purpose.

Kinds of Tables and Their Functions

A table presents data systematically arranged in columns and rows. A series of related facts or a large number of items may be easily seen and followed when displayed in tabular form. Tables are a logical way of analyzing and summarizing numerical and other statistical data. They are invaluable in showing comparisons, trends and quantities of data. They point up significant facts and make it easy for the reader to assimilate and interpret them. According to the function performed, there are three major types of tables: general reference, special purpose and text.

As its name indicates, a *general reference table* presents detailed information for reference purposes. The tabulated results of a questionnaire, for example, are given in Table I, page 156. Here the number and percentage of responses to each question are shown in a columnar arrangement. Points of relationship and comparison of responses can be drawn.

For general reference purposes, tables similar to the example shown might be placed in the appendix of a report, or added as a supplemental exhibit in the case of a short report. The general reference table includes detailed data. It is not selective; accordingly, the reader must draw conclusions from it or have significant details pointed out for him by the writer of the report.

The *special purpose table,* on the other hand, is selective. The reporter may take specific, important points from the general reference table and put them in a special purpose table for emphasis. All of the questions and responses concerning the content of application letters could be taken from Table I and placed in a table emphasizing the content preferred in application letters. In Table II this has been done.

In both Tables I and II, the usual parts of a formal table may be noted. They are identified by number and title caption. Headings designate each column. Items are arranged in a logical sequence on the left, and percentages of each type of response follow to the right of each question listed. There are other details which are generally followed when using a table. In a long column of numbers, the zero preceding a decimal point may be omitted from all entries except the first and the last. Symbols like plus and minus signs, dollar signs and degree signs likewise can be omitted except in the first and last entries. Figures in a column should be aligned by the decimal point. The total column is logically on the right; but when it is going to be referred to frequently it is better on the left. There should be fewer columns than there are items in the left-hand list or stub of the table. For reference, columns may be numbered from left to right on a line below the box head and above the first line of the field (the part of the table that lies to the right of the stub). Items in the stub may also be numbered. Arabic numbers are used. All units in a table should be described in terms of definitely recognized standards, such as feet, dollars or percentages. Where applicable, variable quantities should be arranged in a scale, increasing from left to right and from top to bottom.

Not all general reference and special purpose tables present numerical data. Verbal data may also be arranged in columns. Verbal tables are especially useful in organizing and summarizing. The Research Department of the CBS Radio Network presented all of its data in tabular form in its report, *CBS Radio Clients & Programs,* July, 1953. The page of their report shown in Table III exemplifies the use of a table for presenting verbal information.

The *text table,* or *spot table,* which displays a short single group of facts or figures, is handled like a paragraph inset. Since it is an informal tabulation no number or title is given to the table. Emphasis is on the facts or figures it displays. The break in the paragraph focuses attention on it. Sometimes two or three significant figures are taken from a longer table and emphasized. The following table, for instance, was derived from the special purpose table on page 158.

Employers emphatically want the applicant to state in his letter his reasons for leaving a previous position, and to relate his experience and education to the work of the company. Responses to the questions pertaining to contents were:

	Always	*Frequently*
Reasons	81.58%	14.92%
Education	75.44%	15.79%
Experience	74.56%	14.92%

In this table the white space surrounding the figures displayed also serves to spotlight them.

Setting up tables for presentation of data to the reader is a challenge to the ingenuity of the report writer. Although there are a number of general principles and standards at his command, each set of data presents a different task, and not all tables are set up according to one standard form. Tables must be adapted to the material and purpose at hand. Table IV, taken from the 1950 Annual Report of the Link-Belt Company, is an interesting and effective arrangement of a summary of their year's operations.

TABLE I

EMPLOYERS' PREFERENCES IN APPLICATION LETTERS

Question	Type of Response								
	Total Replies	Always No.	Always %	Frequently No.	Frequently %	Seldom No.	Seldom %	Never No.	Never %
1. Do you want applicants to submit letters of application?	113	50	44.25	35	30.97	19	16.81	9	7.97
2. Do you give consideration to unsolicited letters of application?	116	52	44.83	32	27.59	31	26.72	1	.86
3. Do you give consideration to accompanying letters of recommendation?	116	52	44.83	31	26.72	30	25.86	3	2.59
4. Do you require a photograph of the applicant?	115	22	19.13	18	15.65	34	29.57	41	35.65
5. Do you want the applicant to include a stamped, return envelope for your reply?	116	7	6.03	3	2.59	10	8.62	96	82.76
6. Do you consider the follow-up letter when the first application letter has failed to impress you?	113	7	6.20	34	30.09	51	45.13	21	18.58
7. Do you like a conventional, straightforward approach better than the clever, out-of-the-ordinary application letter?	113	102	90.27	8	7.08	3	2.65	0	0
8. Do you want the applicant to address his letter to a specific person within your company?	108	28	25.93	17	15.74	37	34.26	26	24.07
9. Do you require the applicant to submit a data sheet?	109	34	31.19	23	21.10	24	22.02	28	25.69
10. Do you like the applicant to submit a one-page letter with a data sheet?	108	38	35.19	34	31.48	15	13.89	21	19.44

11. Do you like the applicant to submit a two- or three-page letter without a data sheet?	107	3	2.80	5	4.67	23	21.50	76	71.03
12. Do you like an elaborate presentation of qualifications which might be three to ten pages in length?	114	1	.88	5	4.38	14	12.28	94	82.46
13. Do you give attention to the letter which merely requests an application blank?	117	48	41.02	23	19.66	23	19.66	23	19.66
14. Do you want an applicant to apply for a specific position with your company rather than for just a job?	114	60	52.63	39	34.21	9	7.90	6	5.26
15. Do you like the applicant to state in his letter his reasons for leaving a previous position?	114	93	81.58	17	14.92	2	1.75	2	1.75
16. Do you desire that the applicant relate his experience to the work of your company?	114	85	74.56	17	14.92	7	6.14	5	4.38
17. Do you desire that the applicant relate his education to the work of your company?	114	86	75.44	18	15.79	7	6.14	3	2.63
18. Do you want an applicant to include in his letter his average grades in school?	114	29	25.44	28	24.56	34	29.82	23	20.18
19. Do you want an applicant to include information on extracurricular activities?	113	50	44.25	34	30.09	21	18.58	8	7.08
20. Do you want an applicant to include information on his participation in community activities?	113	44	38.94	33	29.20	25	22.12	11	9.74
21. Do you want the applicant to include information on his family's background?	112	27	24.11	32	28.57	35	31.25	18	16.07
22. Are you favorably impressed if the applicant shows a knowledge of your company?	112	59	52.68	33	29.46	18	16.07	2	1.79
23. Do you want the applicant to state in his letter an expected salary?	113	38	33.63	38	33.63	19	16.81	18	15.93
24. Do you like the application letter to include a request for an interview?	110	65	59.09	30	27.27	11	10.00	4	3.64
25. Do you consider an application letter that contains mechanical errors?	113	18	15.93	37	32.74	52	46.02	6	5.31

TABLE II

EMPLOYERS' CONTENT PREFERENCES IN APPLICATION LETTERS

Question	Percentages			
	Always	Frequently	Seldom	Never
1. Do you like the applicant to state in his letter his reasons for leaving a previous position?	81.58	14.92	1.75	1.75
2. Do you desire that the applicant relate his experience to the work of your company?	74.56	14.92	6.14	4.38
3. Do you desire that the applicant relate his education to the work of your company?	75.44	15.79	6.14	2.63
4. Do you want an applicant to include in his letter his average grades in school?	25.44	24.56	29.82	20.18
5. Do you want an applicant to include information on extracurricular activities?	44.25	30.09	18.58	7.08
6. Do you want an applicant to include information on his participation in community activities?	38.94	29.20	22.12	9.74
7. Do you want the applicant to include information on his family's background?	24.11	28.57	31.25	16.07
8. Are you favorably impressed if the applicant shows a knowledge of your company?	52.68	29.46	16.07	1.79
9. Do you want the applicant to state in his letter an expected salary?	33.63	33.63	16.81	15.93
10. Do you like the application letter to include a request for an interview?	59.09	27.27	10.00	3.64
11. Do you want an applicant to apply for a specific position with your company rather than for just a job?	52.63	34.21	7.90	5.26

TABLE III

ALPHABETICALLY BY *CLIENTS* SPONSORED CBS RADIO PROGRAMS: JULY, 1953

Weeks on CBS Radio	Client and Product	Program	Time and Stations	Agency
6	AMANA REFRIGERATION, INC. Amana Food Freezers	People Are Funny	Tuesday 8:00–8:30 pm Rebroadcast 10:00–10:30 pm 206 CBS Radio Stations	Maury, Lee & Marshall
1064	AMERICAN HOME PRODUCTS CORP. WHITEHALL PHARMACAL DIVISION Anacin, Kolynos, Chlorophyll, Sperti, Biodyne	Our Gal Sunday	Mon. thru Fri. 12:45–1:00 pm 175 CBS Radio Stations	John F. Murray Advertising Agency, Inc.
	WHITEHALL PHARMACAL DIVISION Bisodol, Heet, Sperti, Biodyne	Romance of Helen Trent	Mon. thru Fri. 12:30–12:45 pm 178 CBS Radio Stations	
	AMERICAN HOME FOODS DIVISION Chef Boy-Ar-Dee Quality Foods	Our Gal Sunday	Mon. thru Fri. 12:45–1:00 pm 175 CBS Radio Stations	
	BOYLE-MIDWAY DIVISION Aero Wax, Black Flag	Romance of Helen Trent	Mon. thru Fri. 12:30–12:45 pm 178 CBS Radio Stations	
500	AMERICAN OIL CO. Amoco Gasoline, Lubricants, Tires, Tubes, Batteries	Edward R. Murrow and the News	Mon. thru Fri. 7:45–8:00 pm 81 CBS Radio Stations	Joseph Katz Co.

TABLE IV

1950 OPERATIONS AT A GLANCE

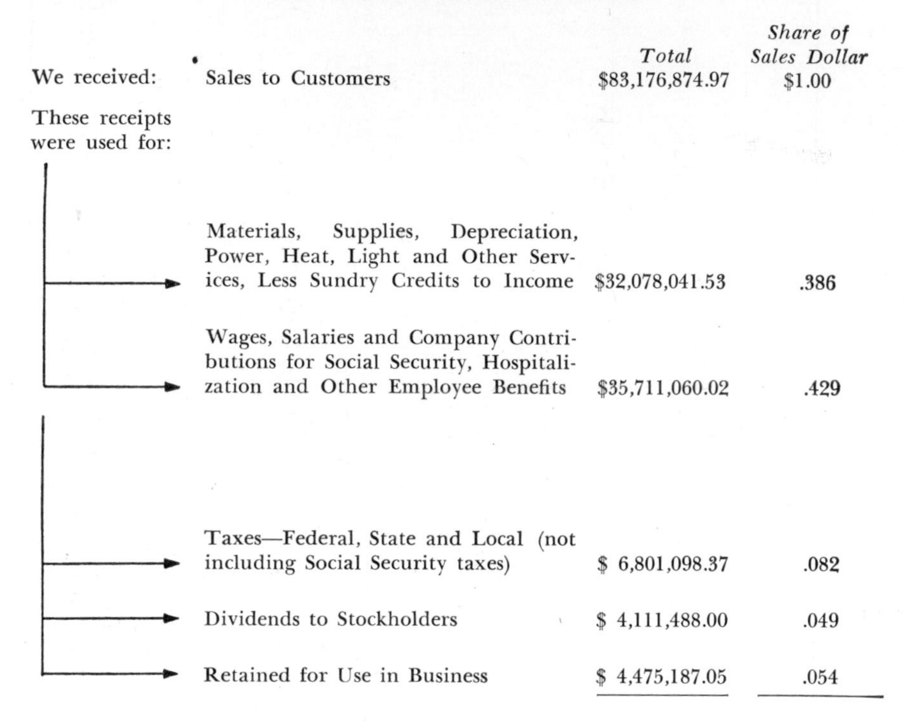

		Total	*Share of Sales Dollar*
We received:	Sales to Customers	$83,176,874.97	$1.00
These receipts were used for:			
	Materials, Supplies, Depreciation, Power, Heat, Light and Other Services, Less Sundry Credits to Income	$32,078,041.53	.386
	Wages, Salaries and Company Contributions for Social Security, Hospitalization and Other Employee Benefits	$35,711,060.02	.429
	Taxes—Federal, State and Local (not including Social Security taxes)	$ 6,801,098.37	.082
	Dividends to Stockholders	$ 4,111,488.00	.049
	Retained for Use in Business	$ 4,475,187.05	.054

Kinds of Charts and Their Functions

A chart is the presentation of data in some visualized form other than tabular. The data are drawn, graphed or mapped to show relationships at a glance. Charts simplify and clarify facts contained in a report. They reinforce the message, emphasize important points and impress and interest the reader.

The types of charts used in a report depend on the nature of the data and what they are to depict. A chart contains less detail than a table and usually shows comparisons of only two or three points. Instead of following a tabular arrangement of data as in tables, charts use bars, columns, lines, curves, blocks and other pictorial devices for visualization. Properly designed, charts tell a story by themselves. Although they should have explanatory notes in accompanying paragraphs to relate their points to the rest of the discussion in the text, they often attract attention and are looked at before the report is read. After the report has been read, they are valuable for a rapid review of important points. When used in conjunction with tables, charts pick up the significant figures for emphasis, and the accompanying tables present the complete numerical data for evidence or reference. The best results of charts are achieved when careful attention is given their selection, construction and use. Charts are constructed according to prescribed standards and used to present information that can be grasped quickly and easily.

Bar charts. Probably the most popular and decorative charts are bar charts. Because they catch the reader's eye and are easily understood, they are used a great deal in advertising and promotional reports — reports written for wide distribution or external use like the company's annual report. Bars are effective for comparing different items of a specified date, comparing items in two or three respects, illustrating simple, complete facts and showing relative importance of items. The Girard Trust Company, for example,

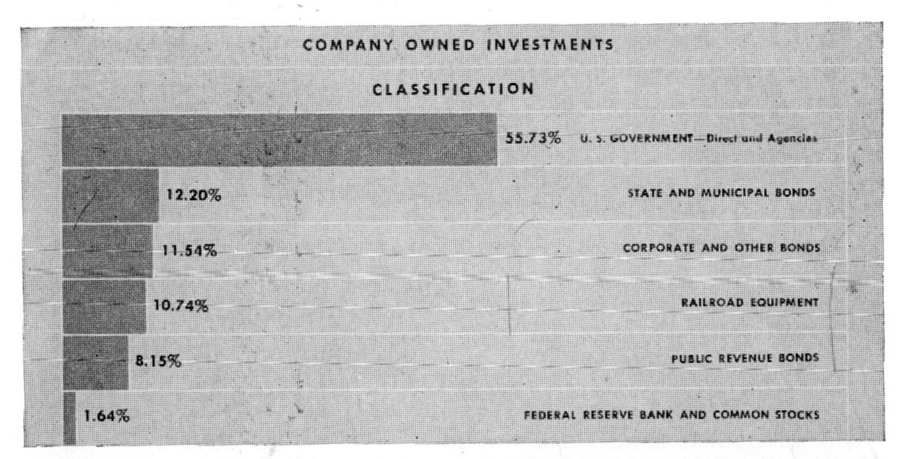

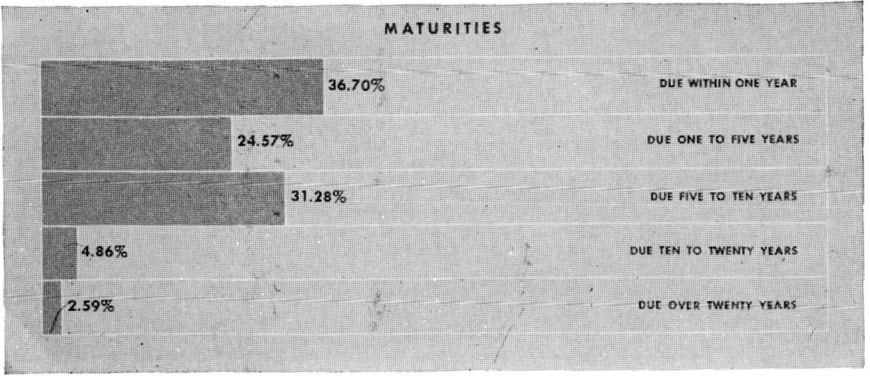

Courtesy Girard Trust Corn Exchange Bank

Simple bar chart.

VARIETY OF WAYS FOR CREATING DIFFERENT EFFECTS IN BAR CHARTS

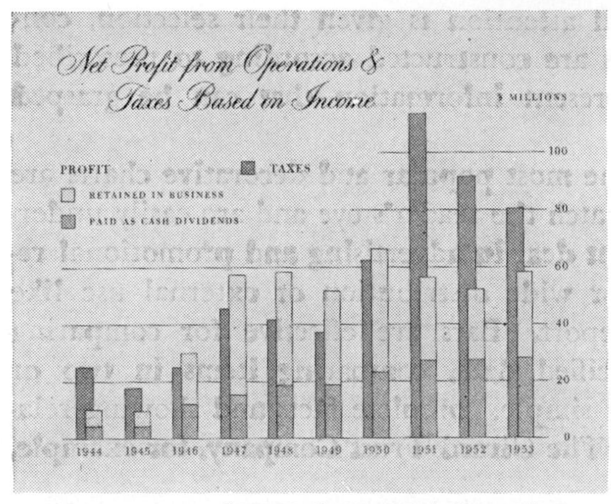

Courtesy International Paper Company

Columns grouped for each time period, and divided to show more than one item, compare two or three items within the same time period.

Working Capital

$ MILLIONS

140 120 100 80 60 40 20 0

'44 '45 '46 '47 '48 '49 '50 '51 '52 '53

December 31,

Courtesy Intern'l Paper Company

Simple vertical bars in chronological order show a trend.

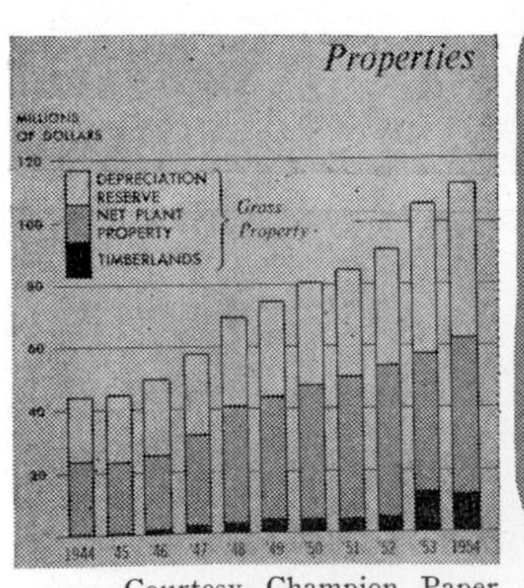

Courtesy Champion Paper and Fibre Company

Shading or crosshatching distinguishes segments of compound bars, giving comparisons for each time period.

TOTAL LIFE INSURANCE IN FORCE

A Ten-Year Growth from 1943 to 1953

1943 1944 1945 1946 1947 1948 1949 1950 1951 1952 1953

Courtesy State Mutual Life Assurance Company

Connected columns accent a trend over a long time period.

used bars arranged in descending order to compare the kinds of investments made and the time periods required for the investments to mature.

Bars may be horizontal or vertical. The *horizontal bar chart* compares several items from the same period or under the same conditions. It measures magnitude horizontally from a vertical zero line at the left. Each bar represents a separate item to be compared for the same condition or time interval that applies to the other items. The *vertical bar chart,* sometimes called the *column chart,* is effective in showing values of a given item over a period of years. The height of the vertical bar or column indicates the percentage or numerical value of the quality measured. The period of time is indicated on the base or horizontal line. Bar charts are used to create a dramatic presentation for public readership. Different arrangements of bars make for a variety of charts as shown on page 162.

A single bar representing 100% shows relationships of its parts to the whole and is called the *100% bar chart.* It may be horizontal, or vertical as illustrated on page 164.

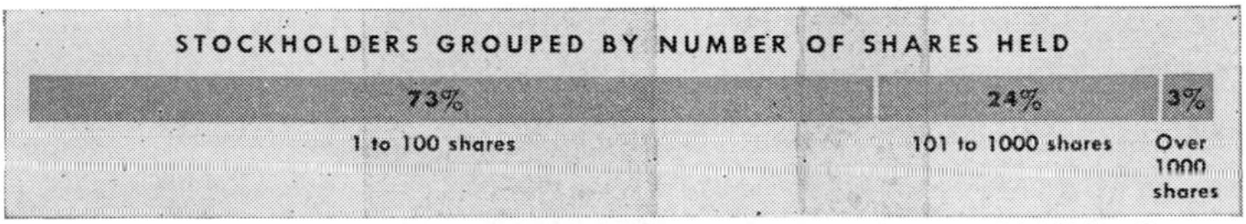

STOCKHOLDERS GROUPED BY NUMBER OF SHARES HELD

73%	24%	3%
1 to 100 shares	101 to 1000 shares	Over 1000 shares

Courtesy Link-Belt Company

Horizontal bar chart.

To conserve space and add interest, symbols instead of captions may be used to identify the various bars on a chart. The symbol must be associated with the subject so that each bar may be readily identified. The use of a row of pictorial symbols instead of bars also creates interest and attracts attention. This is the *pictogram* and is used effectively for popular presentation of comparisons for publicity, advertising and propaganda purposes. Stacks of coins, a dollar bill, geometric figures and pictures of people, equipment or machinery are all favorite pictorial symbols and add variety and interest to a chart. A third dimensional effect can also be obtained as demonstrated on page 165.

Line and Curve Charts. By plotting items of data and connecting the points by a line or curve, a *line* or *curve chart* is formed. It is

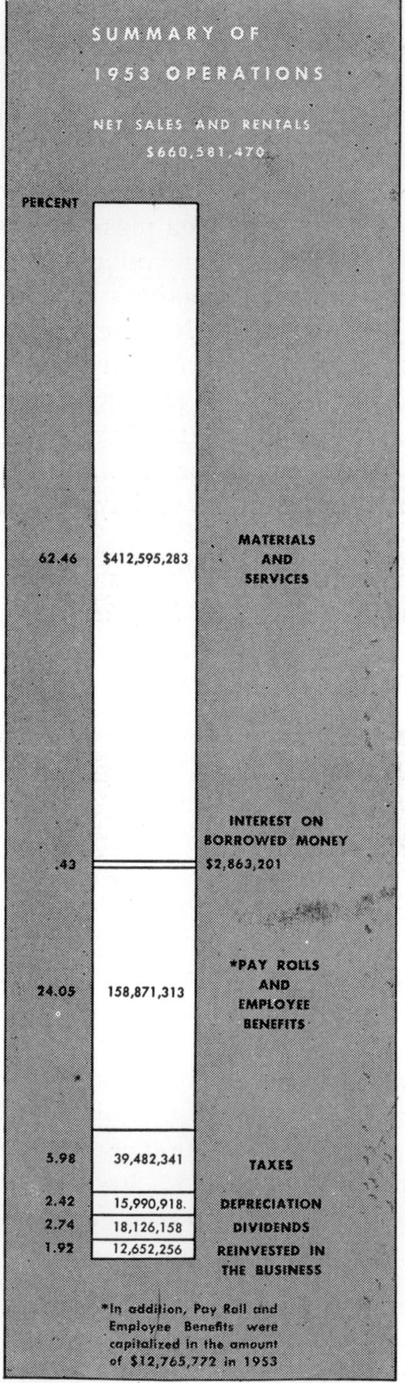

Courtesy American Can Company

Vertical bar chart.

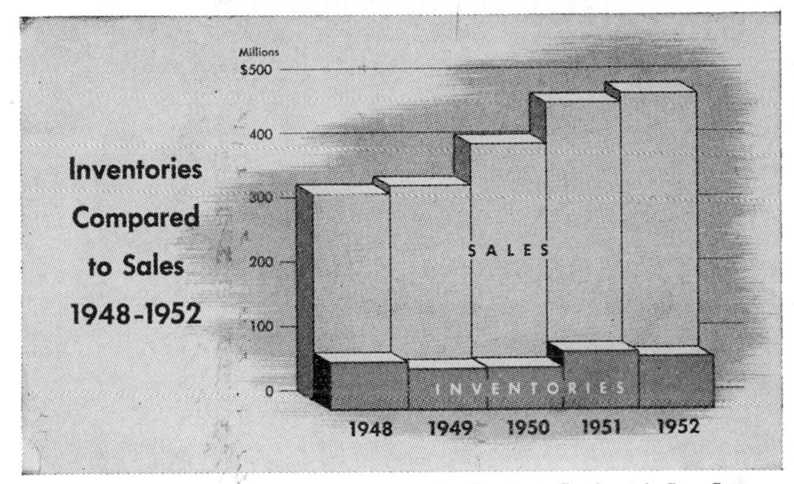

Courtesy Continental Can Company

Third dimensional bar chart.

often called a *graph,* and the plotting is most easily done on graph paper. Especially is it useful for depicting continuous processes over a time period. Generally more detail can be plotted by lines and curves than can be shown in bar charts. When the emphasis is on movement rather than amount, curves depict the data and its trend. The comparison of several series of items, an amount of change, a rate of change, fluctuations, trends, frequency distributions, time series and ratios can all be shown by graphs. The chart on page 166, shows various uses of line and curve charts.

When it is desirable to show the rate at which something is changing rather than the amount it has changed, a *ratio chart* is used. Either logarithms of the values are plotted on an arithmetic scale, or the actual values are plotted on a logarithmic scale, which is the usual procedure because logarithmic paper can be used. The ratio chart should be used only when the reader is likely to be familiar with it. It is therefore rarely used except for internal reports when it is requested. Because it deals with relative movements it is helpful in analyzing the nature of changes taking place, in making sound management decisions and in predicting future growth.

Pie Charts. A *pie chart* presents data in the form of a circle. The names *sector* and *circle chart* also apply. The pie is divided into segments, which make comparisons with each other and the whole. The sections are labeled and percentages given; or guide lines are

LINES AND CURVES CREATE IMPRESSIONS THAT CAN BE QUICKLY GRASPED

INVESTMENTS

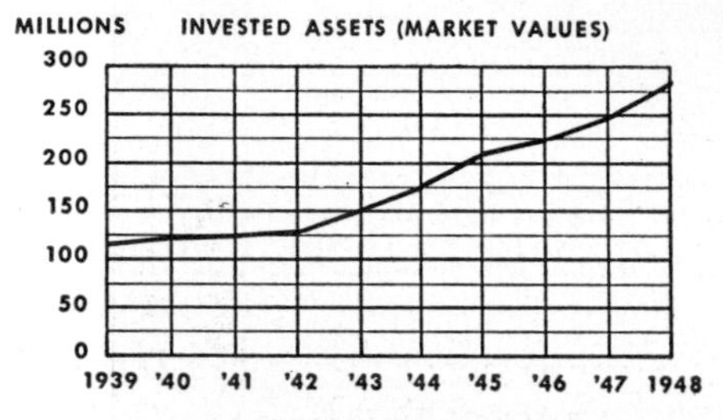

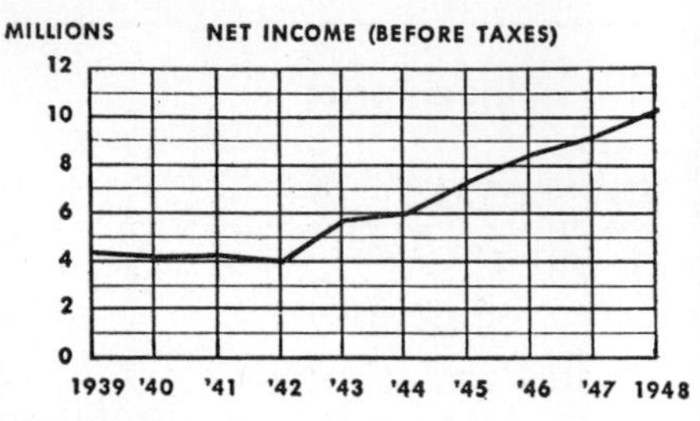

Charts reflect growth of investments, including real estate, and income thereon.

Courtesy Insurance Company of North America

Simple line graph shows a limited set of facts with emphasis on a continuous trend.

Courtesy General Motors Corporation

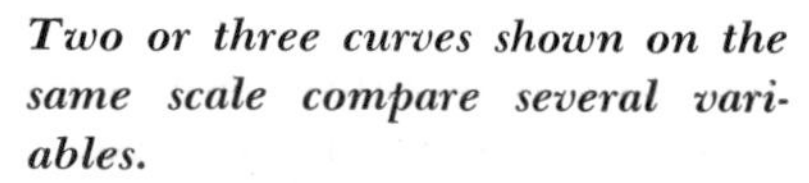

Two or three curves shown on the same scale compare several variables.

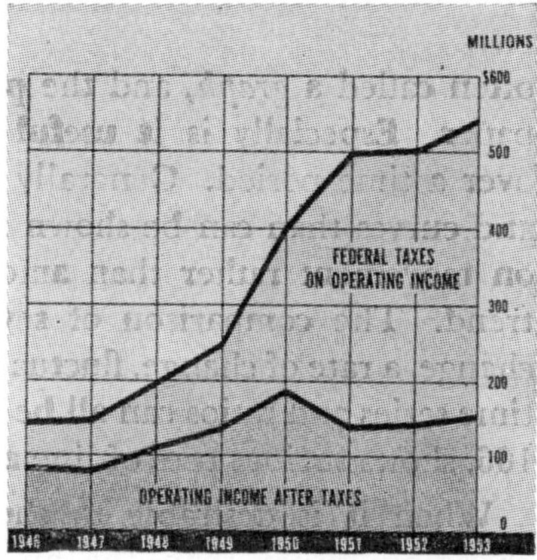

Courtesy E. I. du Pont de Nemours & Co.

Surface chart affords a dimensional or pictorial effect and attracts attention by emphasizing a particular portion of a trend.

used with the information placed outside each sector. Shading or coloring pieces of the pie makes it easier to read. By alternating light and dark, two colors can do the work of four.

When many segments are called for, pie charts should be avoided or used sparingly. If there are not sharp differences the pie can be deceptive to the eye. It does not permit true comparison. Because it is so simple and clear, however, it is a good chart to use when the readers of the report are not acquainted with principles of graphing. It appears frequently in reports presenting information to the public. A favorite use of the pie chart in annual reports is to show the breakdown of the income dollar as demonstrated below. Often pictures of actual coins or other circular objects are used.

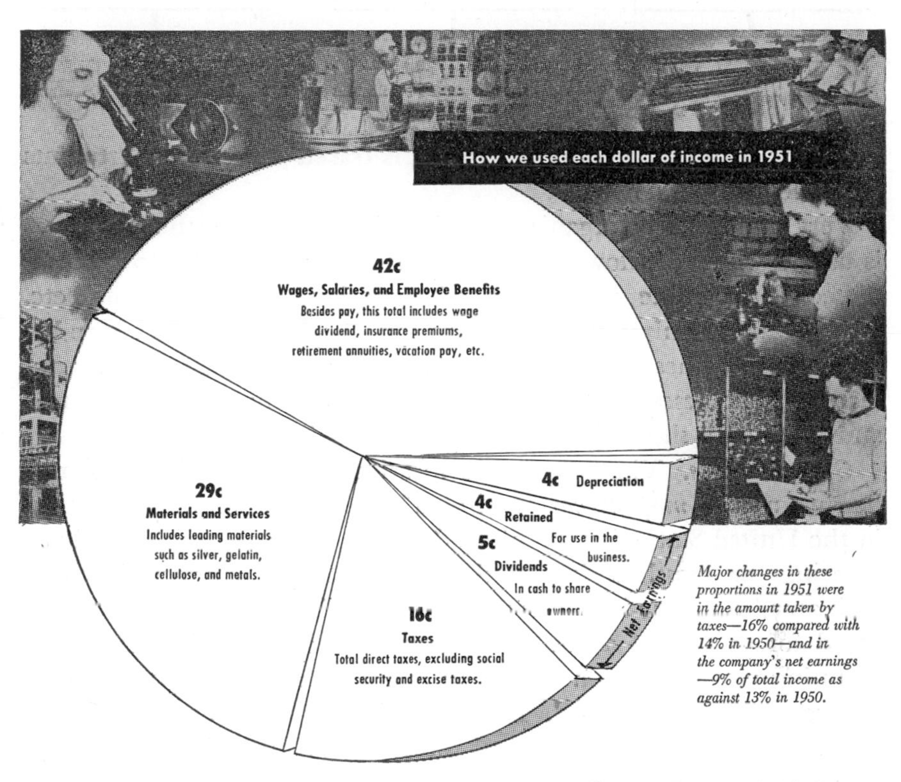
How we used each dollar of income in 1951
42¢
Wages, Salaries, and Employee Benefits
Besides pay, this total includes wage dividend, insurance premiums, retirement annuities, vacation pay, etc.
29¢
Materials and Services
Includes leading materials such as silver, gelatin, cellulose, and metals.
16¢
Taxes
Total direct taxes, excluding social security and excise taxes.
4¢ Depreciation
4¢
Retained
For use in the business.
5¢
Dividends
In cash to share
Net Earnings
Major changes in these proportions in 1951 were in the amount taken by taxes—16% compared with 14% in 1950—and in the company's net earnings —9% of total income as against 13% in 1950.

Courtesy Eastman Kodak Company

Pie chart.

Organization and Flow Charts. Two special charts, not based on statistical information, which are used for reader clarity, interest and emphasis are organization and flow charts. An *organization* chart shows the flow of authority, responsibility and information among positions in a business firm. Starting at the top and branching downward, divisions are indicated by a variety of shapes and shadings with the flow shown by connecting lines. Boxes or rectangles are commonly used and properly labeled:

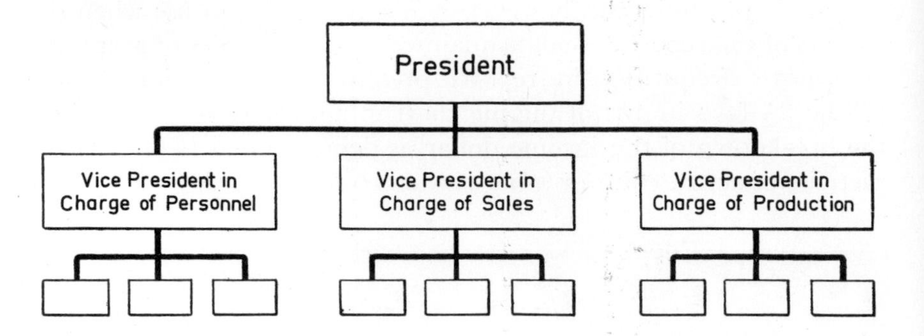

Thus the entire range of organization is traced through departments to the lowest worker.

Very similar to the organization chart in appearance, the *flow chart* is used to show the flow of a product from its beginning to its completed form. The movement of materials, printed forms, etc. through an organizational structure can also be shown as a step-by-step process. These charts are commonly used in production, manufacturing processes and sales. The flow of sulphur into other forms and products is shown in the chart on page 169.

Other Charts. The geographic location of commercial data may be shown on a *map* or *cartogram.* The present economic situation in the United States may be plotted by areas or states with shadings, colorings or crosshatching used to indicate the characteristics of each area. A key or legend is necessary for clear reading. States that voted for or against a law may be marked off. Details helpful in planning moves from one point to another may be shown. Guides and routes may be marked. Dots and pin points are used to present exact geographic distribution of data and to show density or concentration. Pictures and symbols may be added for human interest. The areas providing source materials for a manufacturing firm, the distribution of the stockholders and the distributors of a product are frequently shown by maps in annual reports of companies.

Diagrams make clear the relationship of parts and are very useful in planning. In the 1949 *Annual Report* of the Girard Trust Company a floor plan was diagrammed showing the proposed location of new elevators and approaches. Plans were discussed in the text material. In 1951 they were completed and the report contained photographs of the new elevators and other locations on the first floor. Sometimes blueprints and other scaled drawings are used in a report.

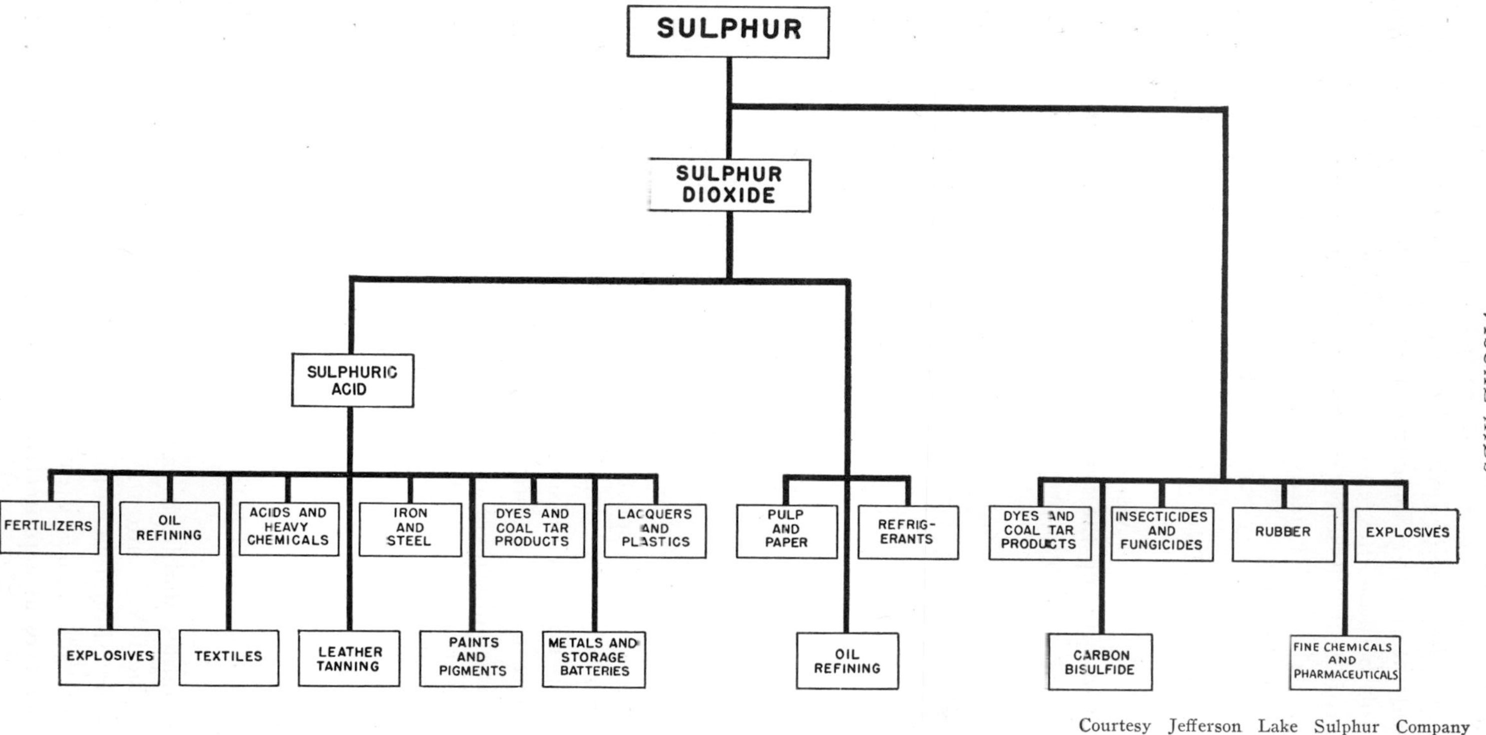

Courtesy Jefferson Lake Sulphur Company

Flow chart.

Photographs provide exact knowledge of appearance and are vivid and interesting. Sometimes they are more confusing than enlightening because they cover outward appearance only. Yet they are realistic and may serve as concrete evidence or proof. They are used when the reader needs to visualize something that the camera can accurately catch.

PRESENTING VISUAL AIDS IN A REPORT

Proper selection of visual aids to use in a report is merely the first step in insuring the report writer of their effective use. They must be appropriately presented in the report and related to the problem at hand.

Placement

Tables may be placed either in the text material or in the appendix. Placed in the body of the report they facilitate the reader's understanding of their analysis. Placed in the appendix they are available for reference when needed. The decision as to where to put a table should rest on its purpose and use. If it is not essential to the text and adds nothing to it, then it should be in the appendix. Often a long table is placed in the appendix for reference, and information is taken from it and arranged in shorter tables placed in appropriate spots throughout the text. An example of this would be a large table showing the results of a questionnaire survey in the appendix, with smaller tables dealing with responses to two or three related questions taken from it and placed in the text where their significances are discussed.

In the text a table should be as close as possible to the discussion point with which it is used. When typing or printing do not allow the table to be accommodated in the available space left on a page, the table should be omitted and the text that follows continued until the page is filled. The table can then be placed on the next page. It is advisable, of course, to continue the text on the next page until the end of a paragraph unless the table will require a full page.

Large tables should be avoided. But when they are necessary they may be folded into the report so as to fit the regular page size used. They should be folded from the bottom up and from the outside in. This makes it easy for the reader to open and read them and also serves as a protective measure for the outer edges. Long tables may be continued from page to page. Each page should have the same table number, title or caption, and the word *continued,* in parentheses, should appear at the top of each page after the first one. All column heads should be set up the same as on page 1 of the table. Wide tables may be placed sideways across the page (broadside), with the caption at the left side of the page, which becomes the top of the table. Two facing pages may be used for still wider tables.

Charts are usually placed in the text of the report and rarely in the appendix, because their main function is to depict data in a way that will interest the reader and save him time. Only occasionally are they used as exhibits in the appendix for reference purposes since they are nearly always a necessary part of the text. Since they are so closely related to the discussion, they should be placed at appropriate spots in it.

A chart is rarely larger than a full page; but when it is, it can be folded in so that it will not extend beyond the page size. Also it is rarely smaller than one-fourth of a page. This size enables it to fit into the material to which it is related. Small charts drawn on graph paper may be cut and mounted on unlined bond paper and thus fitted in appropriately to the typewritten material. (Rubber cement is the best adhesive to use.) For full-page graphs, graph paper the same size as the report page may be used.

Numbering

Tables are numbered consecutively throughout the report. The exception to this would be a book-length report divided into chapters, in which case the tables could be numbered consecutively for each chapter. Either Roman or Arabic numerals may be used. It is important to use a separate numbering system for tables and other types of visual aids. For example, if the tables are numbered I, II, etc., then 1, 2, etc. can be used for charts. More often, however, the distinction is made by using letters for numbering charts. Sometimes the terms *figure* or *illustration* are used instead of *chart.* Consistency should be followed throughout the report in the use of the term. The number designation of the chart is commonly placed on the same line as the title; and, unlike the number and title of a table, it usually appears either *below the chart* or as a part of the body of the chart, spaced, for balance and appearance, in one of its corners. The number of the table is generally centered above the title, at the top of the table.

Captions

By typing the title caption of tables in capital letters and the subtitle in lower-case letters, a distinction is made between them. All captions should indicate what, where and when. They should be specific and concise. The title caption and subtitle apply to the table as a whole and should be descriptive, yet exact. Each column heading, of course, applies only to the material in that particular column by naming the item and the unit in which it is expressed.

Each chart has a title, which is usually typed in lower-case letters and placed with the number below and within the margin limits set for the chart. It can be placed on the chart where it is used similarly to the headline caption in an advertisement. The idea is to attract attention to the chart as well as to let the reader know what the chart contains. Captions are also used to designate units, scales, curves, bars, etc. when appropriate. Only standard abbreviations should be used in captions and then only when space demands their use. Lettering not made on the typewriter should be in India ink. As little vertical lettering as possible should be used. A chart should read from left to right and from bottom up. The title caption sometimes includes the source of data, which may be briefly explained in a footnote placed immediately beneath the title caption.

Footnotes provide supplemental information to a table or chart by explaining or amplifying any one of the entries or headings and giving the source of the data. They are placed at the bottom of the table or chart and are designated by an asterisk or other symbol, which is also used with the item it explains or calls attention to. Footnotes are single spaced and may take up as much but not more line length than the width of the visual aid.

Spacing

Tables may be typed in either single or double spacing; whichever is used should be consistently followed. A crowded effect can be avoided by distributing the amount of white space within the body of the table and in setting up the columns. Triple spacing before and after the table will also help to give it an uncrowded appearance. Whenever space permits there should be a blank line or space between the table number and title and between the title and subtitle or headnote. Also a space should be used between the headnote and top rule of the table, above and below the first and last lines of the column heads, above the sub-headings within the body of the table, above and below each horizontal rule, between the bottom rule of the table and the first line of the footnote and between the footnotes if there are several.

Tables of only two columns should be set up without rules. Tables of more than two columns should be ruled both vertically and horizontally. A double rule is often used at the top and bottom of the table. A two- or three-column table should be indented from each side margin of the page. A table of more than three columns should take up the entire line length, from margin to margin, and is usually boxed in at the sides.

Plenty of white space should surround charts to set them off from the text material and to present an uncrowded effect. It is well to use wider margins for the charts than are used for the text. Of course, several spaces should be left before and after the chart. Usually charts are boxed in by a single-line border with the title caption and number placed below the bottom border, but not extending beyond the side margins of the chart.

WRITING THE DISCUSSION TO ACCOMPANY THE VISUAL AID

Visual aids, which are not ends in themselves but simply means of clarifying data in the report, require explanation and interpretation. Implications of statistics must be discussed; generalizations based on figures need to be given.

Tables, charts and other types of aids should be introduced in the report. The introductory statement should precede the aid, calling attention to it or to some significant point it contains, as:

> The results of the test in Table II . . .
>
> *or*
>
> The data in Table II indicate that . . .
>
> *or*
>
> A glance at Table II reveals . . .
>
> *or*
>
> Fifty percent of the readers, as indicated in Table II, . . .

Where possible, the visual aid should follow its introduction. In any case, the table or chart should be as near as possible to the material with which it is used.

A complete explanation or analysis of each table should be given.

It may include a description of the data and a discussion of the extent to which the figures establish facts and to which they relate to other data, with full explanations of technical terms and details. Attention should be called to maximum and minimum data, to averages, trends and tendencies. The extremes need to be pointed out, exceptions noted and conditions explained. The discussion is organized by considering, in sequence, total figures, significant figures making up the total and conclusions drawn.

Most of these points relevant to the analysis of a table also apply to analyzing charts. An important point to remember, however, is that a chart does not require the detailed interpretation a table does because it presents less detail and is constructed to convey its complete message in itself. But it should be related to the points mentioned in the text and to other charts and material, and this relationship should be discussed as a part of the text material in the report.

Neither charts nor tables are inserted haphazardly into the body of a report. They are put there for a purpose. And to achieve that purpose fully they must add something to the discussion, thus becoming an integral part of the report.

PROBLEMS

1. Take the data presented in Table I and compose several special purpose tables and charts for use in a report to the director of your collge placement bureau. Assume that your report writing class made the investigation.

2. Write the interpretative analysis to accompany the tables and charts you prepared in Problem 1. You may do this in the form of a short report.

3. The following table shows the distribution by media of advertising expenditures in the United States in 1952:

Expenditures for Advertising in the United States, Classified by Media, 1952

Media	*Expenditure (Millions of Dollars)*	*Percentage of Total*
Newspapers	525	32.8
Direct mail	300	18.7
Radio	170	10.6
Magazines	150	9.4
Outdoor	50	3.1
Business papers	50	3.1
Farm papers	17	1.1
Television	300	18.7
Miscellaneous	40	2.5
	1,602	100.0

Assume you work for an advertising agency. Then:

a. Show this information by means of a chart or graphic illustration.

b. Write an interpretative analysis of your illustration. Keep in mind how these figures may be used in helping your clients.

4. Here are several facts concerning the readership of *Life*: 62,600,000 people read at least one of 13 issues; 18,000,000 people read 4 to 7 of 13 issues; 14,800,000 read 8 to 13 out of 13 issues; 29,800,000 people read 1 to 3 out of 13 issues. There are 117,850,000 people (10 years old or older) in the United States. Assume that you are writing a letter report to the firms that advertise in *Life* and that you wish to impress them with *Life*'s value as an advertising medium.

a. Present the above figures in the form of a table or chart (which could be part of the letter report).

b. Write a one-paragraph interpretative analysis of your illustration.

5. The following represents the distribution of the sales dollar in your company:

Materials, supplies and other expenses	47.1¢
Retained in business	1.8¢
Taxes	7.4¢
Wages, salaries and employee benefits	39.8¢
Dividends	3.9¢
TOTAL	$1.00.0

Show the distribution in chart form and write the accompanying text, both to be a part of your annual report.

CHAPTER 12

Measuring Readability

FREQUENTLY USED READABILITY FORMULAS
Flesch's Formulas
The Dale-Chall Formula
Farr, Jenkins and Paterson Formula
Gunning's Fog Index
INFLUENCE OF READABILITY FORMULAS ON STYLE

EVER SINCE THE PUBLICATION OF RUDOLPH FLESCH'S FIRST readability formula in 1943 and of his formula in 1948 for measuring reading ease and human interest in writing, persons having the responsibility of writing various types of business communications have given increased emphasis to making their material readable. A large number of studies similar to Paterson and Walker's[1] investigation of house organs and to Davis and Hopkins'[2] study of employee handbooks have indicated that far too little attention has been given to writing on the level of the reader. Much of the written communication between management and employees and between companies and the general public goes unread because the appropriate readability level has not been maintained.

Readability is that quality of writing that results in clearness and interest for the reader. The level of readability is expressed in terms of the general educational level of the reader. For example, a report from management to a group of unskilled employees, who have probably not attained an average educational level beyond the eighth grade, should be written in terms that could be understood at the eighth grade level of education. Readability

---

1 Donald Paterson and Bradley J. Walker, "Readability and Human Interest of House Organs," *Personnel,* Vol. 25 (May 1949), pp. 438–441.

2 K. Davis and J. O. Hopkins, "Readability of Employee Handbooks," *Personnel Psychology,* Vol. 3 (Autumn, 1950), pp. 317–326.

formulas have been developed for rating material by measurement of its difficulty. Results determine whether or not the measured material will reach its intended reader. If testing indicates that he will be reached, then the writer, in revising, need not be further concerned with readability. If the writing is on too high or too low a level, however, the writer should be concerned with lowering or raising the level when he revises. It should be remembered though that the formula merely indicates the degree of difficulty and leaves correction to the writer. After the report has been revised it is good practice to apply a readability test again.

Because it measures readability in a general way for the general reader, a readability formula is best applied to reports and written communications aimed at a wide audience. Reports from management to employees and from the company to the public, such as policy statements, bulletins, employee handbooks, company magazines and annual reports, fall into this category. In general, readers will prefer an easier version to a more difficult one and will find it more pleasant to read. If well handled, material that is easy will save time for the superior reader.

For reports written by and for readers on the same educational level, there is usually no readability problem. Most of these reports are either of the informational or problem-solving variety; the reader is interested in the information he receives or the solution recommended, and his educational level is sufficiently high for comprehension. For these reasons the report will be read. On the other hand, for a report widely distributed, readership as well as comprehension may be greatly increased by using one of the readability formulas.

FREQUENTLY USED READABILITY FORMULAS

No one formula is definitely superior to another. The newer ones, however, are just as accurate as the older ones and in general are easier to apply. It is important that the report writer be familiar with several of them and know how to use them. Although it is impossible to present enough information about each formula for applying it, four have been selected for discussion here on the basis of their frequent use.

Flesch's Formulas

Rudolf Flesch is more responsible than any other one person for popularizing the readability formula. His formula for measuring reading ease is by far the most widely used, and formulas developed since have made use of it. The first Flesch formula developed in 1943 measured readability by the average sentence length expressed in words, the number of affixes and the number of personal references.[3] It proved to be time-consuming and hard to apply, so he revised it in 1948. The 1948 formula, which measures reading ease by the average sentence length and average word length in syllables and measures human interest by the number of personal words and personal sentences, has become the most widely used of all the readability formulas. Counting syllables instead of affixes makes testing both easier and quicker.

Attempting to get a measurement of abstraction in writing, Flesch in 1950 developed another formula.[4] It is based on the premise that abstract style contains relatively more descriptive adjectives, indefinite pronouns and subordinating conjunctions. Concrete style contains relatively more proper nouns, limiting adjectives, finite verbs, personal pronouns and coordinating conjunctions. Accordingly he determines the level of abstraction by computing the ratio of certain parts of speech. The formula includes a count of 16 categories of definite words and the average word length expressed in syllables. Because it is so new and is difficult to apply, it has not been widely used.

Flesch's latest formula, published in 1954, uses two criteria for measuring readability — specificness and communicative energy.[5] Specificness corresponds to his earlier criterion of human interest. Specific words, including names and places, are counted. Communicative energy bears a close relationship to his earlier concept of sentence length; it includes counting all punctuation marks except commas. There has not been sufficient time for the latest Flesch formula to be adequately used and tested.

The following instructions are for applying the 1948 formulas developed by Flesch.[6]

To determine reading ease score:

1. *Pick samples to be tested.* If under three pages, sample whole

[3] Rudolpf Flesch, *The Art of Plain Talk,* Harper & Brothers, New York, 1943.

[4] Rudolf Flesch, "Measuring the Level of Abstraction," *Journal of Applied Psychology,* Vol. 34 (December, 1950), pp. 384–390.

[5] Rudolf Flesch, *How to Make Sense,* Harper & Brothers, New York, 1954.

[6] Rudolf Flesch, *The Art of Readable Writing,* Harper & Brothers, New York, 1949. Rudolf Flesch, *How to Test Readability,* Harper & Brothers, New York, 1950.

piece of writing. If from three to five pages, select every third paragraph or so. If from 25 to 30 pages, sample every other page or every tenth page. Each sample should start at the beginning of a paragraph.

2. *Count the number of words.* If testing a whole piece of writing, count all the words. If using samples, count each word up to 100 words. Contractions and hyphenated words are to be counted as one word each. Numbers and letters are words when separated by spaces.
3. *Figure the average sentence length.* Do this for the whole piece or total samples combined. In 100-word samples find the sentence ending nearest the 100-word mark—94th word or 109th word, for example. Count the number of sentences up to that point, and divide the number of words in those sentences in all samples by the number of sentences in all samples. Count thought units as sentences even though they may be marked off by a semicolon or colon rather than a period.
4. *Count the syllables.* If testing a whole piece of writing, divide total number of syllables by number of words and multiply by 100. In 100-word samples, divide the total number of syllables by the number of samples. Count syllables by the way a word is pronounced. Symbols and figures are counted as they are normally read; 1916 contains four syllables. If there are a lot of figures, don't include them but add a corresponding number of words after the original 100.
5. *Find the reading ease score.*
   Average sentence length (Step 3) multiplied by 1.015
   Number of syllables per 100 words (Step 4) multiplied by .846 _____
   Added _____
   Subtract the sum from 206.835 to find the reading ease score _____

The reading ease score can be interpreted from the following:

Reading Ease

Score	*Style Description*	*Estimated School Grade Completed*
90–100	Very easy	4th grade
80– 89	Easy	5th grade
70– 79	Fairly easy	6th grade
60– 69	Standard	7th or 8th grade
50– 59	Fairly difficult	Some high school
30– 49	Difficult	High school or some college
0– 29	Very difficult	College

To determine human interest score:

1. *Count the personal words.* If testing the whole piece, divide total number of personal words by the total number of words and multiply by 100. If testing samples, count the personal words in each 100-word sample and divide the total number of personal words by the number of samples. Count as personal words all first-, second- and third-person pronouns except the neuter *it, its, itself, they, them, their, theirs* and *themselves* if referring to things rather than people. Include all words having masculine or feminine gender, but do not count common gender nouns like *teacher, doctor* or *employee.* Count singular and plural forms and group words such as *people* and *folks.*
2. *Count the personal sentences.* If testing the whole, divide total number of personal sentences by total number of sentences and multiply by 100. If testing samples, divide the number of personal sentences in all the samples by the total number of sentences in all the samples and multiply by 100. Personal sentences are spoken sentences (marked by quotation marks or otherwise), questions, commands, requests and other sentences directly addressed to the reader – exclamations and grammatically incomplete sentences where full meaning has to be inferred from the context. If a sentence falls into two or more of these categories, count it only once.
3. *Find the human interest score.*
   Number of personal words per 100 (Step 1) X 3.635 ________
   Number of personal sentences per 100 (Step 2) X .314 ________
   Total is human interest score

The human interest score can be interpreted from the following:

Human Interest

Score	*Style Description*	*Typical Magazine*
60–100	Dramatic	Fiction
40– 59	Very interesting	*New Yorker*
20– 39	Interesting	Digests
10– 19	Mildly interesting	Trade
0– 9	Dull	Scientific

On the inside cover of the *Art of Readable Writing* and in *How to Test Readability* are sets of scales which permit a direct reading of the reading ease and human interest scores without applying the formulas given here. In the case of reading ease, for example, when the average sentence length and word length are known, the score may be read from the scaled chart.

The Dale-Chall Formula

In applying the Flesch formula of 1943, Edgar Dale and Jeanne Chall of Ohio State University found certain shortcomings.[7] Different people would count prefixes and suffixes differently so that they would get different reading ease scores for the same piece of writing. The counting of affixes proved to be time-consuming, as was also the counting of personal references. Therefore, they sought to devise a formula which would help correct the shortcomings.

To get at the upper levels of difficulty they decided on a word list to be used instead of counting affixes. They also discovered that the count of personal references did not add much. This left them with two factors, relative vocabulary count of words outside the Dale list of 300 familiar words known to 80 percent of fourth graders and the average sentence length, which they used in their formula developed in 1948.

Although the Dale-Chall formula may take slightly longer to apply than Flesch's reading ease formula, it gives similar results and has become the second most popular. It also represents about the most satisfactory use of a vocabulary list.[8] To speed up the use of the Dale-Chall formula Klare has developed a table for determining the scores quickly.[9]

Farr, Jenkins and Paterson Formula

Just as Dale and Chall sought to simplify the earlier Flesch formula, so James N. Farr, James J. Jenkins and Donald G. Paterson sought to simplify Flesch's reading ease formula of 1948. They found that counting syllables required a knowledge of syllabication on the part of the analyst. Therefore they modified the formula by substituting the number of one-syllable words per hundred words for the count of the number of syllables per hundred words.[10]

They worked out tests and made a study to show high correlation

[7] Edgar Dale and Jeanne Chall, "A Formula for Predicting Readability," *Educational Research Bulletin,* Ohio State University, Vol. 27 (February, 1948), p. 12.

[8] George R. Klare and Byron Buck, *Know Your Reader,* Hermitage House, New York, 1954, pp. 41–45.

[9] George R. Klare, "Table for Rapid Determination of Dale-Chall Readability Scores," *Educational Research Bulletin,* Ohio State University, Vol. 31 (February, 1952), pp. 43–47.

[10] James N. Farr, James J. Jenkins and Donald G. Paterson, "Simplification of Flesch Reading Ease Formula," *Journal of Applied Psychology,* Vol. 35 (October, 1951), pp. 333–337.

and to prove that the new simplified formula can be substituted for the 1948 Reading Ease formula of Flesch. Tables have also been prepared for computing scores.[11] Since there is no loss in accuracy or reliability and it can be applied faster, the Farr, Jenkins and Paterson formula will probably soon reach a high level of popularity also.

Gunning's Fog Index

In 1944 Robert Gunning Associates set up a firm for readability counseling. They adapted twenty years of research for the use of business writers. Surveys made in business and industry indicated "more than a third of the writing intended for employees and customers is above college reading level. Writing of that degree of difficulty is usually skipped by both customers and employees."[12] They sought to determine the factors of writing style that could be measured and to find out to what degree each affects reading difficulty. They discovered the seven most helpful factors to be average sentence length in words, percentage of simple sentences, percentage of verbs expressing forceful action, portion of familiar words, portion of abstract words, percentage of personal references and percentage of long words.[13]

Gunning uses two elements in measuring readability, the number of words of three or more syllables in 100 words and the average sentence length in words. His method, though related to Flesch's reading ease formula, is much easier to apply and gives very much the same result. One can count the hard-word factor about as fast as he can skim the material, since few familiar words are of more than three syllables.

The following instructions are for applying Gunning's method of measuring readability:[14]

1. *Determine average sentence length.* Jot down the number of words in successive sentences. For long pieces of writing take samples of 100 words. Divide total number of words by the number of sentences.
2. *Find the percentage of hard words.* Count the number of words of three syllables or more per 100 words. Don't count capitalized

[11] *Ibid.*

[12] Robert Gunning, *The Technique of Clear Writing,* McGraw-Hill Book Company, Inc., New York, 1952, p. 7.

[13] *Ibid.,* p. 32.

[14] *Ibid.,* pp. 36, 37.

words, words that are combinations of short easy words (like *book-keeper* and *butterfly*), words that are verb forms made into three syllables by adding *ed* or *es* (like *created* or *trespasses*).

3. *Figure Fog Index.* Add the two factors (Steps 1 and 2) and multiply by .4.

The Fog Index is thus determined in such a simple, easy way that no formula or device for computation is necessary. The following table is for interpreting the Fog Index or readability score: [15]

Fog Index	*Reading Level by Grade*	*Reading Level by Magazine*
17	College graduate	(No popular magazine is this difficult.)
16	College senior	
15	College junior	
14	College sophomore	
13	College freshman	
DANGER LINE		
12	High school senior	*Atlantic Monthly*
11	High school junior	*Harpers*
EASY-READING RANGE		
10	High school sophomore	*Time*
9	High school freshman	*Reader's Digest*
8	Eighth grade	*Ladies' Home Journal*
7	Seventh grade	*True Confessions*
6	Sixth grade	Comics

INFLUENCE OF READABILITY FORMULAS ON STYLE

The use of readability formulas can be carried to the extreme and result in writing faults. A choppy, childish style will result from writing in too many short, simple sentences. The most familiar word may not always be the best choice. Even a short sentence may not be clear. Writing within a limited vocabulary range may become monotonous and deadening.

The formulas should be used for measuring the readability level and not as rules for writing. They do not measure the reader's background and interest nor do they consider many of the factors that go into effective writing. They do, however, measure readability in a general way for the general reader and help the writer to see his material as the reader will or *to adapt his writing to the reader.*

[15] *Ibid.*, p. 38.

Most of the research in readability points to the use of clear sentences and understandable words for making writing readable. Thus emphasis is on clearness in writing, and readability formulas have more or less affected the style of writing to the extent of emphasizing the following principles in writing clear sentences:

Keep majority of sentences short and simple.
Make relationships clear in each sentence.
Vary sentence length and structure.
Use small number of prepositional and infinitive phrases.
Use adequate conjunctions and transitional phrases for smooth reading.
Convey only one or two main thoughts in each sentence.
Let each sentence mean something in relation to other sentences.

The formulas have also emphasized the following principles in using vocabulary:

Use familiar words.
Make words meaningful.
Avoid unnecessary words.
Use short-syllable words.
Select non-technical terms.
Put action into verbs.
Use a variety of words.
Select pictorial words within the reader's experience.
Use concrete rather than abstract words.
Apply concrete analogies, examples and comparisons when abstract concepts must be given.

PROBLEMS

1. Discuss the advantages and disadvantages of using the four frequently used readability formulas.

2. Measure the readability of one of the reports you have written by applying Flesch's reading ease and human interest formulas. What do the scores suggest that you do?

3. Select a company annual report and apply Gunning's Fog Index and Flesch's 1948 readability formula to determine whether or not both indicate the same results.

4. Select an employee magazine or booklet and test it for readability. Why would Flesch's formula be more appropriate than Gunning's in this instance?

5. What general influence have the readability formulas had upon the style of business writing?

CHAPTER 13

Writing, Revising and Editing the Report

WRITING, REVISING AND EDITING THE REPORT IS THE LAST step in the report preparation process. By the time the writer has reached this stage he has already planned and conducted his investigation, gathered his data, organized and interpreted his facts, prepared his tables and charts, reached conclusions, formulated recommendations whenever appropriate and outlined his material for final presentation in his report. In fact, he has accomplished the steps presented in Part II of this book. His notes, data and outline are all in order, and he is ready to apply the principles of effective presentation discussed so far in Part III. The task of writing has been simplified by his having organized and outlined the report.

WRITING THE FIRST DRAFT

With a detailed outline as a guide, a report will almost write itself because it is so easy to go from one point to another. An outline also gives confidence to the writer so that he can focus his attention on the facts he is imparting and on the readers who will absorb them. Because the arrangement has been worked out the writer can go from one item to the next in his outline. He can write rapidly; in fact, he can easily write any short report at one sitting. For long reports he can complete individual sections at a sitting. The important thing is to get ideas down on paper in logical order. By sticking to the outline and not going off on tangents this is possible. The manuscript will grow according to its plan.

Good report writing is achieved by rapid writing based on effective organization for the presentation of facts and ideas. The first draft is written to record facts and ideas within the framework of the outline. The writer at this point is not concerned with punctuation, spelling, grammar and form so much as with the flow and development of facts and thoughts. The correction of mechanical errors comes with revision. A simple easy flow of related ideas is necessary to get the message across to the reader. A lot of attention should be given to the best way to tie material together. Each part of the report should prepare the reader for what is to come. The discussion of each fact should be completed before introducing another.

While writing, the author should keep before him his specific purpose and his audience. The purpose can be used as a device against which to measure ideas as they occur. It will help to keep them in focus, to relate them to each other and to give perspective and shape to the material at hand. In remembering his reader the writer may unconsciously carry on a discussion with him and be stimulated by it. He can also examine his ideas from the other person's viewpoint and will be able to make them more meaningful.

There are times, of course, when the writer will want to depart from his outline, which is merely a guide. When he is expanding it in writing he will be thinking, and thinking is a chain reaction. One idea will generate another. The outline suggests the sequence and subject matter; it does not include the thoughts that will occur to the writer as he develops the points. He should feel free to depart from the outline when his thoughts do – if they are in line with his purpose.

There are times also when the writer will want to sit and think, go over material, find a fresh approach. This will, however, slow down his writing and should not often be necessary if he has done enough thinking and planning before this time.

The report can be thought through as it is being written from its outline. Experienced, capable writers sometimes can write short reports that require very little revision. They write well naturally, thinking through each sentence, selecting words with care, etc. Most report writers, however, will write a first draft, applying all of the principles and techniques of style, tone and of expressing facts clearly, interestingly and persuasively that are applicable to the particular report at hand. Then they depend on improving the report through revision before it appears in its final form.

CRITICIZING AND REVISING

The type of report and how it is to be used, as well as the amount of time available and how well the first draft was prepared, determine the amount of revision needed. A memorandum report, for example, containing information of temporary use does not warrant a lot of time spent on revision. The report is checked, nevertheless, for accuracy of facts, clearness of expression and over-all organization; is tested to see whether it accomplishes its purpose adequately; and is proofread for correction of mechanical errors in form and typing. This procedure is generally followed for all reports of a routine nature or use and, to some degree, for all short or informal reports written for only one specific reader, usually within the company organization. Whether the report gets its message across to the reader is the all-important test, and time is not always available for revision beyond that point.

A report, on the other hand, containing data of permanent value, or one which is to receive wide distribution, certainly warrants time spent in revision. Revision, for such a report, may decide whether or not it is read, and in some cases may even increase its readership. Of course any printed report should be carefully revised and edited before publication. It would be foolish to spend money for printing ineffective or incorrect writing.

Revision varies according to the qualifications of the writer. One who writes competently may have little or nothing to do in the way of correcting mechanical errors such as spelling, punctuation and grammar. One who normally expresses what he has to say clearly, concisely and interestingly will have little revision of that nature to do. In revising lies the opportunity to make up for the deficiencies of the report and the writer so that the finished product is effectively composed to accomplish its purpose as quickly as possible.

Revising a report systematically calls for reading the report several times, each time checking the report for a different purpose. The reading may be done aloud or silently, to or by someone other than the writer.

Checking the Contents

Since the first draft of a report is written for the purpose of setting down facts and ideas, expanding on the outline, and since it is written rapidly, one of the first checks to make on the subject matter is to find out whether it is accurate and complete and whether the purpose of the report has been accomplished. In checking the accuracy of the material, give attention to whether or not the problem is accurately defined and the proper background material provided for the reader to understand the situation. Is the scope properly limited? The original working plan can be used as an aid in checking the introductory material in the report. The plan for conducting the investigation and making the report, checked against the first draft, will indicate whether or not the plans were carried out, and, if not, whether or not the changes can be accounted for and whether they were improvements.

To check further the facts and data presented, the following questions will be helpful:

Are the numerical data exact?
Do the tables and charts contain accurate data?
Are the tables and charts used appropriately?
Do the illustrations conform to standard practice?
Are the illustrations suitable for the purpose and the reader?
Are the quotations exact?
Are the conclusions sound and logical?
Are the conclusions definite and clear?
Are the recommendations workable?
Are the recommendations an outgrowth of the conclusions?

In checking the subject matter for completeness, give attention to whether or not certain repetitions should be omitted or left in for emphasis. There may occur irrelevant material to be deleted, and there may be omitted data or explanations that should be added. It is not sufficient at this point to check merely for the facts and ideas presented; it is also necessary to check on how they are presented. Are the comparisons clear, for instance? Are the analogies appropriate? Are there sufficient examples and illustrative material for clarity and interest? Is there adequate support and evidence for generalizations and conclusions that have been made?

Additional checking of subject matter should disclose whether or not the main issues stand out in proper perspective and whether or not the minor issues are related. What about the flow of ideas from one topic to the next? Is the reader adequately prepared to move forward? Does the report develop logically in one direction? Is adequate transition achieved through transitional sentences, paragraphs, words and ideas? Will the reader reach the same conclusions as those stated? Do the data prepare him to accept the conclusions and to agree with the writer? Are the conclusions a basis for the recommendations? Do the recommendations fulfill the purpose of the report?

Checking Organization

Very closely related to the process of checking the subject matter is that of checking the organization of the report — enough so, in fact, that in most short reports both can be done at the same reading. In long reports, there are times when one might want to check the organization before he delves into the subject matter. The over-all organization of the report should be checked first, then the organization of its parts. Here the outline will serve as a guide in determining the wisdom of the sequence and arrangement of the topics treated. There may, however, have been changes made in writing. Then they should be checked to see whether they should remain or be changed further.

The organization should be logical and make for general coherence. The report should hang together as a whole. Every part should be related and should make sense.

Checking for Clearness of Expression, Mechanics of Style and Form

After he has checked the subject matter and organization, the writer is ready to examine in detail each paragraph, sentence and word that makes up the report, to be sure that clearness of expression and mechanical correctness have been accomplished. The questions, who, when, where, what, why, how much and how many, should all be answered. Important specific details should be included. They make for clearness, interest and conviction.

Sentences should be checked for their thought and structure. Are the ideas clear to the reader? Are their relationships conveyed by proper connection of the sentence elements? Is there ambiguity? What about the phrasing; does it read smoothly? Logically? Does it sound natural? Simple, short sentences outnumbering more complex sentences contribute to clearness and exactness of expression. Yet there should be a variety of sentence types, patterns and lengths. For easy comprehension there should be an average sentence length of 18 to 22 words. But this is an *average*. There should definitely be a combination of long, short and in-between sentences, with the short predominating and the average maintained. The longer the sentence and the more complex its structure, the more difficult it becomes to grasp clearly and quickly. Sentences should also be checked for grammatical correctness. Are unity, coherence and emphasis maintained in each sentence? Does the sentence contain any faulty pronoun reference, dangling modifier, indirect or awkward phrasing?

In checking the words used, try to substitute a concrete word for each abstract one. The concrete word comes within the experience of the reader and will have more meaning for him than the abstract word that deals with concepts not usually within the realm of the five senses. There are of course abstract terms that must be used for want of something better. Then they should be defined or the concept illustrated by specific details. Complex, bookish and trite words and phrases should be avoided. Simple, plain, familiar words make for easier comprehension.

Because they are closely related, the checking of sentences and words can be done at the same time. In working for conciseness, for example, both must be considered. The original copy can usually be greatly reduced in length by shortening sentences, combining sentences, breaking up sentences, cutting out all unnecessary wording and phrasing and selecting words with exact meaning. As thoughts become clarified and concepts simplified, the number of words tends to decrease. Where clarity must be achieved by additional explanation or description, those parts of the report will be longer in the revised copy; but the over-all length will have been shortened merely by applying principles of simplified writing. This is the best way to save the reader's time.

The more one examines the words and sentences, the more likely he is to notice any mechanical errors in English and typing. In most cases he can correct these at the same time. Simply by being conscious of spelling, punctuation and grammar, one can do a great deal toward correcting errors. In some cases, however, a reference handbook or dictionary should be used — to what extent depends on the qualifications and experience of the writer.

The form of a report is determined by its type, its purpose and its use; so each of these factors should be considered in checking the form. This might be done when checking report organization, but usually one is concerned then with a general impression of form rather than with a detailed examination. Does the report conform to a standard form for its type — letter, memorandum, bulletin or some other kind? Then what about details of typing form? Consider here margins, spacing, footnotes, subject headings, etc. Has the proper footnote form been used? Is there consistency in form? Are all headings of like degree typed in the same manner? Are proper degrees of relationship shown in the headings? Have tabulations or quotations been set off rather than run into the other paragraphs of the text?

Checking Readability

One of the readability formulas mentioned in Chapter 12 should be used to measure whether or not the appropriate level of readability is achieved in the report. This should be done normally either after writing the first draft or after checking the subject matter and organization of the report. At any rate it should be done before revising the sentence and language structure, because the results of the test will indicate the extent to which revision is needed to reach the general reader. Either Flesch's reading ease formula or Gunning's Fog Index, for instance, can be quickly used.

Other factors, such as interest, adaptation to the reader and tone, contribute to readability and should be checked. Has the proper tone been maintained? Has the reader been told what he needs to know for understanding? Has the material been adapted to the reader's experience and knowledge? Is interest gained through choice of vocabulary, illustrations, layout and approach to the problem? Has the reader's need and use of the report been recognized?

After the copy has been revised the same or another readability formula can be applied. A second application would depend on the amount of revision that had taken place and also on whether or not the first test had indicated that the desired level of readability had been reached.

General Suggestions for Revising

The purpose of revision is to prepare the report for final typing and distribution. Revision gives the writer an opportunity to correct or rewrite portions and in general to improve and polish the report — all of which may assure its acceptance, increased readership and resultant action. All corrections may be made in the margins or in the text, or an explanatory symbol may be placed in the margin and the error underscored in the text. For inserted material the location may be indicated by a caret. Material may be deleted by marking through it or blocking it out. Material to be added may be written on a separate sheet and attached, with a notation made on the original copy as to where it is to be placed.

After the marked copy has been retyped, it should be proofread for the correction of errors in typing and English. The persistence of errors may warrant another typing. This is not usually necessary. If the report is to be published, a list of proofreader's marks used by the publisher should be checked and used in revising and editing it.

A general check list of what to look for in revising a report follows. The extent to which it is used will depend on the writer's experience and abilities, the type and use of the report and the amount of time available for revision. Not all reports are revised, nor should they be. Most reports, however, can be improved, and careful revision is what does it.

EDITING THE REPORT

Basically editing is the same as revising. Its purpose is to correct and improve the report — to prepare and check the final copy. Although editing is often done by someone other than the author,

CHECK LIST FOR REVISING

Contents

Fulfillment of Purpose

Accuracy and Completeness

- background material
- scope defined
- numerical data
- tables and charts
- quotations
- examples and explanations
- facts and other evidence
- duplication
- repetitions
- irrelevant material
- conclusions

Main Issues

Minor Issues

Logical Development

Flow of Ideas

Emphasis

Mechanical Correctness

English

- spelling
- punctuation
- grammar

Form

- type of report
- parts of report
- margins
- paragraphing
- footnote form
- bibliographical form
- subject headings
- consistency

Organization

As a Whole

Relationship of Parts

Position of Topics

Sequence of Ideas

Transition

Unity

Clearness of Expression

Sentences

- specific facts and details expressed
- varied sentence structure
- short sentences predominant
- average sentence length
- grammatically correct sentences
- smooth phrasing
- use of topic sentences

Words

- concrete
- familiar
- precise
- simple
- abstract concepts defined

Adaptation to Reader

Level of Readability

Tone

Experience and Knowledge

Interest

a number of writers edit their own material. The report rewritten from all of the points noted — with additions, deletions or corrections — is read again for the purpose of checking and improving it before distribution. In the case of a published report editing means preparing the final copy for the printer. The manuscript is checked first for the accuracy, completeness and clearness of subject matter, then for over-all and sectional organization and last for correctness in the mechanics of style and form. In most instances after a report has undergone careful revision, all that is necessary is to correct the few mechanical errors that remain and, if the report is to be published, mark the copy for the printer.

Large companies employ editors to polish material written for wide distribution. The amount of work they do on a report depends on the quality of its writing. In some instances they merely correct mechanical flaws, in other cases technical errors; and sometimes they do a complete rewrite job – retaining only the conclusions of the original. Publishers also have editors who correct and mark material for publication. Usually the editor will make corrections and mark the manuscript for the printer. The printer will then go over it and make his printing plans. The material is checked and returned to the author for approval or changes. When it goes back to the printer he makes the galley proof, which is usually read and corrected by the editor or a proofreader. Page proof is then printed, proofread and returned for final printing.

Throughout the process of publishing, the editor is responsible to the printer for marking instructions and corrections clearly, to the author for preserving his facts, ideas, style and objectives, to the publisher for protecting his publication policies and for increasing readership, to the reader for providing clear and interesting material, and to himself for maintaining his own reputation as an editor. Careful editing is just as necessary for printed reports as careful writing, revising and checking are for typed reports. Effective writing and revising make the editor's task an easy one and assure the reader a clear, well-written report and the writer the fulfillment of his purpose.

PROBLEMS

1. Bring to class a report that you have written for a course other than report writing and discuss the ways in which it should be improved.
2. Obtain a report that has been used by a business firm. Assume that you have been asked to suggest ways it can be improved. In a memorandum to the company present your evaluation, criticisms and recommendations.

Part IV

MOTIVATION OF ACTION THROUGH BUSINESS REPORTS

CHAPTER *14*

Kinds of Business Reports

ON THE BASIS OF FORM
Informal, Short Reports
Formal, Long Reports
ON THE BASIS OF FUNCTION
Reports That Inform
Reports That Analyze
SPECIAL TYPES OF REPORTS

THERE ARE MANY KINDS OF REPORTS AND WAYS OF CLASSIFYING them according to types; for business reports cover a wide range and variety of subjects, dealing with all phases of business activity. They are used for a multitude of purposes and present their messages in a variety of forms. Practices in using reports in one company are not necessarily the same as those followed by another company. Yet through different procedures both companies may accomplish the same purposes. It is important that both businessmen and students become familiar with a large number of types of reports and the manner in which they may be used in different situations. It is also essential that they develop abilities, techniques and skills called for in investigation and in the presentation of material in a report and that they learn to adjust and adapt reports to meet varying circumstances and to solve problems as they arise.

If you were to jot down all the kinds of reports that are used by any one company, you might have a list running something like this:

Policy statements
Periodic reports
Credit reports
Sales reports
Committee minutes
Reports on interviews
Advertising reports
Employee bulletins
Examination reports
Accounting reports
Market surveys
Personnel reports

- Recommendation reports
- Statistical analyses
- Analyses of present business conditions
- Product analyses
- Analyses of processes
- Production reports
- Public relations reports
- Annual reports
- Attitude surveys
- Readership surveys
- Justification reports
- Improvement reports
- Progress reports
- Information reports
- Analytical reports
- Research reports

Although the list is not a complete one, it is representative. When material was gathered for this section of this book, a survey was made of one hundred companies scattered over the United States. Practically every company in replying to the question, "Which types of reports do you use in your company?" stated that at one time or another they made use of every type of report in the above list. Sample reports from the companies, however, showed that the uses of a particular kind of report vary from company to company because of different situations and because of the different functions that reports perform.

The firms surveyed agreed that they presented their reports in a variety of forms and at one time or another used each of the following:

- Memorandum
- Letter
- Informal, short
- Formal, long
- Bulletin
- Booklet
- Blank form
- Other

Reports are used not only within a firm but also as a means of external communication. Within a firm they may move vertically upward or downward, from a non-executive or sub-executive to top management or from an executive down to lower officials and employees. They may move horizontally from one department to another within the firm, from sources outside the company or to outside readers from within the company. On the basis of reports' movement and their use by the company, they could be thus classified as internal or external communications — each report performing a specific function within or outside the company.

Different writers on the subject classify them in various ways, just as companies do. There is frequently a great deal of overlapping among kinds of reports. The same report may be designated by several names. But classification is not as important as understanding different report-writing situations and being able to adapt report material to reader purpose.

Part IV on reports and their uses to motivate action has thus been included to familiarize the reader with a large number of report situations and with the way in which reports function in the business world. Most writers and businessmen agree that there are two fundamental bases for classifying reports: function and form.

ON THE BASIS OF FORM

On the basis of form there are two major types of reports: informal, short reports and formal, long reports. The type used depends on such factors as:

(*1*) Complexity and treatment of the problem
(*2*) Length of the report
(*3*) Interest to the reader
(*4*) Purpose and objectives to be accomplished
(*5*) Time for preparation
(*6*) Permanent or temporary value of the finished report
(*7*) Intended use of the report
(*8*) Formality of the situation

Both major types are treated fully in this text – informal reports in Chapter 15 and formal, long reports in Chapter 16. Thus it is sufficient here to distinguish between them and to enumerate some of the general functions of each type.

Informal, Short Reports

Informal, short reports, as their name implies, are written for informal situations. For example, suppose the advertising manager of a company needs to have a record of sales over a period of time in order to relate his advertising costs to profits. All that would be needed from the sales manager would be an informal memorandum recording the sales, broken down monthly, annually, etc.

Informal, short reports vary in length, usually from one to ten pages. They are often written on subjects of temporary or current interest and speed up the process of keeping someone else informed. They have neither a table of contents nor cover because there is no need for them. The pages are usually clipped or stapled. They are a less-finished product than the formal, long report.

Informal, short reports take on various forms. Memorandum and letter reports are very commonly used. Although memorandum reports are generally distributed internally and letter reports externally, their use may be reversed. A letter report when used internally is sometimes written to someone in higher authority than its author, and a memorandum report may be addressed to a subordinate in the company. Both are personal forms of reports, and their degree of informality depends on the relationship between the reader and author and the purpose of the report. Although the length of letter or memorandum reports may vary, both are usually kept short, from one to three pages.

To speed up the recording and flow of information, mimeographed or printed forms are often used by business firms. The reporter fills in the information required, and it is speeded on its way to be used by someone else. Sometimes bulletins are issued to let employees know what policies or changes have been made. At other times the information is presented in the form of a booklet. An example would be the presentation of the provisions and regulations concerning a company's retirement fund in the form of a booklet circulated among the employees. It would be interestingly written and attractively presented to catch their eye and to interest them in reading it.

There is also a short report form very similar to the formal, long report. The chief differences are that it is shorter, is concerned with a less-involved situation, does not contain all the prefatory elements of the long report and is usually of temporary use. It is like the formal, long report, for it contains the same formal organization and treatment of its subject or problem and is a fairly finished product.

Formal, Long Reports

Formal reports are usually over ten pages long; in some cases they are book length. Their subjects are given comprehensive treatment. The problem being treated is often complicated and involved, covering a wide scope. The report has a cover for protection and is usually bound. Containing a table of contents and several other prefatory elements before the report proper, it usually has an appendix at the end. Its subject, which is of major significance, is broken down into parts. To achieve the purpose, formal organization is used.

The problem arises out of a formal situation, and the report is handled accordingly. To lend impartiality and to make for lack of bias in the treatment, data are presented impersonally.

Not so much variety is used in the long report as is found among short reports. For the long report one form is generally followed. Variations from it are largely omissions or inclusions of parts or adaptations of the text, together with organization to suit the demands of the readers, the problem situation and the use of the report.

ON THE BASIS OF FUNCTION

Although reports are used to achieve a large number of different purposes, ranging from so simple a one as that of stating personnel policy concerning vacation pay to a recommendation for purchasing $150,000 worth of new equipment, basically they are used either to inform or to analyze. Thus, on the basis of function, there are two kinds of reports – informational and analytical reports. Examples and discussion of each of these functional types are presented in Chapters 17 and 18. Here only their major functions are considered.

Reports That Inform

Informative reports serve as a record of data. Facts are organized and presented to the reader to use as he sees fit or to retain as a part of his knowledge on the subject. The report keeps the reader informed, and as a result of being informed he is better able to perform his work. The results of an investigation may also be given for the reader himself to interpret and analyze. Some of the reports that inform are periodic reports, progress reports, policy statements, employee booklets, readership surveys, reports on sales, credit reports, committee minutes, reports on single interviews, some production reports and some public relations reports. Their information may be presented in any of the informal, short report forms or in a formal, long report.

Reports That Analyze

In addition to presenting data, a report may also include an interpretation and analysis of facts or results and recommendations. It then becomes an analytical report. Some specific types of analytical reports are advertising reports, examination reports, accounting reports, statistical analyses, analyses of present business conditions, product analyses, market surveys, employee-attitude surveys, some production reports and some personnel reports. Analytical reports carry the process of report presentation a step further than the informational report. The reader has his data interpreted for him; it is analyzed in relation to his problem, and his task is to decide on the action to be taken. Analytical reports are used often as a basis for a decision.

Analytical reports may also contain conclusions and recommend desired changes. They would then perform three functions – presenting facts, analyzing facts and recommending action. Often used in this way they present a solution to a problem. Although the reader may accept or reject the recommended action, the report itself results in action one way or another and is of greatest use in dealing with business operations, construction or production. Some sales reports, personnel reports, surveys, improvement reports and justification reports fall into this category because of the special function each performs in recommending action.

SPECIAL TYPES OF REPORTS

A few reports cannot be classified according to the functions mentioned, because they may perform any or several of them and still perform additional special functions of their own. The corporation's annual report and reports written for employee publications and trade journals are examples of this type. So much emphasis has been placed on these reports in today's business world that they warrant special treatment in chapters pertaining to them. Chapter 19 takes up the annual report, and Chapter 20 deals with writing for employee publications.

A third special type of report, the research report, has not been included as such in this text. The research report, which is the result of pure research done in the scientific laboratory, is beyond the scope of this book. Such a report is sometimes used by business firms, especially in the development of new products and processes, and the presentation of its data involves the same techniques and procedures used in many of the reports discussed here. The chief difference is in the method of research used to obtain the data – laboratory research. Reports that are the result of applied research are the same as those discussed in the chapters that follow. All business reports, to a great extent, are the result of research or some method or methods of investigation. Therefore, a special research type of business report will not be given further consideration.

An attempt has been made to simplify classification of reports in this chapter and to present an over-all view of the types of reports treated in the chapters that follow. As the reader examines the various kinds of reports, he should be conscious of the procedures and techniques used and seek to understand how they are applied to varying circumstances to accomplish different purposes with different readers. This close attention should help him to write effective reports.

PROBLEMS

1. Why are function and form fundamental bases for classifying business reports?

2. On the basis of form classify the reports given in the problems at the end of Chapter 15. Could any of the reports be presented in more than one form? Why?

3. On the basis of function classify the reports given in the problems at the end of Chapter 15. Do any of the reports perform several functions? Explain.

4. What special functions do annual reports and employee publications perform?

5. Why is it important that there be motivation of action through business reports?

6. Bring a sample business report to class and discuss ways in which it motivates action.

CHAPTER *15*

Arrangement and Format of Informal, Short Reports

LETTER REPORTS
MEMORANDUM REPORTS
BULLETINS
BOOKLETS
FORM REPORTS
SHORT REPORTS

INFORMAL, SHORT REPORTS MAY APPEAR IN A VARIETY OF forms. Because form is a means to an end and not an end in itself, the form selected depends on the reader, the problem, the purpose and the use of the report. Forms also vary from business firm to business firm. At one time or another, however, most companies use all of the forms treated in this chapter.

LETTER REPORTS

Letter reports are business letters that present business information or deal with a business problem. They contain the parts of a business letter, and their general form and layout are the same. They are different from business letters in the organization of the contents and in the style of writing followed.

When the Girard Trust Company consolidated with the Corn Exchange to form the Girard Trust Corn Exchange Bank in 1951, a letter report was sent to the stockholders, employees, customers and friends to inform them of the consolidation, making them aware of

Chartered 1836

Girard Trust Company

BROAD & CHESTNUT STREETS

PHILADELPHIA 2, PA.

JAMES E. GOWEN
CHAIRMAN OF THE BOARD

GEOFFREY S. SMITH
PRESIDENT

To the Stockholders, Employees,
Customers, and Friends
of Girard Trust Company

The Board of Managers of Girard Trust Company and the Board of Directors of Corn Exchange National Bank and Trust Company have both informally approved a proposal for the consolidation of the two institutions.

A detailed plan to effect the combination is being worked out by counsel for both companies. When completed and formally acted upon by each Board, it will then be submitted to the two groups of stockholders and to Federal and State banking authorities for approval.

It is proposed that each stockholder of Girard Trust Company receive one share of stock in the combined institution for each share of Girard stock presently held. Similarly, each stockholder of Corn Exchange would receive one share of the new stock for each share of Corn Exchange stock now owned.

The earnings per share of both companies for their 1950 fiscal years were identical. The relationships of shares outstanding, market value of shares, and net earnings for the fiscal years are as follows:

	Fiscal 1950 Earnings Per Share	Shares Outstanding	Market Value Of Shares (1/10/51)	Net Earnings Fiscal 1950
Girard Trust	$4.75	400,000 (58.4%)	$19,000,000 (59%)	$1,900,330.63 (58.4%)
Corn Exchange	4.75	284,375 (41.6%)	13,152,343 (41%)	1,351,242.76 (41.6%)
		684,375 (100%)	$32,152,343 (100%)	$3,251,573.39 (100%)

The combined bank is to be State-chartered and will be named Girard Corn Exchange Bank and Trust Company.

David E. Williams, now President of Corn Exchange, will be Chairman of the Board. James E. Gowen will be Chairman of the Executive Committee of the Board. I will serve as President.

Courtesy Girard Trust Corn Exchange Bank

Letter report announcing consolidation.

the advantages for both institutions and obtaining their cooperation. The report is presented on this page and the next.

All of the parts of a business letter are used here except the inside address and complimentary close, which are often omitted in form

There will be four Senior Vice Presidents of the combined institutions: two from Girard Trust, J. Malcolm Johnston, and Basil L. Harlow; and two from Corn Exchange, George R. Clark, and Russell J. Bauer.

All personnel of Girard Trust and of Corn Exchange will be needed in the combined organization.

After the consolidation has been completed we will have a united institution with total resources exceeding a half billion dollars. The Girard Corn Exchange Bank and Trust Company will combine an extensive and experienced commercial banking service with a large and profitable trust department. It will provide a completely rounded set of financial and fiduciary services for business organizations, for business executives, and for individual men and women of all income brackets. These services will include savings accounts, special checking accounts, and safe deposit facilities conveniently located throughout the city.

The combined institution will include a foreign department second to none in this area. It will have widespread correspondent banking relationships. A sizable and experienced consumer credit service will be able to meet the needs of individual borrowers, dealers, and small businesses.

In the trust department there will be offered personal trust and estate administration services, custodian and investment advisory accounts for individuals and institutions, as well as corporate trust, pension trust, and profit-sharing trust services for industry and business.

The combined bank will have locations convenient for its customers and strategically placed for the development of new business. There will be nine neighborhood offices, two well-located downtown offices, an exceptional group of three buildings in the heart of the city at Broad and Chestnut Streets, plus an additional excellent midtown office nearby.

The neighborhood offices, particularly in the fast-growing northeast section of the city, will continue to provide on-the-spot service to men and women and business organizations in their respective communities.

It is our belief that this proposed consolidation is a forward and constructive step which will be advantageous for both institutions and their staffs and also for all of the people of the Philadelphia area.

Geoffrey S. Smith

President

February 1, 1951

Letter report **(Cont.).**

letters, especially those sent to a large number of people. The style of writing is factual. Although it lacks the personal touch of most business letters, the report sustains interest by showing consideration for the reader. The facts are pointed out as benefits to him; the material is broken down into short paragraphs, and the terminology used is within the range of his understanding.

INTERNATIONAL PAPER COMPANY

220 EAST 42ND STREET NEW YORK 17, N.Y.

To Holders of Our Common Stock:

It is with real pleasure that we enclose the Common Stock (or Scrip, or both) distributable to you on the stock dividend declared August 8, 1950, by your Directors.

The dividend so declared is payable today to stockholders of record at the close of business August 25, 1950. The rate is 25%; i.e. one-fourth of a share of $7.50 par Common Stock for each share of such stock held on the record date.

If your record date holdings amounted to an even multiple of four shares, only Stock is enclosed. If you held three shares or less only Bearer Scrip for a fraction of a share is enclosed. Otherwise, both Stock and Scrip are enclosed.

On the back of this letter you will find information about the rights represented by the Scrip and how it may be bought and sold.

Effect of Stock Dividend

This stock dividend does not change the percentage of your interest in the Company. Sale of all the Stock and Scrip received on this dividend would reduce your interest in the Company by 20%.

A charge of $60,623,241 ($34 for each share issued) has been made against Earned Surplus as a result of this dividend. The Common Stock account has been credited with $13,372,773.75 ($7.50 a share, the par value) and Capital Surplus with $47,250,467.25 ($26.50 a share).

The amount so charged against Earned Surplus exceeds by $36,216,001 the consolidated net profit, after dividends, during the first half of 1950.

Tax Status

Counsel for the Company have given their opinion, based on present decisions, that this stock dividend is not taxable as income to the recipient under the U. S. Federal Income Tax Law. However, if you sell any Stock or Scrip (whether received through the dividend, or acquired in exchange for Scrip, or previously held by you), this stock dividend must be taken into consideration in calculating the tax basis ("cost") of your holdings in order to determine your gain or loss for Federal Income Tax purposes.

Canadian counsel advise that this stock dividend is not taxable as income to the recipient under the Income Tax Act of Canada.

This information is furnished for your assistance, but it is suggested that you be guided by your regular tax adviser.

Current Cash Dividend

Under separate cover a check is being forwarded to you for the quarterly cash dividend of 75 cents a share payable today to common stockholders of record August 25, 1950. You will note that this cash dividend is being paid on the full share(s) of stock dividend stock enclosed herewith as well as on the shares which were registered in your name on the record date.

JOHN H. HINMAN
PRESIDENT

September 22, 1950

Courtesy International Paper Company

Letter report to stockholders.

Let us take a look at another letter report. Most companies send out a report such as the one on this page to their stockholders when they send the dividend check.

Here again the business letter is readily recognized. Use has been made, however, of subject headings to indicate the nature of the material being presented. They serve as a guide to both the writer and the reader.

Both examples of letter reports presented here are informational, reflecting a specific function of the letter report. Neither of these, however, has presented the results of an investigation, which a letter report may also do.

A distributor of grocery and drug products to supermarkets, for example, might be confronted with the problem of having supermarkets keep fully stocked shelves at all times. In this connection he might make a study of several supermarkets to determine the effect on sales of fully stocked shelves. Sales of several brands in each of ten commodity products could be checked for a two-week period under normal shelf-stock conditions, and then for two weeks under fully stocked shelf conditions. The results of the survey would be of interest to dealers and managers of supermarkets. In fact, a letter report informing them of the survey's results may influence them to keep fully stocked shelves at all times. A report covering this situation follows:

BUCKLEY DISTRIBUTING COMPANY
3204 Laurel Street
New Orleans, Louisiana

June 11, 195_

Mr. James R. Brown
Brown's Supermarket
5200 St. Charles Avenue
New Orleans, Louisiana

Dear Mr. Brown:

Subject: Advantages of Fully Stocked Shelves

Because of increasing inquiries from several supermarket executives concerning grocery- and drug-shelf stocking, I have undertaken an investigation to determine the effect of fully stocked shelves on sales. This survey has been made considering representative grocery and drug products, with attention given to percentagewise increases through mass stocking.

Effect of Diversification

Seven supermarkets were surveyed, with several brands of products checked for a two-week period under normal shelf-stocking conditions, and then for two more weeks under fully stocked shelf conditions. Enclosed is the complete result of the survey; below is a simple breakdown:

Mr. James R. Brown 2 June 11, 195–

TABLE I

SALES IN RELATION TO NUMBER OF ITEMS STOCKED

	On Total Grocery Product Sales	On Total Drug Sales	On All Products
No. of items checked	128	69	197
2 weeks unit sales under normal conditions	8,404	607	9,011
2 weeks unit sales when shelves kept fully stocked	10,287	902	11,189
Change in percentage	+22.4%	+48.5%	+24.2%

If you will notice the change in the percentage of sales resulting from fully stocking the shelves, it is obvious that this procedure is of tremendous value:

Grocery product sales . . . . 22.4% increase
Drug product sales . . . . 48.5% increase
All products sales . . . . 24.2% increase

Margin and Turnover

We all know that it is the desire of every supermarket to offer goods at the lowest possible prices. This can be accomplished only by reducing markup and increasing stock turnover. Now, if you can increase sales on all products by 24.2% merely by fully stocking your shelves, it is apparent that you will be able to reduce markups and offer merchandise at lower prices. By your giving maximum exposure to different commodities, the consumer is afforded the opportunity of seeing more and as a result is motivated to purchase something that would never have entered his mind, had not certain brand appeals caught his eye.

The rise in the general standard of living has caused a proportional increase in the demand for service. By our very nature we cannot offer personalized service; therefore we must do the next best thing—give intensive exposure to a large variety of brands. That is, substitute displays and printed selling appeals of various manufacturers for personal selling. The consumer is still our livelihood; and the more he sees, the more he will buy.

Suggested Policy

I suggest that you keep your shelves fully stocked at all times in order to increase sales of merchandise. It has always been our policy to sell through our retailers and not just to them. Therefore, we want to keep you well posted on the latest developments and surveys which have been brought to light.

Very truly yours,

Frank C. Buckley, Jr.
President

FCB/nlb
Encl.

ENCLOSURE—RESULTS OF SURVEY [1]

On Grocery Product Sales	*Number of Items*	*2 Weeks' Unit Sales Under Normal Conditions*	*2 Weeks' Unit Sales When Shelves Kept Fully Stocked*	*Change %*
Coffee	9	978	1,142	+ 16.8
Frozen foods	31	1,336	2,021	+ 51.2
Paper products and aluminum foil	24	2,953	3,383	+ 14.6
Soap	25	720	836	+ 16.1
Cigarettes	21	1,398	1,602	+ 14.5
Canned beans	16	907	1,035	+ 14.1
Candles	2	112	268	+139.3
Total	128	8,404	10,287	+ 22.4%
On Drug Product Sales				
Total pastes and powders	26	348	479	+ 37.6
Shampoos	22	92	132	+ 43.5
Baby care and first aid	21	167	291	+ 74.0
Total	69	607	902	+ 48.5%
All Products	197	9,011	11,189	+ 24.2%

[1] Figures quoted in this table and report were taken from "New Study Shows Importance of Full Shelves in Supers," *Printers' Ink,* June 5, 1953, p. 43.

To the usual parts of a business letter, in this report the subject line has been added. Although only a few business letters have subject lines, many letter reports contain them. The line may be placed as it is in the example, dropped a line below the salutation, or between the inside address and salutation and flush with the left margin; or it may be centered on the page. Sometimes it may take up two or three short lines and be placed opposite the inside address, where it would balance the address. There are several reasons for using a subject line in a report. It lets the reader know at the outset what the report is about; it gets immediate attention and it is useful in filing the report later.

Subject headings serve as a guide to the reader, letting him know what follows, thus conserving his time in reading the report. For a discussion of subject headings, their use in reports and various possible combinations, the reference section on Appendix page 435 should be checked.

Tables used formally in a letter report should be numbered, given a title, indented and surrounded by space. Figures are arranged in logical columns with headings. Sometimes a spot table which emphasizes a few figures from a larger table is used for emphasis and to help get the point across quickly. The percentages of sales increases are shown in this manner in the sample report. Spot tables are not numbered nor do they have titles; they are used as a paragraph inset. The enclosure gives full results of the survey for further information and use to the reader.

Concluding parts of the letter report are the same as those of a business letter – complimentary close, signature and typist's initials. A second page calls for a heading like that used in the second page of a business letter.

The organization of "Advantages of Fully Stocked Shelves" indicates general characteristics that apply to the organization of most letter reports. The first paragraph is introductory. It mentions the purpose of the survey and introduces the subject of the report. It catches the reader's interest because he is affected by the problem. The next two sections of the report present the important results of the survey and analyze them from the reader's viewpoint. Emphasis here is placed on the way the results affect the reader. The survey findings convince him that he should follow the suggested policy given at the end – that of maintaining fully stocked selves. If he does, the report has accomplished its major purpose. The example report thus follows the simple organizational pattern of beginning with the introduction, presenting facts, interpreting facts and ending with a recommendation, a pattern used generally in short, informal reports. Another commonly used organizational pattern follows these five steps:

(*1*) Authorization for writing the report
(*2*) Statement of problem
(*3*) Summary of findings
(*4*) Development of the report
(*5*) Conclusions and recommendations

The style used in letter reports is factual and definite. The same essentials applicable to all reports and business letters should be adhered to – Completeness, Consistency, Clearness, Conciseness and Correctness. Principles of business letter writing such as using the "you" attitude, emphasizing the positive aspect and being specific should also be appropriately applied. The letter report is one of the most personalized forms of reports, but the degree to which it can be personalized depends upon the relationship of the reader to the writer and the circumstances under which it is used. Used as a means of internal communication in a firm, it is likely to be more formalized and less personal when moving vertically upward to top management than when it is moving downward.

MEMORANDUM REPORTS

The memorandum report is a type of internal communication, usually handling business of a routine nature, but sometimes it is mailed outside the firm. Often it is used for presenting data related to a special problem. In organization, in the use it makes of subject

N. Y. 800L 9-50
PRINTED IN U. S. A.

MEMORANDUM

To | At | Date
From Jean Gordon | At 250 Park Avenue, New York | August 25, 1953

Subject Community Relations News and Notes — Refer to your memorandum dated:

EDITORS USE LOCAL ANNUAL REPORT STORIES

Clippings confirm the fact that editors welcomed the information which most GF units supplied about their operations to supplement newspaper releases on the 1953 annual report.

Some papers used general headlines, but they all used local plant figures in the text. And many papers played these up in headlines. In Waseca, Minn., an agricultural county seat, for instance, the story rated this two-column head on page one:

$860,000 ANNUAL PAYROLL OF
BIRDS EYE PLANT HERE; FIRM
INCREASES SALES FOR 20TH YEAR

In the industrial city of Evansville, Ind., where several large plants also occupy important places in the economy, the story got this one-column head:

IGLEHEART WORKERS GET
$2,346,972 in WAGES

Each headline was calculated to impress even the casual reader with the fact that the particular GF unit in his town makes an important contribution to the community.

* * *

STUDENTS QUIZ LABOR AND MANAGEMENT

Both labor and management representatives met with high school seniors at Manville, N.J., to answer their questions about industry under the sponsorship of Johns-Manville.

Questions which had been raised by students in their classes were used as the basis for panel discussion by executives and union personnel. This first labor-management seminar proved so successful that it has been decided to hold one annually.

Courtesy General Foods Corporation

Memorandum report to general managers of corporation.

headings and in the purpose it may accomplish it is very similar to the letter report. It differs from the letter report chiefly in its form and tone. Although both types of reports are informal and short, the memorandum report is less personal, less formal, shorter and at times more matter of fact than the letter report.

It is most often used to speed up the flow of information from one

- 2 -

PUBLIC RELATIONS IS EVERYBODY'S JOB

In a talk before the American Management Association this summer, President Keith S. McHugh of the New York Telephone Company said:

"Obviously, no one department of a company by itself can do everything that has to be done to carry out the company's policies. No single group of employees can undertake all of the company's public relations activities.

"The public attitude toward a company is a result of many things: the quality of its product or service, its policies and practices and the attitudes and actions of all who represent it, whether on the job or off the job.

"The plain fact is that all employees of all departments are public relations representatives of the company."

* * *

HOULTON, MAINE, PEA INDUSTRY "JUST GROWED"

Current issue of MAINE LINE, magazine of the Bangor and Aroostook railroad, publishes an interesting four-page story of the impressive growth of the pea industry in Houlton, Maine, under the headline: "...it just growed."

The article is illustrated by pictures from the Birds Eye plant, including one of Plant Manager Estel Gallop, Field Supervisor Garold Rideout, and Plant Supervisor Tom Campbell.

What started as a precarious experiment in 1937 with 300 acres of peas has grown into a successful industry in 1953 with 3,000 acres of peas contracted for, the article points out, and continues:

"General Foods provides a useful shot in the arm to Houlton's economy. As an indication, one need only consider the payroll for the six-week summer operation which provides something like $150,000 for the 500 people who daily cross the Bangor and Aroostook main line to the plant. In addition to the payroll for 300 men and 200 women, General Foods pays $125,000 to the farmers who raise the peas."

MAINE LINE has a wide readership among businessmen and civic leaders throughout the area served by the railroad.

* * *

Memorandum report **(Cont.).**

department or office to another within the same company. The information is usually of current, temporary interest. Often it provides figures used in compiling statistics or records what is going on in a firm. It is the means of coordinating the work of various men. Unless it degenerates into a lot of mere paper work and many unnecessary records, it will save the time of a busy executive by providing him with a record of information on the operations of each depart-

- 3 -

WHY HELP RUN COMMUNITY DRIVES?

Business Week commented recently on community relations in general and helping to run community drives in particular.

"To the corporation that runs a plant in one city, or plants in several cities," Business Week said, "community relations has become nearly as important a function of line management as other relations prevalent in business — industrial, public, stockholder."

The article made no bones about the time and energy you have to expend when you head up a community drive. But it pointed out that "businessmen, probably better than anyone else, can put over a successful campaign where even professional fund raisers failed." It concluded:

"The company that is willing to donate the time of a key employe (to head a community drive) can make a much bigger contribution to the community than merely by donating chunks of money.

"Then, there is a selfish angle management should consider If fund drives don't click, there is danger that welfare agencies will be run by people who will put the screws on big employers to carry most of the load

* * *

ROCKLAND FISHERMEN, BIRDS EYE TEAM UP

Fishermen of the Rockland, Maine, trawler fleet and the Birds Eye plant there collaborated in supplying redfish fillets for the Maine Seafood Festival on July 31, August 1 and 2.

Crewmen, owners and captains donated the fish, and Plant Manager Jim Brazier arranged to have them filleted at the Birds Eye plant without cost to the Seafoods Festival. Fried fillets were one of the tasty features of the seafood tray served at what is proclaimed as "the nation's biggest seafood feast." Some 45,000 visitors, including representatives of most of the 48 states and Canada, attended.

Both fishermen and Birds Eye took a bow for this friendly, joint community project, on which they've cooperated for the past three years.

* * *

Memorandum report **(Concl.).**

ment and thus enable him to coordinate the work of the entire firm. It gives him the information and analysis needed for the basis of sound decisions on his part.

The public relations department of General Foods Corporation prepares a monthly memorandum report to keep the general managers up to date on community-relations activities. The information may be used in different ways by the managers who read the report. An example of one of these reports was presented on pages 212 to 214.

Details of form should be observed from the specimen report just presented. There is no letterhead, inside address or salutation such as a business letter would have. Instead are simple "To," "From" and "Subject" lines that convey the needed information. The dateline is used as well as a reference line for referring, if necessary, to previous memorandums. More often than not, however, memorandums are referred to by numbers or by subject matter rather than by dates. Sometimes too a printed letterhead is used at the top of the page; and sometimes there is an identification line or label indicating the department originating the report. Subject headings of one degree are used in the example. There is no complimentary close or signature. Sometimes memorandums are signed or initialed at the end. At other times they may be initialed beside the name on the "From" line. In general the headings are printed like letterheads and filled in as the paper is used. If printed paper is not available the headings are typed at the top of the page. A brief report, which indicates form details of memorandum reports, follows. The form, brevity, tone and purpose of the report should be observed.

SMITH MANUFACTURING COMPANY
1617 South Rendon Street
New Orleans, Louisiana

Date: January 3, 19__

To: Mr. Henry Smith, General Manager

From: John M. Jones, Sales Manager

Subject: Sales by Districts for the Month Ending December 31

Here are the figures of sales reported by districts for the month of December, 19__, which you requested in our telephone conversation yesterday.

District	*December Sales*	*Sales December a Year Ago*
Bookington	$10,465	$12,472
Cooder	15,298	30,364
Northington	25,783	25,750
Misserd	18,590	18,473

Sales dropped about 50% in the Cooder area and about 20% in Bookington. The other two districts held their own. This may be partly explained, in my opinion, by the fact that there is a new sales supervisor in the Cooder area, and half of his sales force are inexperienced men. This does not mean they are to blame for the decrease in sales, but they should be given a chance to prove their worth. I shall see what I can do to help them.

The major purpose of this report is to inform. Sales figures are given with a possible explanation of the decrease in the one instance. There is no need for subject headings because the report is short and contains only a few facts.

Sometimes a memorandum form is used as a cover to route a longer or more formal report through specific channels. It may then contain a request for each reader to initial and send the report on its way to the next person.

Date:

To:

From:

Subject:

Remarks: Please initial after reading and pass report on to the next person.
John Adams
Henry Brown
James Joneson
Alfred Smith

Examples given thus far have not dealt with subjects calling for investigation, nor have they analyzed a problem and recommended a solution. Little investigation is needed for most memorandum reports. There are times, however, when they are used to present an analysis and recommendation in addition to information. The following specimen report indicates this use. Its organizational pattern, as well as its purpose and form, should be examined.

BROWN'S VELVET ICE CREAM, INC.
1332 Baronne Street
New Orleans, La.

October 1, 19__

To: B. T. Brown, Vice President

From: Alfred W. Brown, Jr.

Subject: Failure of Route Drivers to Attend Weekly Safety Meetings

According to your instructions of September 1, 19__, I have investigated the reasons for low attendance of ice cream and milk route drivers at the weekly safety meetings. This report explains why the rate of attendance at the meetings has been so unsatisfactory, and the suggestions at the end of the report should make safety meetings more successful.

The meetings are conducted once each week for the purpose of instructing the ice cream route and milk route truck drivers in traffic safety precautions. Whenever one of the drivers has been involved in an accident of some type, he is brought before the meeting and his accident is discussed by the person presiding over the meeting. Ways in which he might have avoided the accident are pointed out to him and the other drivers. All route drivers are supposed to attend the meetings each week.

At the last four meetings I found that a number of drivers failed to attend. When questioned the following day as to why they failed to show up, they gave the excuse of having had another engagement, or of not having finished their suppers until late. These were the most common excuses. Some of the men who missed the meetings had valid excuses. Still others were out on their routes.

The time and day of the meetings should be changed. At the present time they are being held each Thursday at 7:00 PM. Mondays, Wednesdays, Thursdays and Fridays are "sport" nights either in town or on television. There is boxing both in town and on television on Mondays, Wednesdays and Fridays. There is wrestling both in town and on television on Thursday nights. When asked, the large majority of the drivers favored holding the meetings on Tuesday nights. They also felt that the time of the meetings should be moved up to 7:30 PM. This would give them more time to eat their suppers and get to the meeting. Also most of the drivers are off their routes by this time, and those few who are still on their routes would be excused from attending the meetings.

At the present time drivers who fail to attend a meeting are fined $1.00. Many men who miss the meetings are glad to pay the fine in order to see a good boxing or wrestling match. I suggest that this fine be raised still higher. I do not think that a fine of $5.00 is too high a price to pay for missing a meeting. The proceeds, if any, can be added to the fund for the employees' annual shrimp boil and beer party.

Whenever a man misses a meeting, he should be asked whether he has an excuse. If he thinks that his excuse is valid, he should be made to put it in writing and submit it for approval. In this way he would be exempt from paying the fine if his excuse is approved.

In conclusion, I think that the safety meetings should be moved from Thursday nights at 7:00 to Tuesday nights at 7:30. I further suggest that the fine imposed on a driver for missing a meeting be raised to $5.00, and that if he has an excuse, he be made to put that excuse in writing and submit it to you for your final approval.

I strongly believe that, if these suggestions are followed, the safety meetings will be more successful and most of the drivers will attend them.

BULLETINS

Bulletins are used for both internal and external communication. They are brief and to the point. They nearly always include information of more permanent value than memorandums and are distributed to a sufficient number of readers to warrant their reproduction in quantity. For this reason they are not addressed to any particular person. Nor is any special form necessarily used. Some-

SALES CONTINUE TO INCREASE, EARNINGS IMPROVE

General Foods net sales reached a new high of $324,-243,000 for the six months which ended September 30. Sales for the same period last year were $283,641,000.

A large amount of this $40,602,000 increase was due to the successful promotion of new post war products. Our sale of new products increased $18,700,000—from $33,000,000 last year to $51,700,000 this year.

Included in this group of new products are Instant Maxwell House Coffee, Birds Eye Frozen Orange Juice Concentrate, Swans Down Angel Food Mix, Devil's Food Mix, and Instant Cake Mix, Minute Rice, Jell-O Puddings and Pie Fillings, Post's Sugar Crisp, Cornfetti, and Krinkles, and Baker's 4 in 1 Sweet Cocoa Mix.

Sales of our other products went from $250,-641,000 to $272,543,000 for the six month periods—an increase of $21,902,000. This jump came about mainly as a result of strengthened promotional efforts behind such product lines as Jell-O Desserts, Birds Eye Frosted Foods, and Maxwell House Coffee.

Taxes up 50 per cent

Taxes also set a new high. We provided $19,530.000 for income taxes for the six months, compared with $12,-729,000 for the same period last year. At this rate, our tax bill was roughly three times what we paid in dividends, and nearly two times our net earnings.

Included in our tax bill were $3,224,000 for excess profits taxes. General Foods pays a tax of 82 per cent on everything it earns in the United States above $36,000,-000 annually, or $18,000,000 figured on a six-month basis. Our pre-tax earnings, which also include earnings from some of our foreign operations, were $30,562,000 for the six months.

Earnings equal to $1.91 a share

Despite the higher tax bill, net earnings were up about 28 per cent from the six-month period last year. They amounted to $11,032,000, compared with $8,613,000 the year before. After providing for preferred dividends, earnings were equal to $1.91 a share and $1.47 a share for the respective periods.

Though our earnings improved significantly, they were still well below the $2.75 we earned for the comparable period in calendar 1950, or $2.39 in calendar 1949, when taxes were considerably lower.

Here's how our earnings were used. We distributed $6,683,000 to holders of common stock in the form of two quarterly dividends of 60 cents a share each. We paid two regular 87½-cent dividends on the cumulative preferred stock, totalling $415,000. The balance of our earnings—$3,934,000—was re-invested in the business.

One of the uses of retained earnings is to provide for continued growth. Our major capital expenditures during the six months included further expansion of our Instant Maxwell House coffee operations; additional facilities for producing Swans Down cake mixes, including the new Swans Down Golden Yellow Cake Mix; and construction of General Foods new headquarters in White Plains, New York, which began this Summer and is scheduled for completion in the Spring of 1954.

COMPARATIVE STATEMENT OF EARNINGS
(For periods ending September 30)

	Three months		Six months	
	1952	1951	1952	1951
Net sales	$165,913,000	$146,408,000	$324,243,000	$283,641,000
Earnings before taxes	15,858,000	11,029,000	30,562,000	21,342,000
Income taxes	10,144,000	6,547,000	19,530,000	12,729,000
Net earnings	5,715,000	4,481,000	11,032,000	8,613,000
Earnings a share	$.99	$.77	$1.91	$1.47

Courtesy General Foods Corporation

Monthly bulletin to stockholders.

times they are not even labeled as a bulletin. When they are labeled they have a top form heading similar to the memorandum report. Usually they consist of from one to three pages. Sometimes, however, they are longer and are fastened together as small booklets; in this instance they would have a combination cover and title page on the outside.

A general use for bulletins in most companies is to make announcements. General Foods Corporation, for instance, like other large companies, sends out a news bulletin each month to its stockholders to keep them informed of important company operations and the financial status of the corporation. In the sample issue of the *GF Stockholder News*, its top heading identifies it. It contains news of interest to the stockholders.

Bulletins are used in the same way as memorandum reports, to inform their readers. Louisiana Power & Light Company, for example, issues policy bulletins to its supervisors to keep them informed of personnel policies and changes. The supervisors in turn file the bulletins in policy manuals for reference and inform employees under them of the policy or revision. In the following sample policy bulletin numbered paragraphs have been used for convenient reference.

LOUISIANA POWER & LIGHT COMPANY
POLICY BULLETIN

Date of Issue May 13, 195_

DISTRIBUTION G.O.: WTH-RMS-KJW-ERR-HMW-RWB-WLR-CDB-HLD-ARC-LJO-RAC-TDH-RCP.	SUBJECT: POLICY BULLETINS
STERLINGTON: Supt.–Dept. Heads	SUPERSEDES POLICY BULLETIN(S) OF SUBJECT AND DATE LISTED
DIVISIONS: Mgrs.–Oper. Supts.–Const. Supt.–Ch. Clks.–Sales Mgrs.–Foremen	SUPERSEDED BY POLICY BULLETIN
DISTRICTS: Mgrs.	SUBJECT:_______ DATE:_______

1. From time to time it is necessary to issue Policy Bulletins on matters affecting the operation of the Louisiana Power & Light Company.
2. These bulletins are issued by the executive office or one of the general office departments concerned.
3. This practice will be continued in the future as in the past, but to simplify reference to these bulletins they will be issued on the above Form No. 2393.
4. To prevent occasional overlapping of Policy Bulletins it is recommended that the bulletins carry the signatures of the issuing department head and the approval of this office.
5. Appropriate binders have been ordered for ready reference to these bulletins by those to whom they will be issued. These binders will be distributed as soon as they are received.
6. As you receive Policy Bulletins in the future, please file them alphabetically by subject matter in the binder referred to in No. 5.

7. As bulletins you may have in your binder are superseded by other bulletins, please so indicate on the superseded matter and then transfer them to a section in the binder provided for that purpose.

R. C. Rawls, Vice-President

The top-heading format of the policy bulletin of the Louisiana Power & Light Company is very similar to the top-heading format of a memorandum report. The top heading used by General Foods, however, merely identifies the bulletin by title, volume, number and date. There is no consistency among companies as to the form used for a bulletin or even as to the use of a bulletin. It is important to present its contents in a clear, readable manner, to stick to only one major subject in any one bulletin, to be accurate and to consider the reader and purpose.

BOOKLETS

As a report form booklets are very much like bulletins. In fact some firms use them interchangeably. They do serve the same informative function, and they are used for both internal and external communication. The subject matter of booklets, however, is generally of more than temporary value, and they are reproduced in quantity. Booklets also differ from bulletins in length. They are usually longer than three pages and in some instances practically book length. Instead of having the top-heading identification of a memorandum report or bulletin they resemble books. In this respect they are similar in form to short reports because they have covers, title pages, sometimes tables of contents, and sometimes covering letters or letters of transmittal, depending on their purpose, readers and length.

Booklets run the gamut from formal to informal treatment in their style and general makeup. They should be made so attractive and interesting that they will be sure to be read. When a new employee joins a firm common practice is to give him several informative booklets. One might be on the history of the company, another on employee benefits, another on the company retirement plan, etc. The following selected pages from two booklets used by R. J. Reynolds Tobacco Co. indicate differences between formal and informal booklets. The first examples are from the booklet given to all new employees on the company's retirement plan. Notice the plain formal cover:

The following is taken from the first two pages of the same booklet:

EMPLOYEES' RETIREMENT PLAN
OF
R. J. REYNOLDS TOBACCO COMPANY

BOOKLET OF INFORMATION

INTRODUCTION

The purpose of this booklet is to inform employees in non-technical language as to the benefits provided for them under the Employees' Retirement Plan of the Company. However, this booklet is not a substitute for the Plan and the statements here made are subject to the detailed provisions of the Plan. A copy of the Plan and the Agreement of Trust under the Plan is available to each employee.

The plan provides for payment of retirement allowances to employees who are covered by the Plan and who retire because of age or disability. These retirement allowances are in addition to any old age benefits to which employees are entitled under the Revised 1950 Federal Social Security Law.

In order to provide for payment of the retirement allowances, a Trust Fund has been established which is administered by a Trustee. Each year the Company makes a contribution to this Trust Fund. It is estimated that the contributions made and to be made to the Fund by the Company, together with income on investments held in the Fund, will be sufficient to pay the retirement allowances provided by the Plan.

Employees' Retirement Plan

of

R. J. REYNOLDS TOBACCO CO.

Booklet of Information

Courtesy R. J. Reynolds Tobacco Co.
Simple, formal booklet cover.

GENERAL

Employees Covered

Every regular, full-time employee of the Company is covered by the Plan. However, a person who became an employee after 1946 is not eligible for the benefits of the Plan unless he was less than 50 years of age at the time of his employment.

Retirement Allowance

Retirement allowances are paid monthly. The amount of the allowance depends upon the employee's wage or salary (not including any profit participations or amounts paid by the Company for insurance or retirement benefits) and years of credited service completed before retirement.

Credited Service

Credited service means continuous service and is limited to maximum of 40 years, except that service rendered prior to 1946 by an employee while under age 25 is not included as credited service.

. . . .

The next excerpts are from Reynolds' booklet, "Facts about *Your* Job and Company," which is also given to all new employees. This booklet is informally done with a number of illustrative drawings on nearly every page. Inside an attractive cover, which shows a picture of the main office building at Winston-Salem, North Carolina, is a letter from the president:

R. J. REYNOLDS TOBACCO COMPANY
Winston-Salem, N. C.

Dear

The purpose of this little booklet is to serve as a handy source of information for you about your Company. It tells about its early history and progress, the quality tobacco products upon which our business is based, the benefits each of us as an employee enjoys, and the responsibilities we share together in our work.

Your job is a big part of your life. It affects your future and the future of your family. By working together to make better quality products, we improve our Company and ourselves.

I wish you much happiness and contentment in your part of this job.

Sincerely,

President

On the back of the president's letter in a frame of two shades of blue are these two sentences:

We believe in
Ourselves and in
our Fellow Workers.
We believe in Our
Company and
its Products;
their Good Name
is our Good Name.

The table of contents is presented next, but it is given a more interesting title, "What's Inside."

WHAT'S INSIDE

3

Courtesy R. J. Reynolds Tobacco Company

Interesting table of contents attracts employees' attention.

Two representative pages from the booklet will indicate its informal style, sure to capture the employee's interest.

Benefits and Services to YOU

Your job as a regular employee of this Company brings you more than just the wages you receive. You become eligible for a number of benefits and services which contribute to your well-being, your health and your security.

It is to your interest to know just what these programs are and how they benefit you personally. The several Benefit Plans and Services are referred to below, together with sources of detailed information.

EMPLOYEES' RETIREMENT PLAN

As a contribution to the continued security of regular employees, your Company maintains a Retirement Plan. The plan is supported entirely by the Company at no cost to the employees.

The funds which have already been contributed by your Company to establish this Plan and the additional sums it sets aside each year to maintain the Plan are all placed in trust for the purposes of the Plan and cannot be used for any other purpose.

10

Courtesy R. J. Reynolds Tobacco Company

Inside the employees' booklet.

The booklet you have received on the Retirement Plan outlines its provisions. Your foreman or department head will assist you in getting any additional information you may desire.

GROUP INSURANCE

All regular employees after six months of service have an opportunity to enjoy the protection of a Group Life Insurance Plan at low cost to themselves. Although participation in the plan is voluntary, more than 98% of our eligible employees have subscribed.

Coverage under this plan provides you with insurance benefits in case of sickness, non-occupational accidents, total and permanent disability, and death. You pay your premiums through monthly deductions which you authorize from your pay. Your Company bears a large part of the cost, so the premium you pay for this group protection is extremely low.

Details of this plan are explained in a booklet you have received. Let your foreman or department head know if you have any question on the plan, and he will assist you in obtaining the desired information.

If it becomes necessary for you as the insured to change your beneficiary, by all means do not delay. Simply take your Group Insurance certificate to the Personnel Department, and the change will be arranged.

11

Inside the employees' booklet (Cont.).

FORM REPORTS

Employees in practically every company have probably made the comment at one time or another, "There is simply too much reporting and paper work done around here. It is just so much extra work and should be eliminated." Although some reports are written unnecessarily, many that may seem useless to people who resent having to do them and who do not fully understand their use are really timesavers and provide needed information.

Form reports are used to help cut down on the work of reporting routine information, to keep records and to make decisions. As subject matter and use vary from company to company, so does the form of the report. Printed forms containing appropriate headings calling for blanks to be filled in are used. In this way the information provided in a company is uniform. In reporting the monthly status of group life insurance among its employees, for example, the Louisiana Power & Light Company uses the following form:

LOUISIANA POWER & LIGHT COMPANY
GROUP LIFE INSURANCE REPORT
MONTH OF ________________

	No. of Emps.	*Coverage*	*Company Gift*	*Cost*	*Emp. Contr.*	*Company Contr.*
Executive						
G. O. & Dept. Heads—						
#1						
#2						
Central Billing						
Bldg. Service & Misc.						
Stores & Transformers						
West Bank Division						
Southeastern Division						
Ninemile Point						
Sterlington						
Construction Department						
Sub-Total						
Directors & Legal Staff						
Retired						
Armed Forces						
Sub-Total						
Retroactive Premium Adjustment						
Total						

	Total Amount of P/R	%	Amount	Amount to Be Charged
Constr. Chgs.				
Other				
Totals				

Each month information is presented on a copy of the form; comparisons are made and changes are readily discerned. The information is used for the record and also for analysis and action.

Form 294 15,000 11–53 (Replaces Form 2345)

LOUISIANA POWER & LIGHT COMPANY
INTERVIEW REPORT-------- ELECTRIC

Customer's Name________________ Date Contracted________

Division________ District________ Delivery Point________

Persons Interviewed 1.__________ Position________

2.__________ ________

Where Interviewed________________

(State below: Purpose, Accomplishment and Future Action required)

____
Signature of Company Employee Reporting

Sign and Forward to:
ORIGINAL to President/Vice President
COPY to General Sales Manager/Industrial Sales Manager
COPY to Division Manager/Assistant Division Manager
COPY to Division Sales Manager
COPY to District Manager
COPY to Salesman's File

Courtesy Louisiana Power & Light Company

Form for reporting interviews with customers.

Personnel departments make wide use of form reports for recording facts about employees — not only as records but also as aids in adjusting employees to their jobs and in giving salary increases and promotions. The two examples that follow are used by Swift & Company. The first report is used to rate general office employees as a tie-in with the post-employment interview program. The second

PERSONNEL ANALYSIS REPORT Plant__________ Date__________

Name__________ Position__________ Dept.__________

Birth Date__________ Date Employed__________ Married ☐ Single ☐ Widower ☐ No. Children__________

Education: Grade School ( ); H. S. 1-2-3-4; Business College 1-2; College 1-2-3-4.
(Check number of years in high school and college. If attended college, fill in details.) Degrees__________

Name of College__________ Course Taken__________

Swift & Company Training Completed (Check if completed) S. & Co. Business (YMTC)__________ JIT__________

JMT__________ JRT__________ Safety through Supervision__________ Employe Relations__________ How We Live__________ Conf. Leading Technique__________

Preventive Maint.__________ Swift's Stands. Sys.__________ Swift & Co. Management__________ Others__________

Other Trng. or Educ.__________

Owns or Buying Home: Yes ☐ No ☐ Present Salary__________ Date of Last Merit Increase__________

Experience with the Company

____

____

____

____

____

____

Characteristics

In rating the following qualities, use these symbols: 5 (Outstanding); 4 (Above Average); 3 (Average); 2 (Below Average); 1 (Weak). Rate each oint independently. Usually good men have some weak points and poor men a few strong points.

ABILITY TO GET ALONG WITH PEOPLE: Consider his ability to cooperate, his willingness to accept supervision, and whether he is well liked by fellow workers. __________

ADAPTABILITY: Consider his flexibility. Does he adjust easily to new conditions? __________

APPEARANCE: Consider his dress, facial characteristics, and all-round grooming. __________

DEPENDABILITY: Consider whether he carries out instructions without being checked. Does he readily assume responsibility? __________

ABILITY TO LEARN: Consider how quickly he grasps new ideas and instructions. Does he catch on the first time? __________

QUALITY OF WORK: Consider the correctness of his work and his ability to maintain quality standards consistently. __________

POISE OR BEARING: Consider how well he stands up under pressure; whether he keeps his head; how well he can take criticism. Is he mature? __________

HEALTH: Consider the extent to which his health affects the performance of his duties. Is he physically fit to meet the demands of his job? __________

INITIATIVE: Consider his ability to meet a situation independently. Is he alert for improvements through the development of new ideas and better ways of doing things? __________

LOYALTY: Consider how faithful he is in his support of the company and supervision. Is he resentful and overly critical or does he accept company policy and work accordingly? __________

QUANTITY OF WORK: Consider whether he completes assignments on time. How does his output compare with others? Does he have the will to work? __________

VERBAL EXPRESSION: Consider his ability to express his ideas in a convincing manner both in conversation and in written form. __________

(Over)

PO Form C 586 4-15-52 Printed in U. S. A.

Courtesy Swift & Company

Form for evaluation of employees.

report is on the progress of a new employee and is used also as a part of the interview program in following up his progress in the company.

It is important that form reports be carefully planned so as to secure only the needed information. They must also be clearly

Supervisory or Management Characteristics

The following qualities are to be filled in only on those *employes who supervise others or on those who are ready to assume management responsibilities,* using the same symbols as used on the other side of this sheet.

ABILITY TO DEVELOP MEN: Consider his success in selecting and improving his subordinates. Is he capable in training them to assume specific responsibilities? ________

ANALYTICAL SENSE: Consider whether he can quickly size up a problem relating to markets, products, earnings, savings, policies, or personnel. Can he evaluate facts properly and reach sound decisions that will produce favorable results? ________

LEADERSHIP: Consider whether he has the respect of subordinates; whether he does a good job of delegating work and supervising its execution; whether he gets the maximum efficiency out of the people working for him. ________

OWNERSHIP POINT OF VIEW: Consider whether he is result conscious and makes his decisions in the light of their ultimate effect upon expenses and results. ________

Additional Information

Along what lines can he develop?________ in which department?________

What is his chief weakness?________

____

Have you discussed with him how he is fitting into the organization?________

General Comments:

____

____

____

____

____

Is he available for transfer? Yes ☐ No ☐ If yes, when?________

If not why not?________

Over-all Personnel Analysis ☐ **(Insert symbol that applies as explained below.)**

Analysis by________ **Approved**________ (*Supt. or Auditor*) **Approved**________ (*Manager*)

DEFINITION OF SYMBOLS

Weak

1 —An employe who is unsatisfactory and should be replaced without delay.

Below Average

2A—An employe who is only fairly satisfactory, lacks ability to grow, and therefore should be worked out as soon as can be done so advantageously.

2B—An employe who is only fairly satisfactory, lacks ability to grow, but whose age and years of service entitle him to consideration.

Average

3A—An employe who is doing an average job, is satisfactory on the kind of work he is now doing, but probably lacks ability to grow.

3B—An employe who is doing an average job but looks like good material for development.

Above Average

4A—An employe who is doing better-than-average work but who, because of age or other reasons, lacks capacity for further growth.

4B—An employe who is doing better-than-average work and is the type who should grow with the company in his present or other lines of work.

Outstanding

5A—An employe who is doing excellent work, has experience, but who, because of age or other reasons, cannot take on additional responsibilities.

5B—An employe who is doing excellent work, has experience, and is ready for additional responsibilities in his present or other lines of work.

C 686

Form for evaluation of employees **(Cont.).**

New Employe Progress Report

Name ______ Starting Date ______

Department ______ Position ______

Starting Salary ______ Transferred to ______

Test Scores ______

Personnel Ratings	Training Class Grades

Appearance

Well-groomed				
Satisfactory				
Somewhat careless				
Slovenly				

Personality Characteristics

Attitude	Personality	Poise	Adaptability

Self-Improvement and Leadership Activities

______

Suggestions and Remarks

______

(Continue if necessary on reverse side)

Interviewer and Date ______

PO Form C 3610 9-16-46

Printed in U. S. A.

Courtesy Swift & Company

Form for reporting progress of new employees.

worded so the person filling them out can do so quickly and accurately. Whenever the information is to be tabulated and compiled into a larger report, the forms should be planned to make tabulation of figures possible.

SHORT REPORTS

The body of the short report described in the rest of this chapter resembles that of the formal, long report treated in Chapter 16 in organization, contents and treatment. The major differences between the two concern scope, purpose, length and the inclusion or exclusion of prefatory elements. Most of the prefatory elements of the long report are omitted in the short report, and the writer begins the development of his subject at the outset.

To facilitate the writing of effective reports, most companies devise report writing manuals for the use of their report writers. Although details of form and of developing the text differ among business firms, there are certain elements that are commonly agreed upon. The comments made by Caterpillar Tractor Co. in the manual, "A Guide for Writing Technical Reports," used in their research department, typifies the general practice of most firms. The principles are so appropriately presented by them that they are worthy of inclusion here:

In general it is recommended that the report contain the following divisions, when applicable, in the order named:

1. Title
2. Introduction
3. Conclusions
4. Summary of Results
5. Recommendations
6. Discussion
7. Description of Apparatus and/or Details of Procedure
8. Signature of Writer
9. Performance Curves, Photographs, Drawings, Sketches

1. Title

The title should state clearly, concisely, and specifically the overall scope of the project. This title should convey the same meaning, as much as possible, as that implied on the Job Sheet. Do not use such terms as "to determine," "to test," "to observe," and "to evaluate."

As an example, we might say:

Performance Characteristics of a Self-priming Water Pump

If all the desired information has been obtained and no further work is contemplated, the results may be compiled in one report under this title. This report will be called Report No. 1 and the title written:

Performance Characteristics of a Self-priming Water Pump
Report No. 1

If in the course of the investigation, it is found that several major avenues of investigation are necessary, the results of these several phases will no doubt be reported in several progress reports. In order not to lose sight of the original objective, the title should be stated in full followed by the title of the progress report. For example:

Performance Characteristics of a Self-priming Water Pump
Report No. 1

Failure of Shaft Seal to Properly Control Leakage

In this way we will maintain the overall objective and highlight a particular phase of the test. This same scheme should be used for all succeeding reports under a particular project.

2. Introduction

In writing the "Introduction," the writer should keep in mind that many of the readers of the report have had no contact with the work prior to reading the report. He should present reasons for the investigation, its relation to other work in the laboratory or field, expected use of the results and, in general, any background information that will equip the reader to see the investigation in its true perspective.

3. Conclusions

A conclusion, as we use it in the report, is your *opinion* which is based upon consideration of the data obtained in the investigation. A conclusion should be brief and to the point and should not include supporting evidence which normally appears under "Discussion." It is your best *interpretation* about what has or has not been accomplished.

Conclusions and recommendations must be based on sound deduction and interpretation of data. Many times data can be interpreted in various ways, and the interested parties may disagree with the conclusions of the report writer. Rather than attempt to dictate conclusions and recommendations in such instances, the other interested parties should indicate such differences of opinion in their comments on the report flyleaf. These comments should be restricted to pertinent information and should not reflect personal prejudices.

It is well to bear in mind that normally conclusions are based on information obtained in one specific project and that they apply directly to this one project. Therefore it is not good sense to word your conclusions or recommendations so that they may be interpreted as applying to all allied subjects not covered by the current project. Often, however, these conclusions may apply to other related subjects not necessarily investigated in the current project. In such cases, broader conclusions are desirable but must still be closely related to the project under investigation.

In general a conclusion should be more than a simple statement of an observed fact. For example, in a project calling for the determination of cause of failure of the 6B5523 elbow, the following statement would not constitute a conclusion but would be a simple statement of fact: "The 6B5523 elbows were found broken on both machines at the flanges adjoining the inlet manifold."

Descriptive information of this type should be included in the "Discussion" section of the report. However, from the illustration cited above, any one or all of the following conclusions could be drawn:

1. The design, in general, is not satisfactory, as there is no way to support the manifold to prevent failure.
2. The design is unsatisfactory since there is no support for the overhanging weight.
3. The material is not sufficiently strong to support the overhanging weight.

Although, for the sake of the reader, conclusions have an early place in the report, it is well not to formulate your conclusions until your discussion has been written or at least well outlined. When more than one conclusion is drawn, it is well to put each one down separately and enumerated in 1, 2, 3 order.

4. Summary of Results

In some cases the nature of the work is such that conclusions cannot be drawn. Such a project might call for the determination of the capacity of a fuel tank. When the work is completed the result should be set apart and labeled as "Summary of Results."

"The capacity of the 42B4785 fuel tank was 42 gal. at 68°F."

In certain types of projects, such as literature or data survey, diversified opinion or lack of data does not allow the writer to arrive at justifiable conclusions. In such cases a short synopsis of the information gained may be included under "Summary of Results." This information should be enumerated in 1, 2, 3 order.

5. Recommendation

Recommendations should represent the writer's best thinking as to the direct application of his findings to the solution of problems pertinent to the project. They can include your ideas about the continuance or termination of a project, suggested changes in test materials or procedure, the suggestion that the new material or design be adopted for production. Since your recommendations properly are based on your conclusions, these two subjects are closely related.

Like Conclusions and Summary of Results, Recommendations should be enumerated 1, 2, 3.

6. Discussion

Discussion is the detailed reporting of the many things that lead up to conclusions and recommendations. What you write under this heading should support and explain your conclusions and recommendations.

The Discussion may well begin by including and amplifying those subjects touched upon under Introduction. This is particularly true if these subjects need further description and explanation in order to thoroughly acquaint the reader with the premise.

An orderly arrangement of all the significant, pertinent observations should then be made in full detail, together with the important figures from the data sheets. (Tabulation of original data in its entirety rarely, if ever, should appear in the discussion.) Coherency and readability are desirable here rather than a simple enumeration of facts and observations. *This discussion of the observation might well be considered as the body of the Discussion.* Details relating to apparatus or procedure may be discussed here if they have an important bearing on the interpretation of results.

When the discussion includes figures extracted from the data sheets or from curves or charts plotted therefrom, make reference to the source. This is best done by such parenthetical indication as "(See Liner wear data on Sheet B.)" or "(See curve on Sheet D.)" Similarly, when describing a condition of a part that has been photographed, the clarity of the report and the ease of locating the right photograph is helped by following your description with, "(See photograph of piston No. 4 on Sheet E.)."

In order to have the record complete, a paragraph at the end of Discussion can be devoted to describing the status of the test as it was when you completed your work on which the report was written.

7. Description of Apparatus and Details of Procedure

In this section the writer should present a description of the equipment and methods used in the investigation. The purpose of such a discussion is twofold; first, it provides a record of the instrumentation and methods used and second, it gives interested parties an understanding of the methods used. Details, step-by-step recounting of the procedures used in the investigation should be avoided unless they have an important bearing on the results.

The Description of Apparatus should include the major items of apparatus used, including serial number, if any. (Minor items, such as thermometers, buckets, rubber hose, etc. need not be listed.) Photographs and sketches are particularly useful in discussing the apparatus and the details of procedure.

8. Signature of Writer

   In order to lend greater legal stature to the report, all copies must be signed by the writer on the final page of the body of the report.

9. Performance Curves, Photographs, Drawings, Sketches

   Drawings, sketches, photographs and graphical representation of results add greatly to a report's value. To be most effective these various illustrations should be well integrated with the text material. It is important to refer the reader specifically to the various illustrations in such a way that they serve to illustrate or amplify the text material. Once referred to a particular illustration, the reader should find there all the information necessary for his complete understanding of the illustration. This can be accomplished by care in labeling and lettering. All curve sheets and other original material should be signed and dated.

   Particular attention should be given to titling curve sheets so as to make clear what is being presented in the plotted curves. As an example a title might read "Comparison of Performance of 6B5647 and 7B5148 Water Pumps." Although such a title probably would be an accurate statement of the nature of the investigation, it does not tell the reader anything about the pumps being compared. A more desirable form of the title would be "Comparison of Performance of Self-priming Centrifugal (6B5647) and Gear Type (7B5148) Water Pumps." In general titles should be made simple and explicit. Detailed information relative to parts or machines mentioned in the title should be presented in the text of the report or in footnotes on the curve sheet.

A sample report written according to the instructions just given, and presented also as a part of Caterpillar's guide for writing reports, follows:

CATERPILLAR TRACTOR CO. RESEARCH DEPARTMENT

FILE NO. 1S REPORTED BY JOHN FLERTUS 11–16–48

OBSERVED BY R. A. RINDER AND JOHN FLERTUS

9–1–48 to 11–9–48

PERFORMANCE CHARACTERISTICS OF A CENTRIFUGAL SELF-PRIMING WATER PUMP

REPORT NO. 2

THE SELF-PRIMING ABILITY AND CAPACITY OF THE 109876 PUMP

JOB NO. 6104–36A
ORDER NO. 93–1042
JOB SUPV. R. C. BROWN

INTRODUCTION

Cooling requirements of our 4 ¾-inch bore engines have made necessary the design of a self-priming centrifugal water pump of increased capacity. This was indicated in File 9517R. Report No. 1 under this file number has revealed changes that improve the priming ability of the pumps.

In order to incorporate these changes in the 109876 water pump, which is soon to be released for production, a check was made of the priming ability of this pump. This report covers the self-priming ability and capacity of the 109876 pump. The actual capacity was determined to provide verification of the original design calculations and to record the pump output for future reference.

CONCLUSIONS

1. The 109876 pump will prime faster than the original prove design 100351 pump throughout the speed range, if minor changes are made in the pump housing.
2. One of the major considerations in the design of a self-priming water pump housing should be to provide for the free discharge of air contained in the water system as the pump is started.

SUMMARY OF RESULTS

1. The priming speeds were slower than expected in the speed range of 1200–1400 rpm.
2. The suction lift of the pump was 7¾ feet and the inlet pipe length was 22¼ feet.
3. Pump impeller face clearance was 0.034 inches for this test.

RECOMMENDATIONS

1. Changes in the 109876 water pump housing as shown on Layout CP519 should be made.
2. For ease of assembly and disassembly, the use of a straight key for driving the impeller is urged, along with increased wrench clearance for the 119975 bearing mounting bolts.
3. A shoulder in the 119382 bearing should be added to provide a stop for the 119381 seal. This would provide the seal from being pushed in far enough to block off the oil drain passage.

DISCUSSION

The 109876 pump primed in faster times than were reported on

File 9517R for the original prove design 100351 pump. However, in the speed range of 1200–1400 rpm the priming times were slower than expected. Changes were made in the pump housing as shown on Layout CP519 to improve the priming performance in this range. The pump capacity agreed within 2–3% of the calculated design values over the entire speed range.

A 109876 pump was assembled for testing. It was found that installation of the impeller was difficult to perform with the 119354 seal plate assembly because of the use of a Woodruff key in the pump tapered shaft. With this type of key the seal plate had to be slipped over the key before the impeller was installed on the shaft. Alignment and engagement of the seal plate driving ears with the openings in the impeller was difficult and time consuming. Removal after the pump had been used and dirt deposits had accumulated around the ears caused damage to the seal plate since the plate must slip out of the impeller, and will not come off over the Woodruff key. The use of a straight key will eliminate this difficulty.

The 119382 bearing has a counterbore of 2.000–1.998 in which a 119381 lip-type seal presses. It is possible to install this seal so that the oil drain passage would be blocked off. A shoulder to prevent pressing the seal in too far seems desirable.

As the clearance on the attaching bolts for the 119975 bearing is not sufficient for a socket wrench, an open end wrench must be used for installation and removal. Increasing the wrench clearance would result in faster and easier assembly and disassembly.

After assembly the 109876 pump was mounted on the 15 HP dynamometer for the priming and capacity tests. Inlet and outlet piping of 2-inch diameter was provided. The suction lift was 7¾ feet and the inlet pipe length was 22¼ feet. These dimensions serve as a comparative guide as to the volume of air the pump must handle during the priming process. See Sheet B for this piping arrangement.

In running the priming performance it was found that priming time in the 1200–1400 rpm speed range was not as good as was expected. An observation window of Lucite was installed in the top of the pump housing under chamber to observe the priming water turbulence. It was found that with the pump running the upper chamber completely filled, except for an air cavity near the discharge volute. The elimination of this air pocket was attempted by using various baffles with limited success.

The use of baffles changed the pump-priming characteristics so that an improvement at 1200–1400 rpm resulted in slower priming at other speeds.

With the removal of a capscrew holding the Lucite cover (permitting the entrapped air to escape) the pump primed well throughout the speed range. This indicated that the air in the system was not being discharged properly during the priming period.

An auxiliary tank was mounted on top of the upper chamber. This provided a free air space above the level of the water during priming and allowed the air to escape through the outlet line. Performance comparable to that obtained by removing the capscrew resulted.

The final modification of the pump housing to incorporate a means of eliminating the air pocket is shown on Layout CP519.

The priming times as shown on Sheet C were obtained by measuring the time interval from the starting of the dynamometer until water was discharged from the outlet pipe; thus the pump was penalized somewhat for the acceleration time of the dynamometer. The inlet piping was drained before each trial to eliminate extra water being trapped. The method used has been followed on all self-priming pump tests and provides a good comparison of the various units.

The piping arrangement (see Sheet B) as used for the priming test was modified to include a three-way valve and a weighing tank. While a pressure gauge is shown on the outlet of the pump a mercury manometer was used here until the outlet pressures became too large for the manometer.

From the curves of head versus discharge shown on Sheet A, it will be seen that there is a rapid falling off of the head at the maximum water flow obtainable with this piping setup. Cavitation is responsible for this condition, but since this is out of the pump's normal operating range no attempt was made to determine if the inlet piping were responsible.

Pump impeller face clearance was 0.034 inches for this test.

DESCRIPTION OF APPARATUS

109876 Centrifugal Self-priming Pump
15 H.P. Electric Dynamometer No. 819
No. 236 Fairbanks Scale

John Flertus

SHEETS INCLUDED

A–Head vs. Discharge Curves
B–Piping Diagram
C–Priming Times at Various Speeds
D–Photograph of 109876 Self-priming Centrifugal Water-Pump Housing

REMARKS, DISCUSSIONS AND DECISIONS
BY PERSONS READING THIS REPORT

The trend among business firms today is to present conclusions, summary of results and recommendations early in the report. Busy readers can get at the most important parts first then, and in a number of cases do not read the detailed discussion. Beginning a report with conclusions or recommendations is psychologically useful when the reader is familiar with the background of the problem and is interested primarily in the results and action suggested.

In contrast to the psychological order of development of the subject is the logical order in which the background of the study is presented in the introduction, which includes an explanation of purpose, objectives, procedures, definitions, nature of the problem, etc. Next the facts and results are presented and analyzed. They are followed by the conclusions and recommendations. The logical order is used whenever the reader needs to have the background of the problem presented to him to understand the results more easily. It also takes the reader along the investigator's steps to lead him to the same conclusions. A sample report using the logical order of development is presented on the following pages. Here also a formal title page and letter of transmittal are used as prefatory elements, and a bibliography supplements the report text.[1]

---

[1] For a discussion of the title page and letter of transmittal, see Chapter 16, pp. 254 and 260.

HOUSING OUTLOOK FOR NEW ORLEANS, LOUISIANA

An Estimate of Home Construction in New Orleans, Louisiana, for 1953

Prepared for

MR. LEON KLINGER
Vice-President
New Orleans Association of
Homestead Loan Agencies

Prepared by

ALBERT CAPRONI, JR.
Director of Market Analysis
ABC Research Corporation

New Orleans, Louisiana

19 December 1952

ABC RESEARCH CORPORATION
628½ Webster Street
New Orleans, Louisiana

19 December 1952

Mr. Leon Klinger
New Orleans Association of Homestead Loan Agencies
Box 274
New Orleans, Louisiana

Dear Mr. Klinger:

As requested by your letter of November 12, I have completed the report on the housing outlook for New Orleans for the year 1953. In this report I have endeavored to present only those factors which could cause sizeable changes or fluctuations in home construction.

Government regulations pertaining to the financing of new-home purchases and material controls and their effect on new-home construction are considered in detail. Home construction under rent control and under the absence of rent control is analyzed to a considerable extent. Since its removal is entirely conjectural, it was necessary to view both sides of the question.

Other factors that were considered as influencing home construction are the growth in population and the condition and number of existing dwelling units. Present economic conditions of New Orleans and an estimate of those conditions during 1953 were analyzed with respect to their effect on home construction.

As you well know, any predictions regarding the expected home construction for a future year are considerably limited in their exactness. However, I have attempted to be as objective as possible in preparing this estimate of home construction for 1953.

I hope you will find this report complete and adequate for your needs. If you desire any additional information, please feel free to call on us.

Sincerely yours,

Albert Caproni, Jr.
Director, Market Analysis

HOUSING OUTLOOK FOR NEW ORLEANS, LOUISIANA

Introduction

The purpose of this report is to aid the members of the New Orleans Association of Homestead Loan Agencies in preparing their operating plans for 1953 by providing estimates on home construction in the New Orleans area during the coming calendar year.

This report is concerned primarily with construction of homes in the New Orleans area during 1953. Parts of the report, however, are devoted to home construction for the United States as a whole, home construction during 1951 and 1952, and certain factors of rent control which have a bearing on home construction.

Whenever any year is cited, that year is the calendar year unless otherwise stated. As the research for this report was completed on December 7, 1952, complete figures for home construction for 1952 and an up-to-date forecast for 1953 were not available.

The information used in the preparation of this report was gathered from government reports, current magazines, and books related to housing. The report is based to a large extent on the available data for recent years. The conjectural nature of the report limits its exactness to a considerable extent; however, it is believed that the objective analysis of the facts herein lead to a reasonably accurate estimate of home construction in the New Orleans area during the coming year.

Factors Influencing Home Construction

There are a number of factors that influence home construction. Outstanding among these are government regulations pertaining to financing, rent control and materials; population growth and the increased need for housing; and the prosperity or lack of it for the nation and, in this case, New Orleans and its environs.

Government Regulations

World War II and the post-war period have given the United States more regulations pertaining to home construction than ever before in the history of the nation. These regulations and their effect on home construction are considered in the following order: 1) financing the purchase of a home by the prospective home-owner, (2) rent control and its effect on the number of houses for sale and on the construction of new homes and (3) regulations affecting the amount of materials available for home construction.

(The discussion of government regulations and their effect on home construction has been omitted here. The report continues with its analysis of other factors influencing home construction.)

Population Growth and Housing Need

Population. As population grows, the need for housing grows with it. As of April 1, 1950, New Orleans had a population of 686,700. In September 1952, population was estimated at 712,600. As the director of the research department of the Chamber of Commerce of New Orleans pointed out, "From available figures . . . it is evident that the high birthrate which began during World War II days has continued without interruption in the postwar years. The study also shows that the population increase in the New Orleans area continued at an all-time high rate. There is also a trend to suburban living in the region."[1]

Housing Need. "In simple language an estimate of housing needs is nothing more than an indication of how much safe, sanitary, acceptable housing we will need by some specified future *date,* if all the families who will want housing are to have decent homes."[2] While there were no reliable estimates of the housing need in New Orleans, a reasonably satisfactory estimate of the need can be computed by dividing the total population (712,600) by an arbitrary number of persons per house. Assuming four persons per house, New Orleans needs 178,150 houses. This is relatively close to the actual number of houses in New Orleans, which is 173,608. However, of that 173,608, there are 43,690 houses that have no private bath and/or running water and/or are dilapidated as shown by Table II.

TABLE II

Condition and Plumbing Facilities of New Orleans Housing—1950

Subject		*Number*
All dwelling units		173,608
Number reporting		170,082
With private bath, not dilapidated		126,392
No private bath, with running water, not dilapidated	14,293	
No running water or dilapidated facilities	29,397	
No private bath or dilapidated one		43,690
Condition or plumbing facilities not reported		3,526

SOURCE: *1950 United States Census of Housing,* U. S. Department of Commerce, Bureau of the Census, U. S. Government Printing Office, Washington, D. C., 1952, p. 3.

The above table indicates that, although there seems to be a sufficient *number* of houses for the population of New Orleans, there is not enough "safe, sanitary, acceptable" housing. It is improbable that any major changes will be made in the number of substandard dwelling units during 1953 unless additional low-cost municipal housing is developed.

(The discussion of economic conditions in the report has been omitted here. The report continues with the conclusions that were reached.)

Conclusions

A great many factors will influence the amount of home construction in New Orleans during 1953. The most prominent ones are government regulations, size of population and income.

Government regulations regarding the financing of homes have been substan-

[1] "CHAMBER ESTIMATES METROPOLITAN POPULATION 712,600 AS OF SEPT. 1ST," *Chamber of Commerce News Bulletin,* October 17, 1952, p. 2.

[2] E. E. Ashley, *How Big Is the Housing Job? How the Figures Are Arrived At and What They Mean,* U. S. Government Printing Office, Washington, D. C., 1951, p. 1.

tially relaxed through the suspension of Regulation X. Eased restrictions should cause an increase in the effective demand for housing and should increase sales of houses in the upper-price brackets. If rent control continues through 1953, it may continue to exert a downward pressure on the sale of new houses by causing landlords to sell old houses at an uncontrolled price rather than renting at a specified ceiling. If rent control is discontinued, tenants may buy homes rather than pay higher rent. Government regulation of materials will be substantially reduced by April 1, 1953, if not sooner.

New Orleans' population is continuing its growth, and the need for housing is growing with it. Furthermore, there is a trend to suburban living. While there seems to be an adequate number of dwelling units for the population. 25.7% of those units are in substandard condition. However, it is doubtful that residents of those units will be able to find new houses within the price brackets that they can afford.

Economic conditions in New Orleans and the rest of Louisiana seem extremely favorable to a continued high housing-construction rate. Large amounts of capital expenditures in connection with national defense should keep income at a high level.

Government regulations regarding the financing of new homes and the supplies available will encourage the construction of new homes. Rent control should exert a slight downward pressure on sales of new homes. Population growth and the inadequacy of present housing create a need for housing; but it may not be expressed in an effective market demand. Income should continue at a high level. All of these factors together indicate that home construction in 1953 will be at least as high as in 1952, with a more-than-likely possibility that home construction in 1953 will exceed the level of 1952 by 10 to 20%.

(The report in its original form contained a bibliography which has been omitted here.)

A third short report form for presenting material is exemplified in the informational report published by *Boys' Life* magazine and reproduced in part here. The report is of special use to advertisers in reaching the youth market.

THEY WILL INHERIT AMERICA

An Independent Survey and Report on the Opinions of Boys in America. Sponsored by BOYS' LIFE, the official magazine of the Boy Scouts of America.

Courtesy Boy Scouts of America

Combined cover and title page of informal, short report.

A WORD FROM THE BUSINESS MANAGER OF BOYS' LIFE

This report will tell you how the boys of America think on a variety of the issues vital to our life today. It will also give their opinions on some basic industrial problems; their knowledge of the world about them; their ideas and preferences for the future.

It is the desire of BOYS' LIFE to have this report convince you of the ideological strength and the deep convictions American boys have in the principles of democracy. They stand a challenge to American industry to keep them informed on the progress of our institutions and the constant need to work for their maintenance. Since their training has already begun, it is the responsibility of American industry to make sure they continue to believe in and fight for the ideals and principles of free enterprise that help make America strong and her people free.

Letter of transmittal.

HOW THIS SURVEY CAN BE OF USE TO YOUR COMPANY

The following is a working model of the high points of the survey. For the purposes of clarity and conciseness, tabulations have been digested to give only pertinent and representative findings of the whole. However, full and complete tables and statistics are available to all interested in making further analyses. Such additional information as economic status, age, geographic area, urban versus rural, and Scout-non-Scout tabulations of the various questions can be prepared to satisfy the requirements of specific companies concerned with phases of the boy market. BOYS' LIFE is prepared to provide these valuable cross-tabulations on specific questions to authorized companies without cost.

Introduction.

Only a bare majority of the boys have already made up their minds about the work they'll do when they get older. Yet, almost all of them think about the problem.

Direct personal interest and appeal far outweighs other reasons, such as advancement opportunities, good pay or family influence in the choice of their future vocations.

THE MEANING OF SUCCESS?—In terms of weekly earnings, the boys consider $121.50 a good measure of success. Although 15-year-old B. A. of Houston, Texas, a glaring individualist, told us, ". . . would like to be in mortgaging and banking cause it pays well. Would like to earn $3,000 a week."

THEIR VOCATIONAL PREFERENCES—The boys want to be everything from F.B.I. men to professional Masters of Ceremonies but significant is the fact that the largest single group (more than 30%) will become engineers and scientists.

What sort of work do you think you will do when you get older?

	Number of Boys	Percentage
Engineering	149	21.2%
General and Civil (92); Electrical (17); Mechanical (6); Aeronautical (9); Radio, TV (3); Drafting (6); Building, Construction (5); Chemical (4); Other (7)		
Professional	74	10.5
Doctor (29); Lawyer (21); Dentist (11); Architect (10); Veterinarian (3)		
Scientific Work—Research	38	5.4
Forestry, Conservation	36	5.1
Farming	26	3.7
Aviation (Pilot)	25	3.6
Professional Sports	24	3.4
Business	24	3.4
Own Business (12); Business Man (8); Advertising (1); Banking (1); Store Executive (2)		

(A specially prepared "Analysis of Vocational Aspirations of Boys who want to do Engineering & Scientific Work," based on a cross-tabulation of survey questions, is available to authorized companies on request.)

Body of report.

THE INFLUENCE OF NEWS MEDIA—Newspapers and radio still top the heap when it comes to providing news and information on national and world affairs. Despite the fact that 49.0% of the boys have TV sets (May 1952 BOYS' LIFE Survey), television ranks a poor fifth, behind newspapers, radio, school and magazines, as a source of current events.

AND FINALLY, ARE YOU A BOY SCOUT . . . IF SO, WHY?—Almost three-quarters of the boys are. And primarily for two good reasons . . . adventure and education. They go all out for the outdoor life, hiking, cooking, crafts, health and safety . . . just those things the Scout Movement itself stresses in its programs and activities.

IT IS THE INTENTION OF BOYS' LIFE to provide all interested companies with actual detailed breakdowns of questions, cross tabulations, and additional statistical findings that can be gleaned from this survey.

We believe there is a wealth of material on boy opinion of the various topics covered as related to specific company and industry problems in the youth field. We are therefore prepared to provide assistance to all authorized companies requiring further analyses and look forward to the opportunity to do so.

SURVEY FACTS AND A STATEMENT BY A. S. BENNETT-CY CHAIKIN, INCORPORATED, RESEARCH CONSULTANTS — Painstaking preparation was applied to the design of the questionnaire in this survey since it had to be understood by all the lads in the BOYS' LIFE Reader Panel 12-18 age span. The thorough care and thought given to the wide range of questions on diverse subjects reflects a deep interest in the importance of the information the boys were asked to supply.

The method used in this study, as in all BOYS' LIFE Reader Panel studies, was the mail technique. On June 23, 1952, questionnaires accompanying explanatory letters were sent to 1,250 members of the Reader Panel which is composed of a truly representative cross-section of the circulation of BOYS' LIFE.

The response was 56% or 702 questionnaires, an unusually high return particularly since no special inducements were used in this Panel mailing—and no follow-up letters were sent. Moreover, because of the season of the year when the survey was conducted, the cut-off date for the survey returns was extended to September when most all boys had returned from vacations.

Questionnaire design, tabulation and analysis of returns were all handled by A. S. Bennett-Cy Chaikin, Inc., research consultants to the BOYS' LIFE Reader Panel.

Body of report (Cont.).

PROBLEMS

1. You are the branch manager of the Nola Auto Equipment Company, 722 Bridge Street, Memphis, Tennessee. You are having trouble with the knee-action replacement parts for Summit cars. Write a letter report to Mr. Chester J. Gray, Sales Manager, National Auto Equipment Company, 1222 Michigan Avenue, Chicago, Illinois.

In preparing to write this letter, you have made some mental observations and jotted down a few notes on a scratch pad so that you wouldn't forget to include all of the facts in your letter:

. . . having trouble with knee-action replacement units for Summit cars

. . . 50% of customers have complained about units in letter or in person, and a great many have returned them

. . . common complaint: units too stiff

. . . called in Mr. Pratt, manufacturer's representative, who inspected returned units

. . . Pratt said units not defective; but evidently installers didn't make radius rod adjustment properly

. . . instructions are included with units, but apparently disregarded

. . . evidently three reasons for complaints—many installations made by car-owners or unqualified mechanics, average customer fails to read instructions, and car-owner fails to realize any new unit will be stiff until driven a few thousand miles

. . . informed customers, but complaints continue, some accompanied by repair bills

. . . made adjustments in some cases anyway, cost more than original sale price

. . . will send Gray list of complaints, adjustments

. . . tell him business good lately, this spring's 12% increase over last year will hold through summer—maybe

2. Most of the following topics lend themselves to either a letter or a memorandum report. Select a topic and write the report:

a. An analysis of the menus at your school's cafeteria or dining hall during a week
b. A statement of expenses of a team or other group on a trip
c. An analysis of your study hours for a week
d. An analysis of the time you spent in recreation for a week
e. An analysis of degree requirements in your school
f. The financial statement of a bank
g. Drinking fountains in a public building
h. Bulletin boards in a particular building
i. Conditions in the student lounge
j. An account of an exhibit
k. Your hobbies
l. Summary of a report or article read

3. The following topics call for a short report, somewhat longer than a letter or memorandum. Select a topic and write the report. You may assume necessary details of the situation giving rise to the report. In most instances you will need to gather data for your analysis.

a. Increase in enrollment in your school
b. The organization of a department in a factory or some business firm

c. A statement and explanation of a week's production in a small business concern
d. The recreation room in a plant
e. A company's library facilities
f. The layout in an office
g. An analysis of title pages in 12 reports
h. An analysis of 12 letterheads
i. Fraternity rushing rules
j. Scholastic standing of fraternities or sororities at your school
k. Eligibility rules for ________
l. Your college expenses

4. Your company is planning to purchase a postage meter, an addressograph, an accounting machine, an electric typewriter, a projector, a mimeograph and some other business machines. One of them will be used in connection with the work for which you are responsible. Investigate several brands of the machine and prepare a report recommending the best one.

5. On beginning work as research director in the Blank Company, you discover that the clerical staff is very inconsistent in its typing of reports. Prepare a memorandum setting forth some principles and rules of mechanics for their guidance.

6. Prepare a report for your dean on some school problem and its solution. Possible subjects include registration, advising, grading, visiting speakers, assembly programs, business conferences, spring vacation, examinations, scholarships, honors and awards, activity clubs, etc.

7. Write a report to the general office manager of the Lawton Rubber Company, recommending the action he should take in the situation that follows.

The general office of the Lawton Rubber Company employs 185 people. Employees are hired on the basis of interviews and tests. Successful applicants are on probation for three months, during which time they are given on-the-job training under the direction of their department supervisors. Each person in the office is considered every six months for a pay increase; but he may be passed over if the department head does not recommend him. If a pay increase is allowed in the plants of the company, which are unionized, the company attempts to make a corresponding increase in the office.

In the Cost and Factory Accounting Department are four women who have been with the company for five to seven years. Three men, in this same department, have been with the company for about the same length of time. The senior cost accountant and the factory accountant, who are the supervisors of the department, have been changed twice in the last three years; and in each case the positions have been filled by younger men from outside the office staff. The management, while recognizing the worth of the older staff members, has felt that the employees in the department were not eligible for promotion.

The women employees of the department have been particularly displeased with this action; and it has had a noticeable effect on their work. The department supervisors and the office manager have conferred several times to discuss the excessive amount of talking and visiting that has been going on between the older members of the accounting department. Their topic of conversation is well known to the rest of the office force, and it is feared that it will result in a general morale problem.

Problem: What action should the department supervisors and office manager take?

Problem Analysis: Here are some probable courses of action. What are the arguments for and against each proposal?

a. The offending employees should be discharged.

b. The office manager should send a letter to all employees, asking that they refrain from excessive talking and visiting.

c. He should call in the men and women concerned and ask them to discontinue this practice.

d. He should attempt to break up the "talking and visiting" employees by transferring some of them to other departments.

8. You are employed by an automobile insurance company.

a. Prepare a report form to be sent to the office by your representative who investigates accidents and claims.

b. Prepare a letter or memorandum to be sent to the policyholders telling them what to do if they have an automobile accident.

9. Many people in the middle-income bracket find themselves confronted with the problem of how they can best use the money they earn. The high cost of living forces them to stretch income to meet expenses. The publicity awarded this condition has made them budget conscious. As a result the man in the street has benefited by the use of wise-spending procedures and has saved a little for reserve. Now he has to decide how he can invest his money so it will be available when needed and also work for him to yield a profit while he has no need for it. He has a natural fear of losing his money on the stock market; and if he decides to invest in stocks, he doesn't know how to go about it.

Analyze and compare for him the different means and types of investments. Let him know of the opportunities of the stock market for the small investor. Assume that you are an investment house and that a client has asked you for the above information. Prepare the report you would give him.

10. The situation presented in Problem 9 is a common one; and since your investment firm has a number of similar requests, you decide to print a booklet for distribution to prospective investors. Write the material for this booklet.

CHAPTER *16*

Format and Arrangement of Formal, Long Reports

A FORMAL STYLE AND A PRESCRIBED FORMAT HAVE BEEN established for the formal, long report. The treatment of its contents differs, however, depending on company practice as well as on the type and length of report. In order to avoid stereotyped report form there should be variation from report to report. An understanding of the functions of the major sections of a report will keep the writer from overemphasizing form. The parts of a long report fall into three general divisions – preliminary sections, report text and supplemental sections.

Preliminary sections present reference and informational material which explains and identifies the report and the situation for which it is prepared. The report text, often referred to as the "body" or "report proper," presents the facts, their analysis, conclusions and recommendations. Often it is divided into sections having distinct headings for convenience in presenting the data and to facilitate the reader's comprehension and use of the report. Supplemental sections follow the report proper and include material of a general and secondary interest for record and reference purposes. Sometimes material too bulky for inclusion in the text is placed in the supplemental sections.

Although each of the elements discussed here under the major divisions will appear in various reports, it is desirable not to use *all* in any *one* report. It is important that the writer be selective and use only elements that appropriately suit the situation, reader and report.

PRELIMINARY SECTIONS

Cover

The cover identifies and protects the report. Leather, cardboard, heavy paper or other flexible materials are suitable. It should contain the title, author and completion date. If the report is a numbered one, the cover will carry the number. In reports used for internal communication often a printed form is filled out and attached to the outside.

Flyleaf

The flyleaf, a blank sheet preceding the title page, is used only when the report is written for an official or when a very high-quality appearance is desired. The paper may be of the same stock as the rest of the report, but is frequently a thinner paper of a high quality.

Frontispiece

Likewise a frontispiece is neither required nor often used. Consisting of a map, an organizational chart, a photograph of equipment, or a visual presentation of the major results, it can add interest or importance to a prominent feature of the report. Sometimes used in printed reports going to the general reader, it is rarely used with internal typewritten reports. When used it faces the title page.

Title Page

The title page is necessary for long reports and those that are retained for future use. It provides complete identification of the report. Therefore it should include the title, subtitle, author (his position and address), name and address of the person or company for whom the report is prepared, serial designation if in a series, contract or project numbers and date of completion.

A good title tells the reader what the report contains by both attracting his attention and informing him. Thus it must be complete, accurate, concise and descriptive – characteristics seldom found in a catchy title. There is value in conciseness, and when necessary the subtitle can provide details for completeness.

Because the title must be indicative of the contents of the report, the following suggestions should help in composing effective titles:

(*1*) Use subject and verb.
(*2*) Indicate action suggested by the report.
(*3*) Suggest results or findings.
(*4*) Answer who, what, why, when, where and how.
(*5*) Indicate scope or limitations.

The title should not contain such unnecessary words or phrases as "a report on," "an investigation of," "a survey of," etc. Some titles, however, indicate the nature of the report by use of such phrases as "recommendations for," "the progress of," etc. The subtitle is entirely explanatory or descriptive. It explains and gives details of the subject. It may be as long as necessary.

Complete addresses are given for the author and the person for whom the report is prepared, so that inquiries about the report can be easily made. The date aids in filing and keeping records; it also lets the reader know the recency of the data in the report.

For short, routine and most internal reports the cover and title page are combined, and a memorandum form arrangement is generally used:

Subject: ______________________
To: ______________________
From: ______________________
Date: ______________________
Distribution: ______________________
____

Or

Report on ______________________
Submitted to ______________________
Prepared by ______________________
Date of transmittal ______________________

If a report is to be published the title page will follow the arrangement of the title page of a printed book. The printer's type provides a wide variety of faces which can be used for presenting an attractive appearance. Whether it is printed or typed the title page should be carefully arranged to create a favorable first impression on the reader. Words of the title are grouped, lines are broken, spaces are left — all so that the information can be readily seen and understood at a glance. In typewritten reports, the typist relies on the use of capital and lower-case letters, underlining and spacing, to make up an attention-getting title page. Proper balance and proportion need to be achieved. The sample title pages immediately following should be carefully noted for their arrangements. Each title page, although arranged differently, contains the same basic information.

TV, RADIO & COMIC BOOK

EFFECTIVENESS AMONG THE SCHOOL CHILDREN OF

NORWALK, CONN.

Conducted by
The Norwalk Board of Education

Presented by
Dell Publishing Co., Inc.
New York, N. Y.
May, 195_

Improving the Sales Operational Methods of the Audiphone Company of New Orleans

A Comparison of the Sales Programs of Two Companies in the Hearing Aid Industry As Applied Specifically to the Audiphone Company of New Orleans

Prepared for:

Mr. Frank L. Faust
The Audiphone Company of New Orleans
709 Pere Marquette Building
New Orleans, La.

Prepared by:

James Faust
School of Business Administration
Tulane University
New Orleans, La.

January 11, 195_

IMPROVING THE SALES OPERATIONAL METHODS OF THE AUDIPHONE COMPANY OF NEW ORLEANS

A Comparison Of The Sales Programs Of Two Companies
In The Hearing Aid Industry As Applied
Specifically To The Audiphone
Company Of New Orleans

Prepared For:
MR. FRANK L. FAUST
The Audiphone Company Of New Orleans
709 Pere Marquette Building
New Orleans, La.

Prepared By:
JAMES FAUST
School of Business Administration
Tulane University
New Orleans, La.

January 11, 195_

Copyright Page

When the material is copyrighted, the fact is recognized on the back of the title page. Included are the date of the copyright, name of the publisher and a notation similar to: "All rights reserved. No parts may be reproduced without the permission of the publisher."

Letter of Authorization

The letter of authorization is used to establish authority for and to state the terms under which an investigation and a report are made. It precedes the investigation and is written by the person requesting that a study be made to the person who is to do the research and report. Usually a report contains a letter of authorization *only* if the letter is desirable as a record. Most of the time authorization is given verbally or the report arises out of the reporter's work, and there is no letter of authorization.

There are two kinds of letters of authorization — general and specific. A general letter merely states the request for the report and suggests arrangements for its execution. In addition to making a request, a specific letter of authorization gives details of the problem situation and of what is to be done. In the following letter of authorization the problem, the need for the report, a suggested method of obtaining data, scope and limitations, and the use that will be made of the report are all presented. The investigator can begin his preliminary work immediately, for he knows what to do.

The Audiphone Company of New Orleans
709 Pere Marquette Building
New Orleans, Louisiana

December 5, 195_

Mr. James C. Faust
263 Audubon Street
New Orleans, Louisiana

Dear Mr. Faust:

Several of my salesmen have recently called my attention to deficiences in the operations of the sales program of the Audiphone Company. With this problem in mind, would you please present a report analyzing the situation and giving your conclusions and recommendations.

Since the hearing aid field is a limited one, you should make your analysis by comparing my sales methods with those of two of my competitors, preferably the Telex Company and the Sonotone Company, both of which have local offices. Please confine your investigation of the activities of these companies to the states of Louisiana and Mississippi, as this is the limit of my territory.

In your report, you should cover office selling, road work and advertising, for these are the main sales methods used in the hearing aid field today. You may find that some policies are made at a national level rather than at a local one, but they should be included in the comparison because of their effect upon local operating procedures. The sales programs of hearing aid companies are not secret; therefore, perhaps the best way to collect the necessary information would be by personal interview. However, any advertising booklets, sales manuals, or other material relating to the problem should be used in making your recommendations.

In an effort to improve our competitive position, these recommendations will be the basis for changing our methods. For this reason, please present the complete report by January 11, 195_.

Yours very truly,

Frank L. Faust
Manager

Letter of Acceptance

The letter of acceptance is used infrequently. On rare occasions, however, it is included as a record or for publicity purposes. Because it is an answer to the letter of authorization it accepts the request to make the investigation and to write the report. Thus it may include plans pertaining to stipulation of money, time and expense; it may ask for additional information; it may state changes over plans proposed in the letter of authorization and it may make clear what the investigator proposes to do. Occasionally it includes the working plan (discussed in Chapter 3) or even a preliminary outline. In this case it sometimes requests approval of plans before the researcher proceeds with his investigation.

Letter of Approval

There are two possible functions of the letter of approval. If it is written in answer to the letter of acceptance it may approve the working plan, etc., so the investigator can begin his study. In this case it is rarely a part of the completed report. If the letter is written after the investigation and report have been completed, then it approves the final report and may be included as a part of it. In this case the letter of approval is from a superior officer and is written to help the report get proper attention. Sometimes the report, which has been prepared by a subordinate, is submitted to his chief for approval before it is transmitted to a group or an individual.

Once in a while the letter of approval becomes the letter of submittal because it either takes on aspects of the letter of transmittal or is used in its place. A strictly formal report to the public might contain this type of approval and would usually be formal and conventional.

Letter of Transmittal

The letter of transmittal, which forwards the report, is written after the report has been completed and is addressed to the person or group for whom the report has been prepared. Sometimes it is separate from the report and is sent ahead of it. But usually it is a part of the bound report, in which case it may follow the title page, precede the table of contents or follow the letter of approval.

The composition of the letter of transmittal varies from report to report. It may contain any or all of the following elements, and any additional ones that may be appropriate:

(*1*) Reference to authorization
(*2*) Summary of report
(*3*) Scope and limitations
(*4*) History and background
(*5*) Acknowledgments
(*6*) Need of report
(*7*) Use of report
(*8*) Conclusions and recommendations
(*9*) Personal attitudes of writer
(*10*) Personal opinions of writer

The elements of the letter of transmittal are determined by the type of report it forwards, the relation of author and reader and the existing situation. It should increase the reader's interest and confidence in the report. For this reason a natural, conversational but dignified tone is effective. This letter can also be written in an informal, personal style. The author has an opportunity to mention personal ideas which cannot appear in an impersonal report. By being direct and straightforward he can persuade the reader to accept the report. By developing points of interest to the reader he will get his attention and create a desire to read the report. This may be done by calling attention to points of significance and value to the reader.

When a report has no preface or foreword, the transmittal letter performs their functions. Used in a report which has a foreword or preface, the letter of transmittal merely transmits the report or is used as a covering letter separate from the bound report.

The following sample letter to the Audiphone Company emphasizes the analysis and results of the report and was used with a report that did not contain a preface or a foreword.

263 Audubon Street
New Orleans, Louisiana
January 9, 195_

Mr. Frank L. Faust
The Audiphone Company of New Orleans
709 Pere Marquette Building
New Orleans, Louisiana

Dear Mr. Faust:

As you requested, I am submitting my recommendations for the sales operational methods of the Audiphone Company. The report is based on the operating procedures of your firm as contrasted with those of two of your competitors in the Louisiana-Mississippi Area, the Telex Company and the Sonotone Company.

The analysis shows that the road selling and advertising procedures of the Audiphone Company offer the largest room for improvement. Because of a high degree of control over the policies of the company, you should experience little difficulty in making the proposed changes. Road and rural selling is the most deficient phase of your sales program, from the hiring of road men to their remuneration. The policies of the Audiphone Company towards sub-offices and local repair points have been found excellent, for they provide the hard-of-hearing person with necessary extra services.

The high place occupied by the Audiphone Company in the competitive picture is widely recognized, but this is no indication that changes are not necessary. As selling methods progress, the company must progress also; and it is only by change that this can be accomplished. Following the recommendations should strengthen the position of the Audiphone Company in the highly competitive hearing aid industry for many years to come.

Yours very truly,

James C. Faust

Dedication

Rarely does a business report contain a dedication page. When it does, it is handled in the same way as the dedication of a book. The report would have to be very formal in nature and issued on a very special occasion to call for a dedication.

Foreword

Functionally the foreword accomplishes the same purposes as the letter of transmittal and the introduction. Thus one should complement the others. The foreword establishes contact with the reader and orients him to the report. When the report is addressed to the public in general, the foreword usually replaces the letter of transmittal.

The foreword may contain any or most of the following elements:

(*1*) References to purpose, scope, etc.
(*2*) References to circumstances out of which the report developed
(*3*) Statement of the writer's qualifications and experience
(*4*) Indication of the author's interest in subject
(*5*) General orientation of the reader to the subject
(*6*) Reference to the authorization
(*7*) Acknowledgments
(*8*) Pertinent comments
(*9*) References to other related reports
(*10*) Evaluation of work accomplished

For practical purposes the foreword and the preface are the same — they are used interchangeably. Discriminating authors and publishers, however, distinguish between them. The foreword is written by someone other than the author and the preface is written by the author. For this reason a report may have both a preface and a foreword, although it usually does not. The foreword should be written by one who knows the author and his work, because he is able to comment on the author's qualifications and the merit and value of the work — comments which might sound egotistical if made by the author.

Preface

The preface is written by the report's author and gives him a chance to state his opinions and attitudes. It may include his explanation of why the report was written, his thinking that led to the report, a presentation of his background and experience and his explanation of how he intends the report to be used. It is the author's opportunity to talk about himself to the reader.

Often it is informally and personally written. It is not generally included as a part of a report; however, when it is, it may replace the foreword or letter of transmittal.

Acknowledgments

Acknowledgment of assistance by individuals and organizations who have helped in gathering or contributing information and in writing or editing the report may be included in the letter of transmittal, preface, foreword, introduction or in a separate section of the report. A separate listing gives greater emphasis. If placed in the letter of transmittal, acknowledgments should not take up more than four or five lines. If they are included in the preface, foreword or introduction, a paragraph should be given to them. The amount of emphasis desired and the number and length of acknowledgments will determine where they are placed.

Table of Contents

Because the table of contents is a topical outline of the material contained in a report, it facilitates referral to any section of the report by giving page numbers for each topic listed. Repeating the major subject headings and subheads indicates the relationship among divisions and topics. As a rule, however, no more than three degrees of headings are used, for this number is sufficient to give the reader a clear idea of the extent and content of the material in the report. The shorter the report, the fewer the heads that are listed. The longer the report, the more detailed are the subdivisions.

The preliminary and supplemental sections, as well as the divisions of the report text, may be listed in the table of contents. Typing the preliminary and supplemental elements in lower-case letters, and the major headings referring to the divisions of the report text in capital letters (with subheads in lower-case letters), distinguishes the supplemental and preliminary sections from the report text headings. Here, as in an outline, numbers and indention help show relationships.

Notice how the relationships have been indicated in the following table of contents from a report on an analysis of the internal communications system of the Fitzgerald Advertising Agency:

TABLE OF CONTENTS

TABLE OF CONTENTS (*Cont.*)

The outline numbers and also the listing of prefatory and supplemental parts of the report may be omitted as in the following table of contents:

TABLE OF CONTENTS

List of Tables

At various times the list of tables is also appropriately called "Table of Charts," "Table of Illustrations," etc., depending on whether charts, tables or pictures appear in the report. It follows the table of contents and lists the tables in consecutive order as they appear in the text. The list is prepared from the table captions and shows page numbers. Thus it serves the same function for the tables as the table of contents does for the other material. When there are only a few tables in the report they may be listed either at the bottom of the contents page or as subdivisions in their appropriate place in the divisions of text in the table of contents. In the example that follows the same form is used as is followed in the table of contents. An appropriate heading is given to the page and to each column.

List of Tables

Summary

There is some form of summary in every report. It enables the busy executive to get significant facts without having to read through the entire report or to hunt for them. The first paragraph of an introduction may be a summary of the conclusions, designed to call the reader's attention to them. A brief paragraph summary of significant points in the report may also be included in the letter of transmittal, foreword or preface. As a separate part of the report, however, a summary is usually from one to five pages long, depending on the length of the report text. Bound with the other parts of the report, it completes the preliminary elements of the formal, long report and introduces the report proper.

When used separately it may speed action. Twelve people, for instance, may read a copy of the summary and decide on the action to take with only one or two of the group ever reading the entire report. Too, a summary may be published in a book of summaries or in a magazine.

The terms *abstract, synopsis, digest* and *brief* are all used interchangeably for types of summaries, with few or only arbitrary points of difference. The *abstract,* for instance, is an impersonal, unbiased, non-interpretative, non-critical presentation of essential elements of the report. What the author says is given without evaluation. Although its emphasis is on the results to which it devotes about two-thirds of its length, it covers the material in the introduction and the ending of the report. In fact, the same organization and style of writing used in the report is adhered to. Thus an abstract has the flavor of the report and lends itself well to printing or other use separate from the report.

A *synopsis,* on the other hand, is generally briefer than the abstract and lacks both the detailed information and the style of the original report. Rather than present a complete summary of the entire report, the synopsis aims to give only its outstanding features. The reader can see by glancing at a synopsis the development of the subject or problem; but he has to read the report itself for the details. In other words, this type of summary tells in general what the report contains and does not give specific information. The following sentence is typical of a sentence from a synopsis:

"The results of the questionnaire survey are shown in table form and discussed."

To find out what the results are, one must read the report. The synopsis tells that they are there. Sometimes the synopsis is merely an expansion of the title and is used on the title page as the subtitle. It also is appropriately placed as a last paragraph in the introduction section of the report text.

In that the *digest* is a condensation of the entire report, it is similar to the abstract. The chief difference between the two is length. The report, reduced to three-fourths, one-half or one-third of its original content, retaining the author's style, etc., is a digest.

A *brief* is in the form of a sentence outline with connecting words and phrases added.

In all types of summaries direct, concise writing is used. The essence of each main division should be stated in proportion to its importance in the report. Of course, no information should appear in the summary that is not in the report. In writing a summary one should read the report through, then pick out its main points. Afterwards he can go back for the details, visualizing them in proper perspective. Then he is ready to write the summary. Just as the outline is a valuable guide in writing the text, it also serves in writing a summary. In fact, a sentence outline presented in paragraph form makes an excellent summary.

REPORT TEXT

The complete development of the subject or problem is presented as the report text. The body of the report gives the background information the reader needs to understand the report; describes what was done to gather data; relates the results or findings; analyzes, interprets and discusses the data; states conclusions and recommendations. Based on these functions of a report text, there are four general divisions of a report – introduction, discussion, conclusions and recommendations.

Introduction

The introduction of a report presents the subject or problem to the reader and gets his attention. Through reading it he becomes interested in reading the report. The introduction must furnish him with sufficient material concerning the investigation and problem to lead to an easy understanding of the rest of the report. It should thus give the reader a general view of the report before he plunges into the details.

The trend today is to begin the introduction with a summary of conclusions or findings. When the report does not contain a separate summary section, the summarized conclusions may be omitted from the introduction entirely or placed at its end, where they are treated briefly to tell the reader what to expect in the rest of the report. No words should be wasted in informing the reader of what the report is about. In the very first sentence the subject and purpose can be stated.

Each introduction must be arranged to suit the situation and the reader. A good introduction will set up an orderly path for the reader to follow. The following list of contents is a suggestive rather than an exhaustive one, and few introductions will include all of the items:

Explanation of or reference to authorization of the report
Situation giving rise to the report
The author's understanding of the problem
The author's attitude toward the problem
Scope and limitations
Purpose and objectives
Basic principles or theories involved
Methods of gathering data
Sources of information
Procedure in organizing material
Definition of terms
Brief summary of findings or results
Brief statement of main conclusions
Brief statement of chief recommendation

General plan used in developing the solution
General plan of the report

The introduction may contain subject headings such as *purpose* and *procedures* for its subdivisions. Although these are stereotyped headings, they are, nevertheless, significant guideposts for the reader.

The end of the introduction must make for effective transition to the next section of the report. If it ends with an explanation of the general plan of the rest of the report, logical transition is made. It could also end with a discussion of the procedures used to gather data; and then the next section would present the results. A brief synopsis of the findings or a statement of the main conclusions is also a logical transition.

Discussion

The discussion section is the major part of the report. Here information and data are presented, analyzed and interpreted. The writer must decide between pertinent data to include in the text and less important information to omit or relegate to the appendix. Meanings, ideas and facts are made clear to the reader. Comparisons are made; facts are evaluated; significant relationships are drawn. The solution of a problem may be given with an explanation of its advantages and disadvantages. Tables, charts and other media for presenting figures and data are used. Other illustrative material may be included. Emphasis is on the results and their interpretation. *The discussion leads the reader through the same reasoning process the author used to reach the conclusions and shows him that they are sound.*

Consideration should be given opposing contentions in order to show how the data prove otherwise. It is not well to assume that the reader agrees with a concept unless it is generally accepted. Simple, straightforward statements of facts are most easily understood. Different aspects of the problem are treated in the discussion section. Major subject headings are used to guide the reader. Arrangement of points may be used to suit the subject and reader.

Conclusions

The final section of the report contains conclusions and recommendations. They may be treated in the same section or in separate sections. Conclusions are the result of reasoned analysis and judgment of the data in the report and serve as a basis for recommendations growing out of the study made. They may be summary or analytical in nature. If summary, the conclusion section is a recapitulation of the significant points developed in the discussion section. New points are not developed nor is the analysis carried any further. Concluding statements stand alone, supported by the facts in the discussion section. In an information report the conclusion is nearly always summary. An example of this type of conclusion is the following, taken from a consumer-preference survey made by Swift & Company for the molded pulp egg carton vs. the regular self-locking egg carton:

(*1*) The molded pulp carton is decidedly preferred, both by those having used it (77% of them) and those who have not used it (68% of them).

(*2*) Protection is the principal reason of preference for the molded pulp carton.

(*3*) "Hard to open" and "can't see eggs" are the principal reasons for disliking the molded pulp carton given by those who have used it.

(*4*) Fifteen percent of those preferring the molded pulp carton had opening troubles—69% of those preferring the regular type found the pulp carton difficult to open.

(*5*) Forty-five percent of those preferring the molded pulp carton liked to look at eggs before buying, compared to 74% of those preferring the regular type. "Want to see size" and "color" were given as reasons why.

If analytical by nature, conclusions are reached through analysis and interpretation of the data. They are the result of thinking over the facts. Assume, for instance, that you are doing a report on how to select a mailing list. Your discussion section will take up the process step by step. Then the summary conclusion will list the major significant steps. If, however, you have compared the steps in different ways of selecting a mailing list or have analyzed their good and bad features, then you would have an analytical conclusion: "the best way to select a mailing list is ____________," the result of thinking over the facts.

Analytical conclusions are usually discussed in paragraphs and have been reached as a result of logical reasoning. An example follows:

CONCLUSIONS

Up until the final, comparative analysis of sales, there was relatively little to choose between the two cities. Both were certainly well adapted to a location for conducting the pre-testing surveys of a small national-scale advertising agency, although at this point Kansas City has probably shown itself to be slightly more representative of the nation than Cincinnati. The analysis of retail sales, however, completely changed the picture.

Original Assumption of Suitability

As has been stated previously, no city's population can ever be expected to represent an average sample of the inhabitants of the entire country. Income, standard of living, and sales almost invariably will be greater than average. Consequently, the only measure of suitability is the extent to which these factors remain in proportion to one another, and hence, the degree of reliability which they have, after making necessary corrections and adjustments in data.

On this basis, Cincinnati would seem quite adequately and satisfactorily suited for use as an advertising "pre-testing" ground. Kansas City, in view of its retail sales pattern, is certainly far less suitable, although it could probably be used if necessary.

It should be remembered that these conclusions are based on a current analysis, not a trend analysis, and pertain only to the present time. A period of a few years may completely reverse the situation, or it may be found that the present sales pattern in Kansas City is only a temporary distortion.

Choice of the More Suitable City

After the foregoing discussion, it seems hardly necessary to state that Cincinnati, Ohio is by far the more suitable of the two cities. Its population constitutes a better average sample than Kansas City's, and the result of surveys made there should prove more reliable, in the long run, than those made in Kansas City.

Sometimes facts are presented, analyzed and a conclusion reached in the discussion section; then the writer moves on to another set of facts, their analysis and another conclusion. In this case conclusions are reached along with analysis of the material. Then in the conclusions section they are all brought together.

Conclusions may be listed or may be presented in paragraph form. They are usually introduced by an appropriate statement. Sometimes a summary of findings is given first, followed by conclusions.

Recommendations

Recommendations pertain to the action that is to be taken as a result of the report. They are supported by the conclusions, and they are aimed toward accomplishing the purpose of the report. If the purpose of a report, for instance, is to alleviate employee grievances over wage incentive plans, the recommendations will suggest ways that this can be done. Conclusions and results of investigating the problem will support the recommendations.

Like conclusions, recommendations may take the form of a numbered list of details or may be treated in paragraphs. They should answer the questions of "What is to be done?" "By whom?" "When?" "Where?" and "How?"

In following a logical sequence for the textual parts of a formal, long report, recommendations are presented last; such has been the case in the discussion in this chapter. They do not, however, always appear at the end of the report. They may be given first, especially in recommendation reports. They are also sometimes treated very briefly in the letter of transmittal, preface and separate summary section. If the reader is likely to react unfavorably to the recommendation, then it should be given him last. The report can prepare him for it. If he is already familiar with the data or is chiefly interested in the action to be taken, then he should have the recommendation first so he will not have to read through a lot of material before acting on it.

SUPPLEMENTAL SECTIONS

Material of general and secondary interest, or material that is too bulky to be placed in the report text, is placed in the supplemental sections of a formal, long report. Here it is used for record and reference purposes.

Appendix

The appendix is a catchall for all supplementary material which, if placed in the body of the report, might disrupt or delay the reading process. The appendix contains record and reference material such as:

Large tables and charts
Copy of questionnaire used in the investigation
Sample forms, etc., used in the investigation
Extensive quotations and summaries
Detailed data for reference
Plans and specifications
Glossary
Mailing list
Recapitulation tables
Letters

Short and simple reports rarely have appendices, nor do all formal, long reports. It depends on how the report and its supplemental sections will be used. Sometimes all material is placed in one appendix section; at other times it is divided and placed in several, such as: Appendix A — Recapitulation Tables, Appendix B — Letter from ________ on ________, Appendix C – Glossary of Terms. The appendix is what the writer wants to make it, depending on how it is to be used by the reader.

Bibliography

The bibliography may be included as part of the appendix or presented as a separate supplemental section of the report. If presented separately, it may either precede or follow the appendix. It lists all the printed sources used in gathering data and in writing the report. Each source is alphabetized by the last name of the author. Sample entries for different types of sources are shown in the reference section of the Appendix of this book. If only a few sources have been used the bibliography will list them together in one list. If, however, there are several kinds of sources, then all sources of each type are alphabetized in a subdivision of the bibliography. Thus all books are in one list, all articles in one, etc.

The following bibliographies are subdivided; and where there are no authors the titles are used for alphabetizing. Since only a few interviews were used for special information they too are listed. This would not be done if a survey of a large number of people had been taken.

BIBLIOGRAPHY

Advertising Pamphlets:

Hear Again!, Sonotone, Inc., Chicago, Ill., 1950.
New Help for the Deafened, Audivox, Inc., New York, N. Y., 1950.
The New Look in Hearing Aids, Telex, Inc., Minneapolis, Minn., 1950.
Once in Your Lifetime, Telex, Inc., Minneapolis, Minn., 1949.

Book:

Davis, Hollowell, *Speech and Hearing*, The Viking Press, New York, 1950.

Interviews:

Blocker, Charles M. A., Manager, The Sonotone Company of New Orleans, 812 Carondelet Building, December 11, 195_.
Crawford, C. M., Manager, Telex of New Orleans, 508 Canal Bank Building, December 14, 195_.
Faust, Frank L., Manager, The Audiphone Company of New Orleans, 709 Pere Marquette Building, December 10, 195_.

BIBLIOGRAPHY

Books

Baridon, Felix, and Earl H. Loomis, *Personnel Problems*. New York: McGraw-Hill Book Co., Inc., 1931. 550 pp.

Halsey, George A., *Handbook of Personnel Management.* New York: Harper & Brothers, 1947. 650 pp.
Pigors, Paul John, and Charles Andrew Myers, *Personnel Administration.* New York: McGraw-Hill Book Co., Inc., 1947. 415 pp.
Schell, Erwin, *Technique of Handling People.* New York: McGraw-Hill Book Co., Inc., 1946. 216 pp.
Yoder, Dale, *Personnel Principles and Policies.* New York: Prentice-Hall, Inc., 1952. 602 pp.

Articles

Armstrong, A. F., "Summary of a Personnel Program," *Paper Trade Journal,* November, 1950, p. 339.
Stackman, H.A., "Planning Ahead in Personnel," *Personnel Journal,* January, 1951. p. 286.

Interviews

Wellan, Louis, Manager, Wellan's Department Store, December 6, 1951.
White, Charles, Personnel Director, Wellan's Department Store, December 6, 1951.

Index

The index is prepared after the final typing of the report text and is used only with extensive, complicated, long reports. Arranged alphabetically, it lists page references to important words, phrases, facts, names and ideas. Main divisions and subdivisions are also indicated.

In preparing an index, the use of small 3″ x 5″ cards is advisable. On each card one item can be listed with its major heading, subheadings and page references. Then the cards can be arranged alphabetically and the index typed. The completed index to a report is like the index to a book, and it appears as the last part of the report.

SPECIMEN REPORT

The following report is a typical example of the formal, long report. The preliminary sections give the background of the problem and indicate what was done. In the report text are discussed the findings and conclusions upon which recommendations are based. The appendix material is not reproduced as part of the report. In this particular report the appendix included a map of the area selected as the potential market and a list of interviews used in gathering information. The example illustrates the fact that not all formal, long reports contain all the elements discussed in this chapter, but only the ones the writer selects as being appropriate to his problem and purpose.

SHOULD THE AUDUBON ICE PLANT ADD
A FROZEN FOOD LOCKER PLANT
TO ITS FACILITIES?

Prepared for

Mr. Frank A. Herman, Manager
Audubon Ice Company
New Orleans, Louisiana

Prepared by

John E. Herman—Marketing Consultant
The Southern Marketing Research Company
New Orleans, Louisiana

December 18, 195_

THE SOUTHERN MARKETING RESEARCH COMPANY
NEW ORLEANS, LOUISIANA

December 18, 195_

Mr. Frank A. Herman, Manager
Audubon Ice Company
628 Dublin Street
New Orleans, Louisiana

Dear Mr. Herman:

According to your request concerning the conversion of a section of your ice plant into a frozen food locker, I have made a complete investigation and report on the following:

(*1*) The competition in the frozen food locker field.
(*2*) The extent to which the number of potential customers for such an enterprise warrants the expenditure.
(*3*) The conversion of the plant.
(*4*) The operation of the plant after conversion.

The results of my investigation indicate that conversion of a section of the ice plant into a frozen food locker would prove to be a sound business venture.

Sincerely yours,

John E. Herman
Marketing Consultant

JEH/mm

TABLE OF CONTENTS

SHOULD THE AUDUBON ICE PLANT ADD A FROZEN FOOD LOCKER PLANT TO ITS FACILITIES?

I. Introduction

The Audubon Ice Plant, located on the corner of Dublin and Hampson Streets, one block from the intersection of Carrollton and St. Charles Avenues, has been owned and operated by Mr. Frank A. Herman for the past 15 years. Capable of producing 75 tons of ice per 24 hours the year around, the plant for the past four years has been averaging approximately twenty tons output every 24 hours on the year-around basis. This low output is the result of a sharp decline in business.

A. *Need for Additional Business:*

New business is badly needed not only by the Audubon Ice Company but also by all ice companies in the New Orleans Area. Five years ago there were 62 ice plants operating at capacity in the New Orleans Area, whereas today only 22 of them are still operating; and they are operating at only 25% capacity. Every plant operating in the area today is struggling desperately to remain in operation.

The major reason for the decline in the ice business is increased use of electrical refrigeration. Electric refrigerators had replaced ice boxes in 95% of the homes in the United States by 1941. Although this caused only a slight drop in the ice business, commercial electric refrigeration, which came into steady use between 1947 and 1950, knocked the props out.

The Audubon Ice Company at this time was selling 80% of its capacity output to barrooms, restaurants, nightclubs, hotels and motels. By 1950 all of these business establishments had installed ice-making machines on their premises. The machines produced ice more cheaply than the ice man could deliver it, and, on top of that, they were much more convenient. Because the machine is capable of producing 1,000 or more ice cubes per hour, there is little chance of running out of ice. Since ice sales have declined so sharply, the Audubon Plant must find some new and profitable field to enter.

B. *Purpose and Objectives of the Report:*

Because there is only one operator of a frozen food locker in the New Orleans Area and, according to the Chamber of Commerce, no other firms are planning to enter this business, converting a section of its present plant to a frozen food locker might be the solution to Audubon Ice Company's need for additional income. An investigation was made, therefore, to determine whether it is advisable for the company to add a frozen food locker plant to its present facilities. It was necessary to study the competition in the frozen food locker field, to make a survey of the nearby plant area for determining whether or not the number of potential customers warrants the expenditures that would be needed and to study the problem of plant conversion. The results of the investigation follow.

II. The Competition

Approximately two and one-half miles from the site of the Aubudon Ice Company is the one frozen food locker that is operated at the present time in New Orleans. Food Freezers, Incorporated, 4140 Washington Avenue, rents lockers to people all over the city. Eighty percent of their rentals, however, are to people who live within a one and one-half mile radius of their business location.

There are 750 lockers available for rental purposes. Each one is 36 inches long, 24 inches wide and 12 inches high, providing a total of six square feet of storage space. Any game that a customer brings in will be cleaned, wrapped and placed in his locker for three cents per pound. If a customer prefers, however, he can clean, wrap and store his product for himself and save this extra outlay.

There is an attendant on duty at the locker plant 24 hours per day, seven days a week. When a person rents a locker, he is issued a key. He is thus free to go to his locker at any time of the day or night that he chooses.

At the present time, Food Freezers, Incorporated has all available lockers rented at $18 each per year. There is also a backlog of over two hundred applications for lockers when they become available.

III. Potential Customers

A. *The Area Serviced:*

The area bounded by Napolean Avenue, Magazine Street, the Mississippi River, the Jefferson-Orleans Parish line and South Claiborne Avenue was decided upon as the most likely area from which Audubon Ice Company could obtain its customers for frozen food lockers, because of the closeness of the area to the plant. The area covers approximately eight square miles and contains about 32,400 different mailing addresses. Because 10% of the mailing addresses are commercial sites, in the area there would be about 29,160 prospective families.

Since the area past Magazine Street toward the river is largely commercial property, the Magazine Street boundary was decided upon. The Mississippi River provides a natural boundary, and the Jefferson-Orleans Parish line was decided upon because the residential area past the parish line is widely scattered. Compared to the area on the New Orleans side, the population per square mile is very thin.

All other factors being equal, the average person does business as close to home as possible. South Claiborne Avenue is about one-half the distance between Food Freezers, Incorporated, on Washington Avenue, and Audubon Ice Company on Dublin Street. Likewise the Napolean Avenue boundary was set because residents east of this point could hardly be considered as living close to the Audubon Ice Plant.

B. *Results of an Interview Survey:*

A small survey of potential customers was taken in the area just defined. Fifty homes were picked at random, and the residents interviewed were asked questions about the prospect of a frozen food locker in their immediate area. About 40% of the people interviewed were uncertain as to exactly what a frozen food locker was and how it operated. In these cases a short explanation was given by the interviewer. The following four questions were asked:

(*1*) We operate an ice plant located one block from Carrollton Avenue and St. Charles Avenue. We are contemplating converting part of this ice plant into a frozen food locker. If such facilities were available, would you be interested in the use of them?

(*2*) Would you be interested in this locker on an annual basis or only an occasional basis?

(*3*) Would you be interested in more than one locker?

(*4*) In addition to meat, do you think you would be interested in the processing and freezing of vegetables?

If the response to question number one was negative, the remaining questions were not asked.

The responses to the questions were as follows:

Question Number One:

(*1*) Fifteen families or 30% said that they would be interested.

(*2*) Thirty-five families or 70% said that they would not be interested.

Question Number Two:

(*1*) Of the interested families, thirteen or 87% said that they would want the locker on an annual basis.

(*2*) Two families or 13% said that they would want a locker only occasionally.

Question Number Three:

(*1*) Of those interested, five families or 33% said that they would be interested in more than one locker.

(*2*) Six families or 40% said they did not know whether or not they would need a second locker.

(*3*) Four families or 27% said they would not be interested in a second locker.

Question Number Four:

(*1*) Four families or 27% said that they would be interested in the processing and freezing of vegetables.

(*2*) Eleven families or 73% said they would not be interested in the processing and freezing of vegetables.

Of those interviewed, 30% responded favorably to the idea of a frozen food locker plant. Although only a very small sample was taken, applied to the estimated 29,160 residents of the area, there would be approximately 8,748 families interested in a frozen food locker plant. Certainly not all of these can be counted on as potential customers. At the same time, a certain number of potential customers might be obtained from outside the area.

IV. Conversion

The conversion discussed in this section of the report is based on the idea of installing 600 standard-size frozen food lockers in the area presently being used as an ice manufacturing tank. Since there are two such tanks in the plant and one tank can supply enough ice for the present ice trade, the other can very easily be converted to a frozen food locker plant. The locker room would be sixty by twenty feet, providing 1,200 square feet of floor space, of which 720 square feet could be occupied by lockers.

A. *Space Requirements:*

The usual locker is 36 inches long, 24 inches wide and 12 inches high. Where space permits, lockers are usually placed five high, the two lower ones being drawers, while the top three have hinged doors. All lockers have six cubic feet of storage space and hold about two hundred pounds of food.

Customary practice calls for a four-foot aisle between rows of lockers, so it is calculated that of available space, 40% would be used for aisles and 60% for locker space. Five lockers require a headroom of six feet, eight inches. However, coils must be placed overhead, so eight and one-half feet between the floor and ceiling should be allowed for both lockers and coils.

B. *Cost of Conversion:*

Conversion would not require the purchase of very much material since all the coils, valves, insulation, etc., are available from the ice tank that will be removed to make way for the lockers. The estimated cost of installing the locker plant is as follows:

600 lockers @ $5.00 each	$3,000.00
Scales, electric sign, key cabinet, etc.	750.00
2 cold storage doors @ $125.00 each	250.00
4,000 board feet of lumber @ $100.00 per thousand feet	400.00
Labor — the installation of walls and doors	2,000.00
Labor — connecting pipes, valves, etc. with main plant	400.00
Insurance during construction, and incidental items	600.00
Estimated cost of conversion	$7,400.00

To this $7,400.00 would have to be added unforeseen items such as wiring for lights, initial operating supplies, some plumbing for wash basins, rest rooms, etc., as well as initial circularization of potential customers, advertising, etc. By the time the locker plant is ready to open, the cash outlay would be approximately $12,000.00.

V. Operation of the Plant After Conversion

Locker patrons would pay $15.00 annually for the three upper lockers (hinged doors) and $18.00 annually for the more convenient bottom drawers. The gross revenue from these lockers on an annual basis would be $9,720:

240 lockers (drawer type) @ $18.00 each	$4,320.00
360 lockers (hinged-door type) @ $15.00 each	5,400.00
Annual gross rental revenue	$9,720.00

Experience has shown that most locker patrons use double the capacity of their lockers during a year's time, so on the average 400 pounds of food would be stored in each locker per year, or a total of 240,000 pounds per year for the proposed 600 lockers.

A charge of from $.02 to $.04 a pound would be made on everything that went into a locker. The lower rate would be charged when the food received was properly wrapped and frozen. The higher rates would apply when it was necessary to wrap and freeze the food received. Using an average of $.03 per pound, times 240,000 pounds, a potential revenue of $7,200.00 can be anticipated.

Most locker plants sell frozen food containers, wax bags, etc., to their patrons at a reasonable profit. If each patron bought from the Audubon Ice Company an average of $3.00 worth of such supplies each year, at a 40% profit, there would be a potential gross profit of $1,800.

Thus, based on 600 lockers, gross revenues should be approximately as listed below:

Locker rentals	$9.720.00
Processing	7,200.00
Profit on supplies	1,800.00
Approximate gross revenue	$18,720.00

All locker plants keep a stock of frozen foods on hand to sell to customers at a profit. This report does not take this source of income into consideration; however, the profit from this source is sizable.

The actual operation of the locker plant would entail no extra mechanical or clerical help, since the regular ice plant crew could operate the equipment and keep all necessary records. However, there would be some additional cost estimated as follows on a yearly basis:

Locker manager at $50.00 per week, plus an annual bonus of $500.00	$3,100.00
Liability Insurance, Workman's Compensation, Old Age Benefits, etc.	700.00
Refrigeration: one 5" x 5" compressor operating two-thirds of the time	600.00
Maintenance	400.00
Lights, water and telephone	500.00
Operating supplies	600.00
Advertising	600.00
Depreciation ($10,000 at 8%)	800.00
Miscellaneous and unforeseen	500.00
Additional operating cost	$7,800.00

VI. Conclusions and Recommendations

A detailed study of the possibility of converting a section of the Audubon Ice Plant into a frozen food locker plant indicates that a project of this type would fill a real need.

A cross-section of potential customers shows that a locker plant would receive sufficient patronage to make it a very profitable enterprise. The proposed location seems to be excellent, since it is near a very good residential section, and at the same time has plenty of parking space. There is only one competing firm in New Orleans, and it has more business than it can handle.

Should the gross revenue be somewhat less than anticipated, this venture would still show a handsome profit. Expected expenses might also be higher than estimated, but would not be sufficiently higher to reduce profits to any degree. On an approximate investment of $12,000, there would be an estimated annual profit of 91%:

Annual gross revenue	$18,720.00
Annual expenses	7,800.00
Net profit	$10,920.00

From the standpoints of the competition, potential customers, cost and profits, adding a frozen food locker plant to its present facilities would prove to be a sound business venture for the Audubon Ice Company. It is recommended, therefore, that the company convert a section of its plant to a frozen food locker plant.

PROBLEMS

1. Explain the relationship of the preliminary sections, the text and the supplemental sections of a formal, long report.

2. How does the writer decide which parts to include and which parts to omit in a formal, long report?

3. Discuss the fact that each part of the report text serves as a basis for the part that follows.

4. Rewrite the following introduction to a short report on the comparison of illustrations in annual reports:

At your request I have prepared a report on the use of illustrations in our annual report of the past year as compared with the annual reports of four other comparable companies in similar fields of work. I have paid special attention to our report and their use of graphs, charts, illustrations and pictures as you had authorized me to do this week. The scope of this, my report, is confined to the graphic illustrations used by four other companies as compared to ours in their annual reports. Because I have had a week to prepare the report and waited until today to do it, which does not give me much time to give details nor consider the points in the publishing of an annual report, I have tried my best to write as briefly as possible and give you only the essential facts in order that you may better understand my recommendations for improving the illustrations in our next year's annual report.

5. The material in this chapter should be applied to one of the report subjects listed in the Appendix, pages 414 to 419. The instructor may want you to submit all the preliminary sections of your long report for approval before you proceed with the writing of the text. Likewise, the introduction may be submitted before the analysis. Later the report may be put together for final submission.

CHAPTER 17

Informative Reports

POLICY STATEMENTS
EMPLOYEE BOOKLETS
PROGRESS REPORTS
PERIODIC REPORTS
COMMITTEE MINUTES
CREDIT REPORTS
SALES REPORTS

THE HEAD OF EVERY COMPANY WANTS HIS ORGANIZATION to function efficiently. This means an integrated management team and satisfied employees with a sense of responsibility—both groups having trust in the company and working toward common interests. Development of positive attitudes, loyalties, respect and teamwork is essential to obtaining high operating efficiency and profits. Well-informed personnel contribute to the accomplishment of these goals. Informative reports are thus used to develop an understanding of the aims, objectives, organization, policies, regulations, procedures, problems and future outlook of a company. They are also used to provide information essential for making a decision or for determining a course of action.

POLICY STATEMENTS

Take a look at the Parker Pen Company's statement of policy for U. S. military establishments. It was written not only for the company and military personnel who were concerned but also for the interested public. It sets forth in a general way the position of the company on the sale of its products in post exchanges and ships' service stores without giving instructions for carrying out this sales policy. It also discusses the company's attitude and past record, which is a good thing to do. In this way it informs the reader and creates a favorable impression toward the policy.

THE PARKER PEN COMPANY
Janesville, Wisconsin, U. S. A.

Statement of Policy
U. S. Military Establishments

There have been three national emergencies involving armed conflict during the lifetime of this company. The maintenance of a strong military organization seems vital to the prevention of future wars. Thus, a statement of this company's policy regarding the conduct of business with military stores is provided for the information and guidance of all concerned.

This company believes that the needs and desires of the men and women in military service deserve every consideration because of the hazardous and rigorous nature of their responsibilities and because their efforts are devoted entirely to the national welfare.

Our products are made available to military personnel in post exchanges and ships' service stores. We cannot, nor do we attempt to, control the price because the stores are operated on a non-profit basis. We do not condone, in fact we try to prevent, the sale of our products in military stores to civilians. Whenever specific malpractices come to our attention we make the evidence available immediately to the responsible authorities at the particular military establishment so that corrective measures can be undertaken.

Our policy, in substance, is not at variance with that of the other major pen companies whose products are to be found in, or have been offered to, Army Post Exchanges and Naval Ships' Service Stores.

In the conduct of business with military stores, we are convinced that the morale of servicemen and women should be of prime concern. It bears directly and heavily on their capabilities and proficiencies. In turn, morale depends in great measure on a bridging of the distance and time between service people and their families and a bridging of the circumstances separating them from civilian modes of relatively unregimented life.

One means of bridging the gap has proved to be personal correspondence. Fortunately, a high degree of importance was attached by American military leaders to the two-way flow of mail across continents and oceans during the two most recent global conflicts. This was extremely beneficial to not only pen and ink manufacturers but to retailers. ONLY BECAUSE OF THIS CONVICTION AT THE POLICY LEVEL OF THE ARMY AND NAVY WAS THE WRITING INSTRUMENT INDUSTRY CONSIDERED "ESSENTIAL" AND PERMITTED TO CONTINUE THE USE OF SCARCE MATERIALS DURING THE LAST WAR. This company and the retailers cannot easily forget a mutual debt of gratitude to the military authorities.

This company's policy with regard to military business is not now, nor has it ever been, shaped primarily by the profit motive. It was our privilege during the war to engage in the production of rocket fuses and many other munitions parts. Kenneth Parker stated at the time those wartime tasks were started that this company would not undertake to derive one cent of profit from them. That was long prior to any practice of contract renegotiation. Literally millions of rocket fuses alone were produced for the U. S. Navy at a cost lower than that charged by any other fabricator. The entire Parker program of war-goods production eventuated with a profit of less than one-half of one per cent. The only reason that a single dollar of profit materialized was because we could not figure the job any closer to the zero mark. Of all 86,000 U. S. war plants, 4,299 received the Army-Navy E Award. This company received it three times, being one of only 1,810 such recipients. We were proud of that wartime record. We are now.

During war years of scarcity there is constant and perhaps increased danger of unethical business practices. Unscrupulous or misguided individuals motivated by greed have a record of attempting to profiteer whenever the opportunities are great and the risks small.

This company deprecated wartime black- or grey-market activities as a matter of policy. We joined wholeheartedly with the legally constituted authorities in measures to suppress and eradicate them.

Likewise in times which are not characterized by national emergency there has been evidence pointing to misuse and abuse of the privileges and considerations extended in good faith to servicemen and women. This company also deprecates these situations wherein the benefits intended for service people only are distorted to include civilians with a consequent disturbance to regular business competition and in conflict with fair trade practices.

In both of these equally deplorable conditions, the guilt is difficult to isolate and assess. Remedial measures undertaken by manufacturers, retailers or government stores employees have proved insufficient in most instances. This company has reported abuses and has urged action. But it must be admitted that results are temporary and often inadequate. We believe that the proper marketing of writing instruments is clearly defined in military regulations and in U. S. laws. Therefore, we urge a more rigid enforcement of these established regulations and laws by the attitude and insistence of Congress. If necessary we favor a more harsh schedule of penalties against offenders.

We give our full support to any movement or group undertaking to eliminate abuses of trade regulations and laws by action of duly elected representatives in the Congress of the United States.

Now notice the excerpts from a policy statement of Tulane University's School of Business Administration. In this memorandum specific details of the policy are given and definite instructions for carrying out the policy are included.

To: Faculty and Staff, School of Business Administration

From: Robert W. French, Dean

Subject: Procedure to be followed in case of accidents to students

The following procedure should be followed in case of accidents to students which occur in the classrooms, laboratories, or buildings on the campus:

1. An immediate report to the office of the University Health Service, Extension 341. This office is located at 27 McAlister Place and is open from 9:30 A.M. to 5:00 P.M., Monday through Friday, and Miss ______ ______,

Registered Nurse, is on duty there. A doctor of the University Health Service is in this office from 12:00 noon to 1:00 P.M. and from 4:00 P.M. to 5:00 P.M., Monday through Friday. The student should be taken to this office. Miss _____ is on duty also on Saturday from 9:00 A.M. to 12:00 noon.

2. A report by telephone to the office of the dean of the name of the student and the character of the accident. . . .

Policy statements may be general or specific. A general statement sets boundaries or limits and provides flexibility so that the person responsible can carry out the policy in his own way. A specific statement presents details and provides instructions for following the policy. Whether a general or specific policy statement is written depends entirely on its use and its readers. Whenever great flexibility is desired the general statement might be more appropriate. Whichever is used, however, completeness and clearness are necessary for understanding. The examples given here are very readable. There certainly should be no misunderstanding of their meaning.

The forms of policy statements vary according to their use and the reader for whom they are intended. They usually are letters, memorandums, bulletins or booklets. Sometimes loose-leaf notebooks, covering company policy and practice, are prepared by departmental heads for guidance of their employees and are kept up to date by being issued new pages as needed.

EMPLOYEE BOOKLETS

Booklets on many different subjects are prepared in almost all companies for distribution to employees. For instance, there are booklets describing the provisions of various employee benefit plans, such as pensions, savings, insurance, suggestion system, retirements, loans, etc. Booklets are also used in safety promotion programs and for orienting the new employee.

The illustration, page 289, shows not only the range of subject matter covered in employee booklets, but also the variety of attractive covers that have been used by several companies. The cover must be eye-catching to appeal to the reader, or the booklet may be discarded instead of being carried home and read by the employee and other members of his family.

Notice the differences between the two following paragraphs:

Tucked away in one corner of the inner chambers of your mind there may be money! Sound crazy? Could be, but ideas in Scott Paper Company *are* money

Courtesy (*top, left to right*) Louisiana Power & Light Company, Swift & Company, Scott Paper Company, National Biscuit Company, (*center*) Standard Oil Company (New Jersey), (*bottom, left to right*) R. J. Reynolds Tobacco Company, Shell Oil Company, National Biscuit Company

Employee booklets cover a wide range of subjects.

and an idea when it finally reaches the surface of your mind may have that golden hue. A pleasant thought! And that's what this booklet is for . . . to tell you all about 'Ideas in Action'. . . ideas and money. Exchange one for the other. *You can earn up to $1,000!*

Minimum pension provisions are being included in a greater number of conventional plans. In the conventional plans of this study, 63% have minimums.

The comparable percentage in our 1948-50 study was 28%. These figures include only minimum pensions expressed in dollars, and exclude minimums of the type expressed as a percentage of the final average pay of the employee . . .

The first paragraph is quoted from the "Scott Suggestion System," an employee booklet put out by the Scott Paper Company to inform their employees about the suggestion plan and to induce them to present ideas. The second paragraph is taken from page 17 of the 1953 edition of a report by Bankers Trust Company, New York, "A Study of Industrial Retirement Plans." It analyzes employee retirement programs established or amended, 1950–1952, and is of use to executives facing pension-planning problems. The wide difference in the style and makeup of the two reports illustrates one of the chief differences between an employee booklet and other informational reports

The "Scott Suggestion System" booklet appeals to the employee by getting his attention through a human interest approach. It is highly personalized and applies the "you" attitude by emphasizing a benefit to the reader and by using the pronoun, "you." The Bankers Trust Company's report is written in a factual style. It analyzes trends in industrial retirement plans and presents its material in an impersonal manner.

Observe the following excerpts from Shell Oil Company's booklet, "Program For Security."

As a Shell employee, you can look forward to income from at least three different sources after retirement. They are

Shell Provident Fund—Paid for by you and Shell on a 50-50 basis
Shell Pension —Paid for 100% by Shell
Social Security —Paid for by you and Shell on a 50-50 basis

Shell considers these three together as a Retirement Program.

. . . .

The main purpose of the Provident Fund is to permit you to approach retirement age secure in the knowledge that you have a retirement 'nestegg.'

Under its terms you contribute up to 10% of your regular earnings into an account which is established in your name. Your Company contributes dollar for dollar and the money is accredited to your account monthly.

Again the "you" attitude is used, gaining the reader's attention and interest. The employee is being informed about the company's retirement program and is liking it very much! Page 32 of the Shell booklet has been reproduced here on page 291 because it

BILL SMITH RETIRES

Bill Smith, age 60, retires after 20 years service with Shell. His wife, also age 60, is his beneficiary.

1 His Average Final Compensation is $400 a month.

2 He has $16,600 in the Provident Fund of which $8,300 arose from Company contributions. He may leave all or any part of the $16,600 in the Fund to share in earnings.

3 He is entitled to a Full Pension the amount of which, after Provident Fund deduction, is $142.70* a month, OR

4 Under Option 1, he may elect to receive $119.60* monthly and, after his death, his wife will receive one half or $59.80 monthly for life, OR

5 Under Option 2, he may elect to receive $102.93* and, after his death, his wife will also receive $102.93 monthly for life, OR

6 Under Option 3, he will receive $140.37* for life if, at his death, his wife is to receive $500. (This pension would be altered in the event that the lump sum payment is of a different amount.)

7 Bill may use $16,600 of his Provident Fund, or any part of that amount for the purchase of a Supplementary Pension. If he so uses the full amount of $16,600 his Supplementary Pension will be

8 $104.52 monthly if he elects Straight Life settlement under which all payments cease at his death, OR

9 $87.60 monthly if he elects Joint Survivorship settlement with one half of the amount, or $43.80, payable monthly to his wife after his death, OR

10 $75.40 monthly if he elects Joint Survivorship settlement with an equal amount, or $75.40, payable monthly to his wife after his death, OR

11 $86.12 monthly if he elects Cash Refund settlement. At his death his wife will receive the difference between $16,600 and the amount actually paid out to Bill through monthly payments.

12 If Bill was insured under the Shell Group Life Insurance Plan, his coverage, based on the amount of his wages at retirement, was $5,000. This protection will continue at no cost to him in the amount of $4,000 during the first year following his retirement, $3,000 during the second year, $2,000 during the third year, and $1,000 thereafter until his death.

*Subject to Social Security Deduction at age 65.

Courtesy Shell Oil Company

Story of a typical employee dramatizes company's retirement plan.

illustrates the use of narration in an employee booklet. The story of Bill Smith nails down the plan, and the reader visualizes himself as Bill Smith.

PROGRESS REPORTS

At two series of regional sales meetings—one held in New York and the other in Chicago—Doeskin Products, Inc. kicked off the sessions with an informative, fact-filled narrative report accompanied by illustrative slides.[1] It summarized the progress of the company over the past six months. Mention was made of the company's "Crusade to Save the Profit in the Tissue Industry," of the phenomenal 55% increase in sales over the first six months of 1952, and of the progressive, pioneering organization the salesmen were working for. The purpose of the report was to inform the salesmen of the company's progress and to make them want to be a part of it.

The Pennsylvania Railroad mailed a brochure, "A Pictorial Review of Progress," last year to their employees, stockholders and to others upon request. It pictured the progress of their large improvement program, showing projects that have been completed, others actively underway and still others in the planning stage. They all add up to the broad advance the Pennsylvania Railroad is making for the anticipated needs of business and industry, the travelling public and for the national defense effort. The report depicts in an interesting manner an informative study of progress, obtaining the good will of its readers and making them conscious of what Pennsylvania is doing.

In both of these instances company progress is portrayed to inform the readers and to win them to the company's side. In this way the reports build effective employee and public relations. Not all progress reports, however, use their information to strengthen industrial relations. The Georgia Tech Engineering Experiment Station from a research agency's viewpoint, for instance, makes wide use of progress reports from the time a project gets under way until it is completed, in order to keep the researcher on his target objectively, to keep the director alerted to his staff's current investigations, so he can reorient the work toward the desired goal, and to keep alive the sponsor's interest and confidence. Most research organizations use progress reports in the same way.

---

[1] Adrian Hirschhorn, "Don't Put On a Show for Salesmen Unless You Make It Worthwhile," *Printers' Ink,* October 30, 1953, p. 64.

Business management uses progress reports for keeping informed on activities and results in the company, for learning of new developments and for planning and coordinating work. Take a look at the following progress report from Louisiana Power & Light Company. It is used as a record of the work done in the leadership training program of the company and keeps the training director informed concerning each class meeting, so that he can plan and coordinate future training of the group.

LOUISIANA POWER & LIGHT COMPANY

LEADERSHIP IN BUSINESS PROGRESS REPORT

INSTRUCTIONS: This report should be completed by class secretary as soon as possible after the conclusion of each monthly Leadership in Business Meeting. Original (white copy) to be mailed to Personnel Office. Duplicate (blue copy) to be mailed to Division Manager or Department Head, and Triplicate (buff copy) to be retained by class secretary.

GROUP Operating Group, West Monroe

DATE OF MEETING Monday, August 10, 1953 NUMBER PRESENT 51

SUBJECTS DISCUSSED WERE "You've Got the Ball"

NAMES OF VISITORS C. N. Olivier and U. E. Mathis

RECORD ATTENDANCE ON REVERSE SIDE

IDEAS AND SUGGESTIONS BROUGHT OUT:

1. Mr. J. W. Gaines opened the meeting by presenting Virginia Hamel with a 10-year Service Pin and Ed Hodge with a 15-year Service Pin.
2. Mr. Olivier discussed controlling expenses. He stated that the fundamental idea behind expense control is to alert each individual employee to the realization that he or she has "Got the Ball" and that what we do with it will determine our controlling expenses. He stated that anyone could do a good job on unlimited funds, but our goal is to provide modern, efficient service economically. Controlling expenses is a challenge to us all.
3. Mr. U. E. Mathis stated that only by talking and thinking about the expense control constantly can we do something about it. Mr. Mathis led a discussion on expense items controllable by Louisiana Power & Light Company and ways expenses can be controlled.
4. Adjourn.

A progress report is used by committees, associations and other groups to indicate the advancement made in their work. The major use of a progress report, however, is to show successive stages of development of a project. In this capacity a series of progress reports will provide a running account of the work related to a single project from its beginning to its end, and a final progress report can be compiled when the project is completed. Excerpts from a report which indicate plans to be carried out on a project follow:

LOUISIANA POWER & LIGHT COMPANY
NINEMILE POINT — SNAKE FARM
110 KV TRANSMISSION LINE
AND RIVER CROSSING OVER MISSISSIPPI RIVER
AT HARAHAN

1. *General*

This specification covers the material and construction requirements for a 110 kv line from Ninemile Point Steam Electric Station to Snake Farm Substation, including a double-circuit steel tower crossing over the Mississippi River at Harahan.

The line shall consist of double-circuit steel towers with concrete footings, except for a distance of about 1½ miles between the Ninemile Plant and the approach to the Huey Long Bridge, which, except for the angle structures, will be single-circuit wood H-frame construction (future double-circuit), Drawing C-119211.

Both circuits shall be erected on the river crossing and on the line towers from the river to Snake Farm Substation, one circuit of which will be operated temporarily at 13 kv. On the remainder of the line only one circuit shall be installed with provision for adding a second circuit in the future.

Circuits shall be arranged as shown on Drawing B-119216.

A list of drawings covering the river crossing is shown on Drawing A-112495 and for the line on Drawings A-112460 and A-119205.

The following paragraphs are an example of what was written at the completion of a project. They are taken from a report done after the installation of the Slidell-Bogalusa 110 KV Transmission Line. They show how proposed plans were carried out, serve as a permanent record of the project and keep the administration informed.

LOUISIANA POWER & LIGHT COMPANY
SLIDELL–BOGALUSA 110 KV TRANSMISSION LINE

HISTORY GENERAL

General Features

This transmission line was built to connect the New Orleans-Gulfport and the New Orleans-Amite-Bogalusa 110 KV lines and thus provide a closed loop which completely encircles Lake Pontchartrain.

Starting at the Slidell Substation the line runs in a northerly direction, 38.64 miles, to a switching station about two miles west of Bogalusa in the New Orleans-Amite-Bogalusa line.

. . . .

Labor Policy

The M. S. Carroll Company paid the prevailing labor rates for this area.

Nine hours, on the job, were worked for six and seven days per week. Overtime was paid after forty hours of work in any one week.

Safety Program

Safety meetings were held periodically in which the contractor and his insurance company representative participated. There were no lost-time accidents on this job.

Purchasing

Mr. W. L. Rush prepared all purchase requisitions for materials for the entire line. With these Mr. H. M. Warren made the purchases and followed through to delivery. He encountered a great deal of trouble in attempting to get reasonable pole delivery.

Collect shipments were paid for by the Ebasco field office with drafts on the client. A complete file of all orders was maintained in the field office and a list of these orders appears elsewhere in this report.

Accounting

Under the terms of the contract 28 major items of charge were set up. These together with their subdivisions made 56 items on which unit prices were established. . . .

A progress report that shows a phase of development on a large project is fairly easy to organize and will nearly always adhere to a definite general outline pattern like the following:

I. General aim of the project and short summary of latest developments

II. Summary of earlier progress already reported

III. Detailed account of period covered by present report
- A. Obstacles encountered
- B. Methods used
- C. Record of new work done
- D. Accomplishments to date

IV. Forecast
- A. Next work to be done
- B. Anticipation of completion of work

A similar outline with some variations might be followed:

I. Summary
- A. Progress since last report
- B. Suggestions
- C. Forecast

II. Explanation
- A. Description of project
- B. Discussion of earlier progress

III. Details of progress since last report
- A.
- B.
- C.
- D.

IV. Personnel

V. Other considerations

VI. Appendix
   A. Itemized costs
   B. Data

In either of these organizational outlines major emphasis is on the progress that has been made so the reader will know the present status of the project. This, however, is shown in relation to what had been done earlier and what is to be done next. A chronological arrangement is often used to explain the steps taken; or the progress is described in terms of factors vital to the work, such as equipment, personnel, supervision, materials, labor, etc., or a combination of the two is followed. A point of major interest to the reader is the present status or latest development, so that it becomes a good starting point. Consideration must also be given to the purpose and needs of the report. Emphasis may be placed on methods, results, recommendations or any combination thereof.

The information presented in a progress report is usually drawn from records, experience, observation and interviews. Company periodic reports and statistics are also reliable sources. The task of the report writer is to present the progress completely, clearly and concisely, ensuring that the reader will understand the report. A good organizational outline helps to achieve completeness, clearness and conciseness. It is important that points not be overlooked; on the other hand, if the reader has first-hand information, a number of details may be omitted unless they are needed for the record. Keeping the reader in mind will also enable the writer to adapt his language and style to the reader's needs, interest and level of comprehension. This consideration will govern the use of general and special terms, of technical and non-technical language, and will enable the sections to be slanted to the reader.

Facts are presented objectively, but the reporter needs to have a creative imagination, foresight or intuition to look ahead when all the data are not in. He forecasts possible outcomes, although he cannot give definite conclusions and recommendations because at the time of the report they are still in the making. Simple style and language are always best. Illustrations, photographs, charts, statistics, etc. are valuable for the record and usually are placed in the appendix of a progress report. There they are used to supplement the text material.

If a progress report is submitted at a regular interval—weekly, monthly, etc.—it is in one sense a periodic report. Likewise nearly every periodic report indicates progress that has been made and is in one sense a progress report. Because the two types naturally overlap, a sharp line of distinction cannot always be drawn.

PERIODIC REPORTS

Periodic reports record at regular intervals routine activities of a company. The advertising department may give a weekly report

Courtesy American Can Company

Quarterly Report.

PROGRESS ON NEW PLANTS AND FACILITIES

Shown on the front cover of this Stockholders' Quarterly is an airview of the company's new Stockton, Calif., plant, formal opening of which took place on July 10, and which is now producing containers for the fruit and vegetable canners of the San Joaquin Valley.

Although difficulty in obtaining allotments of steel has caused some delays in the company's program of physical improvement, including replacements and alterations, construction of two new factories in the East began in June. Scheduled opening of these plants in 1953 will further enable the company to serve existing markets and meet the rising demands for containers of all types.

One of these new plants, under construction, at Lemoyne, Pa., will manufacture containers for canners of perishable foods in eastern and central Pennsylvania, western Maryland, West Virginia and Virginia. The second, under construction at Plymouth, Fla., 15 miles north of Orlando, will serve the expanding needs of Florida's citrus canning industry.

In June, milk containers were being produced on new manufacturing lines installed at our can manufacturing plant in Portland, Ore. This is the first company unit of its kind in the Pacific Northwest. At our Tampa, Fla., plant, first deliveries of fibre milk containers were made in July to that important and rapidly expanding area.

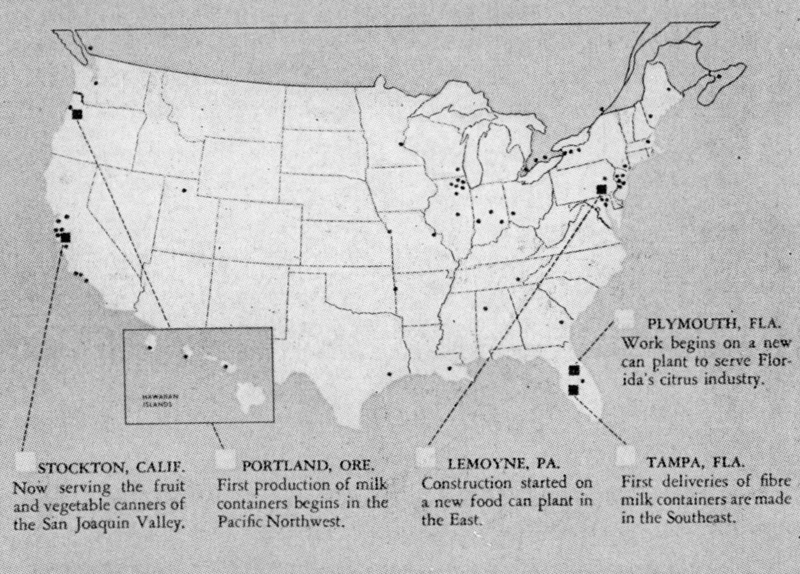

PLYMOUTH, FLA.
Work begins on a new can plant to serve Florida's citrus industry.
STOCKTON, CALIF.
Now serving the fruit and vegetable canners of the San Joaquin Valley.
PORTLAND, ORE.
First production of milk containers begins in the Pacific Northwest.
LEMOYNE, PA.
Construction started on a new food can plant in the East.
TAMPA, FLA.
First deliveries of fibre milk containers are made in the Southeast.

Quarterly report **(Cont.).**

AMERICAN CAN COMPANY
100 PARK AVENUE
NEW YORK 17, N. Y.

In the interest of providing stockholders with timely information concerning its operations, American Can Company will henceforth issue quarterly statements of earnings. Because this first interim report comes at the end of the second quarter of 1952, it reviews the first six months' operations.

TO THE STOCKHOLDERS:

During the first six months of 1952, American Can Company established a new high record of sales. Total sales and rentals amounted to $244,703,188, compared with $228,471,709 for the same period of 1951. This gain of 7.1 per cent is one of actual physical volume, since there have been only minor changes in the price structure since January, 1951. It reflects an increasing demand for the company's products and constantly growing productive capacity as new facilities comprising our expansion and modernization program reach the stage of completion and operation.

We were able to take full advantage of the increased plant capacity throughout the period because at the end of June our operations had not been affected by the crippling steel strike which all but stopped deliveries of tinplate for nearly eight weeks.

While no one could foresee a strike of such duration with its deplorable effect on

Quarterly report **(Cont.).**

the nation's industrial economy, the danger signs in the steel dispute were sufficiently alarming early in the year to indicate the need for a strong inventory position in order to protect our customers who look to the company for container supplies.

This condition prompted the management's decision to make the largest investment in the company's history in inventories of finished products, work in process and in raw materials to the full extent permitted under government inventory regulations.

The management feels there is reason for justifiable pride in the fact that the company's long standing policy of making adequate provision for plate has again enabled us to maintain our proud boast that none of the company's customers has ever sustained a loss of perishable foods by reason of its failure to fulfill its container commitments. With reasonable progress in resumption of operations in the steel mills it is now indicated that despite the tremendous pressure the strike has imposed on the can industry, this record will be maintained. While there will be some temporary curtailment in our production of other types of containers, it appears that there will be a minimum of inconvenience to our customers who pack non-perishable products and whose requirements under government regulations are secondary to protection of the food crops.

❑ EARNINGS

Estimated net earnings for the six-month period, subject to year-end adjustments, were $10,315,428, compared with $11,831,332 for the first half of 1951 Provision for taxes on income amounted to $11,175,047, compared with $14,508,643 in 1951.

These estimated net earnings, after provision for $1,443,166 of dividends on preferred stock, were the equivalent of 82 cents per share on the 10,885,591 shares of common stock outstanding, compared with 95 cents per share in 1951, computed on a basis of the same number of shares.

Sales, rentals and earnings for the second quarter are indicated in the comparative statement of earnings on page 7 of this report.

The statement of estimated earnings reflects reserves which are considered adequate to cover retroactive payroll increases which will evolve from negotiations not

***Quarterly report* (Cont.).**

completed at this writing with the labor unions, also provision for $1,370,000 of interest on the company's debentures and on short term loans required to maintain our strong inventory position.

☐ INCREASE IN WORKING CAPITAL

The management is pleased to report the successful completion of the company's 1952 program of new financing which added approximately $50,000,000 to working capital.

Of this amount $25,000,000 was provided through the sale of thirty-year 3¼ per cent debentures. A sum slightly in excess of $25,000,000 was provided by equity financing based on changes in the certificate of incorporation approved by stockholders at the annual meeting in April.

These changes in the certificate of incorporation made possible a change in the authorized capital stock of the company to 1,760,000 shares of preferred stock of $25 par value, and 15,000,000 shares of common stock of the par value of $12.50 per share.

The plan included a four-for-one split of the $100 preferred stock, a two-for-one split of the common stock and an additional distribution of one share of new common stock for each share of common owned after the split, having the effect of a four-for-one split of the common stock.

The board of directors authorized an offering of 989,599 shares of the new common stock with rights to stockholders to purchase, at $26.50 per share, in the ratio of one share for each ten shares held. The issue was fully subscribed.

☐ THE PRESENT OUTLOOK

While temporary curtailment of production of containers for non-food products to insure protection of the perishable packs calls for an adjustment in early estimates of the year's volume and government crop estimates indicate a more normal food pack than the unusually high level of last year, there is every indication that the company's total 1952 business will equal or exceed the record volume of 1951.

The importance of maintaining a high rate of production is obvious in the light of the pressures on earnings exerted by

Quarterly report **(Cont.).**

increasing tax rates, higher costs of tin-plate growing out of the steel wage settlement and increased payrolls in our own industry. From the standpoint of maintaining volume, the company, by comparison, has fared well. The extent to which the effect of these higher costs can be recovered by an upward adjustment of container prices under government price control will have an important bearing on future earnings. Every effort is being made to obtain a degree of price relief in recognition of the additional costs that will be incurred. Indications are that adjustments will be forthcoming.

* * *

The recent steel strike has subjected our economy to a severe test. There is little reason for national pride in the fact that the wheels of industry came near to a complete halt at a time when every ounce of industrial energy was sorely needed for the protection of the American way of life. Billions of dollars have been lost to the economy and more will be lost before we can return to normal. Our defenses have been weakened and we have surely lost some of our dignity in the eyes of the world. To say that our economy is resilient enough to shake off the effects of such a calamity is to beg the question. The welfare of the country is above factional or political considerations.

Respectfully,

WILLIAM C. STOLK,
President

July 29, 1952

Quarterly report **(Cont.).**

AMERICAN CAN COMPANY
COMPARATIVE STATEMENT OF EARNINGS

Second Quarter April 1 to June 30:	*1952*	*1951*
Net Sales and Rentals	$132,697,965	$114,043,933
Net Income before Income Taxes	$ 10,648,710	$ 12,500,861
Provision for Federal and Canadian Taxes on Income	5,537,329	6,890,947
Net Income	$ 5,111,381*	$ 5,609,914*
Dividends—Preferred Stock	721,583	721,583
Income Available for Common Stock	$ 4,389,798	$ 4,888,331
Per Share**	$.40	$.45

Six Months January 1 to June 30:	*1952*	*1951*
Net Sales and Rentals	$244,703,188	$228,471,709
Net Income before Income Taxes	$ 21,490,475	$ 26,339,975
Provision for Federal and Canadian Taxes on Income	11,175,047	14,508,643
Net Income	$ 10,315,428*	$ 11,831,332*
Dividends—Preferred Stock	1,443,166	1,443,166
Income Available for Common Stock	$ 8,872,262	$ 10,388,166
Per Share**	$.82	$.95

*Net income reported is based partly on estimates, is unaudited and is subject to year-end adjustments.
**Earnings per share are based on 10,885,591 common shares outstanding at present.

Comptroller's Office, New York
July 28, 1952

Quarterly report (Concl.).

on the cost of media used; the sales department may report a weekly volume of sales; an individual salesman may report daily the number of prospects he has, the number of calls made and the number of sales; the production department may report monthly the output of the company and the cost—these are routine business activities reported on at regular intervals. They provide information for further analysis and action. Periodic reports are often the basis for longer progress reports.

The presentation of accurate and complete information is the first requirement of periodic reports. Their organization is similar to that of the progress report. Different situations calling for periodic reports demand different plans. Often forms are provided so that the same type of information can be filled in repeatedly, report after report. They in turn are used as a basis for compiling longer reports over a greater period of time. Periodic reports of various departments in a corporation, for instance, are used as a basis for the company annual report. The annual report of a large corporation is a common example of a periodic report. It has taken on so great an importance and significance, however, that it warrants special treatment in Chapter 19.

The interim report, another periodic report, is much shorter than the annual report. Note the preceding example of a quarterly report of the American Can Company.

The report, which is addressed to the stockholders, presents a resumé of the progress on new plants and equipment. Under various headings it gives a resumé of the present status of the company, a record of the activities of the past six months and the future outlook. All of this is done clearly and concisely and is adapted to the reader's interest. One can readily see here the similarities to the progress report.

COMMITTEE MINUTES

Although committee minutes are not usually thought of as reports, they have enough characteristics of informative reports to warrant brief treatment here. They may be used in carrying out suggestions passed on by a group or in informing others of the group's activities. If the committee meets regularly at a specified time, the minutes become a periodic progress report of the results of each meeting.

Minutes are routine but their contents and arrangement can be varied. Sometimes, however, it is easier and quicker to follow a standardized pattern in recording them. They should contain, for the record, the time and place of meeting and a list of members present. This information is usually placed first. Then the minutes may be arranged chronologically according to the progress of the meeting or by subject headings according to the topics discussed and their relative importance and value.

Most minutes are arranged chronologically because all the secretary has to do is to write the report from the notes taken at the meeting—in the same order. This is a time-saver for the one who writes the minutes. If they are to be arranged by subject headings, the notes will have to be evaluated and rearranged. The reorganized material, however, presents a more interesting and useful report, for the person referring to the minutes can see at a glance the information he is seeking. Minutes must be accurate, complete and clear. Reports, important ideas, motions and opinions should be credited to the individuals contributing them. Emphasis should be given to such items as responsibilities delegated to members of the group, action that is to be taken after the meeting and reports due at the next meeting. When a member receives his copy of the minutes, if they are distributed, he is reminded of the duty he is to perform. This emphasis and distribution help in the proper functioning of the group.

In a company where several committees and departments operate separately and discuss their plans, policies and projects at meetings, the committee minutes serve as an invaluable tool to the executive who coordinates the work of the company. Aside from their value as records and their use in the functioning of the group, this is their chief value as informative reports.

CREDIT REPORTS

The basic purpose of a credit report is to show the extent to which a firm is entitled to credit. It presents a wealth of facts about a company, and the information is used as a basis for making a decision about credit. The banker makes frequent use of the information in credit reports to decide on loans to the businessman. The insurance examiner uses it to study the condition and trend of a business to determine its risk. Equipped with a file of reports on customers and prospects, the credit manager has adequate knowledge to make decisions on accepting or refusing credit; he can establish lines of credit in relation to ability to pay; he can smooth the approach to new accounts and he can be cognizant of important credit changes among his customers and prospects.

A purchasing agent also uses credit reports. They enable him to determine the value of a company and its products. He can verify statements; he can weigh the continuity of a source of supply. Other departments use credit information also. In light of company credit reports, salesmen can analyze what they sell, to whom they sell and on what terms they sell. The advertising manager can select key dealers, study new markets, apportion budgets and select appeals to be used.

A credit report contains essential facts about the history, method of operation, financial conditions and trade relations of a company. They are presented in an impartial way so that the reader can use the information as he sees fit. Dun & Bradstreet, Inc., a nation-wide fact-finding organization with offices in every important trade center of the United States and Canada and with international offices in principal world trade centers, has led the field in credit reporting. In more than a century of growth Dun & Bradstreet has kept pace with the commercial development of the nation and rendered credit-reporting services on all commercial enterprises to suppliers of merchandise and services and to banks and insurance companies.

Behind the information of any credit report is the investigation for facts. Let us follow a Dun & Bradstreet reporter from the time he begins an investigation until his final report is used as a basis for making a credit sale. This story is typical of the routine steps necessary to give the credit man information on the progress, current position and trend of a business. The Dun & Bradstreet reporter, whom we shall call Mr. Gordon, during his regular visit to Long Branch includes a call on Samuel Meyer, President and principal stockholder of General Sales Co., Inc. He studies the window display a moment, then goes inside the store. Mr. Meyer is very cooperative. He gives Mr. Gordon current information on assets and debts, sales and expenses, and answers questions about business prospects as affected by current conditions.

Gordon then calls on Mr. Haydon, Vice-President of the Third National Bank, and asks his opinion of the company and how Meyer is meeting his bank indebtedness. "On our books rather steadily; but we lend on Meyer's endorsement and consider him satisfactory," says Haydon. "Meyer is a wide-awake merchant. Carries low four-figure balances. People here like him."

Gordon drops in to see Mr. Calder, the county's largest wholesaler. "How's Meyer paying his bills?" asks Gordon. "We sell him up to $500 now, owes $300 with $150 past due. Pays reasonably prompt on thirty-day terms," replies Calder.

Back at the office Gordon dictates his report, and the record goes to the dictaphone operator who types the report. Then it is duplicated, distributed and stocked. An example of a finished report is shown on page 308.

The report is placed in the files ready to answer subscribers' inquiries. Additional copies are forwarded to Dun & Bradstreet offices in the trade centers where the merchant makes his purchases.

Now back to the department store of the General Sales Co. to see how the report is used in making a sale. Mr. Walton, salesman for the Acme Jewelry Corporation, is seeking some new business. He has checked the Dun & Bradstreet State Pocket Edition, which lists all the local commercial enterprises, including General Sales Co. Walton has placed General Sales on his prospect list for a call.

Walton enters, makes an effective sales approach and gets a $300 order from Samuel Meyer for novelty jewelry. It is a first order and a new customer for Walton, who mails the order to his home office.

The next morning Mr. Burke, the credit man of Acme Jewelry Corporation, receives the order and looks up the credit rating of the General Sales Co. Since it is a sizable order he calls Dun & Bradstreet for some immediate information on the new customer.

The inquiry is received at the service phoneboard, and the telephone ticket is made out and sent to the files where the report is taken out. The subscriber's number is listed on the card, the ticket is properly marked and the report is sent to the phoneboard. Here the operator reads excerpts to Mr. Burke, the credit man, who makes notes and requests the report be mailed to him. The report is checked and mailed.

When Mr. Burke receives the report he studies it carefully, checks the order and places the report in his files. A few days later Mr. Meyer receives merchandise. Thus credit has been established, and a business relationship has begun between retailer and supplier.

This story is typical of the credit investigation and of the use of a Dun & Bradstreet report. Now let us examine more closely a sample credit report and its elements.

Credit - MAN'S CONFIDENCE IN MAN

Dun & Bradstreet, Inc.

MERCANTILE CREDIT REPORTS NECESSARILY DIFFER IN FORM AND IN LENGTH, DEPENDING UPON THE SIZE AND COMPLEXITY OF THE CONCERN REPORTED . . . . THE POLICY OF THE AGENCY IS TO PRESENT THE ESSENTIAL INFORMATION AS CONCISELY AS POSSIBLE.

RATING UNCHANGED

5912
PENN PINES PHARMACY — CD 1 JUNE 26 195-

BROOKLYN 19 NY
1246 HAZEL ROAD

Miles Gross, Partner — Hannah (Mrs. Miles) Gross, Partner

RATING: E 2

SYNOPSIS

BACKGROUND: Firm formed April, 1946. One partner a pharmacist since 1933.
NET WORTH: $26,865 — SALES: $89,232 (Annual)
PAYMENTS: Discount
CONDITION & TREND: Condition sound. Sales increasing and operations profitable.

HISTORY

Style was registered by partners April 30, 1946.

This firm was formed April, 1946. Starting capital consisted of $10,500 savings $3,500 loan from Teachers Credit Union, and $3,000 loan from partners' families, making total of $17,000. Loans have since been repaid.

Miles Gross, 41, native born, graduated from Columbia College of Pharmacy 1933. Employed as pharmacist by Liggett Drug Co. between 1933 and 1936, and by Ray Drug Co. until this business was started.

Hannah (Mrs. Miles) Gross is 36. She was New York school teacher prior to formation of this firm.

OPERATION-LOCATION

Operates a pharmacy and soda fountain. Drugs and prescriptions account for 50% of sales, with balance equally divided among fountain, sundries, and confectionery. Fixtures are new with twenty-foot soda fountain. Both partners active and three employed. Gross and one employee are registered pharmacists.

Rents first floor of two-story building in good condition. Store measures about 20 x 50 feet. Located in recently developed residential section.

FINANCIAL INFORMATION

A financial statement at April 30, 195--cents omitted:

ASSETS		LIABILITIES	
Cash on Hand	$ 304	Accts. Pay.	$ 3,724
Cash in Bank	1,872		
Merchandise	14,950		
Total Current	17,126	Total Current	3,724
Fixts. & Equip.	10,913		
Station Wagon	2,464		
Deposits	86	NET WORTH	26,865
Total Assets	30,589	Total	30,589

Net sales from May 1, 195- to April 30, 195- $89,232; gross profit $26,181; salary and drawings of partners $4,732; net profit over and above salary and drawings of partners $5,467. Monthly rent $150., lease expires April 30, 195-. Fire insurance on merchandise and fixtures $25,000.
Signed: June 26, 195- PENN PINES PHARMACY By Miles Gross, Partner
Received by mail. No accountant indicated.

-----0-----

Residential construction has stepped up in this section with result that both sales and profits have mounted steadily. Part of earnings have been re-invested in the business to finance its growth.

HC	OWE	P.DUE	TERMS	PAYMENTS May 20, 195-	
2431	2146		10th of Mo.	Disc	Sold 3 yrs to date
340	230		2-10 N30	Disc	Sold since 1946
250			2-10	Disc	Sold 3 yrs
136	136		2-10 Prox	Disc	Sold yrs to date
75			2-10 EOM	Disc	
15			30	Ppt	Sold 2 yrs

6-26-5- (241 29) FOUR

PLEASE NOTE WHETHER NAME, BUSINESS AND STREET ADDRESS CORRESPOND WITH YOUR INQUIRY
The foregoing report is furnished, at your request, under your Subscription Contract, in STRICT CONFIDENCE, by DUN & BRADSTREET, Inc. as your agents and employees, for your exclusive use as an aid in determining the advisability of granting credit or insurance, and for no other purpose.
9H2-2(27704)

Courtesy Dun & Bradstreet, Inc.

Credit report on a retail pharmacy.

Synopsis: The important facts developed in the body of the report are summarized in the synopsis. Sometimes this information serves as an introduction to what follows. At other times it provides a condensation of essential information on which the credit manager can make a decision.

Rating: The financial strength and a composite appraisal of a business are indicated by rating symbol at the beginning and end of the report. It is a device used to classify firms by size and credit standing. The rating consists of two parts. The financial strength is represented by a letter of the alphabet, while the numerical part of the rating symbol reflects the composite of the firm's financial stability, character and payment record. No rating is permanent; changes in ratings are made daily.

Ratings, often studied by sales departments in planning sales programs, aid salesmen in selecting and classifying prospective customers. Manufacturers seeking agencies and dealers for their products also screen prospects by use of the ratings.

History: The names and ages of the principals or owners of a concern, along with their past business experience, are shown in the history section of a credit report. The business history of the proprietor or partner indicates his character and capacity. There are many important uses for the information found under "History"—verifying orders, identifying owners, partners and officers and revealing any outside business interests of the principals. The information also makes it easy to establish business relations because of the light shed on the principals.

Method of Operation: What a concern does and how it does it are important facts described under operations. The section explains the lines of merchandise handled or services rendered, price range, class of customers, selling terms, percentage of cash and credit sales, size of floor space and type of equipment. Knowing facts about the machinery of production and distribution prepares the reader for a clear understanding of the balance sheet and profit and loss figures. Sales departments use this information to determine whether or not a firm would make a profitable outlet for merchandise. Purchasing departments use it in determining the capacity of a manufacturer to deliver an order, maintain schedules and support guarantees.

Fire Hazard: Although in the sample report "fire hazard" is not used as a heading, a brief description of the physical conditions of the premises and adjoining buildings is usually given, since these factors are important from a fire-risk viewpoint. The fire record lists the fires that have occurred, including dates, causes, losses and insurance settlements.

Statement: From the statement the essential facts for determining the financial condition of the company can be obtained. Shown are the amount of capital, how it is applied and how much of it is borrowed. Balance sheet figures are often supplemented by profit and loss details, plus information regarding leases and insurance coverage. Comments following the statement give further explanation of the figures and a description of sales and profit trends.

Trade Reports: The purpose of this section is to record the manner in which the credit seeker pays his bills. Each line under "Trade Reports" represents the experience of a specific supplier. The column on the left shows the amount of highest credit (H-C) granted during the past year. Other columns from left to right indicate the amount now owing, the amount past due, terms of sale, manner of payment, and any explanatory remarks about the account. Trade reports information is obtained from the ledgers of a representative number of suppliers covering all markets and lines.

If a supplier intends to open a new account, he can tell from the paying experiences of others what to expect in his dealings with the prospective customer. If he has already been selling the account he is able to guide his own selling activity and credit policy by checking the relation of his own sales with those of other suppliers. Besides seeing the amount of credit being granted by others, he can also see the terms they have offered. Much of the information found in the "Trade Reports" section leads to further investigation.

SALES REPORTS

The Louisiana Power & Light Company conducted an outstanding sales campaign, the "Whale Hunt," in which districts over the state were organized as whaleboat crews sailing under a commander in search of prospects and sales ("whales"). It lasted for ten weeks and generated much enthusiasm and genuine employee participation. At the end of each two-week period a report was compiled and distributed among the employees informing them of the campaign's progress and inducing them to strive harder to capture more "whales" for their crew. At the close of the campaign final results were reported. The sales reports used during the campaign were periodic reports—consolidated at the close into a progress report—because they reported the sales accomplished.

An example follows of the periodic sales reports used. It should be examined for its special style of writing. The theme of the "whale hunt" runs throughout the report. Salesmen are members of the boat's crew; the district manager is the captain or commander; sales are whales, etc. It thus captures the reader's attention and maintains it, because the language used is well adapted to the theme, purpose and reader. The reader is spurred on to greater effort and teamwork in the "whale hunt."

SALES AND PROSPECTS CONTINUE TO SKYROCKET

With still another reporting period remaining, Louisiana Power & Light Company's "Whale Hunt" had reached staggering heights as the fourth period closed July 10, 1953. During the two-week period, 1,891 whales (sales) were landed by the LP&L fleet, bringing the total for the campaign to 6,489 (which was 58 per cent of the prospects secured).

Lookouts in the division crow's nests were keeping their weather eyes peeled. During the fourth period, 3,072 prospects were added to the whale sighting sheet, bringing the total to a tremendous 11,088 (an average of 22 per employee throughout the service area).

By divisions the accomplishments are:

	SALES		PROSPECTS	
	This Period	*To Date*	*This Period*	*To Date*
Northern	456	1617 (7.2/employee)	687	2794 (12/employee)
Southeastern	715	2531 (18.3/employee)	1233	4276 (31/employee)
West Bank	720	2341 (17.1/employee)	1152	4018 (29/employee)

Nearly 100 Per Cent Participation

All districts have 100 per cent employee participation except Ferriday—(Note to Boat Commander Preston: Please make every effort to secure 100 per cent participation.)

WHALE CATCHES (SALES) BREAKDOWN

	This Period	*To Date*
Home Freezers	299	971
Refrigerators	569	1865
Room Air Conditioners	908	3256
Commercial Refrigerator Cases	80	282
Water Coolers	29	98
Ice Cube Makers	5	11
Dehumidifiers	1	5

With The Division Ships . . .

NORTHERN DIVISION: The crews from this ship have encountered storms with gales and downpours. Then some of the boat crews were becalmed for several weeks with short water supplies. As a result, their catches have been smaller than those of the other whaling ships. However, the outlook for the remaining period is much brighter, and these sturdy individuals should turn in outstanding accomplishments in this closing period.

In spite of the difficulties encountered, the division's boat crews holding top places in sales per employee were as follows:

Haynesville	16.1
Dubach	15.0
Jena	10.9
Springhill	10.7
West Monroe	9.8
Arcadia	9.4
Gibsland	8.4

• • • • • • • • • • • • • • • • • • •

WEATHER IS A GOOD SALES ALLY

Sales of room air conditioners are greater than all other items of the campaign combined. This is true for this period, and for the campaign to date. The kind of weather we are having is a great sales aid to every item in the campaign. Let's all try to do a good all-round job of promoting all items. Examine your list of sales and try to pick up those items that are not going so well. Boat Crew Captain Felix Coleman did that up in Gibsland and reported four water coolers this period. That is good work and similar jobs can be done by other districts.

The next catch report, which is the final wrap-up, is due July 24. Please get them in on time.

The report has an attractive cover and title page combined, picturing a whaleboat. Attached to the report are two pages of figures giving the complete breakdown by districts and divisions and product by product for the period to date. In the text good use is made of subject headings in organizing the material to guide the reader and present important sales figures in simple table form.

Excerpts from the final progress report on sales are presented below. Here credit and acknowledgments are included to give the employee a sense of pride in having done his job well.

WHALE OF A CAMPAIGN

With practically every district boat crew reporting whopping catches during the fifth and final expedition, Louisiana Power & Light Company closed out one of the most outstanding sales campaigns in its history. In the words of experienced campaigners, "This sales activity has generated more enthusiasm and genuine employee participation than any past activity. The results will certainly be reflected in added revenue and should help many districts to improve their kilowatt-hour standing among residential, farm and commercial customers."

Before going into the actual results a word of strong praise is due Division and Assistant Division Managers, Division Sales Managers, and the Dealer Service Representatives for their splendid support in making this a successful campaign. Despite their many other problems and duties the Division Managers were in behind the campaign from the start and contributed materially to its success. We in the General Office are grateful for this support and feel that it will continue in campaigns to follow.

Of course, the results bespeak the fine efforts of our District Managers, Salespeople and District forces. With only few exceptions outstanding jobs were turned in by all district crews. Never before have they worked so closely as a team in accomplishing their objectives. The 100% employee participation alone is strong testimony to the teamwork and cooperative spirit that prevailed during the campaign. This sales activity proves beyond any doubt the value of our district employees in getting a good sales job done. In many instances the competitive spirit among district employees gave added impetus to the campaign. A good majority of our boat crew commanders have every reason to be extremely proud of their district's accomplishments. . . .

And lastly, it may be said with real conviction, that through this sales activity we have helped to solidify our dealer relations. No one can deny that this campaign has proved extremely successful for those dealers that chose to tie in with us and capitalize on our combined promotional efforts. We are a non-merchandise utility; every sale reported was a dealer sale, and there were 9,038 during a ten-week period. This campaign will go a long way toward making our dealer cooperative program a living reality.

REVIEWING THE FLEET CATCH

With the fifth and final expedition producing the biggest catch to date, LP&L whalers wound up their ten-week whale-hunting campaign in a blaze of glory. Total sales stood at 9,038 out of the 14,886 prospects developed during the furious and exciting campaign. One of the noteworthy accomplishments in the campaign was the 100% participation achieved among all district boat crews. Although there were many outstanding accomplishments, this 100% participation stands as a tribute to the boat crew commanders who saw to it their crews got behind the campaign and pulled their oars in perfect team spirit. . . .

DIVISION BREAKDOWN ON SALES OF MAJOR REFRIGERATION ITEMS

Division	*Home Freezers*	*Refrigerators*	*Room Air Conditioners*	*Commercial Refrig. Cases*	*Water Coolers*
Northern	434	603	937	160	41
Southeastern	440	958	1816	124	72
West Bank	626	1430	1244	100	26
State Total	1500	2991	3997	384	139

As we close out this whale of a campaign we should bear in mind that we have had to put aside a few of our day-to-day chores to make it the success that it was. With another major activity scheduled some few weeks away, it would be well for us to clean up those chores that we have had to put aside before the next activity starts. Remember our over-all sales job is far from done. We still have a long way to go before we reach the national average in kilowatt-hours per residential customer. We can reach that goal, and with several more successful campaigns like "The Whale Hunt" we'll be there.

We of the General Office want to express genuine appreciation to all for your contributions to this campaign. We hope that in the campaigns to follow you will demonstrate the same enthusiasm and teamwork that was displayed in this one.

Some informational sales reports deal with sales accomplished; others are used in promotion of sales. Insurance companies today are emphasizing the services they perform for their clients. It is common practice to compile information on a particular insurance plan or policy for an individual and to organize the facts as a report which is presented to the prospective customer. The representative then meets with the prospect to answer his questions and to further discuss the material in the report, which has interested the customer and "paved the way" for the salesman. A sale of a policy should result if the representative has followed through well. At the birth of a prospect's son, such a report from John Hancock Mutual Life Insurance Company explained plans for an educational fund. Several paragraphs of this report follow. Here the explanatory style should be noted and also the way in which facts are expressed in terms of reader interest.

PLANS AVAILABLE

There are two general plans for providing an educational fund through life insurance. These are by insuring the life of a child under an endowment to mature when he is ready to enter college, or to insure the life of the father so that the savings accumulated will equal the fund desired. . . .

The following policies will meet the need discussed above. Results at the end of the 18th year are included. If the child is ready to enter college at some other year, figures would be slightly higher or lower depending on the length of time the policy is in force.

Policy	*Annual Deposit*	*Total Deposits*	*Cash Value & Dividends*	*Total Cost*	*Cost per Year*
$ 5,000 Endowment Age 18	$311.30	$5,603.40	$5,449.50	$ 153.90	$ 8.55
$10,000 Preferred Risk	307.90	5,542.20	5,238.40	203.80	11.32
$10,000 20 Payment Life	442.00	7,956.00	7,879.60	76.40	4.24
$ 5,000 Preferred Risk with Family Income Provision of $50**	190.70	3,814.00	2,771.40	1,042.60	52.13

$5,000 Endowment Age 18—This policy covers the life of the child providing an endowment at age 18. Also included is a provision waiving premiums to be paid after the death or disability of the father. Thus the educational fund is assured whether or not the father lives, dies or becomes disabled. The life of the child is also insured for $5,000.

$10,000 Preferred Risk—This policy provides for the payment of $10,000 in the event of the father's death. This may be used to provide $5,000 for an educational fund and the remaining $5,000 received as monthly income until the child enters college. If the father lives, savings will have accumulated to approximately $5,000. Provision is included to waive premiums in the event of the father's disability.

$10,000 20 Payment Life—This policy is included to indicate how accumulated savings may be built up at a rapid rate by use of a limited payment life plan. If larger amount is to be provided than that mentioned above, this policy may be used to provide rapid accumulation at low cost. This policy also provides for waiving of premiums in the event of the father's disability.

$5,000 Preferred Risk with Family Income Provision—This policy provides for an income of $50 per month to be paid to the mother from the time of the father's death until the child reaches age 15, in addition to the $5,000 sum insured. Approximately $2,500 will be available if the father lives. Provision is included in case of the father's disability. Emphasis in this policy is placed on minimum annual deposit and maximum protection in the event of death.

Method of Settlement—The manner in which the funds are paid by the company to cover the cost of tuition, books, room and board, etc. can be arranged in any way desired. No decision is necessary until the time arrives for the boy to enter college.

** The cash value and dividend estimates are not available at the end of the 18th year. The figures for this policy are the results at the end of the 20th year.

One method of settlement of $5,000 proceeds might be:

$250 lump sum payment in September and February of each year for four years	$2,000
$65 payment each month from September to June of each year for four years	2,600
$50 payment in July and August of each year for three years	300
Total	$4,900

The remaining $100 plus interest on the unused balances may be presented as a graduation present in June of the fourth year.

With the emphasis on *assuring* a fund to provide for the education of your son, the $10,000 Preferred Risk policy is best. Consideration must be made, of course, of how much you desire to provide, how much you desire to save and the degree of protection you would like. This plan will provide approximately the same savings at age 18 with approximately the same annual deposit, as will the $5,000 endowment. The increased protection, however, is considered an important factor.

Of course not all sales reports are informational; some are analytical and others are recommendation reports. There are also sales promotional reports on finding new markets, developing new markets and changing product to meet demand of market, and sales operational reports on operating an existing department under existing policies. The purpose in presenting the examples of sales reports here is to show how they can be used as informational reports. It must be realized, however, that the term, "sales report," refers to a classification of reports according to business function; and on that basis there are production reports, advertising reports, accounting reports, finance reports, administrative reports, etc., each dealing with its own particular function in a business. The basis for classification of reports followed here is according to the general purpose of the report —to inform or to analyze. In this sense the sales reports mentioned here are typical of reports that might be written in connection with any phase of business activity.

PROBLEMS

1. In the past your company has sponsored business speaking courses for employees. Numerous requests have been submitted through suggestion boxes, by letters and verbally that the course be repeated this year. You have arranged for Mr. John Kinson, an outstanding authority in the field of business speech, to teach the course this year. There will be a series of ten dinner meetings on Mondays from 5:30 P.M. to 8:30 P.M. in the company dining room. The company will pay the tuition cost and expenses other than for the dinners. Each dinner will cost $1.75 per employee. Meetings will start the first Monday in February. Regular attendance is expected. Enrollees will gain practice in speaking before the group.

Prepare the report you would send to the employees informing them of the course and making provision for them to enroll if they wish.

2. You are personnel director in your firm. There has been difficulty with one department in keeping open the flow of communications. An open door policy exists in the company; but in this particular department complaints are stopped by the supervisor and go no further, although he does not always handle them satisfactorily. The men are afraid to go over his head, thinking their jobs may be at stake.

Finally, through the grapevine, complaints have reached you. Upon checking them, you find they are well founded. You also decide, after talking with the men, to establish a grievance committee and to set up a suggestion box for the employees' benefit. It is your responsibility to formulate a policy statement and circulate it among the employees. It should cover points such as composition and makeup of the committee, organization of the committee, duties and responsibilities of the members and functioning of the committee as a group.

You may need to do some reading in books and articles on industrial relations or labor problems to help you formulate your policy; or perhaps you can draw from knowledge you have obtained from a course in the subject.

3. To reduce the company's cost of benefits granted to employees under Workmen's Compensation laws, to maintain good personnel relations and to reduce the number of accidents among employees who attempt to work while ill or injured, you have formulated the following policy concerning leave of absence due to illness or accident:

(*1*) Wages or salary are to be paid, based on the standard work week and the employee's base rate or salary.

(*2*) Wages or salary are to be paid only to the extent the applicable statutes provide.

(*3*) Sick leave with pay is to be given to employees absent from work because of illness or injuries received in an accident.

(*4*) The maximum amount of leave shall be eight weeks.

(*5*) Each employee must have been in the company at least sixty days to be entitled to sick leave.

(*6*) Up to the first full year of employment, one day of leave of absence for each month of service shall be given.

(*7*) For each additional year of service with the company, one additional week of leave of absence shall be given.

Prepare the copy for your leave of absence due to illness or accident policy to be included as part of a company booklet on employee benefits to be distributed to all employees.

4. Bring an employee booklet to class. Discuss its purpose and use. How does its tone and style differ from other types of reports?

5. Write a progress report on the work you have completed on your long report for this course.

6. Find out the financial or operational history of one of the firms in your community and write a report showing the progress that has been made.

7. Obtain a quarterly or semiannual statement from your bank and write a two-page periodic report to be sent to the bank's clients.

8. You are an insurance representative and have a client who is interested in a retirement income endowment policy, maturity age 65. You have gathered the following information from your company:

Premiums:	*Quarterly*	*Semiannually*	*Annually*
Basic policy	$66.93	$131.93	$257.42
Additional benefits available:			
Premium waiver	2.33	4.60	9.01
Double indemnity	2.08	4.03	7.88

Results at Maturity Age 65:

Guaranteed value	$10,231.20
Dividend accumulation	4,097.58
Total value	$14,328.78

Dividends:

End of year	*Dividend*	*Premium less dividend if applied*
1	$28.41	$229.01
2	30.93	226.49
5	38.87	218.55
10	52.22	205.20
15	65.08	192.34

Dividends are according to the current year's dividend scale and interest rate credited on accumulations, and are not guarantees for the future. No company guarantees dividends. However, your company has paid substantial dividends for 125 years. It is the insured's option at any time to withdraw the cash value and dividend accumulations or to apply the cash value and dividend accumulations to policy settlement options for income.

Protection:

Creates immediate estate of $6,300.00, including any dividend accumulations.

Fully paid-up:

If dividends are allowed to accumulate, policy may be declared paid up in 25 years.

Guaranteed monthly income for life, age 65	$63.00
Additional income from dividend accumulations	25.26
Total monthly retirement income available	$88.26

Emergency Values:

End of year	*Guaranteed cash value*	*Div. acc. at 3%*	*Paid up endowment, age 65*
1	$ 55.69	$ —	$ 113.00
2	241.61	60.23	485.00
5	837.90	177.72	1,575.00
10	2,018.33	453.98	3,421.00
15	3,221.57	843.89	4,933.00

Results after 20 years:

Guaranteed value	$4,597.36
Dividend accumulation	1,366.09
Total value	$5,963.45

Prepare the report to be used in helping to sell the client the retirement policy.

9. Write a Dun & Bradstreet type credit report from the following information on the Horowitz Products Company:

40% of sales are to real estate concerns, 15% to hotels, 20% to institutions and 25% to commercial houses. The trade style was registered by Benjamin Horowitz on January 2, 1942. He is married and was born in 1901 in Lima, Ohio. Business (not incorporated) was established in 1942. 261 Main Street, Dayton, Ohio. Benjamin Horowitz in 1921 became a partner in a local retail men's clothing business, but sold his interest in 1928. Sells wholesale janitor supplies, including disinfectants, brushes, mops, detergents, waxes and metal refuse containers. Storage and office space 2,500 sq. ft. on ground floor, six-story building. In good condition in downtown wholesale district.

Net sales year ending December, 1954: $174,587.64. Gross profit $58,195.88. Six employees, two salesmen, three clerks, one driver. One truck is used for delivery purposes.

Terms 2% 10, net 30 days (85%) cash 15%.

125 accounts in Dayton and nearby counties. Rating: E 2. Operations have been profitable and tangible net worth has steadily increased. Sales have shown steady upward trend. With assistance of moderate bank support trade invoices are generally discounted. Two salesmen on commission basis against drawing account.

Improved conditions in respect to availability of merchandise following the war. In 1947 withdrawals exceeded profits by $3,724.27. Withdrawals included $6,725 used to purchase a residence at 27 Park Street, Dayton. The owner's wife is named Ocelia. Balance sheet of December 31, 1954 reflects satisfactory condition. After he sold his interest in the retail clothing business in 1928, Horowitz was employed as salesman for five years by Royal Janitor's Supply Co., Columbus, Ohio. In 1941 he resigned to start this business as of January 1, 1942, with $7,500 representing his life savings. Seasons: steady throughout the year. Net profit December 31, 1954 was $10,168.73. Withdrawals $14,873. Annual rent $2,940; lease expires in 1955. Inventory valued at cost. Fixed assets net of $610.30, reserve for depreciation. No reserve for bad debts, but $450 of bad debts was charged off in 1947. This concern uses one bank (local). Balances ranging from four to five figures are maintained. Occasionally, medium four-figure straight paper loans are obtained for making bulk purchases at advantageous prices. The last such loan was November, 1950 and was retired January 15, 1954. No loans requested since that date.

Fire record: no fire reported. In December, 1950 a fire broke out in a warehouse next door to Horowitz, and through damage a loss of $10,000 was sustained. No damage to Horowitz's business. Building in good condition. Wood construction.

A son was born in December, 1933. He is a senior at Ohio State University.

Inventory valued at cost. Residence is valued at cost of $16,725 and is subject to 4½%, mortgage of $10,000; this lien held by local bank. Payments $77.25 monthly. On July 8, 1954, David Horowitz stated that sales for the first six months of 1954 amounted to $136,267 and were approximately 25% larger than for the same months of 1953. Inventory was estimated at $18,000, and liabilities at $13,000. Debt was stated to be covered by cost of $8,000 and accounts receivable of $14,000. Benjamin Horowitz has a brother named David. Financial statement was prepared by Jack Guidon, C.P.A., Dayton, Ohio. Benjamin is a high school graduate and attended the University of Indiana for two years. He married Ocelia in June, 1930.

10. Write a Dun & Bradstreet type of credit report, using the following information on the Del Grande Service Station:

A financial statement as of September 16, 195_:

Assets		*Liabilities*	
Cash in bank	$ 2,055	Accts. Pay.	$ 1,900
Accts. Rec.	3,800		
Mdse.	5,000		
Notes Rec.	120		
Total Current	10,975	Total Current	1,900
Fixts., Machy., Tools	700	NET WORTH	9,775
Total Assets	$11,675	Total	$11,675

REAL ESTATE	TITLE	VALUE	MTG.
1568 Sixth St., Home	Jointly	$11,000	$4,000

On March 3, 195_, Del Grande reported volume steady to increasing slightly at $15,000 monthly. Unregistered trade style. Uses advertising. Starting capital $4,118. His first business venture. Purchased station on July 16, 1951 from Leonard G. Makes. By staying open nights this summer hopes to make $20,000 monthly. Started 1951. Net worth $9,775. Sales $15,000 monthly. When he started his station the total debt was less than $2,500 and consisted entirely of current bills. Home exempt under state laws.

A record of payments follows:

HC	OWE	P DUE	TERMS	PAYMENTS MARCH 2, 195_	
450	275		2% 10–30	Disc.	Sold 8 — to date
600			Net 30	Prompt	Sold 19 — to date
350	135		2%–10–30	Prompt	Sold 10 — to date

Carl Del Grande was born 1924. Married, native of Eureka, Calif. He was a professional baseball player for Detroit and Pittsburgh Pirates minor leagues for several years. Except for some slowness in collections, finances in good shape and he is making money. Texaco Service Station is in Humboldt County, at Fourth and Broadway Streets in Eureka, Calif. He retails gasoline and oil, tires, batteries, accessories. He also does car washing, lubricating and towing.

Rating is G 3½. Owner is active. Five people are employed. Prior to purchasing the station Carl was employed as laundry and dry cleaning route man for three years. He rents a typical one-story steel and wood building. Is located on a well travelled street. Building is in good repair. Premises are usually neatly maintained.

Payments: discount and prompt. Sales from 7-24-__ to 8-31-__, $19,612. Monthly rent, $100. Lease expires August 11, 195_. Option to renew. Has fire insurance on $2,500 merchandise. Operations are profitable.

Has $2,000. Receivables now $5,100 and good but 25% slow. Plans to adopt tighter credit policies. Inventory now $5,000 and equipment $1,100.

CHAPTER *18*

Analytical Reports

STATISTICAL ANALYSIS
ANALYSIS OF CONDITIONS
RECOMMENDATION REPORTS
Organization
Special Functions

ANY REPORT IN WHICH THE MAJOR EMPHASIS IS ON AN analysis of the results of an investigation or the proposed solution to a problem is an analytical report. It continues from where the informational report stops; it analyzes the facts and, in the process of interpreting them, reaches conclusions. The analytical report informs, analyzes and may also recommend.

Look at the following excerpts from an analytical report used by Swift and Company to determine consumer preference for a copper-bottom skillet that the company was considering as a premium. A combination interview-questionnaire was used for gathering data which were presented and analyzed. No action was recommended, but a conclusion was reached as to customer acceptance of the skillet.

CC: Messrs. Wm. B. Traynor — 3rd floor
E. A. Moss — 2nd floor
L. A. Shepherd (TMA) — 4th floor
V. D. Beatty (WCM) — 2nd floor
M. L. Westering — 2nd floor

October 26, 195_

Mr. M. L. Westering (RMW)
Second Floor

7″ COPPER-COATED STEEL PANS — CHROME INSIDE

In your letter dated October 9, 195_, you requested that the Commercial Research Department obtain consumer reactions to a seven-inch, copper-coated, chromium-lined skillet, which is being considered as a premium in connection with Swift's Cleanser. Because the manufacturer of the skillets must get his orders placed for the necessary raw materials as quickly as possible, we conducted a very short opinion survey among Chicago housewives.

Normally an investigation of this type would involve setting up several stores and equipping them with the pans and POP material and actually measuring sales; in other words, as closely approximate the actual situation facing the housewife as possible. We have found from experience that we get a bias toward "yes" answers when we *ask* people whether or not they *think* they would buy something, as compared with a sales test where housewives actually have to put out their money for the item. Therefore, you can see that this investigation is *not* a measure of *how many* or *how well* the skillet will sell, but rather housewives' opinions regarding their reactions to the skillet when having an opportunity to look it over. From this investigation we can decide whether or not the skillet will meet with public acceptance.

The field work was conducted in Chicago, October 17, 18, 19 and 20.

Objective

To investigate consumer opinions on a seven-inch, copper-coated, chromium-plated skillet so a decision can be made as to whether or not the skillet should be offered as a premium in connection with Swift's Cleanser.

Method

Two field investigators, hired especially for this study, conducted 385 interviews in 13 large grocery outlets, which were located in several sections of the city. The interviewing was accomplished in large grocery outlets because it has been proposed that the skillet be distributed at the retail store level. Also, this was a quick way to talk with a lot of housewives. The interviewers were each equipped with one of the skillets, so each respondent had an opportunity to see and handle the pan.

The interview was opened by displaying the pan to the respondent and asking her what she thought about it. No mention was made of Swift's nor of the actual deal (75 cents with the purchase of two cans of Swift's Cleanser) until the end of the interview. During the interview likes, dislikes and possible uses for the skillet were obtained.

The findings that follow break down the answers to each question by those housewives wanting a skillet and those not wanting a skillet.

Findings

1. The interview opened by handing the respondent the pan and asking her what she thought about it. Favorable comments far out-weighed the unfavorable ones, even among the group who said that they didn't think they would get a pan.

WOULD YOU PLEASE EXAMINE THIS PLAN
AND TELL ME WHAT YOU THINK ABOUT IT?

	Housewives Who Thought They:			
	Would Get Pan		*Would Not Get Pan*	
	No.	%	No.	%
Favorable Comments				
Good looking, attractive	92	34	37	34
Very nice pan	66	24	16	15

WOULD YOU PLEASE EXAMINE THIS PLAN
AND TELL ME WHAT YOU THINK ABOUT IT?

	Housewives Who Thought They:			
	Would Get Pan		*Would Not Get Pan*	
Well constructed, made well	55	20	10	9
Nice weight, good weight	48	18	10	9
Good size, handy size	45	16	10	9
Like copper bottom	10	4	1	1
Smooth edge, beveled edge	9	3	1	1
Ornamental	5	2	2	2
Nice shape, deep	3	1	1	1
Easy to handle	3	1	–	–
Easy to keep clean	3	1	2	2
Copper holds heat	1	–	3	3
Miscellaneous	19	7	5	5
Unfavorable Comments				
Don't like copper	–	–	11	10
Too small	1	–	10	9
Looks like one I got from Swift's, no good	–	–	5	5
Doesn't appeal to me	–	–	5	5
Don't like handle	3	1	4	4
Difficult to keep clean	–	–	3	3
Too light	1	–	3	3
Miscellaneous	1	–	4	4
Number Answering	273		109	

. . . .

5. The "pay-off" question was saved until the end of the interview so that we could get as unbiased a reaction as possible to the pan. About 7 out of 10 of the women questioned thought that they would like to get a pan if offered in her favorite store for 75 cents with the purchase of two cans of Swift's Cleanser. As has already been pointed out, this is no doubt biased toward "yes" answers. But the lack of any severe criticisms throughout this study would indicate that a decision to use the pan as a premium would probably be the proper one.

IF THIS PAN WERE OFFERED IN YOUR FAVORITE STORE
FOR 75 CENTS WITH THE PURCHASE OF TWO CANS
OF SWIFT'S CLEANSER TODAY, DO YOU THINK YOU WOULD GET ONE?

	No.	%
Yes	274	71
No	111	29
Total	385	100%

6. Those housewives who indicated that they didn't think they would get a pan were further questioned as to why they didn't want one. The principal reasons consumers gave for not wanting one were nothing against the pan itself, but rather that they just didn't have a need for a pan of that size and type.

Reasons Given for Not Wanting Pan

	No.	%
Have enough pans already, have one that size	50	45
Don't like copper, hard to keep copper clean, prefer other types of metals, don't like copper bottoms	19	17
Too small	17	15
Got one from Swift's, no good	6	5
Not a good value, too high, cheap	5	5
Don't like Swift's Cleanser	3	3
Handle hurts hand	3	3
Miscellaneous	8	7
Total	111	100%

Conclusions

It would seem that from all indications in the study that a decision to accept the seven-inch skillet would be the proper one. An indication that housewives have a need for a skillet of this size and type has been borne out by the overwhelming success of the first skillet offer. Of course this survey did not put the skillet to use, but it is our understanding that it did receive thorough testing in the laboratory. Two of the top complaints registered for the old six-inch skillet apparently have been remedied—lightness and rusting.

As pointed out in the beginning of this letter, it was beyond the scope of this survey to measure how much success this premium will enjoy. Nor did we measure the merit of the proposed "in-store" method of distribution of the pan. We have merely established that upon a quick inspection of the pan, 7 in 10 housewives thought they would like to get one for 75 cents with the purchase of two cans of Swift's Cleanser.

R. W. COFFMAN

Commercial Research Dept.
Marketing & Sales Research Div.
RIT:MH

Classifying analytical reports must necessarily be on an arbitrary basis. Emphasis upon the analysis of the findings is a common characteristic of all analytical reports. On the basis of kinds of analyses presented, there are three general types of analytical reports discussed here: those that use statistical analyses, those that report on present conditions of a business, process or department and those that examine an idea, process or object — examination reports.

STATISTICAL ANALYSIS

A statistical report emphasizes the use of statistical methods either in gathering data or in analyzing them. When the emphasis is on statistical methods, an explanation of them is usually presented in detail at the beginning of the report. Here they serve the function of orienting the reader so that he will have a complete understanding of what has been done. An excellent example of this use is the discussion presented under "Method" in the *Consumer Analysis of the Indianapolis Metropolitan Market,* compiled and published by *The Indianapolis Star* and *The Indianapolis News* in 1953.

Method

The CONSUMER ANALYSIS type of survey long has been recognized and accepted by advertisers, agencies, distributors and manufacturers for its ability to determine consumer brand preferences and buying habits in a given market.

In Metropolitan Indianapolis—a rich, diversified, $2,000,000,000 market—the CONSUMER ANALYSIS permits individual, personal contact with a representative group of families for careful checking of all information obtained.

In order to study the final flow of goods to the consumer, this study actually questions the consumer and correlates the information obtained with a thorough check on the availability of the product through a store distribution survey.

The data for this study came from questionnaires filled in at home by 3,586 housewives and returned, in person, to the survey office. The questionnaires covered brand preferences, buying habits, ownership and other pertinent information embracing a wide range of products. A copy of the questionnaire is included at the back of this book.

The various operations involved include the sample, mailing, editing, bag pack, tabulation, reporting and the store sample and store check for ascertaining product distribution.

Sample

The number of families in Marion County on January 1, 1953, was estimated to be 179,300. Several sources were used to arrive at this figure. They were residential building permits; electric, gas and water meters; annual rate of increase in families in Marion County from 1940–1950; U.S. rate of increase since April, 1950, and the portion of this which is in Marion County.

3,586 returned questionnaires would give a straight 2% sample. From past experience it was known that approximately 15,840 questionnaires would have to be mailed in order to get the 2% sample or a questionnaire mailed to one out of every 11 homes. The 1951 City Directory of Indianapolis and suburban areas was used for selecting every eleventh name. In other parts of the county not covered by the City Directory information from the Post Office was used for this purpose.

Mailing

The envelopes were addressed to the housewife and separated into census tracts. Then each census tract was separated into three groups. Starting December 30 and continuing through January 15 questionnaires were mailed daily to every fifth census tract. After the first five days, when all areas had been covered, the second group of questionnaires was mailed in the same manner. Adjustments, based on returns from the first two groups, were made on the third group of questionnaires.

Several changes were made that were effective in increasing the ratio of returns. It was necessary to mail 12,582 questionnaires or 3,258 less than the original estimate of 15,840. Of these 3,885 were returned, or they were returned at the rate of 309 per thousand mailed. In addition 62 of the questionnaires were mailed in and 1,061 were returned by the Post Office because of change in address, etc. This gave a net rate of return of 343 per thousand mailed.

The surplus of 299 questionnaires was laid aside and not used when the quota was filled for each census tract.

. . . .

Tabulation

After the questionnaires are edited they are filed in groups of 50 and prepared for the first tabulating process, which is coding. Coding each of the 250 questions is the biggest job as far as time is concerned. This year 1,300 man hours were spent by 14 people who were trained for this job.

The information is then punched on cards—it takes 9 cards for each questionnaire. International Business Machines, which are used for this purpose, are permanent installations in the Research Department of THE INDIANAPOLIS STAR and THE INDIANAPOLIS NEWS.

The cards are sorted and trained personnel tabulates and totals the final results. They are then projected to the 179,300 families in the Indianapolis Metropolitan Market. For example, if 3,400 of the housewives answering the questionnaire say that they use white bread, this projected shows that 170,000 of the 179,300 families use white bread. Brand popularity is handled in the same manner.

Reliability of the method followed and its sensitivity, even in small segments of the over-all area, has been cross-checked against known facts in the Indianapolis Metropolitan Market.

Extensive studies have been made which show that a stability point of a brand's standing is reached easily with a 2% sample.

Sometimes the use of statistical methods is briefly explained in the introduction with details given in the appendix at the end of the report. Placed here they are used for reference, and more emphasis is given to the results than to the method. This procedure was followed by the CBS Television Research Department in their report on *U.S. Television Ownership by Counties, May 1, 1953*. The brief explanation in the "Introduction" is:

In this report, we have used statistical methods to estimate television ownership by counties for May 1, 1953. In essence our method involved a standard statistical technique of forecasting from past data. We grouped all counties by: 1) level of set penetration on May 23, 1952; and 2) length of television service in the area. Using the data from the Census and Nielson surveys, we were able to draw curves for these groups of counties and to project their future growth to May 1, 1953.

The details of this estimating process are presented in the appendix. We feel that the needs for such data are so great the errors inherent in any estimating process are relatively inconsequential.

When the emphasis is upon the statistical analysis of data, the facts are usually presented in tables, and an interpretative discussion is given. Often a comparison is made of data in several tables, and relationships are pointed out for determining significant trends. Note the way this has been done by Bankers Trust Company, New

York, in their 1953 edition of *A Study of Industrial Retirement Plans*. In the section on "Trends in Retirement Plans," the following analysis of the eligibility requirements of conventional plans is given. Two tables are compared here for determining trends.

Conventional plans—The eligibility requirements in a conventional plan usually refer to the years of service which must be completed and the age which must be attained by an employee before he may become a member of the plan and may start to accrue benefits. These requirements define the earliest date on which an employee may become a member of the plan. In Table II, the eligibility requirements in the 217 conventional plans of this study are summarized and compared with those of the 1948–50 plans covered by our 1950 edition.

TABLE II
Conventional Plans

Eligibility Requirements	*1948–50 Plans*	*1950–52 Plans*
None	14%	21%
Age only	5	1
Service only	30	35
Age and Service	51	43
Total	100%	100%

A detailed analysis of the eligibility requirements of the conventional plans of this study is shown in Table III. In plans which have more than one set of requirements, we have used the set that would probably be applicable to the average employee.

TABLE III
Conventional Plans

Service Requirements	*Number of Plans by Age Requirements*			
	No Age	*Age 25 % under*	*Age 30*	*Age 35 % over*
None	47	1	1	–
1 year or less	43	15	23	6
2 years	10	2	8	1
3 years	8	7	9	3
4 years	2	–	–	–
5 years*	13	1	13	4
Total	123	26	54	14

* Includes one plan having a service requirement of 6 years.

A comparison of the figures in Tables II and III with similar figures for the 1948–50 plans and 1943–47 plans covered by our previous studies shows the following interesting trends:

(1) The use of an age requirement is diminishing. In the 1950–52 conventional plans, 44% included an age requirement compared with 56% in the 1948–50 plans and 52% in the 1943–47 plans.

(2) Among the plans using an age requirement, the tendency is toward a lower age requirement. However, age 30 continues to be the favored age by a large majority of the plans using an age requirement. Age 35 is being used less, and age 25 is being used more often.

(3) A service requirement is found in about the same percentage of plans as in previous years. In 1950–52 conventional plans, 78% included a service requirement compared with 81% in the 1948–50 plans and 85% in the 1943–47 plans.

(4) Among the plans using a service requirement, the tendency is toward reducing the requirement. Only 18% of the conventional 1950–52 plans with service requirements had a requirement as long as five years, while 64% had a requirement of two years or less. Among the 1948–50 plans, the percentages were 39% and 43%, respectively. Among the 1943–47 plans, the percentages were 45% and 38%, respectively. . . .

Many times an analysis of figures and percentages in tables and charts is made for drawing conclusions. Then relationships of significant items are pointed out, and the entire discussion is used as a basis for the conclusion that the reader reaches and accepts. The following report excerpts illustrate how a conclusion is reached from the analysis of the data given.

COMPARATIVE ANALYSIS OF GEORGIA AND IOWA TO DETERMINE WHICH CONSTITUTES THE LARGEST POTENTIAL MARKET FOR LOW-PRICED MEN'S SUITS

INTRODUCTION

Purpose

The purpose of this analysis is to determine which of two states, Iowa and Georgia, offers the better general conditions for introducing and selling a low-priced—$22.50 to $48.75—line of men's medium-weight, wool suits. The manufacturer of these suits is located in Cleveland, Ohio, and is a relatively new producer who has been expanding rather slowly, a state at a time, developing the largest potential markets first. Sales are made through a number of widely scattered, but carefully selected, men's clothing stores.

The primary consideration and objective is to determine which state offers the larger potential market.

A second objective, almost as important as the first, is to determine the availability of suitable advertising media and the comparative costs for a similar advertising campaign in each state.

Finally, the analysis includes a study of various other less important matters which may, nevertheless, have some effect upon the ultimate selection. These minor factors are:

(*1*) Freight costs
(*2*) Climatic conditions
(*3*) Competition
(*4*) Racial distribution

Scope and Limitations

. . . .

Methods of Analysis

. . . .

ANALYSIS OF THE POTENTIAL MARKET

Determination of Number of Potential Customers

The market for a low-priced line of men's suits is limited to a special segment of the total population. The city dweller will generally be a better customer than a person living in a rural area. A suit in this price range—$22.50 to $48.75—will appeal only to a certain income group. If income is too little, the person simply does not have sufficient buying power to be a good potential customer; if income is too high, the customer begins to demand better material and tailoring than is available at these prices.

Number of Inhabitants

The outward, physical characteristics of Georgia and Iowa are almost identical. As Table I shows, the area of both states is almost equal. Georgia, however, has a somewhat larger population, 3½ million, as compared to 2½ million for Iowa.

The potential market for men's suits is obviously limited to male inhabitants over a certain age. The age of 14 has, somewhat arbitrarily, been chosen as the point below which these suits would have no market. As the Table shows, the male population, over 14 years of age, remains in approximately the same proportion as the total populations of each state.

TABLE I

CHARACTERISTICS OF THE POPULATION[1]

. . . .

Distribution of Population

Since it is believed that the major towns and cities—being the primary "habitat" of the suit-wearing businessman—are, by far, the most important market areas, the population has been divided in that manner. Table I also shows that, while Iowa has a somewhat larger proportion of urban[2] dwellers than Georgia (40% to 35%), Georgia still has the substantially greater number of urban inhabitants.

The urban/rural breakdown for "males over 14 years of age" is only an estimate, or approximation, based upon the apportionment of the total population. However, the figure obtained for "urban, male population over 14 years of age" is the primary basis for choosing the better potential market. On this basis, Georgia (with 410,000) constitutes a considerably larger market than Iowa (with 330,000).

. . . .

[1] Tables I, II, III, IV, and VI and Chart A of this report have been omitted here.

[2] The term "urban" is used throughout this report to mean the combined population of those cities and towns having more than 10,000 inhabitants.

Income and Buying Power Distribution

The determination of the better potential market cannot be placed solely upon a physical basis of urban, male population. Within the group of urban males over 14 years of age, this low-priced line of suits will largely appeal only to those within certain income brackets. For this analysis, it is assumed that this group will be limited to persons with an annual income between $1500 and $5000. This certainly does not completely eliminate all other persons as possible customers. (Students, without any income, will probably be interested in suits of this nature.) However, it is felt that the $1500 to $5000 segment represents the major part of the market for these suits and serves as a fair, relative index of market potential.

TABLE II

BUYING POWER DISTRIBUTION: 1952

. . . .

Table II serves primarily as a control factor, demonstrating that there is not an appreciable difference in the over-all buying power of the two states.

Chart A and Table III show clearly the number of persons (males over 14 years of age) falling within the stipulated wage bracket in the two states.

CHART A

COMPARISON OF NUMBER OF POTENTIAL CUSTOMERS IN GEORGIA AND IOWA BASED ON DISTRIBUTION OF INCOME FOR MALE PERSONS OVER 14 YEARS OF AGE IN 1950

. . . .

Probably, due to its larger Negro population, approximately one-third of the Georgia population falls below the $1500 lower limit. Consequently, Iowa has a slightly greater number of inhabitants that come within the desired wage bracket. Iowa has the greater number of potential customers.

TABLE III

DISTRIBUTION OF INCOME FOR MALE POPULATION OVER 14 YEARS OF AGE: 1950

. . . .

Buying Habits

However, the number of potential customers is not the final criterion; rather, the "total sales potential" is.

An examination of buying habits—Table IV—shows that in Georgia general merchandise sales constitute 14% of total retail sales; while in Iowa they constitute only 9%. Table V shows essentially the same information from a different source, including, however, a breakdown of apparel store sales only. Here the relation of general merchandise sales to total sales is virtually the same: 16% for Georgia, 10% for Iowa. This relation, for apparel sales only, is 6.2% for Georgia, 5.4% for Iowa.

TABLE IV

RETAIL SALES DISTRIBUTION PATTERN: 1952

. . . .

TABLE V

RETAIL SALES OF APPAREL AND RELATED ITEMS: 1951

	Georgia	*Iowa*
Total Retail Sales	$2,548,435,000	$3,069,120,000
Apparel Store Sales	160,059,000	165,990,000
Percent of Total Sales	6.2%	5.4%
Gen. Mdse. Sales	411,231,000	313,391,000
Percent of Total Sales	16%	10%
Apparel Stores: Number of Retail outlets, 1948	1,566	1,681
Sales per Store	$102,200	$98,800

Source: Standard Rate and Data Service, Inc., "Consumer Markets": 1952/1953.

Neither general merchandise sales nor apparel store sales give a true picture of total clothing sales: general merchandise sales include some other items besides clothing; apparel store sales do not include all clothing sales. (Sales of clothing departments of department stores are not included.) Consequently, it is felt that the percentage of clothing sales to total retail sales lies somewhere between the 16% and 6.2% for Georgia, and between the 10% and 5.4% for Iowa.

To arrive at a reasonable index factor for clothing sales, these respective percentages were averaged, giving a figure of 11.1% for Georgia, 7.7% for Iowa. Using 11.1% as a base of 100, the index factors are: Georgia, 1.00; Iowa, .69.

These index factors are only approximate measures of clothing sales. For want of more detailed statistics, it is assumed that they are also representative of sales of men's suits priced between $22.50 and $48.75.

Because the total retail figures for 1952 (Table IV) are so nearly equal, it was not deemed necessary to adjust the index factors to compensate for any differences appearing here.

TABLE VI

POTENTIAL MARKET INDEX
ADJUSTMENT OF THE $1,500–$5,000 INCOME GROUP
TO THE INDEX FACTORS FOR BUYING HABITS

. . . .

Availability of Retail Outlets

There is an entirely adequate number of retail apparel stores in either state; every county has at least one such outlet. Table V shows that the total number of apparel stores in the two states is very nearly equal. Iowa has slightly more than Georgia; however, this is of little importance, other than to prove that there is a more than ample number of outlets for the desired method of distribution.

ADVERTISING

Suitable Types of Media

There are three major forms of advertising media, suitable for use with this product, on a state-wide basis:

(*1*) Newspapers
(*2*) Radio
(*3*) Television

Georgia and Iowa lend themselves well to a comparison of advertising facilities and costs. Each state has one large central city—Atlanta in Georgia, and Des Moines in Iowa—with one large newspaper and one high-power radio station. Each state also has three minor but distinct areas of population concentration: Augusta, Columbus and Savannah in Georgia; Cedar Rapids, Davenport and Sioux City in Iowa. Each of these areas has newspapers and radio stations of comparable size, distribution and power.

As a further point of comparison, one of these areas, in each state, lies on a state border: in Georgia, Columbus lies on the Alabama line; in Iowa, Davenport is just across the Mississippi River from Illinois.

However, Illinois, having a population of roughly 10 million, has presumably already been developed as a market area. Consequently, if an advertising campaign has already been undertaken in this area, it has certainly overlapped the state line, thereby making Iowa an "economical" state to enter now. Or else, if this area has hitherto been neglected, part of the cost of an advertising campaign in Davenport can be apportioned to the Illinois area.

Alabama, on the other hand, having a small potential market, is presumably undeveloped at this time. In any event, the area opposite Columbus is "barren" territory. Consequently, the full cost of a campaign in the Columbus area must be borne in the Georgia territory. As a result of this situation, Iowa might initially be considered the slightly more advantageous area.

Newspapers

The analysis of comparative costs of newspaper advertising, Table VII, is very simple. By dividing the most desirable coverage (depending on various combinations of morning, evening, and Sunday editions) into the applicable line rate, the cost per person per line is derived. This should be a reasonably accurate index to the comparative cost of a similar campaign in either state.

. . . .

CONCLUSION

Although there is relatively little difference in either the potential market or anticipated costs of advertising, Georgia has consistently shown itself to be superior, by however slight a margin, to Iowa. The most significant point is the relative cost of radio advertising; the same commercials would cost roughly 40% more in Iowa than they would in Georgia. Newspaper advertising, likewise, is somewhat more economical in Georgia, but only by a matter of approximately 5%. Georgia's potential market is approximately 18% greater than Iowa's, both for the entire state and for urban areas only.

Consequently, Georgia is the preferable state for this manufacturer of men's suits to enter.

TABLE VII

NEWSPAPER COVERAGE AND COMPARATIVE COSTS: 1953

	City and Newspapers		Population	Coverage	and Line Rate	Relative Cost Per Person (thousandths of a cent)
GEORGIA	ATLANTA	CZ*	563,192	272,283	M. & E. – .95	
	Constitution	RTZ*	1,052,303	213,632	Sun. & M. – 1.30	
	Journal	Total	1,615,495	724,024	Sun. & E. – 1.40	194
	AUGUSTA	CZ	117,675	40,656	M. & E. – .25	
	Chronicle	RTZ	278,297	28,760	Sun. – .23	
	Herald	Total	395,972	71,774	Comb. – .48	670
	COLUMBUS	CZ	104,368	38,413		
	Ledger	RTZ	317,461	10,250		
	Enquirer	Total	421,829	49,329	Flat – .22	447
	SAVANNAH	CZ	135,595	50,855	M. & E. – .25	
	News	RTZ	363,820	25,421	Sun. – .25	
	Press	Total	499,415	79,495	Comb. – .50	630
	AVERAGE: OF SAVANNAH, COLUMBIA AND AUGUSTA					582
IOWA	DES MOINES	CZ	212,792	112,536	M. & E. – .85	
	Register	RTZ	918,795	291,091	Sun. & E. – 1.45	
	Tribune	Total	1,131,587	771,463	Sun. & M. – 1.55	201
	CEDAR RAPIDS	CZ	78,212	26,952		
	Gazette	RTZ	195,342	26,092		426
		Total	273,554	58,775	Flat – .25	
	DAVENPORT					
	Times Democrat	CZ	185,875	47,064	M. & E. – .24	
	Democrat Times	RTZ	326,178	14,963	Sun. – .26	
		Total	512,053	63,602	Comb. – .50	786
	SIOUX CITY	CZ	90,639	29,477	M. & E. – .28	
	Journal	RTZ	662,124	49,619	Sun. – .24	
	Journal Tribune	Total	752,763	82,456	Comb. – .52	635
	AVERAGE: OF SIOUX CITY, DAVENPORT AND CEDAR RAPIDS					616

Source: Standard Rate and Data Service, Inc., "Newspaper Rates and Data," 1953. (* CZ – City Zone; RTZ – Retail Trading Zone)

ANALYSIS OF CONDITIONS

One of the best examples of a report on present conditions of a business is the operations letter which the controller uses to give to top management a bird's-eye view of the entire business for the accounting period. Here the operational results and financial status of the company are presented, as well as the measurement of actual performance against the predetermined blueprint or budget. Profit and loss results are stressed, and a permanent reference is recorded for all phases of business activity. Exhibits showing necessary financial data accompany the report. As an example, note the following paragraphs: [3]

Net sales billed for April amounted to $400,000 and resulted in a net profit after taxes of $14,400. A brief summary of April results compared with March, Year to Date and Budget 1953 is shown in Exhibit 1.

EXHIBIT 1	APRIL RESULTS				YEAR TO DATE		BUDGET
	April 1953		*March 1953*				
	Amount	*% NSB*	*Amount*	*% NSB*	*Amount*	*% NSB*	*1953*
Net Sales Billed	$400,000	100.0%	$350,000	100.0%	$1,600,000	100.0%	100.0%
Cost of Sales	310,000	77.5	280,000	80.0	1,248,000	78.0	76.0
Gross Profit on Sales	90,000	22.5	70,000	20.0	352,000	22.0	24.0
Comm'l. & Adm. Exp.	48,000	12.0	46,900	13.4	208,000	13.0	12.0
Net Profit from Operations	42,000	10.5	23,100	6.6	144,000	9.0	12.0
Other Income & Deduct.	7,600	1.9	7,000	2.0	30,400	1.9	2.0
Net Profit before Taxes	34,400	8.6	16,100	4.6	113,600	7.1	10.0
Federal & State Taxes	20,000	5.0	8,400	2.4	59,200	3.7	6.0
Net Profit After Taxes	$ 14,400	3.6%	$ 7,700	2.2%	$ 54,400	3.4%	4.0%

Net profit before taxes in April was 8.6% of net sales billed, compared with 4.6% in March. This improvement was primarily due to increased sales volume and a greater profit ratio at standard manufacturing cost. Although net profit before taxes was 1.4 percentage points below that budgeted, unfavorable overhead variance was 2.1% of net sales billed and was again the primary cause of failure to realize budgeted profit this year.

NET SALES BILLED AND
GROSS PROFIT ON SALES

Gross profit on sales of 22.5% in April represented an improvement of 2.5 percentage points over March and 0.5 percentage points over year to date. However, this was still 1.5 percentage points under budget, due primarily to overhead variances and heavy scrap losses.

Hot-forged scissors made in United States again produced a gross loss on sales. As discussed in report sent you under separate cover, it would appear

[3] Paul L. Smith, "The Operations Letter As the Controller's Medium of Expression," *The Controller,* November, 1953, pp. 505 and 507.

advisable to terminate manufacture of this line and purchase from our Swedish supplier.

Net sales billed were $400,000, or $15,300 less than budgeted. Year to date billing of $1,600,000 was $192,800 less than budgeted. By product class, as shown in Exhibit 2, these differences were confined principally to pinking shear sales, where production has been restricted during a period of engineering changes.

Profit at standard manufacturing cost was 30.0% of net sales billed compared with 27.2% in March. Most significant improvement over the prior month was in the cast product class, which showed a 5.2 percentage point gain. This resulted from absence of sales in April of the unprofitable 190 Line. Discontinuance of this line and substitution of the profitable 179, recommended in November 1952, was fully accomplished by final clearance of inventories in March. In addition, costs of several low margin cold forged steel items, commented upon in the February operations letter, were reduced through changes in the method of assembly.

April standard profit was also 1.0 percentage points higher than budgeted. Favorable performance was due to cold forged steel cost reductions and proportionately smaller sales volume of the lower margin purchased goods and defense-forgings.

It is important in making an analysis of conditions that the proper perspective be realized and that accuracy of interpretation be maintained. This is true whether it be an analysis of conditions of a business, process or department.

The writer is largely concerned with financial data in analyzing conditions of a business, enough so that the type of report ensuing may be an accounting or financial report. So much has been written about each of these in their respective special fields that no treatment is considered necessary here.

Reporting on the conditions of a department or process might emphasize the need for changes or for a continuation of the present setup or procedures. A report on conditions may also explain the results of an examination of a process, an object or an idea. When it does this, it is commonly referred to as an examination report. Largely expository by nature, the examination report is used to enlighten its reader, who in turn may apply the information he receives as a basis for making a decision or taking action. The analytical treatment of facts in such a report is similar to that in other reports. Use may be made of comparison and contrast; the known and familiar may be compared with a similar process or idea. Sometimes two plans are compared to reach a conclusion as to which is the better. An evaluation of each is given. At other times the present situation may be compared to the ideal. A criterion is selected and applied to the points being considered.

Since the major emphasis is either on the results of an investigation and their analysis or on the conclusions reached, the conclusions are generally presented first in the text of an examination report. Two general outlines for organizing this report type follow:

Conclusions	Conclusions
Explanation of investigation	Analysis of data for reaching conclusions
Discussion	Facts considered or results of investigation
Data	Summary (briefly given)
Interpretation	
Final Summary	

Presenting conclusions first facilitates their use and helps to obtain reader interest.

RECOMMENDATION REPORTS

Analytical reports that perform a recommendation function are often referred to as recommendation reports. The analysis and conclusions become a basis for recommending action. The report usually deals with the problem, the solution of which consists of a program of action. Although recommendation reports vary widely in scope and subject material, they nearly always deal with some phase of business activity, such as personnel, marketing, sales, accounting, advertising, production, equipment, plant location and distribution.

Organization

The order of arrangement in the recommendation report may vary according to the order of the factors analyzed or of the steps taken in the investigation. Adding a recommendations section to either of the two general outlines mentioned for examination reports produces a general outline for the recommendation report. Several general outline patterns follow:

I	II	III
Recommendations	Introduction	Introduction
Conclusions	Conclusions	Analysis
Discussion of data	Recommendations	Conclusions
Summary	Analysis of data	Recommendations
	Summary	

IV	V
General recommendations	Statement of problem
Present conditions	Main issues
Proposed plan	Discussion of data
Discussion of details	Conclusions
Recommendations	Recommendations

Whether recommendations are at the beginning or end of the report, they may be the point of major emphasis; and the other sections of the report lend support to them and prove that the recommended action should be taken. Placed at the beginning they are a point of chief interest to the reader. At the end they draw supporting facts from the analysis of the data which the reader has read by that time. The reader's degree of familiarity with the problem, the report writer's authority or the immediacy of the recommended action may be used to decide which position the recommendations section should take.

Recommendations are the logical outcome of the conclusions, which are derived from the analysis of data. In other words, they involve reasoning out a definite and positive course of action that applies the conclusions in accomplishing the purpose of the report. They may be treated in a section with conclusions or presented in a separate section. They may be given in an itemized list or in paragraph form. Often only one course of action is suggested. When several recommendations are given they may be grouped to show their relative importance and value. Sometimes recommendations include specific points for further investigation or treatment. A good principle to follow in writing up recommendations is the journalistic one of telling who, what, when and where—explain what is to be done, who is to do it, where it should be done and when.

The following recommendation section is taken from the Swift & Company recommendation report, "Analysis of Employee Attitudes and Participation in the Swift Suggestion Plan." The report itself, as indicated in its introductory statement, contains only the main points of the analysis:

> The following summarized report has been prepared to provide a brief and concise review of the research which has been done. Only the main points are presented; the details and complete analysis are found in the extensive report which is separately bound.

After a 15-page presentation of results and their analysis, the following recommendations are given:

WHERE DO WE GO FROM HERE?

Based on the survey results, there are a number of areas which seem to call for critical examination with the thought of making changes or taking action in specific directions:

Recommended Action	*Basis for Recommendation*
Thoroughly acquaint new employes with the Suggestion Plan — how it works, awards, types of suggestions they can make, etc.	17% of the employes know nothing about the plan and 27% know nothing about the operation of the plan. The rate of suggesting is extremely low among employes with few years of service.
Familiarize employes with the suggestion form.	40% of the employes did not recognize the form when it was shown to them. A larger proportion of people are familiar with the plan than recognize the form—the major vehicle of the plan.
Have a vigorous campaign for the Suggestion Plan in dairy and poultry units.	Dairy and poultry is very low in rate of suggesting. Dairy and poultry is extremely low in percent of people familiar with the plan and its operation. Only 25% know anything about the operation of the plan. These units have a disproportionate number of "low service" employes—those who seem to require special indoctrination.
Review the method of handling suggestions in branch houses.	There is indication that some branch house suggestions never get to Chicago—i.e., 10% of the branch house people said they turned in suggestions during 1951 and the Suggestion Department records show a rate of 5 per 100 employes. Interviewers got the impression that many branch house employes are completely unfamiliar with the channels through which their suggestions are processed.
Publicize changes made as a result of suggestions. This might be done by putting signs above changes, promoting them more in the Swift *News,* etc.	46% of the employes know of no changes as a result of suggestions.
In preparing promotional material, keep in mind that the largest group of untapped suggesters is among younger people, women, and those with little education.	These groups are the lowest in rate of suggesting.
Review eligibility rules from the standpoint of either changing them or more adequately explaining to employes why they are fair and necessary—especially to mechanical people.	Only 36% of the mechanical employes who know about the eligibility rules think the policy is fair. There is a group of employes who do not turn in suggestions because they are unhappy with the eligibility rules.

Recommended Action	*Basis for Recommendation*
Make a personal contact a "must" in connection with every suggestion.	A much larger proportion of Fort Worth employes say there is personal contact than do those at other plants, and Fort Worth is one of the most successful plants suggestionwise. Some employes who think that the turn-down letters do not give enough explanation feel that a personal contact would help out.
Make an attempt to educate office-sales people that the plan is for them as well as for production employes.	A large percentage of these employes do not suggest because they feel that they have no opportunity to see things to change.
Review the effectiveness of the supervisor in promoting the plan and to what extent he should be utilized.	About half of all non-supervisory employes say that their "boss" has mentioned the Suggestion Plan to them.

Other types of action which have been suggested by interviewers or which have come up in discussions, but are not necessarily based upon statistical results are:

Consider raising the minimum monetary award and, at the same time, give small merchandise awards in lieu of money for minor suggestions.

Develop a system to insure prompt handling of suggestions, personal contact, proper posting, etc. A form, a cardex system, a peg board, etc., could be used.

In an attempt to find out what is the secret of a good closeout letter, get samples of letters written by various plants and see if there is reason to believe that plants high in suggestions have good letters. If so, these could be used as guides.

Itemize, on the back of the suggestion form, the channels through which suggestions go.

Have all Suggestion Committee members wear frocks with "Suggestion Committee" written on the back—a form of advertising.

Utilize the back of the pay envelope for promoting the Suggestion Plan.

HOW CAN THIS RESEARCH BE USED?

As a guide for forming policies about the Suggestion Plan.

As ammunition for promoting the plan.

For guidance in focusing attention in the most productive areas from the standpoint of potential suggestions.

As a guide in tapping heretofore unproductive areas by overcoming the barriers revealed by the study.

As a reference book for those charged with the responsibility of running the plan.

To help solve special problems that come up from time to time.

To help local administrators of the plan in their job through informal discussions of the findings and/or a discussion outline or film strip distributed.

The example just given combines conclusions and recommendations in one section. Here the close relationship of the two can be clearly seen, with major emphasis of the whole report on the recommendations.

A brief and more general type of recommendation section is sometimes used. The following, for instance, recommends what should be done but does not give specific suggestions for doing it. It is from a recommendation report which analyzes the personnel policies of a department store. A numbered list is used here.

RECOMMENDATIONS

The following recommendations are suggested to improve the personnel policies of Wellan's Department Store:

(*1*) More frequent rest periods to relieve the strain of consistent work.
(*2*) More store parties in order to develop closer relations between employees themselves and employees and management.
(*3*) Lounges for both men and women employees where they can rest during their rest periods without leaving the store.

If these policies are carried out along with the policies already established at Wellan's, improved personnel policies and a closer relationship between personnel and management should result.

Recommendation reports may be presented in any of the forms treated in Chapters 15 or 16. The recommendation sections just given as examples came from a short and a long report format. The report that follows is an intra-office memorandum. Here recommendations, present duties and proposed duties are given — all emphasizing the recommended changes. It was used as a basis for deciding what to do in handling mail.

R. J. REYNOLDS TOBACCO COMPANY

Winston-Salem, N. C.

April 26, 195_

MEMORANDUM FOR: Mr. C. B. Wade, Jr.

SUBJECT: Recommendations for Change in Handling of Mail on the 9th Floor of the Main Office Building.

1. No change in assignments of the Messenger in the Sales Accounts Department or in the Advertising Department are recommended except as they will be affected by the changes made in the duties of the Messenger stationed at the dumb waiter.

2. Present duties of the Messenger at the dumb waiter. Supervised by: Mr. Nelson.

A. Receives mail from 7th floor Mail Room and 8th floor in folders marked to:

Mr. J. W. Nelson
Mr. C. B. Wilkinson
Mr. R. D. McKenzie
Mr. L. E. George
Mr. C. B. Wade, Jr.
Mr. Wm. H. Maddrey

Distributes mail to Mr. J. W. Nelson and Mr. C. B. Wilkinson and places other folders in basket at dumb waiter.

B. Receives telegrams from dumb waiter. Takes telegrams to Mr. J. W. Nelson and to others in Mr. Nelson's Department.

C. Occasionally makes trips to the 17th floor.

D. Files future orders and similar items in a distributor. This is not a continuous operation.

E. Distributes inter-departmental correspondence in the Sales Checking Department.

3. Proposed duties of person at the dumb waiter. Supervisor: Mr. L. E. George.

Change in work place: It is recommended that the mail distributor now in Mr. George's Department be moved to a position near the dumb waiter.

A. Receive mail from the 7th and 8th floor in folders on the dumb waiter. Place the mail in the distributor and return folders. Pick out mail requiring attachment and place in folder for Mr. L. E. George. Take out all folders from distributor that go on the 9th floor. Deliver to Mr. George, Mr. Nelson, and Mr. Wilkinson. Carry remainder of folders to Messenger at Mr. McKenzie's Department for distribution as is now the practice. Pick up out-going mail from Messenger at Mr. McKenzie's Department. Repeat this operation as folders are received from the 7th floor, approximately every thirty minutes.

B. Deliver telegrams received at the dumb waiter to Mr. Nelson.

C. Make occasional trips to the 17th floor as needed.

D. Help with Salesmen's mail (opening) in the morning.

JCM:bs Industrial Engineering Department

Special Functions

Sometimes recommended action must be justified, shifting the emphasis of the report to the evidence for the recommendation. The report is thus written for the sole purpose of convincing the reader that the recommendation is sound. More often than not such a report is unauthorized, and the person for whom it is intended does not know it is being prepared until he has seen the finished product. It is also used when immediate action is called for and when justification is sought for a request for new equipment or construction.

With emphasis on the evidence or proof, the report begins with a statement of the recommended action, and everything that follows is marshaled to the end of proving that the action must be taken. An argumentative style of writing is tactfully followed, so that the reader feels each argument presented is his own and is ready to say at the end, "Yes, that's right." Care must be taken that the reader is never put on the defensive. Emphasis is placed on the positive aspect; and if disadvantages are given, they are shown to be far outweighed by the advantages. The following report, which performs a justification function, should be examined for its organization and style of writing.

EVANS DEPARTMENT STORE

1100 Grand Avenue

Kansas City, Missouri

November 2, 195_

TO: Board of Directors

FROM: Office Manager

SUBJECT: Recommendation for Purchase of ____ Addressograph Machine

In order to increase efficiency and to save time and money in billing customers each month, a ____ electric addressograph machine should be purchased by Evans Department Store.

A comparison of present billing procedure with addressograph procedure revealed that with an addressograph:

Board of Directors 2 November 2, 195_

(*1*) Costs for addressing bills would be less than one-ninth present addressing costs. This is a saving of $292.75 per year.

(*2*) Four working days per month could be eliminated from billing work and devoted to other office work.

(*3*) Billing to incorrect addresses would be eliminated, thus doing away with the cost of second mailings.

(*4*) Space for storage and operation of the machine is ample and convenient.

These advantages would greatly enhance the efficiency and reduce the cost of monthly billing. The saving of $292.75 per year alone is a benefit the company cannot afford to overlook.

Present Costly and Inefficient Method of Addressing Bills

Our store has 2000 customers. Each of these customers is billed every month, whether he has a balance or not. At present this billing procedure requires the work of two girls for two days each month to type addresses. This is a total of four working days per month that is required for typing addresses. At a rate of pay of $40 for a 48-hour week, this is an outlay of $26.67 per month or $320 per year for typing of addresses.

An additional expense is incurred through errors in typing. The girls who type addresses are frequently interrupted by phone calls and personal inquiries during peak-activity hours. The rushing which results from this added work placed upon them is one reason for errors in typing. Approximately 25 letters are returned each month because of incorrect addresses. Each of these must be mailed again. This is an added expense of $.75 per month or $9 per year. Table I shows an itemized list of present addressing expenses.

TABLE I

PRESENT COSTS OF ADDRESSING BILLS

Per Year:	
Wages: 48 days @ $6.66⅔ per day (12 mos. at 4 working days/mo.)	$320
Second mailings: 25/mo. @ $.03 ea. for 12 mo.	9
Total	$329
For 20 Years: 20 x $329	$6580

This table shows that the yearly cost for addressing bills is $329. For a 20-year period this would amount to $6580. Huge savings may be realized by the purchase of an addressograph machine.

Economies of the Addressograph Method of Addressing Bills

The initial cost of the ____ addressograph, complete with cord and tax, is $325. Its estimated life is 20 years. The Smith Supply Company gives a year's free service and guarantees the machine against mechanical defects for a full year. One address plate for each customer would cost $.05. This would amount to $100 for 2000 customers. Properly amortized over a 20-year period of useful-

Board of Directors 3 November 2, 195_

ness, the machine and plates would represent a cost of $21.25 per year. Not more than 25 changes per month, or 300 changes per year, are required in the mailing lists. Replacements at $.05 each would amount to $15 per year. Table II itemizes these costs.

TABLE II

COST OF ADDRESSING BILLS WITH A _____ ADDRESSOGRAPH

Per Year:	
Cost of addressograph: $325 (initial cost) amortized over 20 years ($325 ÷ 20)	$16.25
Cost of plates: $100 (2000 x $.05) amortized over 20 years ($100 ÷ 20)	5.00
Cost of address changes: 25 changes a month at $.05 each for 12 months	15.00
Total	$36.25
For 20 Years: 20 x $36.25	$725.00

Table II shows that the cost of addressing bills for 20 years with a _____ addressograph is only $725. This is only $67 more than it costs to address bills under the present method for two years. This is a saving of $5855 over a 20-year period.

Increased efficiency is assured through the use of the addressograph. The added expense, inaccuracy and inconvenience of 300 incorrectly addressed bills each year would be eliminated.

The use of an addressograph would create no storage or operation problems. It is portable, so it does not have to be installed. It is small enough to be placed on a desk top when it is in use and it can be easily stored in the storage closet when it is not in use.

Just compare the present addressing method with the addressograph method:

Present Method	*Addressograph Method*
(*1*) Yearly cost: $329.	(*1*) Yearly cost: $21.25. This is less than one-ninth the present method.
(*2*) Loss of four working days per month for typing addresses.	(*2*) No working days expended on operation of addressograph.
(*3*) Approximately 25 bills per month returned because of errors in typing.	(*3*) No bills returned because of typing.
(*4*) Space required for typing: 2 desks.	(*4*) Space required for operation of addressograph: 1 desk.

This comparison is evidence of the superiority of the addressograph method. Its purchase means increased efficiency and savings in time and money for Evans Department Store.

Another special function of recommendation reports is to improve a situation, policy, procedure or practice. The report which performs this function may be organized in a similar manner to other recommendation reports and may be in any appropriate report format. It is less argumentative, however than the justification report, and it emphasizes the need for the recommended improvements. Equal attention is usually given the analysis of the present situation, what is weak or at fault about it and what the suggestions will do to help.

Throughout the report emphasis is on improvements. Thus it is logical to begin with an analysis of the present situation and to end with an analysis of the results of the improvements. Sometimes a possible development in the future is examined; often the suggestions are applied and tested before the report is written. The conclusions and recommendations section is the most important part of an improvement report.

The following conclusions and recommendations section from "An Analysis of the Sales Operational Methods of the Audiphone Company of New Orleans" begins with a summary of the analysis of data as a basis for the conclusions and recommendations. The entire report emphasizes, through comparisons with sales programs in other hearing aid companies, the weaknesses and good features of the present sales program in the Audiphone Company, pointing up necessary improvements that are recommended.

CONCLUSIONS AND RECOMMENDATIONS

Conclusions

That there are deficiencies in the sales operational methods of the Audiphone Company has been proved; their correction should not be a serious problem because of the high degree of control over policies held by the local office.

The road selling methods of the Audiphone Company offer the greatest room for improvement, in all phases. The training of the salesman, when done locally, is not sufficient unless the man has a knowledge of basic selling principles. High-pressure tactics in the hearing aid field are an ever-present danger and can be combatted effectively only by a very complete sales training program. The local office has neither the time nor the facilities to provide such a program without national help, and herein lies the value of the national sales training given to Sonotone and Telex men.

Territory coverage in the Audiphone Company is not complete, for there is only one road man, who must serve about 300 people, which is too large a task for him to do effectively. This incomplete territory coverage, when coupled with the present methods of remuneration, do not keep incentive of salesmen at a peak. The high base salary, while perhaps an effective method of combatting high-pressure tactics, does not give the salesman the very necessary motive to sell a service rather than just a product.

It is in office selling procedures and policies that the Audiphone Company excels. While the actual selling methods used in the office are highly standardized, the policies concerning sub-offices and repair work help to strengthen customer satisfaction. Sub-offices provide the rural user with a place to get his necessary services and also give the Audiphone Company complete coverage in the smaller cities and adjacent areas in which they are located. The high degree of freedom given to these sub-offices is an excellent method of discouraging high-pressure selling tactics; and in spite of the extra expense of maintaining these offices, they are well worth it. The same is true of repair work; for even though the service department makes no profit, its contribution to customer satisfaction is invaluable. These services set the Audiphone Company apart from its competitors and have an excellent effect upon its sales program.

The advertisements used by the Audiphone Company, while stressing the important hearing qualities of the aid, place too little emphasis upon its characteristic features. Good hearing is of prime importance to any hard-of-hearing person, and the fact should be stressed heavily and frequently. However, a well-rounded advertising program should include the other characteristics that are of interest to the prospect; for these features appeal to a very important buying motive, that of desire for physical comfort.

The one remaining factor that the Audiphone Company needs to complete its advertising program is increased emphasis upon direct mail. This is particularly important to present customers, for it promotes repeat sales.

In summary, then, the final recommendations are based on these conclusions as brought out by the analysis:

(*1*) Sales training is not complete when done by the local office.
(*2*) Territory coverage in the Audiphone Company is far from sufficient.
(*3*) The incentive of salesmen is not kept at high levels because of expensive methods of remuneration.
(*4*) The policies of the Audiphone Company towards sub-offices and local repair points are the strongest and most effective part of their sales program.
(*5*) Although the media of advertising are standardized, there is room for improvement in ad content.
(*6*) There is not sufficient emphasis upon the use of direct mail.

Recommendations

The first and most important changes necessary in the sales operational methods of the Audiphone Company are in its road operations. It might be beyond the power of the local office to establish a centralized sales training point, but the branch should certainly start pressing the national office for these facilities. Until such time as a centralized sales training program can be established, the Audiphone Company should carefully screen all men to be hired in an effort to discourage high-pressure tactics. In spite of this carefully supervised screening, more salesmen should be employed to provide the Audiphone Company with complete territory coverage. These men should be assigned only to rural routes and small towns with each having about 100 customers to serve. Sub-offices should be established in those cities where population and territory limitations permit. The Audiphone Company needs at least four more sub-offices, in the cities of Lake Charles, Baton Rouge, Biloxi and McComb. Each of these offices should have its own service department. Four road men could cover the rural routes between these sub-offices. In order to keep the incentive of these salesmen high, and still discourage high pressure selling, a commission of 25 percent, a base salary of $100, and expenses should be paid. This will be enough to keep the road man from worrying about financial troubles and still give him the incentive to sell.

As a final step in the improvement of the sales program of the Audiphone Company, the nature of its advertisements should be changed to include the special features of the Audivox. Stress good hearing, but bring out these extra features more often in advertisements and direct mail. Increase the frequency of mailings to about seven times per year, concentrating on customers and prospects. The Audiphone Company of New Orleans rates high in the local competitive picture in spite of the present methods, not because of them, which indicates that it has efficient personnel and a good product—these facts plus the recommended improvements should move them to the top competitive position and keep them there.

PROBLEMS

1. You have been asked to recommend to Mr. Jonathan Jones whether or not he should invest his savings in a self-service launderette. He has $6,000 in personal funds with which to open a business. He is 30 years old, a high school graduate, married and has a son aged 5. He attended your state university's school of business administration for three years, but he went into the army and did not graduate. He has been driving one of the buses for your city transportation service since he was discharged from service. He plans to run the business himself with the help of his wife.

Assume that the community in which he lives and plans to open the business has no self-service laundry, has a population of 10,000 and has two commercial laundries.

In estimating his monthly expenses for operating the laundry, you would list the following items:

Rent	$ 75.00
Heat, electricity, water	100.00
Telephone	10.00
Depreciation	50.00
Miscellaneous (taxes, insurance, supplies)	100.00
Total	$335.00

You would also estimate the following items as initial costs of opening the business:

10 automatic washers at $185 each	$1,850.00
1 extractor	265.00
1 dryer	450.00
1 parts and tool kit	175.00
Gas heating equipment	625.00
Plumbing installation	1,000.00
Electrical installation	350.00
Other fixtures	400.00
Total	$5,115.00

The best location for such a business would be near a large supermarket or some similar spot with a heavy flow of traffic. The surrounding neighborhood should include residents of an economic status that prohibits their buying washing machines or hiring washwomen. Such a location is available.

The customary charges for a self-service laundry include:

Soap	5 cents
Bleach	5 cents
Each machine load	25 cents
Use of dryer	25 cents

For a nine-hour day, eight to five, about 15 wash loads per machine can be run through, taking about 36 minutes to load, wash, unload, etc. Most launderettes do not operate at 100% capacity, but only 50% capacity, to be successful. Prepare the report for Mr. Jones.

2. After collecting first-hand information write an examination report on one of the following subjects:

a. The check-out counters in a supermarket
b. Arrangement of shelves in a drugstore
c. The layout of your neighborhood grocery
d. The general reading room facilities of a public library
e. Washing operations at a commercial laundry
f. Cleaning operations at a dry cleaning plant
g. The service at a particular restaurant
h. Reservation system at a hotel
i. Distribution of mail in an office

3. Write a memorandum report to Mr. Drum, Office Manager of the Orton Tool Company. Recommend what he should do in the following situation in which he is dealing with an employee who is a good worker but possesses a disqualifying trait.

A total of five hundred employees, of whom sixty are office workers, are employed by the Orton Tool Company. The company has a fine reputation and specializes in the production of machine tools. The company pays top wages and is recognized as being progressive in its methods and procedures. The Office Manager, Mr. Drum, is capable and very well liked by the employees.

Miss Fleming, the senior employee in the Machine Bookkeeping Department, has fallen into the habit of reporting for work fifteen to twenty minutes late each morning and of returning from lunch ten to fifteen minutes after the hour. Although tardy, Miss Fleming can put out more work each day than can the other operators.

When questioned by Mr. Drum, Miss Fleming stated that the transportation and lunch facilities were adequate and that she enjoyed her work. She gave as her reason for being late the fact that she could complete her assigned work so much faster than other operators. She seemed to feel that she would be just wasting time by coming earlier. Miss Fleming is recognized by the other workers as being very capable; but her failure to be on time has created a morale problem in the office. The Office Manager finds that the other staff members are beginning to acquire the "late" habit.

How should Mr. Drum handle this personnel problem? Here are some possible courses of action. Discuss the arguments for and against each proposal.

a. Mr. Drum should discharge Miss Fleming.

b. He should call Miss Fleming to his office and point out the fact that she is a senior member of the bookkeeping section and that he expects her to set the proper example for the rest of the employees.

c. He should point out to Miss Fleming that, because she is the most efficient and able operator, her opportunities for promotion and salary increases are very good—if she can overcome the habit of being late.

d. The office manager should seek to keep Miss Fleming busy by saying to her: "Miss Fleming, please come and tell me whenever you have completed your assigned tasks and I will find additional work for you."

e. He should call all members of the office staff together and give a lecture on punctuality.

4. The top management of your company asked you to check up on the attitude of the employees toward the company magazine, of which you are the editor. They had in mind the possibility of cutting the publication's budget unless its readers indicated that the cut should not be made.

You inserted a postcard questionnaire in a recent issue and received the following responses to your questions:

(*1*) Do you like *Company Life?*
86.8% checked *Very Much*
12.5% checked *Fairly Well*
.7% checked *Not at All*

(*2*) Do members of your family read it?
92.6% checked *Yes*
7.4% checked *No*

(*3*) Do you read the following sections?

	Always	*Occasionally*	*Seldom*
Jokes	86.5%	10.7%	2.8%
Cartoons	86.3	11.0	2.7
Personals	80.5	15.2	4.3
Appointments	79.8	15.2	5.0
Safety articles	75.7	20.1	4.2
Editorials	74.8	22.7	2.5
Back cover features	73.5	21.6	4.9
Economic articles	72.9	22.0	5.1
Feature stories	72.5	24.9	2.6
Woman's page	55.9	19.0	26.0

Several of the favorable comments about the magazine were:

It's tops with us.
It's very good as is.
Have always enjoyed *Company Life.*
A fine magazine as it stands.
Keep up the good work. You are doing fine. I'm retired and will be 83 this year.
Company Life is tops.
You have a well-balanced magazine.
It's like getting a letter from home.
We all think it's a splendid magazine.
Just keep up the good job of putting out a swell magazine.
Keep it as good as it is.
Company Life is as good as they come.
A fine magazine.
It's a welcome addition to our home.
It couldn't be better.
I do enjoy *Company Life.*
It's the best reading one can get for the family.
Best I've ever seen.
We read it from cover to cover.

Several of the unfavorable comments were:

Company Life covers lots of people but few are ever heard of.
Grow up—get some hair on your chest.
Some of your stories should be censored.
Always the same names in the news from *Company Life.*

Several suggestions for improvment were also given:

More articles of national interest.
Let's get a sporting page.
More personal plant news.
My wife says add another page for women.
Let's hear about old-timers.
Purchasing hints.
Have longer and more detailed articles on economics.
More jokes and cartoons.
More educational short articles.
Add a fiction continued story.
How about plant histories?
More technical features.
More on economics.
Enlarge the magazine.
More stories about labor problems.
Encourage readers' comments.
More about "Free Enterprise."
More safety articles.
Something for children.
Add some religious reading.
Articles on training.
Children's column or page.
Crossword puzzles, recipes, fashions.
Put in plans for small homes.
More about hobbies.
Something for teen-agers.
Send it out more often.

Prepare a memorandum report to top management. Do you have the basis for recommending continued publication? Do you have plans for improving your magazine?

5. Write a special recommendation report, justifying the purchase of some equipment for your company.

6. Study some work method or procedure being followed in a company and suggest improvements.

CHAPTER *19*

Annual Reports

Annual reports have always been a direct and vital tool with which a company can tell its story. The very name given this means of communication suggests its scope and its responsibilities – it is annual and it is a report. An annual report can be a mere compilation of figures that only an accountant can readily understand or it can be an informative and analytical report of status and progress of a company expressed in terms readily comprehensible to all its readers. Every firm has a constructive story to tell. It should neither neglect reporting it nor hide it in a maze of statistical information. The annual report should effectively present a broad coverage of topics for an expanded readership. It should speak up for the company and for industry.

First of all the annual report is a financial report. It accounts for the company's finances and operations to its owners. But it should do much more than that. In the last twenty-five years or so the company annual report has changed from a formal, technical, forbidding document to an attractively printed, illustrated booklet. Solicitous care and thoughtful concern of company officers responsible for annual reports have helped to bring about the change. Alert managements recognize the annual report as a dynamic force in constructive public relations that foster a wholesome understanding of industry among stockholders, employees, dealers, customers and members of communities in which their products are manufactured or distributed.

Annual reports are being made a part of a company's public relations program. This has naturally changed their tone and character. As a public relations medium they are aimed toward reaching all publics. Modern philosophy of annual reporting would:

(*1*) Make the report of company operations and finances as nearly complete as possible.

(*2*) Interpret company operations in terms of human experience so as to make the report understandable to the average reader.

(*3*) Use illustrations, color, visual aids, good paper and legible printing to make the report interesting reading.

(*4*) Give the report wide distribution among all groups whose approval of the company will create a healthy atmosphere for American free enterprise, for industry and for the company.

An up-to-date annual report can be a strong, interesting and convincing review of the company, welding together, for the general good of the corporation, all of the elements on which it depends.

PURPOSES

Broad, general purposes of the annual report are: to etsablish goodwill for the company; to tell the company story to stockholders, employees and anyone interested; to build interest in the company; to create better understanding among the report's audiences and to improve industrial public relations. The annual report accomplishes specific purposes with each group of readers to whom it communicates its message.

To the stockholder the report gives an account of stewardship. By creating an understanding of the financial and business operations of the company, the report keeps him interested and satisfied that things are going well. By making the business live, the report sells the company to the stockholder. As a result he is satisfied; favorable attitudes and good relations have been maintained; he will retain his holdings and may even invest further in the company.

To the employee the report gives specific facts and general information about his company that he can get in no other way. As employees are oriented to the inner workings of the firm, misconceptions are corrected and misunderstandings avoided, so that the worker develops a sense of identity with his company. With high company morale, intelligent understanding and a facing of problems cooperatively the way is paved for greater productivity. A well-informed worker is usually receptive to his responsibilities and willingly does his part in the company. He also represents the company to others, and in his contacts in his community he will sell the company to others, recommend its products and further create favorable public opinion.

To aim the annual report toward public relations means considering the interests of credit men, banks, security analysts and financial officers of corporations. In many instances the annual report is the most important means of contact with hundreds of analysts all over the country in brokerage offices and investment advisory concerns, which hold stock of record for thousands of beneficial owners. Furthermore, many individual stockholders of record depend primarily on their bank, brokerage or investment advisory concern for advice about the companies in which they hold stock and for interpretation of the financial statements, even though they may themselves receive copies directly from the company. By providing financial data and focusing attention on company earning power, stability and future outlook — all centered around financial analysis, ratios and trends — the annual report places the analyst in a position to give advice to clients.

Among other readers of the annual report are the government, customers and the general public. For the government the report establishes the proper basis for taxes and regulations. The customer who is sold on the company and its products will buy more, will be willing to pay the price and will be satisfied.

More and more companies are accepting the social obligation of explaining to the general public their contribution to American industry. There is a recognition of and concern for the company's part and place in the free enterprise system and general economic order. Each report is a part of the story of the achievements of that order and seeks to win favorable opinion and attitude to its side.

In utilizing the annual report to foster constructive public relations, managements must place the report in the hands of as many thinking people as possible. For the corporation that wishes to expand the readership of its annual report, *Financial World* has listed two classes of audiences as targets: (*1*) the "national level" and (*2*) the "community level."[1] Their suggestions for specific groups included in each target are presented here and on the following page. By making the information in the report available to as many people as possible the company broadens the understanding of its activities for all those to whom the report is aimed.

TARGET

1

Distribution of the Corporation Annual Report

at the

NATIONAL LEVEL

(In Addition to Stockholders and Employes)

Associated Groups:
- Suppliers of Raw Materials, etc.
- Agents and Representatives
- Dealers and Jobbers
- Distributors
- Retailers (Chain Stores)
- Customers
- Trade Associations
- Professional Societies

Press and Radio:
- Big City Newspapers
  - Financial Editor
  - Business News Editor
  - Selected Columnists
  - Selected Financial Writers
  - Editorial Writers
- Press Services
- Financial Publications
- Journals of Commerce
- Business Magazines
- Selected Trade Papers
- Accountancy Journals
- Advertising Publications
- Graphic Arts Magazines
- Washington Newsletters
- Public Relations Publications
- Women's Magazines (If appropriate)
- Feature Writers and Columnists
- News Syndicates

Press and Radio (cont.):
- Radio News Rooms
- Selected Radio Commentators

Financial:
- Big City Commercial Banks
- Big City Trust Companies
- Investment Bankers
- Stock Exchange Member Firms
- Security Analysts
- Dealers in Securities
- Investment Counselors
- Statistical Agencies
- Financial Services
- Investment Trusts
- Mutual Funds
- Insurance Companies
- Trustees of Estates
- Credit Agencies

Government Officials:
- SEC, ICC, FTC, FCC, etc.
- Department of Commerce
- Department of Labor
- Other Selected Cabinet Members
- Library of Congress
- U. S. Senators (All or selected)
- Representatives (All or selected)
- Governor of State Where Incorporated
- Secretary of State Where Incorporated

---

[1] Weston Smith, "Stockholder Relations Guide-Book," *Financial World*, Guenther Publishing Corporation, 1950, p. 15.

Government Officials (cont.):
- States Where Plants Are Located

Other:
- Big City Public Libraries
- Leading Universities and Colleges
  - Schools of Business Administration
  - Schools of Commerce and Finance
- Philanthropic Institutions

On Request—Through Paid Advertising:
- Big City Newspapers
- Financial Publications
- Journals of Commerce
- Business Magazines
- Selected Trade Papers
- Selected National Magazines
- Selected Women's Publications
- Labor Publications

TARGET

2

Distribution of the Corporation Annual Report

at the

COMMUNITY LEVEL

(In Addition to Stockholders and Employes)

Associated Groups:
- Suppliers of Raw Materials, etc.
- Union Leaders
- Employment Agencies
- Transportation Services
- Chamber of Commerce Members
- Rotary, Kiwanis and Lions Club Members

Press and Radio:
- Editors of Local Newspapers
- Editors of County Weeklies
- Suburban and Community Magazines
- Local Broadcasting Stations
- Chamber of Commerce Paper
- Board of Trade Bulletin

Financial:
- Local National Banks
- Local Savings Banks
- Savings and Loan Associations
- Brokerage Office Managers
- Trustees of Estates
- Small Loan Associations

Opinion Leaders:
- Heads of Local Business Firms
- Judges and Police Officers
- The Clergy
- Professional
  - Physicians
  - Dentists
  - Hospital Directors
- Officers of
  - Fraternal Societies
  - Women's Clubs

Opinion Leaders (cont.):
  - Welfare Organizations
  - Parent-Teacher Associations
- Principals and Teachers of
  - Grade Schools
  - High Schools
  - Business Schools
  - Colleges and Universities
- Leaders and Youth Groups
  - Boy and Girl Scouts
  - Y.M.C.A. and Y.W.C.A.
  - Junior Achievement, Inc.
  - Sunday Schools

Municipal or Township Officials:
- Mayor or Borough President
- Members of Board of Supervisors
- Department Heads

Other:
- Local Libraries
- Movie Theatre Owners
- Barber and Beauty Shop Managers
- Druggists
- Gas Station Operators
- Chain Store Managers

On Request—Through Paid Advertising:
- Local Newspapers
- County Weeklies
- Community Magazines
- Suburban Publications
- House Organs or Tabloids
- Church and Fraternal
  - Publications
  - Programs
- Local Labor Union Publications

KINDS OF ANNUAL REPORTS

Classified on the basis of the main group of readers aimed at and the major purposes to be accomplished, there are joint stockholder-employee reports, separate stockholder and employee reports, combined stockholder-employee-public reports and reports prepared for *many* groups. There is a marked trend away from separate reports toward the joint or combined group. There is sufficient overlapping of interests among the different groups so that the information any one group wants is also of interest to the other groups, and when the report is adapted to one group it can be adapted at the same time to other groups for readability and understanding. In appealing to several groups in the same report firms have generally tended to speak to each group in separate paragraphs or sections. This is the natural result of thinking about each group's characteristics and interests and adapting to them. A merging, however, if it is to be successful, should bind all groups together. Because the groups have mutual interests, those interests should be welded together with group lines broken down in the final report.

Annual reports may be printed, mimeographed, lithographed or reproduced by some other method. The larger the company the greater the need for a printed report. But in some very small firms a typewritten report may serve its purpose well. Emphasis in this chapter, however, is on the printed corporation report aimed at reaching as many readers as possible and toward accomplishing as many purposes as possible. Here there may be a choice between the conservative, conventional report and the humanized, popularized report. Impressions gleaned from examining hundreds of annual reports of the last decade have indicated definite trends toward the humanized report, through which the corporation can reach a vast, varied audience and make fullest use of the annual report.

CONTENTS

What to Include

What does a company talk about in its annual report? Details of financial condition and operational activities are of paramount interest to all readers of annual reports. Some readers are more interested in details than others. Not all parts of an annual report will be read by all; nor will those that are generally read receive the same amount of interest. The reader will read what he needs to and what appeals to him. Therefore, in determining the contents of an annual report the writer should consider two main questions: What does the reader want and need for his purposes and what do I need to tell him to accomplish my purposes? In many cases the information the reader wants is also necessary for accomplishing the company's purposes.

The following check list of information for stockholders, although not all-inclusive, is suggestive of what is necessary for the stockholder's information and for the company in maintaining appropriate relations with the stockholder. Probably no annual report would include all of the items listed as subject possibilities, but the company would select and use those items that apply to their particular situation.

Check List
of
Information for Stockholders

Financial Narrative

Sales
Earnings
Dividends
Taxes
Reserves
Net Worth
Exports and Imports
Inventories
Unfilled Orders
Capital Inventories
Fixed Assets
Intangible Assets
Investment per Employee
Capital Requirements
Supplies
New Policies
Research
Employee Relations
Community Relations
Dealer and Consumer
Prospects
Trade Recognition
Future Outlook

Financial Statistics

Financial Highlights
Balance Sheet
Operating Statement
Explanatory Notes
Auditor's Certificate
Earned Surplus Statement
Capital Surplus Statement
Financial Position
Sales
Earnings
Dividends
Taxes
Reserves
Income Other Than Operations
Income Distribution
Capital Expenditures
Working Capital
Payroll
Investments
Depreciation and Depletion
Value of Plants
Net Worth

Non-financial Narrative

Operational Facts About the Company:
Brief History of Company
Summary of Growth of Industry
Contributions to Growth
Production Process
Distribution Facilities
Plant Size, Location, etc.
Advertising and Sales Promotion
Departmental Operations
Company Publications

Employee Statistics:
Number of Employees
Average Age
Length of Service

Employee Benefits:
Pension Plan
Insurance
Health and Safety Practice
Vacation
Work Productivity
Employee Training
Personnel Development

Stockholder Statistics:
Issues
Number
Sex
General Distribution

Check List (cont.)

Management:
- Thumbnail Biographies
- Organization Chart

Selling Industry:
- Management as a Trusteeship
- Employment and Sales Volume
- Price and Wage Increase
- Lower or Higher Costs

Additional Information:
- List of Officers
- Stock Transfer Agents
- Registrars
- Attorneys
- Auditors
- Proxy Notices
- Date of Annual Meeting

Year to Year Comparisons

- Sales
- Earnings
- Dividends
- Market Value of Stock
- Reserves
- Taxes
- Financial Progress

Treatment of Social and Economic Aspects of the Business

- Business Partnership
- Employee Relations
- Research Development
- Industry Education
- Taxation
- Legislation
- Labor
- Wages and Selling Price
- Economic Conditions
- Company Contributions
- Capital Assets
- Sales Dollar Breakdown
- Income Dollar Breakdown
- Earnings, Dividends, Taxes and Payroll Compared

The stockholder is chiefly interested in the financial condition and operational activities of the company. He wants to know how the business is being run and its prospects for the future. Details that will show him the stability of the firm and its successful operation will satisfy him; he will retain his holdings and invest further in the business.

According to the American Management Association, the criteria for the effectiveness of a corporation annual report are completeness, interest and clarity of expression.[2] Completeness requires that the report contain all the information necessary to meet the needs of the audiences which the firm considers to be the most important. It should answer all the questions that a stockholder, employee or the general public might ask.

The topics in the check list of information for employees that follows overlap somewhat with those in the list for the stockholders. They do, however, indicate what the employee is interested in knowing and what he may have questions about. Although the list is not all inclusive, like the stockholder list it is suggestive and can serve as a reminder. Employees are principally interested in operational facts affecting their jobs, which are their first concern. What makes

[2] *Preparation of Company Annual Reports* (Research Report Number Ten), American Management Association, New York, 1947, p. 14.

the job? What keeps it? How does it fit into the work of the company? How secure is the employee in the job? What are his promotional opportunities? These are questions an employee wants answered. A stable firm means security to him, and he is interested in the financial condition from that standpoint. He wants to know how the running of the business affects him, who the real boss is, who the owners are. In giving him facts that he wants, the company report is likely to be read by him, and as a result he will be a better informed and more productive worker.

Check List
of
Information for Employees

General Information

The Company's Position in the Business World
The Worker, Stockholder and Consumer in American Industry
Discussion of Capitalistic System of Free Enterprise
Basic Economics of American Business Growth

Employee Benefits

Employee Training Program
Opportunities for Advancement
Job Evaluation
Safety Practices
Health Practices
Insurance
Pension Plan
Medical Plan
Wage Plan
Bonus Plan
Incentive Plan
Credit Union
Company Loan Plan
Paid Vacation
Social Security
Suggestion System
Recreational Facilities
Activities Program

Facts About the Company

History and Development:
Personnel
Executives
Products
Sales Record
Production Record
Expansion of Facilities
Research
Company Competition
Community Relations
Stock Issues
Owners of the Business
Manner of Growth

Business Operations:
Raw Materials Used
Supply and Supplies
Sales and Advertising
Employment Statistics
Stockholder Statistics
Distribution
Inventories
Plant Maintenance
Company Awards
Prices
Government Regulations
Income and Disbursements
Assets and Liabilities
Future Prospects

The contents of an annual report that are of interest to the employee and the stockholder also interest the general public. By informing the public and encouraging them to think favorably about the company, the firm has gone a long way toward creating good public relations. A policy of frankness and sincerity in reporting facts helps. Emphasizing how the company serves human needs and contributes to the general well-being of the community also goes a long way toward obtaining favorable public reaction.

Deciding what to include in the annual report is simply selecting items based on the interests of the audiences and the purposes of the report. Two other aspects of annual report preparation loom as greater problems: arrangement of facts in the various parts of the report and the style of presentation and writing.

Arrangement of Parts of the Report

Annual reports differ in makeup and arrangement, but there are some similarities among them. Most of them begin with a summary or highlights-of-the-year section, followed by a letter to the stockholders from the president of the company. A financial and operational review of the year is presented next. It is followed by the financial statements, notes and auditor's certificate. Sections on employee activities, on the advertising of products and on the future outlook of the firm come last. The order varies from report to report as does also the treatment of specific details in each part.

Cover. Westinghouse Electric Corporation had one of the most outstanding covers of the reports published in 1953. In full color, the design depicts in terms of the atom the contributions of Westinghouse to the age of industrial atomic power. The illustration presents the artist's conception of tomorrow's atomic power plant and the atomic submarine of today. Thus two of the company's traditional products, power generation and marine propulsion equipment, are joined to this new source of energy. The atom as a motif is used through the report as an added introductory or theme touch to each section.

In recent years the trend in covers has been to make them as attention-getting as possible so as to attract the reader. This is in line with the tendency to popularize annual reports. Thus color and illustration are widely used to obtain a favorable first impression. A large number of covers highlight the chief feature of the report, present a new product or old products in use, show product benefits or depict the character and activities of the company.

In the illustration showing annual report covers, page 362, the Nash-Kelvinator Corporation 1953 report shows its products in use. The Eastman Kodak Company illustrates the result of using its product, a beautiful photograph of Grand Canyon taken from the north rim. A dramatic night view of *Hazel* blast furnace and cast house at United States Steel's Fairless Works, Morrisville, Pennsylvania, is on United States Steel's report for 1953. The General Motors 1951 report pictures the changing shifts which characterize a combination of a free industry and a free people as part of the American heritage. The Champion Paper Company's reports always emphasize the use of a trademark.

Other successful covers might show a manufacturing operation, an aerial view of a plant or factory, an entrance, sources of raw materials, new additions or future plans. Pictures of employees at work and at home or in some recreational activity add human interest too. More and more corporations are making use of the back cover and the inside of the front and back covers. Inside the front cover favorite items used are a list of officers and directors of the company, the table of contents, highlights of the year or some point of major importance. The back cover is used mostly for advertising and selling the company's products.

Highlights. The most important parts of the annual report are selected and highlighted by brief statements with supporting figures. When a summary statistical table is used it is made up of items extracted from the financial statements included in the report. Sometimes outstanding developments of the year are listed with no figures. Facts and figures are selected to reflect the progress during the year and are sometimes presented entirely in graphic form. Comparisons with the previous year or several years make the figures significant and point up the progress of the company. The summary may cover such items as sales figures, earnings before and after income taxes, income per share of common stock, dividends per share of common stock, net working capital, capital expenditures, long term debt, number of employees, number of stockholders, investments, book value per common share and any special features of the particular company. The highlights from the 1953 Nash-Kelvinator Corporation report follow, pages 364, 365. Comparative figures for five years are presented in tabular form, and on the opposite page the major activities of the company during the year are emphasized and interpretative figures given.

President's Letter. Specific items included in the president's letter fall into a number of categories: finance and accounting, production, employee relations, marketing, research development, relation of company to the industry, economic and political condition of the country, etc. They are frequently presented under main headings and in summary form or in the light of current conditions or future plans. The president's message should be brief and should deal with important points only. A few letters are long; in some instances, the entire report is written in letter form. The letter is an opportunity for the president to merge his group of readers into one. He should recognize that business is a human affair and thus present points of human interest — not mere, cold facts. He should be sincere, clear and informal. The letter should reflect a certain amount of human warmth toward the people to whom it is addressed. A personal conversational style is good.

In essence the letter is a letter of transmittal and a summary of the report. It should result in gaining the interest of the reader and in his reading the report. Synchronized with the report, it sets the tone for what follows. The letter, page 366, from the 1953 Westinghouse report is typical of what is done in most annual reports.

Table of Contents. Reproduced here, the "Table of Contents," also from the Westinghouse 1953 report, is typical of what is done in most annual reports. It shows what is in the report and serves as a page reference for turning to items of special interest to the reader.

Table of Contents

Annual Report
1953
UNITED STATES STEEL CORPORATION
Annual
Report
EASTMAN KODAK COMPANY
NASH-KELVINATOR
CORPORATION
Annual Report
1953
Westinghouse
ANNUAL REPORT • YEAR 1953
GM
ANNUAL REPORT

Generally the table of contents is either on the inside front cover or first page of the report. Sometimes placed in the same position is a list of officers and directors of the company. This list may also be on the inside back cover or at the end of the report.

Narratives. Together the operational and financial narratives make up the bulk of the report. Here no one plan or order of subjects is followed. Often a central theme is selected and the topics are organized with it in mind. For example, on the company's 25th or 50th anniversary emphasis would be on the historical development and progress made during the period of operation. Topics would be related to the anniversary theme.

The narratives in the annual report are financial and non-financial, depending on the basic subject matter. Non-financial narrative takes up subjects such as history of the company, what the company does, its products and sales methods, production, sales, advertising, employee relations and benefits, public relations and research. The financial narrative discusses such subjects as dividends, earnings, sales, cost, taxes and income. The following outline of the narrative material in the General Motors 1951 report is typical of annual report organization:

I. A full year of combined operations
  A. GM's role in national defense
  B. Civilian production curtailed
  C. Diesel products in strong demand
  D. Allison a major defense producer
  E. Fourteen million Frigidaire refrigerating units
  F. Passenger car prices
  G. Overseas operations
  H. Engineered for transportation service
  I. Continued technological improvement

II. Teamwork was '51 keynote
  A. Six employment objectives
  B. Adjustments under the wage formula
  C. GM plants are good places in which to work
  D. Fine response to improved suggestion plan
  E. GM training programs

Courtesy (*top, left*) United States Steel Corporation, (*top, right*) Eastman Kodak Company, (*center, left*) Nash-Kelvinator Corporation, (*center, right*) Westinghouse Electric Corporation, (*bottom*) General Motors Corporation

A handsome cover, illustrating the company's contribution to industry, is an important feature of many annual reports.

Statistics

	FISCAL YEARS ENDED SEPTEMBER 30	1953	1952	1951	1950	1949
Operating	NET SALES	$478,697,891	$358,400,502	$401,148,293	$427,203,107	$364,193,360
	NET EARNINGS	14,123,026	12,603,701	16,220,173	28,836,326	26,229,930
	NET EARNINGS PER CAPITAL SHARE	$3.25	$2.90	$3.73	$6.64	$6.04
	DIVIDENDS	$2.00	$2.00	$2.50	$2.95	$1.40
Financial	NET WORKING CAPITAL	$ 67,755,415	$ 70,040,713	$ 85,895,898	$ 79,123,751	$71,822,366
	LONG-TERM DEBT	18,000,000	20,000,000	20,000,000	20,000,000	20,000,000
	PROPERTY, PLANT, AND EQUIPMENT (GROSS)	107,123,206	94,103,622	74,468,593	73,616,759	63,460,266
	ACCUMULATED DEPRECIATION	41,020,167	34,982,262	32,028,581	29,059,447	26,748,751
	PROPERTY, PLANT, AND EQUIPMENT (NET)	66,103,039	59,121,360	42,440,012	44,557,312	36,711,515
	STOCKHOLDERS' INVESTMENT	129,085,801	123,644,993	119,755,828	114,550,014	98,701,069
	BOOK VALUE PER CAPITAL SHARE	$29.73	$28.48	$27.58	$26.38	$22.73
Production	AUTOMOBILES	166,918	137,587	177,613	178,827	139,521
	APPLIANCES	638,204	456,981	678,039	803,600	702,110
Employment	AVERAGE NUMBER OF EMPLOYEES	25,745	21,126	24,613	26,662	24,321
	GROSS PAYROLL	$110,536,336	$87,725,443	$96,110,408	$95,264,885	$86,417,725

Courtesy Nash-Kelvinator Corporation

Annual report to stockholders.

F. Employes purchased $82 million of savings bonds
G. New insurance program popular
H. First year of new pension program
I. Bonus plan

III. You and your neighbors benefit from GM ownership

IV. Financial Review

A. Factors affecting 1951 financial results

Highlights of 1953

Because of the return of normal competitive conditions in most industries in 1953, an unusual feature of the present annual report is a discussion on Pages 4 and 5 of the important competitive factors in the automobile and appliance industries as they affect Nash-Kelvinator Corporation. The following subjects are covered:

a. The sizeable portion of the automobile market available to the independent companies;

b. Ability of the independent companies to buy parts and components as cheaply as the large producers;

c. Savings in Nash-Kelvinator costs resulting from close integration of manufacturing facilities;

d. Nash-Kelvinator's postwar expenditures of $72,000,000 for expansion of plant and equipment and investment in unconsolidated subsidiaries, $27,000,000 for engineering, and $61,000,000 for tooling for new products.

e. Broadened and improved lines of Nash and Kelvinator products;

f. Earnings and dividends of subsidiary companies, which have become an important source of income for the parent corporation

The foregoing factors, it is pointed out, will be of the greatest importance to Nash-Kelvinator Corporation in the competitive period ahead.

•

Nash-Kelvinator's sales in the 1953 fiscal year totaled $478,697,891. This was $120,297,389 in excess of the previous year, and 12% greater than in the previous record year 1950. Three factors contributed to the gain — sales of defense products, addition of laundry equipment to the Kelvinator product line, and increases in production of automobiles and appliances

Net earnings amounted to $14,123,026, or $3.25 per share, against $12,603,701, or $2.90 per share, in the 1952 fiscal year.

•

Dividends paid during the 1953 fiscal year totaled $2.00 per share, the same as in the previous year

•

The Nash Division produced 166,918 automobiles compared with 137,587 in the preceding fiscal year

•

The Kelvinator Division produced 638,204 electric appliances compared with 456,981 in 1952. Much of this gain was accounted for by the entry of Kelvinator into the laundry equipment field

•

Expenditures of $21,673,951 were made during the 1953 fiscal year for plant facilities, tooling for new automobile and appliance models, and other capital investments

•

Net working capital at the close of the fiscal year was $67,755,415 compared with $70,040,713 a year previous. Inventories at the close of the fiscal year were in line with present and anticipated retail demand

•

Stockholders' investment in Nash-Kelvinator at September 30, 1953, was $129,085,801, equivalent to a book value of $29.73 per share. This is without consideration of an additional $10,913,956 equity in the accumulated undistributed earnings of its subsidiaries, which is not included in the above total This amounts to $2.51 per share

Annual report to stockholders **(Cont.).**

1. Taxes
2. Price ceilings
3. Rising costs
4. Nature of defense business

B. Disposition of earnings
C. Real estate, plants, and shipment
D. Advances to steel producers
E. Investments outside the United States

PRESIDENT'S LETTER

Fellow Stockholders:

I am happy and proud to report that 1953 was a truly notable year in your Company's history. Among the many things which contributed to this achievement, I believe that these were the most significant:

- For the fourth consecutive year, the Company established a new record for output, in terms of both production and dollar volume.
- Westinghouse was assigned by the Atomic Energy Commission to develop the world's first atomic power reactor for the generation of electricity, thus opening the era of industrial application of this great new source of energy
- The sale of consumer products was the greatest in the Company's history

The new record in output was achieved mainly through the more intensive utilization of existing facilities, although there was an initial contribution from new facilities coming into operation during the year.

Net income was moderately higher than in 1952. It would have been larger except for substantial expenses incurred in preparing new plants for production, training new employes for their tasks, and amortizing new facilities for which certificates of necessity were obtained.

It was with a great deal of pride that Westinghouse accepted the award of a contract to develop the world's first large-scale atomic power reactor for the generation of electricity. The Company's pioneering research in atomic energy, its long experience with turbine and power equipment development, and its outstanding work in building the world's first atomic submarine engine have now matured in a truly revolutionary undertaking. We look forward with enthusiasm to this great new era of power generation.

Our Consumer Products Divisions recorded a sales increase of 21 per cent, and enhanced the market position of their lines generally. This increase is a substantial step toward our goal of expanding considerably the proportion of this business to our Company's total volume.

The Apparatus and General Industrial Products Divisions, whose shipments represented about half of our 1953 billings, increased their output by three per cent over 1952, while the backlog of unfilled orders remains at approximately a year's capacity production.

The billings of our Defense Products Divisions exceeded 1952 by 10 per cent. This was less than we hoped for at the beginning of the year, and resulted from development delays which prevented full-scale production of certain equipment for the military services.

All of you, I am sure, want to know how we view the prospects for our business in 1954. Earnings will be affected by our ability to maintain profit margins in the face of increased competition. With this in mind, we have been stressing reduction in costs and expenses for the past year, and we shall continue to do so.

We expect continued high operations. In industrial products, output will be benefited by a sizable backlog; on defense contracts, we plan to achieve a higher rate of production than in 1953; and in consumer products, sales plans are directed to the full utilization of considerably expanded facilities, notably the new Columbus, Ohio, plant.

Essentially all of the projects in our $296,000,000 expansion program have been initiated (see tabulation, page seven), and many of the new facilities are already in production. Expenditures through 1953 amounted to approximately $189,000,000. While the entire program will not be completed until 1955, new facilities now in production, and those to be completed in 1954, will add substantially to our volume in the year ahead.

Even, therefore, if the level of general business activity for 1954 is moderately lower than in 1953, as has been predicted, we are planning for and aiming toward larger billings and profits in the coming year. Looking ahead to 1955 and 1956, however, there is one disturbing factor from the viewpoint of the heavy electrical manufacturing industry. This is the increasing competition from manufacturers abroad. The situation is discussed in two paragraphs at the top of the left-hand column on page seven.

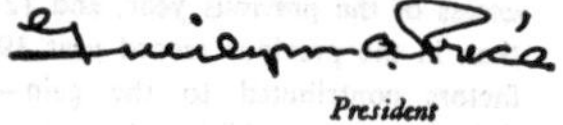

President

Page 2

Courtesy Westinghouse Electric Corporation

Message from the president.

F. Common stock held in treasury
G. Pension program

Financial Statements. The majority of the companies include a consolidated balance sheet and income statement. The balance sheet is the hub around which all the rest of the report, especially the financial data, revolves. This may be the reason for placing it in the center of the report as most firms do. The center position also has a mechanical advantage, allowing the double-page spread when putting the report together. Two other favorite positions for financial statements are at the end of the report and following the president's letter. The statements are followed by explanatory notes and the auditor's certificate. Because not all readers are familiar with accounting practices explanatory notes are necessary. They may be in the form of footnotes to the statements or on separate pages succeeding the statements. The auditor's certificate is customary practice and reflects a standard pattern.

Statements are further clarified by the use of simplified terminology and form. They must, however, conform to accepted accounting practice and are thus standardized by accountants. To be of value statements should be for two years or more, showing changes. For one year they are somewhat meaningless. Care should also be taken to avoid incompleteness for simplification. The statements should contain figures which will enable those readers desiring to do so to compute such ratios as that of expenses to net earnings and that of total sales to total money employed in the business. Of course, figures for this purpose may be given in comparative statistical tables. At any rate, adequate financial information must be in the report.

The "Consolidated Statement of Financial Position" reproduced, pages 368, 369, from the 1953 Westinghouse report follows the trends just discussed. Simplified form and terminology are used. Comparative figures for three years are given, with emphasis on the last year.

When the financial statements are in the middle of the report, the narrative sections are divided and part of the narrative follows the financial section. Usually the emphasis in the narrative sections is on such items as stockholder data, employee information, sales and advertising. The end of the report, particularly the inside back cover, lends itself to product advertising and activities surrounding the product or services offered for sale. If the statements are at the end of the report, the center spread may be devoted to advertising copy and a layout of the products.

Presentation of Data

Use of Visual Aids. In recent years there has been tremendous increase in the number of tables, charts, graphs and pictures used in

CONSOLIDATED STATEMENT OF FINANCIAL

(Balance

THE COMPANIES OWN:	1953	1952	1951
Cash	$ 49,975,473	$ 65,096,211	$ 66,648,783
U. S. Government and other marketable securities (*at lower of cost, less amortization of premium, or market*)	170,382,774	170,691,410	80,902,254
Amounts owed to the companies by:			
Customers (*less allowance for doubtful accounts*)	204,415,595	192,718,576	165,163,656
Wholly- and majority-owned companies not consolidated	631,682	1,140,362	1,024,125
Materials, supplies, products in process of manufacture and finished products (*inventories—less valuation reserves*)	497,454,081	412,847,144	387,647,734
Other amounts recoverable	31,563,516	37,551,913	21,424,091
Total	954,423,121	880,045,616	722,810,643
Less: Progress and advance billings, included above, on products not shipped	124,827,279	101,749,159	68,924,094
TOTAL (*Current Assets*)	829,595,842	778,296,457	653,886,549
Investments:			
U. S. Government securities, short-term—from proceeds of sale of debentures—acquired for expansion program	111,000,000	149,000,000	125,000,000
Wholly- and majority-owned companies not consolidated	1,206,882	1,716,527	301,598
Westinghouse Electric Corporation—Common stock (*at cost*) (*December 31, 1953 market $802,654*)	739,429	59,934	411,743
Other securities (*at lower of cost or market*)	15,716,943	17,561,441	17,271,275
Land, buildings and machinery (*reduced for wear of facilities at December 31, 1953 by $213,246,955; 1952 by $191,432,100; 1951 by $174,555,148*)	285,498,168	230,289,165	187,460,560
Patents, charters and franchises	8	9	9
Insurance premiums and other expenses paid in advance	4,605,117	4,833,152	4,583,275
Receivables not collectible within one year (*less allowance for doubtful accounts*)	10,009,765	9,943,842	10,000,981
Working fund under special purpose contracts—U. S. Government	1,803,063	3,198,298	5,027,130
Other assets	5,178,500	393,215	434,917
TOTAL OWNED BY THE COMPANIES	$1,265,353,717	$1,195,292,040	$1,004,378,037

(Continued on page 15)

Double-page financial statement

annual reports. They add not only interest to the report but also understanding. Figures presented in the balance sheet and other financial statements mean more to the general reader of the annual report if they are lifted from the financial statement and displayed in appropriate charts. Figures on sales, earnings, taxes, reserves and dividends lend themselves to visual treatment in chart or graph form.

POSITION AT DECEMBER 31, 1953, 1952, AND 1951

Sheet)

THE COMPANIES OWE:	1953	1952	1951
Wages and salaries	$ 26,498,938	$ 27,728,058	$ 22,777,650
Suppliers of materials and services	56,955,259	60,235,492	39,484,366
Federal income and excess profits taxes	75,938,000	102,058,728	104,560,000
Other taxes (*Federal, state, local, etc.*)	9,194,250	10,852,734	10,725,288
Product guarantees	13,163,009	10,882,849	8,315,771
Miscellaneous	18,120,919	13,326,701	12,744,155
TOTAL (*Current Liabilities*)	199,870,375	225,084,562	198,607,230
Amounts borrowed from the public through debenture issues:			
Debentures, 2⅝%—Due September 1, 1971	23,842,000	23,842,000	23,842,000
Debentures, 3½%—Due December 15, 1981	300,000,000	250,000,000	125,000,000
Due U. S. Government under special purpose contracts	1,803,063	3,198,298	5,027,130
Other amounts owed including product guarantees beyond one year	6,010,735	5,804,674	6,060,598
TOTAL OWED BY THE COMPANIES	531,526,173	507,929,534	358,536,958
TOTAL OWNED—AFTER DEDUCTING TOTAL OWED	733,827,544	687,362,506	645,841,079
Less: Allowance for contingencies	15,015,196	15,223,098	17,324,877
STOCKHOLDERS' EQUITY (*Net Worth*)	$718,812,348	$672,139,408	$628,516,202

STOCKHOLDERS' EQUITY EVIDENCED BY:	1953	1952	1951
Preferred stock, cumulative, par value $100 per share. Authorized 570,026 shares; issued, 3.80% Series B, 500,000 shares	$ 50,000,000	$ 50,000,000	$ 50,000,000
Common stock, par value $12.50 per share. Authorized 18,000,000 shares; issued and outstanding (*at December 31, 1953*) 15,985,262 shares†	199,815,775	197,055,325	194,371,212
Income retained in the business:			
For inventory and plant contingencies	21,978,859	21,978,859	21,978,859
Other retained earnings	352,401,009	314,411,169	277,957,223
Amount paid the Company for capital stock in excess of par value	94,616,705	88,694,055	84,208,908
TOTAL STOCKHOLDERS' EQUITY	$718,812,348	$672,139,408	$628,516,202

† Excludes 3,614 shares, treasury stock at $12.50 par value per share, 169,027 shares reserved for Employe Stock Plan and 491,710 shares reserved for Restricted Stock Option Plan.

The accompanying notes on page 18 are an integral part of this statement.

Page 15

Courtesy Westinghouse Electric Corporation

covering three years' operations.

Frequently used is a pie chart, showing the breakdown of the income dollar which can be conveniently and quickly understood.

When each page is illustrated with some form of visual aid, attention is attracted to that page, and the interested reader will be encouraged to start reading the accompanying text material. Probably as much as 50% of the space could be filled with interpretative charts, pictorial graphs, maps, photographs and other appealing illustrations. The remainder of the space should be devoted to explanatory text material and the financial statements. The visual aids help the reader grasp the facts presented in the textual message and create attention and interest. The explanatory material presents facts and indicates their significance and relationship. Thus the reader's understanding and favorable opinion and action are obtained.

Almost all of the visual aids used as examples in Chapter 11 were taken from annual reports. They indicate the wide variety of aids that may be used and the variety of information they can display in annual reports. Pies, bars, columns, flow diagrams and all their variations are easily comprehended and are interesting to look at. Photographs of the company president, major officers and board of directors are used to show the stockholders and employees what they look like. An employee pictured at work on the production line, a group of employees shown participating in some form of recreational or operational activity and pictures of plant facilities and equipment add interest. A map may be used to show the distribution of the stockholders or of the product. An organizational chart may also be useful. In general the more visual aids used, the more likely the report is to be looked at and read by the layman. The specialist will read the financial statements and more serious text material because he needs to make use of the data and his position and background qualify him to comprehend all parts of the report.

Humanized Style. Much human interest can be achieved in the annual report just by a careful selection of visual aids. Illustrations help dramatize the important points. For the report to be highly humanized, however, the style of writing in the textual parts must also create human interest. Basically this is achieved largely through the use of the "you" attitude in writing. Material is presented on the basis of what the reader wants, needs and is interested in reading.

Very much in contrast to the objective, impersonal and impartial tone used in problem-solution reports, the humanized, "you" style in annual reports is personal and subjective and reflects the human warmth felt by the company towards the reader. In a sincere, friendly, cordial manner the facts are presented. All three persons of personal pronouns are used with emphasis on you. "Your company," "your dividends," "improvements that will help you," "your benefits," are expressions indicating the unlimited possibilities in the use of the second person pronoun. The style is conversational. The report, which represents the company, is talking with the readers. Both are put on the same level. Only in this way can the annual report become humanized, because to become so it must take on the characteristics or personality of a warm, friendly individual.

Also in line with humanizing the style of writing one must consider adapting the terminology to the reader's understanding. Many readers have not gone beyond the second year of high school. To reach the various publics, the annual report must be written simply. In this way it can be understood by all; and, as long as he is not talked down to, the educated reader will appreciate the simplicity because it saves him time and energy. The trend toward simplified terminology in financial statements is not altogether a new one nor one that is followed by all companies. Firms are using "Statement of Financial Position" or "Financial Condition" now instead of "Balance Sheet," replacing "company owns" for "assets," "company owes" for "liabilities," and using other descriptive phrases like "allowance for" instead of "reserves." The example statements shown on pages 368 and 369 reflect the trend in simplified terminology for convenient and easy comprehension.

Make the narrative readable by presenting it interestingly, clearly and convincingly; by sticking to short sentences; by using the "you" attitude; by writing as you talk and adding personal touches; by letting the text reflect characteristics of human personality. This will go a long way toward obtaining readership of the report and favorable reaction. Enlivening the annual report by attractive appearance and use of visual aids, and by making the statistics, financial statements and text comprehensive yet clear, will also help tremendously in making it a public relations document. Business is a service to the public and needs all the goodwill and public confidence that it can get. A humanized style of writing is the means to accomplishing this function of the annual report.

Design Factors. Typographical appeal is vitally important. Advertising art and book design are used to influence opinion in favor of the company. Expert printer's advice on paper, printing processes, illustrative techniques, printing colors, type faces and type sizes should be secured and followed.

The 8½″ by 11″ size is that of the majority of the reports today. The wide pages allow for the balance sheets, other financial statements and statistical tabulations. With this wide a page the text should be broken into two or three columns for readability. The type should lend dignity and clarity. It is an aid to the accomplishment of the total communication process. Appropriate good taste should be followed in selecting colors in the report. Reports with a four-color cover may use only two or three colors throughout the text material or even be done entirely in black and white.

The usual report varies from 16 to 32 pages in length. A report that is less than 16 pages usually will lack visual aids and will be too brief to be interesting. Likewise one longer than 32 pages will tend to be too wordy and drawn out, may have too many visual aids and may lose its readers.

PRODUCTION

Although annual reports are signed by a company's board chairman or president and sometimes by both, it is unrealistic to believe that these reports are actually prepared by these executives, who are pressed by too many other duties. To whom do they delegate the responsibility for the planning, writing, publishing and distribution of the report? An annual report production survey of 194 selected companies conducted by Monsanto Chemical Company in 1953 showed responsibility delegated as follows:

In 6.6%of the companies, the board chairman or the president actively directed the preparation of the report.

In 28.1% of the companies, the public relations department did it.

In 23.4% of the companies, a group of officers handled the job. Invariably the public relations department was more consistently responsible than any other group.

In 16.1% of the companies, it became the company secretary's responsibility.

In 7.2% of the companies, the job went to the treasurer.

In 5.4% of the companies, the comptroller was in charge.

In 3% of the companies, the assistant to the president took over.

In 1.8% of the companies, it was in the hands of the advertising manager.

In 8.4% of the companies, various other people had the responsibility.

The public relations department has the responsibility in about 50% of the companies. That does not mean that they do all the work. The report is the result of the work of many people in every department and division of the company. The accounting department provides the financial figures, the personnel department information about employees and so forth. If the report is to emphasize its accounting and public relations functions over all others, then the people in those departments are best qualified to handle the planning, writing, publishing and distribution details. The report then becomes the combined efforts of a number of people, and an outside agency is hired to do the art work and printing.

The question always rises as to the amount to be spent on the annual report. The Monsanto Survey shows that the average prices compare favorably with other printed material. The lowest cost per copy was $.05; the highest was $1.50 (reported by two companies). The lowest cost per page was $.002; the highest was $.125. The average cost per page was $.0203. (The individual copy cost was divided by the number of pages, exclusive of covers.) The longer the report, the greater the cost will be. Use of color and professional art work always increases the cost. During the 1940's, when glamorization of annual reports reached its peak, cost was not an important factor. Since then, companies have raised the issue: what did glamorization gain for us? Some of the companies are de-glamorizing their reports and relying on simplicity and clarity of style rather than on elaborately printed pages to tell their story to the public.

Another factor affecting cost is the number of copies to be printed. The more copies, the lower the printing rate. The Monsanto Survey found the average number of copies distributed per report to be 62,127. The smallest distribution was 3,000 copies and the largest 1,307,456 copies. The survey also found that 55.1% of the companies used third-class mail, the cheapest mailing method. In spite of extra expense, however, 37.9% used first class to shorten the delivery time period. Because their reports were too heavy for third class, 6.4% used fourth-class mail.

According to the Monsanto Survey the period from the end of the fiscal year to the annual meeting is divided into the following phases in the preparation of an annual report:

Phase 1—While the accounting department closes its books and prepares its final figures.

Phase 2—While the auditors check the accounting reports and prepare to issue their certificate of audit.

(The average time for the accounting phase is 29 days. The average time for the auditing phase is 20 days. The shortest time was one day; the longest period was 90 days.)

Phase 3—Final printing and binding of the annual report and preparing it for distribution.

(Some typesetting, art work and even printing can be completed while the accountants and auditors are at work. But the final printing and binding must wait until the accounting and auditing phases have ended. The average time for the final printing phase is 23 days. The range was from four to 73 days.)

Phase 4—Delivery time for reports before proxy material is mailed.
Phase 5—Proxy mailing and solicitation period.

(The average waiting time between mailing annual reports and proxy material is 11 days. The average time for proxy solicitation is 31 days.)

Typical of the time and work schedule for most reports is the following one quoted from a letter from Mr. William A. Hanway, Secretary, International Paper Company:

As Secretary of this Company I have the responsibility for assembly of the component parts and for the production and distribution of the report, but preparation of text and statements is a cooperative job in which a great many people take part. Our time schedule runs about as follows:

1. Planning:
   (a) Within the next sixty days [September and October] we will block out the general form of the report and decide what if any changes will have to be made in the standard material, what special supplementary information and material is to be included, etc.
   (b) A tentative outline of the text will then be prepared and responsibility for having different sections drafted will be assumed by various people – primarily Mr. H. R. Weaver, our First Vice President; Mr. John L. Tower, our Director of Public Relations, and myself. The actual drafting in many cases will be done by the particular department most directly concerned.

2. Preparation and Composition (1953 time schedule):
   (a) Covers – We try to have the art work and any incidental text material completed by January 15 so that the plate-maker and printer will not be rushed and can give us a top quality color printing job. (A top quality job of printing and binding 60,000 copies of a 32-page report is a matter of weeks at best, and additional time is required for process color work. We therefore avoid use of process color in the body of the report, which cannot go to press until the auditors complete their certificate of the financial statements.)
   (b) Text of Report:
   January 15 – All preliminary drafts of individual report sections.
   February 1 – Integrated draft of complete report.
   February 15 – Final draft subject only to minor figure corrections to printer for composition.
   March 9 – Semi-final proofs to auditors for final check.

(c) Financial Statements:
March 1 – Preliminary copy to printer for composition.
March 9 – Semi-final proofs to auditors for final check.

3. Presswork and Mailing (1953 time schdule):

March 11 – Press date.
March 12 – Unbound advance black and white sheets released to press.
April 1 – First delivery of final bound copies.
April 6 – Mailing to stockholders completed.

TRENDS

In the last decade of progress in annual reporting several main areas of improvement stand out. There has been a great gain in clarity of presentation and exposition. The report is much easier for the reader to understand than it was ten years ago, mainly because clear, simple charts and graphs are used more extensively to help tell the company's story. Simplified, non-technical statements and terminology are used, and the explanatory discussion is better than in the past.

More consciousness of the social responsibilities of the company is apparent. If free enterprise is to prevail the company's responsibilities must be met.

Data are presented in comparable form and cover two years or more for comparison.

Considerable improvement is noted in the form of annual reports. The 8½" by 11" size is used more often than other sizes. Color is used in the covers and throughout the report.

The appearance and content have been improved. The report is made attractive and interesting, is clearly and concisely written, yet gives wide coverage of the company's financial and operational condition. Thus annual reports are increasing their readership and accomplishing several public relations functions, as well as accounting for the company's financial progress of the year.

PROBLEMS

1. Discuss how an annual report accomplishes various purposes with different readers.

2. Bring to class a recent annual report and show how it is or is not following the trends in annual reporting in its makeup and presentation.

3. How does the style of writing in an annual report differ from that in other types of reports? Why?

4. In an annual report the president wants to include these facts in his letter to the stockholders and employees:

Expenditures for new addition, $50,000
New pension plan established
Taxes increased 11%
Poor sales in southern district
New employee magazine started
Profits last year $85,000; this year $38,000
Sales increased 8%, total $2,095
Heavy advertising expense
New product did not sell well
Training course started
Have new sales manager
Employed 75 more men
Expenses increased 6%
Small labor turnover
Prospects for next year look good
Selling cost up 10%

Develop several paragraphs making use of this information, interpreting and analyzing relationships and significance. Assume that what you write will be a part of the president's letter. You may supply other details consistent with the ones listed.

5. Write a summary, suitable for mailing to stockholders, of a company annual report.

6. Making use of pertinent summary information in an annual report, prepare a full-page newspaper advertisement aimed at obtaining public interest and goodwill for your company.

7. Write a summary of an annual report for publication as a feature article in the January issue of your employee magazine.

8. Select one of the following features of an annual report and suggest ways for improving a particular report:

a. Presentation of financial statements
b. Use of visual aids
c. Design factors
d. Style of writing

9. The American Management Association has set up three criteria for evaluating the effectiveness of an annual report—interest, clearness and completeness. Select an annual report and criticize it on this basis.

10. Make a study of selected annual reports of one company over a period of years to find out changes, progress, trends, etc. Your results are to be presented to top management as a basis for recommending improvements.

CHAPTER 20

Employee Publications

EMPLOYEE PUBLICATIONS IS A GENERAL TERM EMBRACING ALL forms of written communication, excluding routine correspondence, between a company and its employees. These publications may take the forms of newspapers, magazines, tabloids, news magazines, picture magazines, bulletins or handbooks. They are distributed to employees free of charge. Occasionally companies find it desirable to send these publications to persons outside of the company for advertising or public relations purposes.

The bulk of employee publications being printed today is newspapers, magazines and handbooks — the last often referred to as manuals. The purpose of this chapter is to indicate the types of employee publications, their contents and the necessity for presenting information to the employees so clearly and interestingly that they will not only read the publications but will understand them.

HISTORY AND GROWTH

Employee publications, sometimes called house organs, were very few in number prior to World War I. The number greatly increased in the latter 1920's, but the depression years forced companies to reduce the number and cost of such publications to a minimum. The big boom in employee publications began with World War II.

Industry needed production quickly and in mammoth quantities. Therefore it was necessary to enlist employees' aid by informing them of the nation's urgent need for production and of the importance of the individual in the war effort. The quickest and most effective way to communicate these facts and ideas to employees was through attractive easy-to-read publications. The United States Government urged firms to start using employee publications by helping to staff them and by providing material to keep them going. The rise in quantity and cost of publications has never stopped since World War II, and size and appearance are still changing.

It is almost impossible to estimate accurately the number of employee publications today; but the 1954 *Printers' Ink Directory of House Organs* listed more than 6,300 publications by name, and there are undoubtedly several thousand more not reported. The combined circulation has been estimated at over 150,000,000, which is more than the combined circulations of all daily newspapers in the United States, and the budgets have been estimated to be over $115,000,000. Some large companies publish scores of publications. General Motors was distributing 37 publications in 1952, including *Folks* with a circulation of 500,000, the *Executive Bulletin* for 90,000 salaried personnel, and 35 newspapers with a circulation of 300,000. Standard Oil (New Jersey) published in 1952 about 85 magazines and newspapers in 24 countries and in 13 languages. Individual budgets vary from the part-time salary of one man assigned to get out a company newsletter, to International Harvester's budget of $500,000, excluding salaries and overhead, on three slick-paper magazines.[1]

Some publications contain only local office chit-chat, bowling records, births, awards, jokes and items like "What machine operator with initials A. C. is eyeing what blonde in Section 22 with initials B. G.?" Others, such as the publication of Standard Oil (New Jersey), *The Lamp,* are written with a much broader coverage, containing stories of general interest that may be only slightly related to the company or its employees. The selection of the type of publication, the contents and the style of writing will vary entirely with the purposes and objectives that the company wishes to accomplish with its publication.

PURPOSES AND OBJECTIVES

It is every company's goal to have employees working harmoniously with management, feeling a sense of responsibility for the success of the company and happy in their jobs. Industry has realized that much labor friction results from management's and labor's misunderstanding facts and attitudes toward each other. In many companies employees have little information about the company and therefore have a natural suspicion of the company's actions. Unless the company plans a program to explain its operations, objectives and problems – unless it takes employees into its confidence and makes them feel a necessary part of its operations – it cannot expect them to work smoothly and happily for the company.

Toward this end industry has spent millions of dollars in training programs, recreation buildings, pension programs, hospitals, insurance plans, profit-sharing plans and many other employee benefits. Industry promotes a mutual understanding by showing employees that the company is genuinely interested in their welfare and that cooperation between management and employees is mutually desirable and profitable. Therefore the company must communicate with employees in such a manner that they will understand their rights and responsibilities and have faith in the company. This is the role of employee publications.

Before any company begins an employee publication it should first set down the purposes and objectives that it hopes to accomplish.

---

1 "How to Play the House Organ," *Fortune,* October, 1952, p. 145.

This will guide the editor in determining the contents and approach to use in writing. The three general purposes of employee publications are to provide information, to educate and to entertain.

Information

The most common aim of all employee publications is to inform. One company official expressed it this way: "Employees should be kept informed about *what* the company is doing, *why* they are doing it, and *how* it will affect each one of them." This involves telling employees about the financial condition of the company, its sales and production problems, plans and achievements. The informed employee is made a part of the company, which enables him to better understand the actions of the company and creates a desire on his part to cooperate.

Education

Every company wishes to increase the loyalty and morale of its employees by giving them a better understanding of the work they do, in an interesting and dramatic fashion. Information about the company's product, like the source of raw material and the end use of the product, helps employees to realize that they are important contributors to the company's success. An employee will take pride in his workmanship and his company if the story is written to emphasize his individual importance and the importance of everyone's working as part of a "family" or "team" to get products to consumers.

Also included under educational aims are stories about benefits rendered to employees by the company, such as hospitalization, pensions and insurance. This is usually done in detail through handbooks, but newspapers and magazines usually supplement the material by using specific illustrations to emphasize the benefits.

Following World War II the idea swept industry that employee relations would improve if employees understood the "free enterprise-profit" system better. Many companies published and still publish articles, stories and vignettes that educate or remind employees that their job and high standard of living are made possible by a democratic, capitalistic system.

Entertainment

Most publications contain items written solely for the entertainment of employees — articles about social activities, sports and hobbies: women's pages; cartoons; jokes; news of promotions and human interest stories about individuals. In addition, each story in the employee publication, whether educational or informational, should be written in an interesting or entertaining fashion; otherwise, the story will probably not be read by the majority of the employees.

A company may have information, education or entertainment as the main goal for its employee publications; or, more likely, the publications will have elements of each. A survey of goals of editors of 88 publications revealed the following list: [2]

Aims of Employee Publications	*Number of Editors Mentioning*
To give information on company operations, policies, and problems	51
To draw individuals into closer contact with the company	41
To make employees feel they are members of a single organization	33
To help employees understand each other	19
To keep employees informed on the progress of the industry	5
To promote safety	6
To stimulate employees in work	6
To promote better industrial relations	5
To make employees understand the principles and philosophy of the company	5

FORMAT

There are several formats that companies may use for publications, and each format has certain advantages and limitations. The format chosen by any particular organization will vary with the character of the company, the urgency of the news, budget limitations and the taste of its employees. Also the format may vary if the publication is distributed to a wide reader group. For instance, the format of a publication distributed to employees, the community and stockholders may be different from one that is distributed to employees only.

[2] Excerpt from *Employee Publications,* available exclusively to Metropolitan Group Policyholders. Copyright, 1952 by Metropolitan Life Insurance Company. Reproduced by permission.

Magazine

The magazine is the most commonly used format of employee publications. It is usually published once a month and varies in length from four to fifty pages. It has a separately illustrated

Courtesy (*top, left to right*) Standard Oil Company (New Jersey), Monsanto Chemical Company, (*bottom, left to right*) Southern Bell Telephone Company, Lykes Brothers Steamship Company.

Representative covers of four widely distributed employee magazines.

cover and is usually printed on a high-grade slick paper. The magazine is most effective when presenting company or employee news in feature-story form with illustrations and layout designed to make the story attractive, interesting and easily understood. Many companies spend large sums of money in making covers and illustrations

Add 1835 CSF Members
(See Page 5)

Industry Control Man Is Grid Expert
(See Page 12)

Vol. 37—No. 39 Published Weekly for the Men and Women of the General Electric Company, Schenectady, N. Y. Friday, October 1, 1954

Top Suggestion at KAPL

KAPL'S Highest single award of $420 was presented to Joseph Bartman, center, liquid metal tester, for perfecting and improving the technique and equipment for liquid metal disposal. Unit Supervisor Donald Kerr, left, and Foreman William McGroty, right, join Mr. Bartman in admiring the check. Mr. Bartman has won two previous awards of $10 and $5, respectively.

Voting Registration Dates Listed

Qualified voters in Schenectady County who are to vote in the fall election on Nov. 2 must register this week end or next.

Residents of the City of Schenectady and the Village of Scotia will have their first opportunity to register today. On the first three days of registration, Oct. 1, 2, and 8, hours will be from 10 a.m. to 10 p.m. On the fourth day, Oct. 9, residents of these personal registration areas may register to vote from 7 a.m. to 10 p.m.

The first day for residents of the five towns in Schenectady County, which have non-personal registration, will be tomorrow from 7 a.m. to 10 p.m. The other day for them is Oct. 9, when registration will be held from 1 to 10 p.m. The towns which have non-personal registration are Niskayuna, Princetown, Rotterdam, Duanesburg, and Glenville.

For further information on registration, call the Election Commissioners on Tel. 6-1269.

Just One of the 'Boas' . . .

Guest Performer at the recent ASME smoker at the Edison Club was this 10-foot boa constrictor, owned by New York Zoological Park. Holding the reptile's head is Dr. James A. Oliver, curator of reptiles at the zoo, who spoke at the smoker and displayed this boa together with a python. Cautiously clutching a couple of coils are ASME members, left to right, Dr. Linden Saline, G.E.L.; Bob Jackson, LST-G; and Nick August, LST-G. The snake is a lady. Ladies weren't invited to the smoker, but who wants to argue with a boa, especially when she's out of sorts due to shedding her skin. Additional information in "Around GE," on page 3.

GE Waives Pension Plan Provisions To Enable All Pensioners to Benefit From Recent Social Security Increase

Also Announces Increase in Payments to Pensioners over 65 Retired Prior to Social Security

General Electric announced today that it would waive provisions of its Pension Plan to enable all of its more than 14,000 pensioners to benefit by the recently increased Social Security payments.

In addition to waiving the provision which calls for deductions in Company payments when Social Security benefits are increased, General Electric announced that it would also increase its payments by $7 a month to its retired employees over 65 who were retired before Social Security benefits became payable and who thus are not able to benefit from Social Security. This amount will match the average Social Security increase which other GE pensioners will receive.

Effective Sept. 1

The extra GE payment of $7 a month will be effective as of September 1, the same as the new higher Social Security benefits. It is expected that the first payment will be included in pension checks sent out at the end of October.

The Company stated that under the GE Pension Plan the majority of its present and future pensioners will automatically receive the benefits of increases in Social Security payments. However, for a number of its present and future pensioners to receive the larger income it is necessary for the Company to waive provisions of its pension plan which call for offsetting pension payments by Social Security increases.

The purpose of the Company's action, which is subject to approval by its board of directors, is to make certain that all of its pensioners over 65 either receive the benefit of Social Security increases or the extra payment by the Company comparable to the Social Security increase. The pensioners have been notified of the Company's proposed action by letters from local management.

150 Affected

Of GE employees retiring in the next year, about 150 of those who might be affected may be represented by unions. Before making this program effective for these employees, the Company will ascertain that the interested union has no objections to GE making higher payments than those called for by continuing contracts which run to September 15, 1955.

General Electric plans thus contemplate that all present pensioners as well as employees retiring in the future will, as they qualify for Social Security, have their incomes increased as a result of the 1954 increases in Social Security benefits.

W. W. Trench, Company Secretary For 24 Years, Stood Alone as Pioneer In Educational, Benefit Plans

Few General Electric men have had as profound an effect upon the Company's employee relations program as had W. W. Trench, who died last week. He was secretary of the Company when he retired.

"What we remember most about Bill Trench," remarked one of his close friends and associates, "was his enthusiasm and his ability to inspire others."

An ardent exponent of the philosophy that the Company should help employees to help themselves, Mr. Trench worked tirelessly to develop and gain wide acceptance of many of our current employee benefit plans.

From the time of his appointment to the Relief and Loan Plan board of directors in 1927 until his retirement in 1952, his persistence in improving our employee relations program was tremendous.

Mr. Trench's work in employee benefits went beyond the confines of General Electric since many of his programs were adopted by other industrial firms.

He headed and was long a guiding force in the Company group insurance plans, educational programs and other employee benefit plans. Service as chairman of the pension board and education committee was a vital part of his busy GE career.

The suggestion system as it is presently constituted was another of Mr. Trench's closest projects. He also served as secretary of the former GE Employees' Security Corp., during its 25 years of existence.

All this was in addition to his countless duties as secretary of GE for 24 years and a widely recognized Schenectady civic leader.

Bill Trench will be remembered for a myriad of activities in and out of the Company but above it all, his greatest contribution was the thought and philosophy that the "human touch" must never be forgotten when dealing with people.

Though Bill Trench is no longer with us, his ideals, philosophies, and objectives in employee relations will be evident for many years. He leaves behind a living memorial in the form of employee relations programs which have proven unique in American industry.

Joseph Cotten Makes TV Bow on GE Theater

Joseph Cotten, one of Hollywood's leading actors, makes his television debut on "The General Electric Theater" Sunday, at 9 p.m. over station WRGB when he stars in an adaptation of Evelyn Waugh's "High Green Wall."

Courtesy General Electric Company

Employee newspaper.

(often in color) so attractive that the magazine is looked forward to by employees and taken home to be read at leisure by themselves and their families.

The magazine has the main disadvantages of being expensive to publish and of requiring a great amount of time and work. News stories often have less punch in a monthly magazine because the magazine is published after the occurrence of many events. However, editors can counter this to some extent by slanting the news to show how it affects the lives of employees.

Newspaper

When a company wishes to contact its employees frequently with straight news, the newspaper format is usually chosen. It may be issued daily, weekly, semimonthly or, rarely, even monthly, and is most often used by large companies with many thousands of readers. It may be issued to employees and to supervisors separately. Employees accustomed to reading news in their daily newspaper find the company newspaper easy to read because of the similarity. The stories are laid out in columnar fashion with heads, which makes the publication easy for editors to plan and for employees to read.

For the very reasons that the company newspaper has appearance advantages, it also has disadvantages. The employee is likely to skim over the headlines, read news items selectively and discard the issue quickly. The stories necessarily must be short, which leaves little chance for informational or educational material to be presented in an interesting and complete manner. Each company must decide between newspaper timeliness and sensational appeal and magazine flexibility in style and layout.

Tabloid

A tabloid format is similar to that of a newspaper and is best used in situations where company newspapers can be used effectively. Tabloids contain many pictures, with catchy captions; the stories are extremely short, often written in narrative style. Surveys have shown that the readership of tabloids by employees is usually high, but that employees often read them for entertainment alone and remember little of what they have read. There is little place in a tabloid for good articles of an educational or informational nature.

Bulletin

If a company does not wish to publish either a newspaper, tabloid or magazine, it may decide to publish a bulletin. These publications are usually from four to eight pages long and may be issued regularly or whenever the company wishes to publicize some particular news. The format may vary between newspaper or magazine, and it may be reproduced by any number of processes – printing, offset, mimeograph or multilith. The bulletin has the disadvantage of being small in size, but this may prove to be an advantage to some companies.

Handbook

The handbook is a publication distributed primarily to new employees to inform them of company policies or to all employees to announce a new policy. This publication is discussed in a later section of this chapter.

CONTENT

Company and Employee News

In deciding which items will be included in employee publications the company must draw a balance between:

(*1*) What the company wants the employees to read and

(*2*) What the employees want to read.

This is an extremely difficult balance to strike, for the company is naturally interested in building friendliness and understanding by giving employees certain information about the company. Editors have learned, however, that information that the company wants employees to read is very often not what the employees want to read. Therefore, it is a challenge to the editor to present company information in such a manner that employees want to read it. This requires that articles be written or illustrated so that, *with little effort,* the employee can see that the information affects his job. Otherwise he is not interested. Mistakes have been made by companies in thinking that whatever they print in their publications is being read and understood by employees simply because it is published and handed to the employee. Nothing could be farther from the truth.

The employee is under no obligation to read any publication; nor is he under any compulsion to believe what he reads. Company officials are vitally interested in production, sales and profit problems, and often they assume that the employee is equally interested in the same information. The employee *is* interested in this information, but not in the same way, for he sees these problems from a different viewpoint. Companies who continue to write stories from the management point of view and who publish only information that they want the employees to know are wasting thousands of dollars and man-hours.

One of Our Raw Materials — What It Is and How Obtained

HUGE SCOOPS (left) bite out ten-cubic yard mouthsful of the reddish-brown phosphate ore found just below the earth's surface. Then hydraulic washing of the phosphate matrix (above) frees it from unwanted clay and dirt before being sent to the furnaces.

Phosphates, the chemical being unloaded from the hopper car by Al Peterson on the opposite page, has been used in manufacturing synthetic detergents like Lever's Surf, only since the end of World War II. But phosphate rock, the ore from which phosphates are [illegible] in the [illegible]

ous, which is then broken mechanically and stored under cover. It's carefully mixed with coke and silica sand before it is put into the furnaces.

Huge furnaces [illegible]

Courtesy Lever Brothers Company

Company tells employees about its product.

To know what will interest employees the editor must listen to employees talk, be a good judge of human nature and have some broad knowledge of sociology, philosophy and psychology. What does John Phillips on Machine #14 think about wages? What is on his mind when he reads about a new expansion policy or a company million-dollar profit? What are his basic wants?

Employees are becoming more and more interested in information about the company, provided management is honest in presenting both good and bad information. Employees want to know about office planning; and companies are beginning to tell them something of the plans for the future, as illustrated by the article on page 388. If employees know about the strength and weaknesses of the company, they are more likely to be understanding when problems arise that affect both them and management.

Edgewater

John Cooney

Phil Tarabola (Surf) was married to Tena Cioffi of New York City on October 28, 1950.

Eleanor Pesquera (Case Packing) was married to Robert Renner of Ridgefield Park on November 12, 1950.

Charles Ecklin (Surf lab.) was married to Evelyn Anema of Clifton, New Jersey on November 4, 1950.

Martha Lusa (Office) was married to Rocco Toscano of Ridgefield on November 4, 1950.

Cosmopolitan Club

Twenty-eight members of the Cosmopolitan Club crossed the Hudson River to see the Broadway Hit "Gentlemen Prefer Blondes." The gals had a wonderful dinner at the Red Coach Grill before the show. After a very enjoyable evening, our girls returned to Jersey with Carol Channing's show-stopper still ringing in their ears, but not fully convinced themselves, that "Diamonds Are a Girl's Best Friend."

Bowling

The Edgewater Plant Bowling League has completed its tenth week of competition and the team standings are relatively the same. The "Electricians", "Refinery" and "Catalyst" are all tied

Pete Newcomb Goes West

MORE than seventy-five persons attended the farewell dinner party for Pete Newcomb, Edgewater shift superintendent before he was transferred to our new Los Angeles plant. At a party held in Sautter's Restaurant, Fairview, N. J., Pete's friends presented him with a metal bench lathe, complete with motor and attachments. Pete and his wife are shown directly behind the lathe.

Softball Dinner

On Saturday evening, November 18, the Annual Softball Dinner was held at Jerry's Restaurant, Fort Lee, New Jersey. Approximately

inaccurate pitching during the 1950 Season.

Joe Schwartz was

Courtesy Lever Brothers Company

Publication includes news about employees.

At the same time that company information is being published, it must be remembered that employees are human beings. They do not want to read company news exclusively; they also want to read about themselves. They like to read what their friends are doing, see pictures of fellow employees and read reports of social activities. This can be carried too far unless an editor is careful. Some editors, believing that names make the news, fill publications with birthdays of employees, service records, pictures of the deer that Paul bagged on his vacation, cheesecake and office gossip. This sort of publication has high readership in small companies; but in larger companies, where few employees know each other, this kind of news means nothing to the majority.

Planners D. A. Howard, Jr., William Bang, R. W. Darwin, W. R. Knight, and R. F. Sewell.

Long Range Planners Figure . . .

What's In Store for 19XX?

By Al Arnett

A TECHNICALIZED FUTURE is pressing hard on the heels of our modern age. In the span of one generation, Southern Bell's long range planners predict some astounding changes for the telephone business; changes geared to meet the demands of a nation grown accustomed to round-the-world flights and push-

ing. By 1975, for example

creased

sibilities for new and increased uses of communication services."

A city without wires, perhaps? The idea

possible today than

Courtesy Southern Bell Telephone Company

Magazine keeps employees informed of company's plans.

Two-Way Communication

An editor must always keep in mind that an employee publication should be a two-way communication medium — from management to employees and from employees to management. If the editor consistently communicates one way to employees, there will probably be a growing stack of unread magazines in the waste-paper baskets. If an employee has a question about the company or his job that he wants answered, he will not be receptive to any other information until his question is answered. He will come to regard the company publication with more respect if he feels that it is his medium for communication also.

Many companies make a practice of publishing employee questions with answers credited to a responsible official. Occasionally the questions may be embarrassing for the company to answer in print, but a company that answers openly will build employee morale and confidence in management. The following are typical questions taken from several publications, illustrating the variety of employee interests:

What is the deadline for rest periods in the morning and afternoon? Can anyone save his 15-minute rest period until the end of the morning or the end of the afternoon and leave for home 15 minutes early?

Is there a chance of equalling other shops regarding overtime in the near future?

Does our hospitalization limit us to only 31 days of hospital care in a calendar year, or is it really 31 days of care for each different type of illness?

I understand that all merit-rate increases have been suspended in view of the current economy drive, regardless of the quality of the individual's work. Is this true?

How many different models does the company make?

The employees' side of the picture can also be presented by reporting discussions and conferences between management and employees and by printing side by side statements representing differing points of view.

The following is a sample check list of some of the types of company and employee news that might be included in an employee publication: [3]

EMPLOYEE EFFICIENCY

- Effect of absence from the job
- Increasing production
- Waste reduction
- Good housekeeping
- Suggestion system
- Vocational training
- Technical explanations

---

[3] K. C. Pratt, *House Magazine Copy,* The Champion Paper and Fibre Company, Hamilton, Ohio, 1946.

COMPANY POLICY

- Hours and wages
- Bonus and incentive plans
- Union relationships
- Recruitment of new employees
- Supervisory training
- Litigation affecting company status
- Rules and regulations
- Striking and insubordination
- Vacations and sick leave
- Solicitation on company property
- Contributions to community welfare
- Board of directors meeting reports

BUSINESS AND FINANCIAL INFORMATION

- Balance Sheet
- Profit and Loss statement
- Earnings
- Taxes
- Wages (laws affecting)
- Costs of operation
- Business conditions
- New property and equipment
- Dividends
- Financing
- Investments
- Prices
- Sales
- Markets
- New products

GENERAL INFORMATION ABOUT THE COMPANY

- Seniority and age groups
- New officers and directors
- Mergers
- Raw material sources
- Customers
- Exports
- Company history
- Departments and branch plants
- Corporate structure
- Plant expansion
- Advertising
- Public relations
- Contests
- Stockholders

INFORMATION ABOUT INDUSTRY

- Contribution to industry
- Relative position
- Industry as economic factor

Contribution to other industries
What other members of industry think about company
Competitive and non-competitive aspects
Inter-industry personalities
The industry and government

EMPLOYEE BENEFITS

Hospitalization
Insurance
Credit union
Company's publications
Stock ownership
Library
Cafeteria
Pension plan
Profit sharing
Recreational facilities

EMPLOYEE RECOGNITION

Service awards
Promotions
Heroism
New employees
Retired employees
Obituaries
Service anniversaries
Hobby stories
Family stories
Personals
Birthdays, weddings, births
The old timer
Community contributions
Unusual performance
Exemplary activities

EMPLOYEE WELFARE

Health and nutrition
Safety
Venereal disease
Medical and dental facilities

GENERAL STORIES

Economic information
Community activities
Citizenship
Adult education
Income taxes
Social security
Legislation affecting the company
Politics (local and national)

MISCELLANEOUS

- Fiction
- Children's page
- Comics
- Fashions
- Interior decorating
- Recipes and homemaking
- Sons and daughters of employees
- Classified ads
- Crossword puzzles, bridge, chess
- Cartoons and jokes
- Inspirational articles
- Poetry
- Prize contests
- Questions and answers
- Other quiz-type features
- Reader's forum
- Religious material

SECURING READER INTEREST

Journalistic Techniques

Much of what has already been written about securing reader interest in earlier parts of this book will apply to employee publication writing. The essential difference is that the average business report is designed to be read by one person or a small group of persons. Usually these persons want to read the report because it is directed to them personally or because it is their job to read such reports.

Employee publications are distributed to large numbers of people who are not required to read them, and the publications will be thrown away unread if the readers are not interested or entertained to some degree. It is the responsibility of the editor, therefore, to secure readership by presenting the information to employees in such style that they will want to read each issue and will understand what has been written.

Because the editor must write to interest employees the style of writing for employee publications is very similar to that of daily newspaper and popular magazine writing. In fact many of the editors of employee publications today have had some prior experience in the journalistic field. This background is helpful, but not essential, for there are some differences between journalistic and employee publication writing.

Journalism involves objective reporting of facts — who, what, where, when and why — with little interpretation of the facts. A newspaper reporter collects and reports facts with no intent to influence reader attitudes, except on editorial pages. The newspaper audience is large and varied, and the value of the news lies in its timeliness or sensational appeal.

An employee publication is aimed at a specific group, which has as a common bond the fact that its members work for the same company. Therefore only the news that affects the lives of those individuals need be reported. The news stories in employee publications can be written and interpreted according to the way they affect the lives of employees. Because employee publications are usually published more infrequently than daily newspapers, their stories are seldom timely. Thus the news item is written to interpret its effect on the company and employees.

Therefore journalism is essentially objective writing, whereas employee publication writing is generally more interpretative, or subjective, writing. One partial exception is the employee newspaper that is published daily or weekly. The layout and style of writing follow to a great extent that of daily newspapers, but the news is selected on the basis of its interest to employees and is adapted in presentation on the same basis.

For example, a story written in journalistic style about the construction of a new plant might be written in this manner:

> The Teasdel Corporation will construct a modern plant next June, Jay B. Teasdel, president, announced today.
>
> The plant, to be located on the same site as the present plant, will be soundproofed and air conditioned.

Written for the employee publication, the story might be written in this style:

> Wouldn't it be nice if you could come to work in the morning, leave the heat outside, and step into a cool, quiet building? Instead of the slam-bang clatter of the presses, there would be only a soft hum and pleasant music.
>
> A dream?
>
> No. This will be true next June when the new air-conditioned and soundproofed plant is constructed. . . .

Personalization

"How does this affect me?" an employee usually asks after hearing news about the company. This is probably the most important single question to be remembered when writing for employees, and, as simple as it may seem, it is probably the most often forgotten point.

An employee picks up a company magazine; he reads that the company is spending $545,656 per year on company benefits, and the story states that this expenditure is made solely for the employees' welfare. The company naturally expects employees to feel somewhat grateful after reading this. However the chances are that the individual employee understands little from such a statement; for the figures mean nothing to him in particular – Jim Garrison, office janitor. If the story had been written to show that the company was spending $425 per year on each employee for employee benefits, it would have had much more impact. Jim Garrison has a mental image of $425, for he can visualize what that amount of money will buy – suits, washing machines or groceries. He could see what the company is doing for *him*.

If an article tells about a new product that the company is adding to its line, the story should be written, not just about the product itself, but also about how the addition of this product will affect the employee's pocketbook and working conditions. For example, an article in one employee magazine headlined a story, "HOW OUR COMPANY HAS GROWN . . . AND WHAT IT MEANS TO YOU."

Remember that foremost in any employee's mind is this question: "How does this affect me?" If the personalization is not presented so that the employee can understand how the story affects him, he probably will not read the article. Nor will he retain any of its information if he does read it.

Language

If one person wishes to communicate with another it is logical that he will choose the language that the other can understand. If he is speaking to a person in a foreign country he uses the foreign language. Persons speaking English to each other should realize the necessity for speaking exactly the same language. The language spoken by the president very often varies from the language of the man on an assembly line. They use different expressions to convey a thought. Language used frequently by management may sound stilted or complicated to employees. An employee may look at an article and say, "I know what it says; but what does it mean?"

Editors must remember that employee publications are written for the employees, not the board of directors or top management, to understand. Yet editors often subconsciously think of the manner in which their bosses would write a story and then turn out formal writing or jargon sometimes used in management conversations. The employee does not understand jargon and is not interested in literary prose — he wants to read about himself and the company in language he can easily read and understand. Thus, an editor must know the language of the employees if he is to communicate with them. He must evaluate the level of understanding of employees and then write for them on that level. One method is to choose a typical employee and write to him in the language he understands; it might be Nigel Rafferty in the meat department, but he is the one the editor wishes to communicate with — not the president.

One company wanted to tell its employees about the necessity for profits in business. Instead of writing the story in straight prose with economic theory and a mass of statistics, the company wrote the story in this fashion: [4]

ABOUT THOSE PROFITS. . . .

"They tell me," said George Golightly, waggling his coffee spoon across the table at his friend, Steve Steadfast, "that the company made $134 million last year — just from its own chemical operations. How do you like that? Why should those guys get 134 million bucks when I'm working for . . . "

"Wait a minute, George," Steadfast interrupted. "How many of 'those guys' do you think there are? There are 110,000 of them. George, suppose you had $11,000."

"Don't change the subj . . ." Golightly dropped his coffee spoon in astonishment. "Who me? $11,000?"

IF YOU HAD A STORE

"Yes, you. Suppose you had $11,000 and bought a grocery store with it. How much would you expect to clear in a year after you'd paid for your stock, your clerks, taxes and other expenses?"

"Gee, I don't know. One or two thousand, maybe. But what's that got to do with $134 million?"

"Just this, George. The company has 110,000 stockholders, 110,000 owners, where your grocery store had just one. . . ."

Simple, easy writing makes for easy reading. Newspapers have discovered in writing for a mass public that it is necessary to use simple, familiar words in fairly short sentences. There should be few complicated sentences and a minimum of adjectives. Paragraphs

---

[4] "About Those Profits . . . ," *The Blender,* Martinsville Nylon Plant of E. I du Pont de Nemours and Company, Inc., Martinsville, Virginia, May, 1950, p. 2.

should be short and frequent headings should be used to break type into easily read portions. This is not to say that the writer must reduce his style to that of a first-grade primer; writing can be easy without being childish.

Words

There is a common, erroneous assumption that words mean the same thing to everyone. Each person learns a word meaning by relating it to experiences he has had. The experiences of one person are not likely to be exactly like those of another in learning a word, so each person may have a slightly different meaning attached to it. Both persons will have a rough understanding of what is meant, but it will be difficult to have both persons interpreting the word exactly the same way.

For instance, "profit," "work stoppage," "capitalism," "incentive plan" and many other abstract words set up different mental pictures for different persons. What is management thinking of when it uses the word "wage" or the word "salary"? Are they just symbols for a method of determining compensation, or do they also carry symbols for status in the company organization? The meaning of the word "capitalist" has been so distorted that to some people the word brings a mental image of an excessively rich man who squeezes his living from the hard work of employees. When a writer uses abstract words, he should explain their exact meaning if he knows that employees associate the words with unpleasant mental images.

There is no exact rule for choice of words that an editor can use, except that he should be aware of the dangers of variation in the meaning of abstract words and try to use concrete words and specific examples as often as possible.

Ideas in Small Doses

Trying to put across too many ideas in one story may cause an employee to get confused, lose interest or miss the major idea completely. The more that is written into a story, the less the reader is likely to read. Restrict the story to one or two major ideas or facts.

This principle also applies to the frequency of issue of publications, for there is a point where the company may be distributing more publications to employees than they can or care to read. One monthly publication of eight pages might better be broken into bi-monthly publications of four pages each. The eight-page publication may look long and forbidding, but an employee might read every word in a shorter, four-page issue.

Accuracy

One of the main purposes of employee publications is to present accurate information for refuting erroneous rumors and grapevine gossip. If the publication is consistently accurate, employees will come to regard it as an authoritative source of information. Errors in dates, places and names can earn a publication a reputation for inaccuracy, and the entire publication may be disbelieved or unread. Accuracy requires double checking the original copy for inaccuracies of fact and careful reading of the printer's proof.

Drama

Everyone likes to hear a good story, and everyone likes to read a good story. The top management of one company was considering the purchase of a competitor's plant in order to increase its product line. It involved a major expenditure and the executives debated for months. Finally they decided that it was a wise purchase and they announced it in the employee publication. Later a poll revealed that few employees were interested and many had never even read the story. Why?

The story was written as a factual, straight-news release. There was no interest or drama to make an employee take an interest in the story and realize that the purchase would affect *his* job. It is not the duty of an employee to read a company publication. It is the duty of the editor to interest the employee with writing that snags his attention, holds his interest right to the end and is clear enough for him to understand.

The editor of *The Lamp* began his story about the importance of ship fueling in world commerce in this fashion:

> At 5:06 o'clock on a Monday afternoon, the telephone rang on the fifth floor of the Esso Building in midtown New York.
>
> The Tarpaulin Steamship Company wanted 7,500 barrels (about 1,168 long

tons) of bunker fuel oil delivered at eight o'clock next morning to its steamship *Hawser,* lying at Pier 1234 in Brooklyn.

The *SS Hawser* was loading bathtubs, cotton shirts, soup in tins, wrapping paper and road scrapers for the Far East and was due to sail on the tide at 11:18 Wednesday morning.

After that, things happened fast. . . .

The most important sentences in a story from an attention-getting angle are the first sentences. The writer is competing for the employee's attention with the daily newspaper, radio, television, movies, books, wife, children, friends and an urge not to read anything requiring effort. The employee will take about five seconds on the story in the hope that it may prove to be of interest. If the opening sentences don't arouse his interest there probably will not be a reader for the rest of the story and the publication will have misfired.

To the British they are Dakotas; to American flyboys, C-47's; and to many businessmen who eased themselves into their deep, soft seats—just plain old DC-3's. These same businessmen and their wives or sisters or sons will remember slim, trim stewardesses rushing up and down the aisles carrying trays or kind words; pillows or post cards. . . .

This was the beginning of a story about a new Monsanto Chemical Company product used in DC-3 airplanes, published in the employee publication, *Monsanto.*

The opening sentences are called the lead. They set the atmosphere for the rest of the story; therefore it is dangerous to begin a story with a routine expository style, no matter how well the story is developed thereafter. Create a picture in the employee's mind and set the stage for what is coming. Tell the story in terms of people and not inanimate objects.

An article about old age and survivors insurance published in The Champion Paper and Fibre Company's publication, *The Log,* was written interestingly. Instead of presenting a set of uninteresting and complicated rules and regulations, the entire story is told in terms of how the laws affect a typical employee. The story begins:

"Yes, I've got a good job at Champion . . . I make pretty good money, and I have a fair chance for promotion.

"But I haven't done much figuring on the future. How will I be fixed a few years from now? What about when I retire? Or if I die, what will my family live on?"

A story about the facilities of the company library may be dead reading to most people, but a personal interview with the librarian about the library will often develop interest. Use incidents and anecdotes to illustrate principles, rather than dry reasoning throughout the story. If there is no real incident, make up one by using a hypothetical case, such as, "Let's see what the company president does after getting to the office on a typical morning."

The following is a good check list of techniques that may be used to develop reader interest.[5] In addition to editorial techniques, the list includes layout suggestions.

EDITORIAL GIMMICKS

1. **Use easy-to-read story treatments.** Interview style (dialog, short sentences); case histories (problem, solution, results); check lists, prime points in staccato, like the one you are now reading.
2. **Invite the reader into succeeding pages.** Problem, question or teaser in front of book, answer or details on latter pages. "What Did John Jones Say to the Boss?—see page 18."
3. **Get continued interest** from issue to issue through a correlated series, say a series of pictorial visits to plant cities, product-by-product development, etc.
4. **Use a come-hither slogan** or subtitle under the name of the publication.
5. **Q. and A.'s are good** for the I.Q. They tie in with the current quiz fad, are a challenge to the reader, appeal because of their brevity and offer wide variety in small space.
6. **Use short breakers for variety,** one-sentence items, usually humorous or statistical, set less-than-column-width, in small type, between longer items.
7. **Be sure you give the readers what they really want,** not what you think they want or ought to have. A yearly post-card survey or more frequent cross-section surveys will give you the facts on which to act. One house organ was about to drop a regular monthly feature that had been running for a long period. A simple survey showed, somewhat to the astonishment of the editor, that this was the most popular feature.

HEADLINE TREATMENTS

8. **Pictorial headlines denote action.** The headline, NOVEL CONTEST PRODUCES RESULTS, had intertwining sketches showing a woman pushing a wheelbarrow filled to overflowing with contest entry blanks; a silver dollar to denote the awards; and a photograph of an actual award presentation, all this compressed into a headline six inches wide.
9. **Design in the headline.** In the headline, SAFETY IN OPERATING TRUCKS, the word SAFETY was set in type and superimposed on a sketch of a flying pennant.
10. **Headline modifying a well-known saying.** A fire insurance company pulls a switch with DON'T KEEP THE HOME FIRES BURNING.

[5] Kenilworth H. Mathus, "How to Develop Reader Interest in Your House Organ Through These Techniques," *Printers' Ink,* June 13, 1952, pp. 48–50.

11. **Photos inside the headline.** An internal house organ reported the *Jackson Picnic* by running these words as a headline in huge block letters—inside each letter was a photo of the day's activities.
12. **Use color to show cause and effect.** TELLING (in black) = SELLING (in red).
13. **Headline framed within the product picture.** A molding or pipe manufacturer can enclose his headline with a reproduction of the finished pipe or molding strip.
14. **Experiment with a double headline.** This reads two ways, horizontally and vertically:

	HOW TO MAKE THE
USE SHOWMANSHIP FOR	SALES MEETINGS
	APPEAL TO ALL

15. **Surround the headline with plenty of white space.** A lot of "nothing" is sometimes the best attention-getter of all.
16. **Use newsy headlines:** historical present tense; verb in every headline; avoid negatives; put first things first. Not TRAIN WRECK INJURES EISENHOWER but EISENHOWER INJURED IN TRAIN WRECK.
17. **Make occasional use of hand-lettered headlines** for special feature; because they're different and perhaps slightly irregular, they arouse interest.
18. **Utilize other psychological factors:** alliteration, contradictory, question, provocative, how-to.

DEPARTMENT HEADINGS

19. **Use a snappy come-on.** For gossip columns or department news, try something like HAVE YOU HEARD THE LATEST?
20. **Put imagination into the headings.** Instead of ENGAGEMENTS, WEDDINGS AND BIRTHS, one house organ uses RINGS, RICE AND RATTLES.
21. **Embellish them with sketches.** CALLED TO THE COLORS shows, besides the American flag, caps of the Marine, Army, Navy and Air Force; news of retirements is pictured with a montage of garden tools, fishing equipment, golf bags, etc.

LAYOUT

Possibilities almost endless. Here are just two, as indicative:

22. **Change the column treatment.** On a few pages, shift from three to two columns, or vice versa. Or even use nonstandard width for a special feature or department, like the Editors' page in *Printers' Ink.*
23. **Try the newspaper technique** of The Inquiring Photographer with similar format.

TYPO TRICKS

24. **The humble dotted line** (vertical) has possibilities. But be sure it points down to something important at the bottom of the page, not just fades off into nothingness.
25. **Consider the type arrow.** Set a block of type flush on one side like the point of an arrow, pointing to some spot requiring emphasis.
26. **Use short 6-pt. rules** staggered between lines of type, to draw eye down to focal point below type panel. This gives the effect of art without the cost factors of art or engravings.

PHOTOS

27. **Cheesecake should be pertinent,** not remote and forced. A company advertising Lastex yarn shows bathing beauties attired in swim suits made from this yarn.
28. **Dramatize.** One concern has a series of wall maps showing, by company departments, location and addresses of men in the armed services. The house organ not only showed a typical map, but got live action and human interest by having a pretty girl employee point to the location of her boy friend.
29. **Utilize picture-magazine treatment.** Similar-size photos, uniform block captions, continuity of theme depicted.
30. **Human interest-ize your photos.** Winner of suggestion system award is shown in the arms of his wife at home, receiving *her* happy congratulations.
31. **An occasional silhouette or vignette** captures attention, because of contrast, irregular shape, etc.
32. **Special effects.** Two kinds of halftone screens—gray effect for supporting background, main figures in bold, black screen, combination line and halftone, etc.
33. **Unusual poses.** A feet-first exposure of employees at the beach; a baby crying.

MAPS

34. **Pictorial maps** tell a real picture story and can be highly decorative.
35. **A progress story** can utilize several photos or sketches, all tied together by a portion of a map (color) in background. Flow of raw material into final finished product.
36. **National scope of operations** is emphasized by outline map in background, say a map of U. S., spotting distributorships, branch offices, service stations, allocation of investments, recruitment of manpower, proportion of sales, etc.

HANDBOOKS

The relationship between employees and employers has been growing more complex in recent years. Formerly employers talked to new employees personally to explain to them the conditions of their employment, such as working hours, the nature of the job, pay, information about the company and employee responsibilities. Today the men who set these policies in large companies seldom have a chance to talk to employees when they are first employed, and their contacts thereafter are exceptional.

Employee handbooks were designed to replace to some extent this lack of personal contact in explaining the company to new employees and in defining employees' rights and responsibilities on their new jobs. The first of these handbooks were the old "rules and regulations," which set forth a series of "don'ts" in brusque, cold fashion. The employee may have known exactly what he should and should not do; but the company certainly incurred no goodwill, nor was any basis formed for future cooperation. It is basic psychology that people will conform as requested if they are asked politely and can be shown a good reason for following that course. When a new employee reports to a job, the handbook is his first contact with the company, and this first impression may be a lasting one.

The editors of handbooks today generally recognize that principle. Gone is the old style of listing "do's" and "don'ts," and substituted is a straightforward, conversational style explaining company policy in terms of how management and employees benefit by mutual cooperation. "We" and "our company" are used, helping the employee feel that he is welcome and that he is identified with the company.

A well-written handbook leaves the employee with a feeling of pride in his new job and a feeling of security, which may influence him to remain with the company on a permanent basis. Titles of modern handbooks reflect this thinking: "Welcome," "Let's Get Acquainted" and "Our Business and Yours."

The following is a partial list of the most frequent subjects found in 237 handbooks studied by The National Board of Fire Underwriters: [6]

Vacations
Personnel Records, Changes
Group Insurance
Company Business History
Pay Day
Office Hours
Holidays
Use of Telephones
Salary, Advancement, Promotion
Suggestion Plans
Absence (How to report, excessive, etc.)
Attendance (Encouragement of regularity as aid to production, promotion, efficiency)
Accident Prevention
Hospitalization
Retirement Benefits
Resignation, Discharge, Lay-Off
Medical Examination
House Organ
Overtime
Activities (Recreational, dramatic, etc.)
Canvassing, Charity, Soliciting
Bulletin Boards
Payroll Deductions
Message from President
Smoking Privilege
Social Security Benefits
Disability, Sick Leave
Cafeteria
Wage Policy
General Welcome
Uniforms, Dress, Cleanliness
Care of Records, Equipment
Company Club
Workmen's Compensation
Lunch Hours
Job Security

[6] *Planning Effective Employee Handbooks,* The National Board of Fire Underwriters, New York, 1948, pp. 58 and 59.

The points which have already been discussed in writing for other employee publications also apply to handbook writing — simple, specific, clear, interesting writing. The communication problem is the same, the company wants employees to have certain information and at the same time wants to create an atmosphere of mutual understanding and cooperation.

In the beginning, a new employe will find the surroundings strange, the work unfamiliar. There is a great deal to be learned. But you have only to remember this fact: that your job and every employe's job in Shell carries with it certain definite duties and responsibilties—and privileges. Your supervisor will tell you what they are you will soon feel at home. He will introduce you to your fellow workers, show you where you will work, explain your duties, and tell you of the safety precautions. Don't be afraid to ask him questions.[7]

PROBLEMS

1. Critics have said that employee publications represent an attempt on the part of management to propagandize employees and that this is inherently bad. Comment.

2. What formats can be used for employee publications and what are the advantages and disadvantages of each?

3. What differentiates employee publication writing and journalistic writing?

4. Why is it important to have two-way communication in employee publications?

5. What are employee handbooks used for? Why is the style of writing important?

6. You are the editor of an employee magazine which is published by a steel company employing 6,000 men in plants over several states. Your company has recently installed a new pension system—one of the first companies in the industry to do so. A plant survey reveals that most of your employees are young men and that only a few will benefit directly in the next few years. Using basic details which your instructor will supply, write a story to appear in the employee magazine announcing the new pension plan.

7. The Elliott Oil Company, a large oil exploration, refining and distributing company, reports $11,000,000 net income for the current year. The company has 10,000 stockholders. Wage negotiations with employees are in progress, and the president fears that publication of the earnings figure in the employee magazine will cause employee resentment over "high profits." The president asks you to submit a story that you would publish in the employee magazine announcing the earnings figure.

8. A 76-year-old employee is retiring after 45 years of service with the Eaves Sugar Refining Company. He started as a bookkeeper when the company first started operations and rose to his present position as head of the Cost Accounting Department. At a banquet two days ago he was presented with a service key and a scroll by the president of the company.

a. Write the story for an employee newspaper as a straight news story.

---

[7] *What Shell Means to You,* Shell Oil Company, New York, 1950.

b. Write the story for an employee magazine as a human interest story, assuming facts about the employee as necessary.

9. Your company has announced a suggestion plan whereby an employee will be rewarded for a suggestion that improves production processes or increases the general efficiency of the plant. The suggestion plan was announced through notices on the bulletin boards, on slips in the pay envelopes and over the loud-speaker system. There has been only one suggestion to date. It was a suggestion that a door be swung outward instead of inward, a change that resulted in only a minor increase in plant efficiency. The employee was rewarded with $25. The company is disappointed by the small response received so far and asks you, as editor of the employee magazine, to write a story about the award in such a manner that it will encourage other suggestions. The company will pay a minimum of $25 for any suggestion actually used, and if savings of over $1,000 result from the suggestion, an employee will receive 5% of all savings.

10. The president of your company has just completed a tour through the plant. He discovered several employees smoking in front of a "No Smoking" sign. He lectured them and then came to you, the editor of the employee hand-book. "I just caught several men smoking today right in front of a 'No Smoking' sign. This has got to stop. You tell those men that I'll fire any man I see smoking anywhere near one of those signs and I mean it." Write this regulation for the next edition of the employee handbook.

11. The editor of an employee magazine published by a large local manufacturing company comes to you, a college student, and says that he is writing a series of articles on the local community and wants to tell his employees about college life. He states that he believes most of the employees think students spend their time drinking beer, going out on dates and learning nothing but a lot of theory. The editor asks that you write a brief story for the magazine telling employees something about college life and the value of education. He says that the level of understanding of the employees is fairly low. He requests that the story be written in third-person style.

APPENDIX *A*

Bibliography

PART I. EFFECTIVE COMMUNICATION THROUGH BUSINESS REPORTS

Ball, John and Cecil B. Williams, *Report Writing,* The Ronald Press Company. New York, 1955.

Bearsley, Monroe C., *Thinking Straight,* Prentice-Hall, Inc., New York, 1950.

Brennecke, Ernest and Donald L. Clark, *Magazine Article Writing* (rev. ed.), The Macmillan Company, New York, 1949.

Crouch, W. G., and Robert L. Zetler, *A Guide to Technical Writing,* The Ronald Press Company, New York, 1948.

"Economic Facts for Executives," *Modern Industry,* December, 1952, Vol. 24, pp. 48–51.

Elfenbein, Julien, *Business Journalism. Its Function and Future* (rev. ed.), Harper & Brothers, New York, 1947.

Fitting, Ralph U., *Report Writing* (rev. ed.), The Ronald Press Company, New York, 1942.

Gaum, C. G., H. F. Graves and L. S. S. Hoffman, *Report Writing* (3rd ed.), Prentice-Hall, Inc., New York, 1950.

Glover, John C., *Business Operational Research and Reports,* The American Book Company, Chicago, 1949.

Hayakawa, S. I., *Language in Thought and Action,* Harcourt, Brace and Company, New York, 1949.

Hodges, John C., *Harbrace College Handbook,* Harcourt, Brace and Company, New York, 1951.

Johnson, Wendell, "Fateful Process of Mr. A Talking to Mr. B," *Harvard Business Review,* January, 1953, Vol. 31, pp. 49–56.

Kerekes, Frank and Robley Winfrey, *Report Preparation Including Correspondence and Technical Writing* (2nd ed.), The Iowa State College Press, Ames, Iowa, 1951.

Lee, Irving J., *How to Talk With People,* Harper & Brothers, New York, 1952.

Marcoux, Harvey Lee, *A College Guide to Business English,* D. Van Nostrand Company, Inc., New York, 1939.

Marsten, Everett C., Loring M. Thompson and Frank Zacker, *Business Communication,* The Macmillan Company, New York, 1949.

Osborn, Alex F., *Applied Imagination, Principles and Procedures of Creative Thinking,* Charles Scribner's Sons, New York, 1953.

Peters, Raymond W., *Communication Within Industry,* Harper & Brothers, New York, 1950.

Pigors, Paul, *Effective Communication in Industry,* National Association of Manufacturers, New York, 1949.

Reddick, DeWitt C., *Modern Feature Writing,* Harper & Brothers, New York, 1949.

Redfield, Charles E., *Communication in Management,* The University of Chicago Press, Chicago, 1953.

Saunders, Alta Gwinn and Chester Reed Anderson, *Business Reports* (2nd ed.), McGraw-Hill Book Company, Inc., New York, 1940.

Ulman, Joseph N., Jr., *Technical Reporting,* Henry Holt and Company, Incorporated, New York, 1952.

Wolley, Edwin C. and Franklin W. Scott, *College Handbook of Composition* (rev. ed.), D. C. Heath & Company, New York, 1949.

PART II. STEPS IN THE PREPARATION OF BUSINESS REPORTS

Bingham, Walter Van Dyke and Bruce Victor Moore, *How to Interview* (3rd rev. ed.), Harper & Brothers, New York, 1941.

Blankenship, Albert B., *Consumer and Opinion Research—The Questionnaire Technique,* Harper & Brothers, New York, 1943.

Blankenship, Albert B., editor, *How to Conduct Consumer and Opinion Research,* Harper & Brothers, New York, 1946.

Blankenship, Albert B., Archibald Crossley, *et al.,* "Questionnaire Preparation and Interviewer Technique," *The Journal of Marketing,* October, 1949, Vol. 14, pp. 399–433.

Bradford, Ernest S., *Marketing Research,* McGraw-Hill Book Company, Inc., New York, 1951.

Brown, Lyndon O., *Marketing and Distribution Research,* The Ronald Press Company, New York, 1949.

Cantril, Hadley, *Gauging Public Opinion,* Princeton University Press, Princeton, New Jersey, 1947.

Coman, Edwin T., Jr., *Sources of Business Information,* Prentice-Hall, Inc., New York, 1949.

Eigelberner, J., *The Investigation of Business Problems,* McGraw-Hill Book Company, Inc., New York, 1926.

Heidingsfield, Myron S. and Albert B. Blankenship, *Market and Marketing Analysis,* Henry Holt and Company, Incorporated, New York, 1947.

Hertz, David B., *The Theory and Practice of Industrial Research,* McGraw-Hill Book Company, Inc., New York, 1950.

Hutchins, Margaret, A. S. Johnson and M. S. Williams, *Guide to Use of Libraries* (5th ed.), The H. W. Wilson Company, New York, 1936.

Northrop, F. S. C., *The Logic of the Sciences and Humanities,* The Macmillan Company, New York, 1947.

Parten, Mildred, *Surveys, Polls and Samples: Practical Procedures,* Harper & Brothers, New York, 1950.

Payne, Stanley L., *The Art of Asking Questions,* Princeton University Press. Princeton, New Jersey, 1951.

Robinson, R. A., "How to Boost Returns from Mail Surveys," *Printers' Ink,* June 6, 1952, Vol. 239, pp. 35–37.

Whitney, F. L., *Elements of Research* (rev. ed.), Prentice-Hall, Inc., New York, 1942.

Williams, Cecil and Allan H. Stevenson, *A Research Manual,* Harper & Brothers, New York, 1951.

Winchell, Constance M., *Guide to Reference Books* (7th ed. based on 6th ed. of Mudge, I. W., *Guide to Reference Books*), American Library Association, Chicago, 1951.

Worthy, James C., "Attitude Surveys As a Tool of Management," *General Management Series No. 145,* American Management Association, New York, 1950.

PART III. EFFECTIVE PRESENTATION IN BUSINESS REPORTS

Boyd, William P., *Good Style and Form in Report Structure,* Hemphill's Book Store, Austin, Texas, 1949.

Brinton, Willard Cope, *Graphic Presentation,* Brinton Associates, New York, 1939.

Chase, Stuart, *Power of Words,* Harcourt, Brace and Company, New York, 1954.

Chase, Stuart, *The Tyranny of Words,* Harcourt, Brace and Company, New York, 1938.

Croxton, F. E. and D. J. Cowden, *Applied General Statistics,* Prentice-Hall, Inc., New York, 1946.

Dale, Edgar and Jeanne S. Chall, "The Concept of Readability," *Elementary English,* January, 1948, Vol. 26, pp. 19–26.

Dale, Edgar and Jeanne S. Chall, "A Formula for Predicting Readability," *Educational Research Bulletin,* Ohio State University, January, 1948, Vol. 27, pp. 11–20.

Dale, Edgar and Jeanne S. Chall, "A Formula for Predicting Readability: Instructions," *Educational Research Bulletin,* Ohio State University, February, 1948, Vol. 27, pp. 37–54.

Dale, Edgar, editor, *Readability,* National Council of Teachers of English, Chicago, 1949.

Davis, K. and J. O. Hopkins, "Readability of Employee Handbooks," *Personnel Psychology,* Autumn, 1950, Vol. 3, pp. 317–326.

Dolch, E. W., *Problems in Reading,* The Garrard Press, Champaign, Illinois, 1948.

Farr, James N., James J. Jenkins, Donald D. Paterson and George W. England, "Reply to Klare and Flesch re 'Simplification of Flesch Reading Ease Formula,'" *Journal of Applied Psychology,* February, 1952, Vol. 36, pp. 55–57.

Farr, James N., James J. Jenkins and Donald G. Paterson, "Simplification of Flesch Reading Ease Formula," *Journal of Applied Psychology,* October, 1951, Vol. 35, pp. 333–337.

Farr, James N. and James J. Jenkins, "Tables for Use with the Flesch Readability Formulas," *Journal of Applied Psychology,* June, 1949, Vol. 33, pp. 275–278.

Flesch, Rudolf, *The Art of Plain Talk,* Harper & Brothers, New York, 1946.

Flesch, Rudolf, *The Art of Readable Writing,* Harper & Brothers, New York, 1949.

Flesch, Rudolf, *How to Make Sense: How Improvement in Specific Speaking, Reading and Writing Can Be a Means to a Better Way of Life for You,* Harper & Brothers, New York, 1954.

Flesch, Rudolf, *How to Test Readability,* Harper & Brothers, New York, 1950.

Flesch, Rudolf, "Measuring the Level of Abstraction," *Journal of Applied Psychology,* December, 1950, Vol. 34, pp. 384–390.

Flesch, Rudolf, "Reply to 'Simplification of Flesch Reading Ease Formula,'" *Journal of Applied Psychology,* February, 1952, Vol. 36, pp. 54–55.

Graves, Robert and Alan Hodge, *The Reader over Your Shoulder,* The Macmillan Company, New York, 1944.

Gray, William S. and Bernice Leary, *What Makes a Book Readable,* University of Chicago Press, Chicago, 1935.

Guide for Air Force Writing, Air University, Air Command and Staff School, Maxwell Air Force Base, Alabama, 1951.

Gunning, Robert, *The Technique of Clear Writing,* McGraw-Hill Book Company, Inc., New York, 1952.

Guthrie, L. C., *Factual Communication,* The Macmillan Company, New York, 1948.

Hall, Ray Ovid, *Handbook of Tabular Presentation,* The Ronald Press Company, New York, 1943.

Kilduff, Edward J., *Words and Human Nature,* Harper & Brothers, New York, 1941.

Klare, George R. and Byron Buck, *Know Your Reader,* Hermitage House, New York, 1954.

Klare, George R., "Measures of the Readability of Written Communication: an Evaluation," *Journal of Educational Psychology,* November, 1952, Vol. 43, pp. 385–399.

Klare, George R., "A Table for Rapid Determination of Dale-Chall Readability Scores," *Educational Research Bulletin,* Ohio State University, February, 1952, Vol. 31, pp. 43–47.

Linton, Calvin D., *How to Write Reports,* Harper & Brothers, New York, 1954.

Lutz, R. R., *Graphic Presentation Simplified,* Funk & Wagnalls Company, New York, 1950.

McElroy, John, *Techniques of Clear Informative Writing,* Government Printing Office, Washington, D. C., 1950.

A Manual of Style (11th ed.), University of Chicago Press, Chicago, 1949.

Miller, George A., *Language and Communication,* McGraw-Hill Book Company, Inc., New York, 1951.

Modley, Rudolf, *How to Use Pictorial Statistics,* Harper & Brothers, New York, 1937.

Naylor, J. S., *Informative Writing,* The Macmillan Company, New York, 1942.

Neikirk, W. W., "Organizing the Business Report," *National Association of Cost Accountants,* October 15, 1948, Vol. 30, pp. 193–204.

Paterson, Donald G. and Bradley J. Walker, "Readability and Human Interest of House Organs," *Personnel,* May, 1949, Vol. 25, pp. 438–441.

Perrin, Porter G., *Writer's Guide and Index to English* (rev. ed.), Scott, Foresman and Company, New York, 1950.

Riggleman, John R. and Ira N. Frisbee, *Business Statistics* (2nd ed.), McGraw-Hill Book Company, Inc., New York, 1938.

Santmyers, Selby S., *Practical Report Writing,* International Textbook Company, Scranton, Pennsylvania, 1949.

Skillin, Marjorie E., Robert M. Gay, *et al., Words into Type,* Appleton-Century-Crofts, Incorporated, New York, 1948.

Smart, L. Edwin and Sam Arnold, *Practical Rules for Graphic Presentation of Business Statistics,* Ohio State Universtity, Columbus, Ohio, 1947.

Spear, Mary Eleanor, *Charting Statistics,* McGraw-Hill Book Company, Inc., New York, 1952.

Stockton, John R., *An Introduction to Business Statistics,* (2nd ed.), D. C. Heath & Company, Boston, 1947.

Style Manual, Government Printing Office (rev. ed.), Washington, D. C., Government Printing Office, 1953.

Thouless, Robert H., *How to Think Straight,* Simon and Schuster, Inc., New York, 1946.

Weld, Walter E., *How to Chart: Facts from Figures with Graphs,* Codex Book Company, Norwood, Massachusetts, 1947.

Wood, Clement, *More Power to Your Words,* Prentice-Hall, Inc., New York, 1940.

PART IV. MOTIVATION OF ACTION THROUGH BUSINESS REPORTS

Allison, T., "Employee Publications: There's Room for Improvement," *Personnel Journal,* July, 1954, Vol. 31, pp. 56–59.

Andrews, M. B., "This Company Newspaper Helps the Mill Community," *Textile World,* October, 1953, Vol. 103, p. 145.

The Annual Report, S. D. Warren Company, Boston, 1947.

Baker, Ray P. and A. C. Howell, *The Preparation of Reports,* The Ronald Press Company, New York, 1938.

Bell, William H., *Accountants' Reports* (4th ed.), The Ronald Press Company, New York, 1949.

Bentley, Garth, *Editing the Company Publication,* Harper & Brothers, New York, 1953.

Building a Balanced Communications Program, American Management Association, New York, 1954.

Case Book of Employee Communications in Action, National Association of Manufacturers, New York, 1950.

Chase, Stuart, "How to Read an Annual Report," *The Lamp* (Standard Oil [New Jersey] House Magazine), March, 1948.

Clapp, John M., *Accountants' Writing,* The Ronald Press Company, New York, 1948.

Communications and Employee Publications, University of Illinois, Institute of Labor and Industrial Relations, Champaign, Illinois, 1952.

Company Annual Reports to Stockholders and Employees, The Champion Paper and Fibre Company, Hamilton, Ohio, 1948.

Doris, Lillian, *Modern Corporate Reports to Stockholders, Employees and Public,* Prentice-Hall, Inc., New York, 1948.

Employee Communication, Parts 1 and 2, General Electric Company, Employee and Plant Community Relations Services Division, New York, 1952.

Employee Communications for Better Understanding, National Association of Manufacturers, New York, 1950.

The Employee Manual, S. D. Warren Company, Boston, 1948.

Employee Publications, Metropolitan Life Insurance Company, Policyholders Service Bureau, Group Division, New York, 1952.

Employees' Handbooks, National Industrial Conference Board, Inc., New York, 1942.

Gardner, J., "Get Your Ideas Across in Language Your Employees Understand," *Textile World,* June, 1951, Vol. 101, p. 170.

A Guide to the Preparation of Reports in the School of Business, The University of Chicago Press, Chicago, 1946.

Heussner, A. E., "Editing for Employees Who Hardly Read Anything," *Personnel Journal,* April, 1954, Vol. 32, pp. 423–427.

"How Effective Is Your Employee Magazine?" *Factory Management,* June, 1953, Vol. 111, p. 270.

"How to Analyze an Annual Report," *Modern Industry,* May, 1953, Vol. 25, pp. 41–44.

"How to Play the House Organ," *Fortune,* October, 1952, Vol. 46, pp. 144–147.

"How to Put Human Interest in Your Annual Report," *Industrial Marketing,* June, 1948, Vol. 33, p. 83.

How to Read a Financial Report, Merrill Lynch, Pierce, Fenner & Beane, New York, 1947.

Inglis, John B., "Recent Statements Show New Techniques in Annual Reporting Are Being Widely Used," *Journal of Accounting,* December, 1950, Vol. 90, pp. 474–478.

"Is Your Employee Publication an Employee Publication?" *Journal of Retailing,* Spring, 1951, Vol. 27, pp. 1–7.

Knowlton, Don, "Semantics of Annual Reports," *Accounting Review,* October, 1947, Vol. 22, pp. 360–366.

Lorimore, Max, "Corporate Reports Directed Toward Four Major Groups, No Longer for Shareholders Alone," *Journal of Accounting,* June, 1951, Vol. 91, pp. 836–837.

McCoy, R. C., "Speeding Factory News to Employees—Weekly Newsletter," *Factory Management,* May, 1954, Vol. 112, p. 113.

McLaren, Norman L., *Annual Reports to Stockholders,* The Ronald Press Company, New York, 1947.

Maloney, Martin, "Semantics: The Foundation of All Business Communications," *Advanced Management,* July, 1954, Vol. 19, pp. 26–29.

Marting, Elizabeth, editor, *Reports to Top Management for Effective Planning and Control,* American Management Association, New York, 1953.

More Business Through House Organs (rev. ed.), S. D. Warren Company, Boston, 1948.

Nelson, J. Raleigh, *Writing the Technical Report* (2nd ed.), McGraw-Hill Book Company, Inc., New York, 1947.

Newcomb, Robert and Marg Sammons, "Management Learns What to Talk About in Company Magazines," *Industrial Marketing,* October, 1952, Vol. 37, p. 68.

Newcomb, Robert and Marg Sammons, "What Does Management Do?" *Industrial Marketing,* June, 1953, Vol. 38, p. 116.

Opinion-Forming Annual Reports, Charles Francis Press, Inc., New York, 1947.

Opinion-Forming Employee Handbooks, Charles Francis Press, Inc., New York, 1947.

Paterson, Donald G. and James J. Jenkins, "Communication between Management and Employees," *Journal of Applied Psychology,* February, 1948, Vol. 32, pp. 71–80.

Planning Effective Employee Handbooks, The National Board of Fire Underwriters, New York, 1948.

Pratt, K. C., *House Magazine Copy,* The Champion Paper and Fibre Company, Hamilton, Ohio, 1946.

Pratt, K. C., *House Magazine Layout,* The Champion Paper and Fibre Company, Hamilton, Ohio, 1946.

Preparation of Company Annual Reports, American Management Association, New York, 1946.

The Printers' Ink Directory of House Organs, Printers' Ink Publishing Co., Inc., New York, 1950.

Ridley, Clarence E. and Herbert A. Simon, *Specifications for the Annual Municipal Report,* The International City Managers Association, Chicago, 1948.

Sanders, Thomas H., *Company Annual Reports to Stockholders, Employees, and the Public,* Graduate School of Business Administration, Harvard University, Boston, 1949.

Selvage, James P. and Morris M. Lee, *Making the Annual Report Speak for Industry,* McGraw-Hill Book Company, Inc., New York, 1938.

Sigband, Norman B., "Writing the Annual Report," *Advanced Management,* January, 1952, Vol. 17, pp. 20–21.

Smith, H. Graham, "Humanizing Annual Reports," *Commercial and Financial Chronicle,* October 12, 1950, Vol. 172, pp. 1,398 and 1,419.

"Some Conclusions Drawn from New Study of Annual Reports," *Journal of Accountancy,* February, 1951, Vol. 91, pp. 300–303.

Tolleris, Beatrice K., *Annual Reports—How to Plan and Write Them,* National Publication Council, New York, 1946.

Turabian, Kate L., *A Manual for Writers of Dissertations,* University of Chicago Press, Chicago, 1947.

Whyte, William H., Jr., *Is Anybody Listening?* Simon and Schuster, Inc., New York, 1952.

"World Reads Over Our Employees' Shoulders," *Railway Age,* August 11, 1952, Vol. 133, pp. 51–53.

APPENDIX *B*

Course Outlines

MANY INSTRUCTORS WILL WANT TO TEACH *Effective Business Report Writing* in a different order from the one in which the chapters are arranged. Two suggested course outlines follow.

The first outline is based on the idea of orienting the student to business reports and giving him early practice in writing short reports that require little or no research for data. Then as he studies and as he develops his ability to apply the techniques and principles of writing reports, he can progress to longer and more complicated problems, culminating in his writing a formal, long report for which he does his own research.

OUTLINE ONE

1. The Need for Effective Business Reports (Chapter 1)
2. Communication Through Reports (Chapter 2)
3. Kinds of Business Reports (Chapter 14)
4. Arrangement and Format of Informal, Short Reports (Chapter 15)
5. Informative Reports (Chapter 17)
6. Organizing and Interpreting Data (Chapter 7)
7. Outlining the Report (Chapter 8)
8. Characteristics of Factual Writing (Chapter 9)
9. Expressing Facts Clearly, Interestingly and Persuasively (Chapter 10)
10. Analytical Reports (Chapter 18)
11. Using Visual Aids Effectively (Chapter 11)
12. Writing, Revising and Editing the Report (Chapter 13)
13. Planning the Investigation and the Report (Chapter 3)
14. Securing Data Through Bibliographical Research (Chapter 4)
15. Securing Data Through Questionnaires (Chapter 5)
16. Securing Data Through Interviews and Other Research Methods (Chapter 6)
17. Arrangement and Format of Formal, Long Reports (Chapter 16)
18. Measuring Readability (Chapter 12)
19. Annual Reports (Chapter 19)
20. Employee Publications (Chapter 20)

The second outline is based on the idea of having the student get his long report project under way very early in the semester, and, as he works on it, of orienting him in the techniques and principles of report writing. He, in turn, applies these to short reports requiring very little research. Writing principles should be taught along with the type of report to which they best apply. For instance, the teaching of analytical reports offers an opportunity for the accompanying presentation of effective visual aids usage.

Outline Two

1. The Need for Effective Business Reports (Chapter 1)
2. Communication Through Reports (Chapter 2)
3. Planning the Investigation and the Report (Chapter 3)
4. Securing Data Through Bibliographical Research (Chapter 4)
5. Securing Data Through Questionnaires (Chapter 5)
6. Securing Data Through Interviews and Other Research Methods (Chapter 6)
7. Organizing and Interpreting Data (Chapter 7)
8. Arrangement and Format of Formal, Long Reports (Chapter 16)
9. Outlining the Report (Chapter 8)
10. Kinds of Business Reports (Chapter 14)
11. Arrangement and Format of Informal, Short Reports (Chapter 15)
12. Characteristics of Factual Writing (Chapter 9)
13. Informative Reports (Chapter 17)
14. Expressing Facts Clearly, Interestingly and Persuasively (Chapter 10)
15. Analytical Reports (Chapter 18)
16. Using Visual Aids Effectively (Chapter 11)
17. Writing, Revising and Editing the Report (Chapter 13)
18. Annual Reports (Chapter 19)
19. Measuring Readability (Chapter 12)
20. Employee Publications (Chapter 20)

A third teaching possibility would be to present informative reports integrated with bibliographical procedure, analytical reports with questionnaires and interviews, etc. This would entail the teaching of research procedures along with the special type or types of report to which they are frequently applied.

APPENDIX *C*

Suggested Report Subjects

THE FOLLOWING LIST OF REPORT SUBJECTS FOR FORMAL, long reports is presented as an aid to instructors and students in assigning and selecting report topics. It is merely suggestive. Many of the subjects need limiting. Although some are too general to use as they are, they can be readily made specific by applying the subject to a specific problem in a specific company or area or by changing the point of view. Most of the subjects have been used by students in the author's classes and have proved to be very satisfactory.

Accounting as a useful tool to management

The accounting, bookkeeping and cost control record systems of the ________ Cafeteria

How to combat the friction between labor and management caused by accounting terminology

The value of membership in accounting associations

An adequate private library for an accountant

Differences between accounting reports and other types of business reports

A critical analysis of financial statements in current annual reports

Reorganization of the budget department at ________ Tire Company

Reconciling the differences in tax theory and accounting theory

An analysis of the wage control system in ________ Company

A study of the uses of accounting statements

A cash budget system for gasoline service stations

Incorporation of ________ Restaurant

Recommendations for improving the inventory practices of ________ Plumbing Specialty Company

---

Selling the free enterprise system through annual reports

How do annual reports of corporations help the average investor?

Contents and organization of the president's letter in annual reports (based on analysis of one hundred company annual reports)

A municipal report

What manufacturers and distributors can do to make advertising more effective at the retail level

What the small businessman with limited budget and limited market can do through advertising

The influence of television on direct-mail advertising

An advertising campaign for __________ attic fans

Simplified interchange of information between advertising and other divisions of management and operations

Forms and procedures for simplifying advertising department operations

Consumer demand for quality in products

The advertising department of __________ Company and how to improve it

The allocation by counties of advertising for Venetian blinds

Methods of preparing direct-mail advertising

Advertising for a casualty insurance company

Using direct-mail advertising for a furniture store

Readership study of campus newspaper or magazine

Constructing men's permanent dormitories on the __________ University campus

Analysis of the personnel policy of the campus cafeteria

Survey of student listeners to __________ Station

The accounting system at __________ Fraternity and how to improve it

Student opinion of the __________ campus laundry

Summer activities of __________ students

A five-year program in accounting in a college of business administration

Recreational facilities at __________ University

How to improve the parking facilities at __________

Earnings of students during the college year

College grades and vocational success

Students' library habits

Insurance as an aid to financing education

Causes of failures in college work

Students' radio habits

Night football at __________ University

An evaluation of the collection policy of __________ Florists

A proposed system of collection procedure at __________ Hospital

The collection problems of the Southeastern Branch of the __________ Company

---

The internal communications of the __________ Oil Company

The external business reports of the __________ Manufacturing Company

Communications within management

Written communications at __________

Correspondence supervision in __________ Company

Management's use of employee publications

An evaluation of the _____ _____ employee magazine published by _______ Company

How industrial publications can strengthen a company's public relations program

How to make the employee publication easy to look at and to read

The vital responsibility of the employee publication to American freedom

Analysis of the __________ employee magazine at __________ Company

Humanizing the technical feature article

The industrial editor's responsibilities to management

A study of municipal bond issues and bidding procedures for a securities broker

How to finance a new home

Insuring against business risks

A profit sharing plan for employees of the __________ Company

Better publicity improves public relations

Selling a credit union to employees

Selling the company pension story to employees

Human relations in __________ Oil Company

The retirement plan of __________ Company and how to improve it

The best way to tell the business story to employees

What can be done about the older worker in industry?

The employee wage incentive plans of __________ Drug Company

Management's relations with employees and their families

Labor relations in __________ Company

Improving employee morale by using economic incentives

A look at __________ Company's employee benefit programs

Explaining company profits to the employees and to the public

Government intervention in industrial relations

Unionization of white-collar workers in __________ City

Employee attitudes toward __________

Introduction of music in an industrial plant for purpose of increasing efficiency

---

The effect of the Internal Revenue Code of 1954 on the individual wage-earner with income of $5000 or less

State sales tax law

State minimum wage law

Government supervision of commercial airlines

Personal property tax assessment in your state

Influence of tax rates on types of business organizations

Reducing shipping costs of __________

Reducing warehousing costs of __________

The cost of owning and operating company warehouses compared with the cost of leasing bonded warehouses

Streamlining administrative procedures used by __________ Manufacturing Company

Streamlining production methods used by __________ Manufacturing Company

Comparison of owning trucks with renting trucks for distribution of company products

Sales operations of the __________ Food Store

Layout of the __________ Food Store

Improving the reservation system of __________ Air Lines

Revising the mailing system of __________

A market analysis of the facilities of a self-service laundry

Opportunities and problems in starting and operating a small retail grocery store in __________

Selecting the best wrapper for _____ _____ bread

Reaching the student market with local newspaper ads

Consumer attitudes toward department stores in your city

Cigarette brand preferences of students

Locating a men's summer clothing plant in Miami, Florida

Consumer attitudes toward fair trade

Choosing a Canadian market on the basis of risks and trade restrictions

How to meet the increasing competition facing a small insurance agency

Consumer habits in buying automobiles

A study of the used-car market in __________ to determine whether or not to establish a used car lot

Establishing a steel barge fabricating plant in the __________ Area

Establishing a motel in __________

The need for a youth center in __________

Opening a dining, dancing and entertainment establishment in __________

A guide in planning successful oil station openings

Relocating the __________ Church

The outlook for home construction next year in __________

Should the __________ Ice Company expand its facilities for retail house-to-house delivery of frozen foods?

Should the __________ Chemical Company remodel or build a new plant?

Expansion of delivery service of __________ Cleaners
Expanding the __________ Inn
Determining location for a service station
How will the plastic industry expand?
Locating a paper bag factory in the mid-west
Designing and planning a new plant for __________ Mattress Factory, Inc.
Expanding the __________ Music Home of __________ City

The executive training program of the __________ Company
Job evaluation, its objectives and benefits as applied to the medium-size business firm
A wage incentive system for __________ Company
How job analyses fit the employee to the job
Alterations of the sales personnel policies of __________ Store
Analysis of departmental personnel relations of the __________ Hotel
An evaluation of company training programs for college graduates
The hiring policy for extra Christmas employees at __________ Department Store, and how to improve it
Training extra Christmas employees at __________ Department Store
The use of job aptitude tests in industry
The establishment of an interview policy for __________ Products Corporation
A study of application blank items as an aid in the selection process
The use of diagnostic interview guides as an aid in the selection process
What is the foreman's part in the company's personnel relations program?
Labor turnover of the office force of __________ Company

The purchase of food for __________ Fraternity
Adopting a group purchase plan by __________ University fraternities
The problems of purchasing and stock control of __________ Company

---

The maintenance problems of a large apartment house development
Improving production operations of the milk department for __________ Dairy
The maintenance department procedures at __________ Sewerage and Water Board
Safety's contribution to production efficiency
A study of accidents in __________ and their reduction

A comparative analysis of Sales Promotional policies of __________ Company and __________ Company
Sales compensation plans
An analysis of the effectiveness of the men's sportswear department of the __________ Company

The training program for selling in __________ Company

The California market for selling men's slacks

Increasing sales in radio advertising at __________ Station

The relationship between the manufacturing department and the sales department of __________ Company

Improving dealer and distributor relations of __________

Combating the seasonal slump

Advising prospective buyers concerning purchase of imports

Training program for life insurance agents

Prefabs as summer homes

Daytime supervised recreation for children

The history of the __________ YMCA

Public housing in __________

Housing plan for a denominational men's convention

A survey for determining the need for bus route extension of the __________ line

APPENDIX *D*

Practical Suggestions

ABBREVIATIONS

Acceptable standard abbreviations may be used in some personal, informal short reports – if used consistently. In general, however, abbreviations should be avoided, especially in formal reports.

It is good business practice to use the following abbreviations when the company uses them as part of its firm name:

Co.—Company	*Inc.—Incorporated*
Bros.—Brothers	*Ltd.—Limited*

Standard abbreviations used in footnote and bibliographical references are indicated in the suggestions presented under those headings.

BIBLIOGRAPHY

A bibliography is a list of sources of information used in gathering data and writing a report. It must include all those mentioned in footnotes and may include any other references which would be helpful to others in pursuing further the subject of the report.

(1) *Placement.* The bibliography is always at the end of the report. It is part of the supplemental material included for reference purposes. It may be a separate section appearing before the appendix, although it usually follows it. Sometimes it is a part of the appendix, in which case it may be either first or last.

(2) *Organization.* The entries in a bibliography are classified either according to subject matter or according to types of publications and sources of information. Thus there would be sections of the bibliography corresponding to the main subject divisions of the

report, or there would be a section listing books, one listing articles, etc. Within each classified section of the bibliography individual entries are alphabetized by authors' last names, or by titles when the authors are not known.

When subject divisions are used to classify items of the bibliography, it may be necessary to have one section called "General References" for listing those pertaining to several subject divisions of the report or to the report's subject as a whole. When the items are classified according to sources, it may be necessary to have a section called "Miscellaneous" for entries that do not warrant a separate section.

(3) *Arrangement of Elements.* The arrangement of elements in both footnotes and bibliographical references follows the same general pattern. The major difference is that the bibliographical items list the last name of the author first, because they are arranged alphabetically.

Sample bibliographical book entries are:

Smith, James F., *Advertising Media.* New York: Harper & Brothers, 1949.
Smith, James F., *Advertising Media,* Harper & Brothers, New York, 1949.

Sample magazine article entries are:

Smith, Genevieve. "New Convenience Foods Set Off Promotion Battle," *Printers' Ink,* Vol. 249 (November 26, 1954), pp. 29–32.

Smith, Genevieve. "New Convenience Foods Set Off Promotion Battle," *Printers' Ink,* CCXLIX: 29–32, November 26, 1954.

Smith, Genevieve, "New Convenience Foods Set Off Promotion Battle," *Printers' Ink,* November 26, 1954, Vol. 249, pp. 29–32.

A good reference manual like the Chicago *Manual of Style* should always be consulted for forms less commonly used than those which have been presented in this section.

It is very important that consistency in form be observed throughout a bibliography.

Bibliographical references are single spaced, with a double space between entries. Items are unnumbered. Indentation of five to ten spaces may be used at the beginning of each entry. Each entry, however, may be blocked with no indentation, or hanging indentation may be followed.

The total number of pages may be given for each book when the whole book has been used. Of course, if only part of the book or reference has been consulted, inclusive pages are indicated for the chapter or section used.

(4) *Abbreviations.* The following abbreviations are used as necessary within the bibliographical entries:

anon.	—No author known
2nd ed.	—Second edition
et al.	—And others (when more than three authors, first author's name is used and *et al.*)
n.d.	—No date known
p, pp.	—Page, pages
pp. 50–60	—Pages 50 to 60, inclusive
vol., vols.	—Volume, volumes

BINDING

Typed reports are usually bound on the left side. Sometimes they are bound at the top. Adjustments in the margins are made on the side or top and according to the binding used.

The report may be bound:

(*1*) with staples or wire stitching
(*2*) with paper fasteners, in which case holes must be spaced and punched to match the spacing of the fasteners
(*3*) with spiral bindings
(*4*) in a two- or three-ring note book
(*5*) by the use of a gummed-tape covering on the stapled side
(*6*) in a semi-rigid or rigid leather-like cover

Not all reports are bound. Often they are merely stapled at the top left-hand corner and enclosed in a self-cover or manila folder. If the report is to be used permanently or handled a great deal, it should be bound. The binding insures that the pages will be kept intact and provides a protective cover for the report. Information to identify the report should be placed on the cover. It usually consists of title, author and date of completion.

BOXING AND RULING MATERIAL

Material to be set off for emphasis in a report – both figures and facts – may be surrounded by lines or a decorative border. The advertising principle of always leaving a lot of white space around the material may also be followed.

It is easier to read tables when lines are drawn between groups of items and between columns.

Tables of more than three columns are generally boxed at the top and bottom. They may also be enclosed in a complete box by ruling the sides, or the sides may be left open. Consistency should be followed throughout any one report.

FOOTNOTES

Footnotes should be used to give credit for the source of quoted material in the text, to lend authority to a statement not generally accepted, to explain or give additional information, to give an appraisal of the source or to provide a cross reference to material presented in some other part of the report.

(1) *Placement.* They should be placed at the bottom of the page and separated from the report text by a solid line partly or all the way across the page. After typing the last line of the text, one should single space, type the solid line, double space, then indent about five to ten spaces from the left margin and begin the first line of the footnote entry. Succeeding lines of the footnote should be spaced even with the margin. The footnote entry should be single spaced. A space should be left between entries.

(2) *Numbering.* Footnotes are numbered consecutively by Arabic numerals in unbroken series throughout the report. The reference figure in the text should always follow the passage to which it refers and should be placed after the punctuation marks and slightly above the line.

The reference figure in the footnote should be typed one-half space above the line, without punctuation, and at the beginning of the footnote entry.

(3) *Arrangement of Elements.* For a *book,* footnote *items* should be arranged as follows:

> Author's name with given name or initials first, title of the book, place of publication, publisher's name, date of publication and page reference.

A sample footnote following this arrangement could be punctuated as follows:

[1] Dale Yoder, *Personnel Principles and Policies* (New York: Prentice-Hall, Inc., 1952), p. 95.

Or a simplified form might be used:

[1] Dale Yoder, *Personnel Principles and Policies,* Prentice-Hall, Inc., New York, 1952, p. 95.

When a bibliography accompanies the report, a short form for footnotes may be used:

[1] Yoder, *Personnel Principles and Policies,* p. 95.

For a book with two or more authors, an example entry is:

[2] C. G. Gaum, H. F. Graves, and L. S. S. Hoffman, *Report Writing,* 3rd ed. (New York: Prentice-Hall, Inc., 1950), p. 25.

When there are more than three authors, the first-named author is given and the Latin abbreviation, *et al.,* is used to designate *and others.*

For an *article* or component of a larger work, *items* should be arranged as follows:

> Author's name with given name or initial first, title of the article or section or chapter, title of the magazine or work, the volume number, the date and page reference.

Following this arrangement, a sample footnote would be punctuated as follows:

[3] Paul W. Cook, Jr., "Decentralization and the Transfer-Price Problem." *Journal of Business,* Vol. 28 (April, 1955), p. 90.

or

[3] Paul W. Cook, Jr., "Decentralization and the Transfer-Price Problem," *Journal of Business,* April, 1955, p. 90.

or

[3] Paul W. Cook, Jr., "Decentralization and the Transfer-Price Problem," *Journal of Business,* XXVIII:90. April, 1955.

For a *newspaper item,* the name of the paper, the date and the page reference are usually given:

[4] *Chicago Tribune,* May 16, 1954, p. 10.

For a reference to *letters, interviews,* etc., the items given depend on the significance for the particular report. There may be:

[5] Statement by Mr. Henry Jonson, personal interview.
[5] Personal interview, Mr. Henry Jonson, Personnel Director, Union Oil Company, New Orleans, Louisiana, May 10, 1954.
[6] Letter from Mr. Henry Jonson, Personnel Director, Union Oil Company, New Orleans, Louisiana, May 12, 1954.
[6] Statement by Mr. Henry Jonson, letter, May 12, 1954.

(4) *Short Footnote Forms.* After the first full citation of a par-

ticular work has been given, the full form need not be repeated in a footnote entry. The last name of the author, appropriate Latin abbreviation and specific page reference are given.

Where references to the same work follow without intervening footnotes, *ibid.* (for the Latin *ibidem,* meaning *in the same place*) should be used. If the reference is to the same page, merely *ibid.* is sufficient; for a different page, cite the page, as: *Ibid.,* p. 10.

When there are intervening footnotes and it is necessary to refer to a previous entry for a reference, *op. cit.,* meaning *work cited,* should be used for reference to a different page of the book cited, as:

[7] Jones, *op. cit.,* p. 150.

If reference is to the same page in the book, *loc. cit.,* meaning *the place cited,* is used. *Loc. cit.* is also used for repeated reference to an article or part of a work.

[8] Zirkle, *loc. cit.,* p. 121.

(5) *Abbreviations.* In footnote and bibliographical entries abbreviations are used for words designating parts when followed by numbers:

Bk. I (plural, *Bks.*)—Book I
chap. 2 (plural, *chaps.*)—Chapter 2
col. 2 (plural, *cols.*)—Column 2
2nd ed. (plural, *edd.*)—Second edition
fig. 2 (plural, *figs.*)—Figure 2
no. 7 (plural, *nos.*)—Number 7
l. 9 (plural, *ll.*)—Line 9
p. 7 (plural, *pp.*)—Page 7
pp. 7 f.—Page 7 and page following
pp. 7 ff.—Page 7 and pages following
pp. 5–7—Pages 5 to 7 inclusive
sec. 9 (plural, *secs.*)—Section 9
vol. III (plural, *vols.*)—Volume III

Other abbreviations commonly used are *cf.* for compare and *ed.* for editor.

(6) *Numerals.* Roman numerals (capitals) should be used for designating volume, book, part or division:

Volume I *Book II* *Part III*

Roman numerals (lower case – i, ii, iii, iv, etc.) should be used for designating introductory or prefatory pages in a book.

Arabic numbers are used for designating pages, lines and references to chapters:

pp. 10–15 *p. 5, l. 3* *chap. 2*

(7) *Continuation of Long Footnotes.* When it is necessary to continue a long footnote from one page to the next, it should begin on the page where reference to it is made in the text and should be arranged so that the note will break in the middle of a sentence, ending on the next page, to indicate that the note is continued.

MARGINS

Throughout the report uniform standard margins should be maintained on each page. The same width of margin, varying from one to one and one-half inches, should be followed on each of the four sides of the typewritten page. Or the top and bottom margins may be the same, preferably one and one-quarter inches, with the left margin wider than the right, preferably one and one-quarter inches on the left and three-quarters of an inch on the right.

If the manuscript is bound at the top, an additional three-quarters of an inch or one inch is allowed for the top margin. If the manuscript is bound on the left side, an additional one-half to one inch is allowed as needed for the left margin.

An over-ragged margin on the right should be avoided. An even margin should be maintained without having to divide many words.

NUMERALS

The rules for writing numbers have not been standardized for business writing. Most businessmen agree, however, on the desirability of writing out the number *ten* and all numbers below, because they are simple and easy to remember when so written, and on the desirability of expressing most other numbers in figures.[1]

(1) *Numbers.* Many numbers are used in business writing. Although they offer no trouble on invoices, orders, and statements, recording them in letters and reports does pose a problem. The general rule is that all numbers should be expressed in figures when there are several numbers in a paragraph, letter or report. For quick readability and clarity the following modifications are recommended:

(a) *If a sentence begins with a number, the number should be expressed in words:* This rule is used when the sentence cannot be effectively revised.

---

[1] Material presented here concerning numerals is reprinted by permission, Committee Report (Robert D. Hay, chairman), *American Business Writing Association Bulletin,* April, 1953, pp. 6-11.

Correct: Fifty applicants were interviewed for the position.

(b) *When a number standing first in the sentence is followed by another number to form an approximation, both should be in words:*

Correct: Fifty or sixty will be enough.

NOTE: *Try not to begin a sentence with a number:* Rewrite the sentence to place the number within or at the end of the sentence.

Correct: The confirmation request was answered by 559 businesses.

(c) *When a sentence contains one series of numbers, all members of the series should be expressed in figures:*

Correct: There were 25 applicants from Arkansas, 15 applicants from Texas, and 10 applicants from Oklahoma.

(d) *When a sentence contains two series of numbers, the members of one series should be expressed in words while those of the other series should be expressed in figures:* If this rule is not followed, confusion results because of too many groups of numbers.

Correct: Five students scored 95 points; seventeen students scored 80 points; and eleven scored 75 points.

Correct: Three senior accountants made $50 a day; two semi-seniors made $40 a day; and five junior accountants made $35 a day.

NOTE: More than two series of numbers should be tabulated for clarity.

Name of Accountant	*Daily Rate*	*Estimated Working Days*	*Total Estimated Earnings*
Barlow, Helen	$50	3	$150
Dickinson, Al	35	2	70
Oman, Charles	40	1	40

(e) *When an isolated number is ten or below, it should be expressed in words:* This rule does not apply to exact dimensions.

Correct: He hired 56 women employees.

Correct: The new salesman sold eight refrigerators last month.

(f) *When numbers are expressed in words, as at the beginning of a sentence, a hyphen should be used to join the compound numbers, twenty-one through ninety-nine:* A compound number usually acts as a compound adjective. Compound adjectives are usually hyphenated.

Correct: Fifty-six; twenty-one; ninety-three

(g) *When one number immediately precedes another number of different context, one number should be expressed in words; the other, in figures:*

Correct: The specifications call for twenty-five 2 × 4's.
Correct: The deposit slip listed four 5's as the only currency.
Correct: You ordered 275 three-inch bolts.

(h) *When a numerical quantity contains more than four digits, each group of three digits (starting at the right) should be set off by a comma:* Obviously, this rule does not apply to dates, street numbers, serial numbers, and page numbers.

Correct: 1000; 1021; 5280
Also correct: 1,000; 1,021; 5,280
Correct: 1,000,000; 1,253,878; 35,000; 43,120

(i) *When large numbers (more than three digits) are to be tabulated, special care should be taken to align them properly:* When tabulating, the right or last digit of the longest number should be used as the main guide. Consequently, the longest number is found and the plan made accordingly.

Correct:	
	1,150
	1,000
	25,150
	500
	325,200
	25
	1,250,000
	5
Total	1,603,030

(2) *Money.* Amounts of money, generally speaking, should be expressed in figures. This is particularly true when a sentence, a paragraph, a letter, or a report mentions several different amounts of money. However, some questions invariably arise on how to use numbers in money amounts. The following practices are recommended.

(a) *When several amounts are written close together, all should be expressed in figures:*

Correct: The assets were $17,000; the liabilities were $3,000; and the net worth was $14,000.

(b) *When an amount of money consists of dollars and cents, the amount should always be expressed in figures:* The dollar sign should precede the amount (unless in a tabulated column).

Correct: The invoice total was $50.51.
Correct: The bonds were sold at $999.50 each.

(c) *When an amount of money consists only of dollars, it should not be followed by a decimal point and a double zero:* The double zero is not necessary, unless the amount is tabulated in a column which includes both dollars and cents.

Correct: The invoice total was $150.

Correct:

$ 250.80
200.00
312.70
286.50
$1,050.00

When a series of money amounts contains mixed figures, all even figures should include the double zero for consistency.

Correct: The committee raised amounts of $15.00, $33.75, and $75.00 in the three rummage sales.

(d) *An amount should not be written in both figures and words:* This procedure is acceptable only in legal documents and financial documents.

Correct: The check was for $57.

Correct: The total assets are $23,000.

(e) *An isolated amount of money of more than ten cents but less than one dollar should be expressed in figures:*

Correct: The piggy bank yielded $.57.

Correct: The piggy bank yielded 57¢.

Correct: The piggy bank yielded 57 cents.

Correct: The piggy bank yielded nine cents.

(f) *An isolated amount of money in even dollars should be written in figures. When the even amount is ten dollars or less it should be written in words.*

Correct: The check was for $57.

Correct: The other check was for five dollars. (Assuming an isolated amount.)

(g) *When amounts of money are to be tabulated, care should be taken to align the numbers correctly:* The right-hand digit of the largest amount governs the tabulation. All decimals, commas, and dollar signs should be aligned properly. A dollar sign should be used both at the beginning of a column and at the end of a column after the underline. It should be set far enough to the left to take care of the longest amount.

Correct:	$ 50.00	**Correct:**		$1,000.50
	100.90		$5,000.00	
	1,100.10		475.00	
	10,133.10			5,475.00
	$11,384.10			$6,475.50
				1.00
				35.00
				$6,511.50

(3) *Miscellaneous.* The following numbers should be expressed in figures.

(a) *Dates:*

Correct: October 10, 1951
10th of October
tenth of October

Correct: 10 Oct 51 (Military)
Your letter of October 10 was most welcome.

(b) *Street numbers:*

Correct: 1503 Garland Street

(c) *Numerical names of streets:*

Correct: 110 First Street*
110 69th Street

Correct: 110 110th Street
110 110 Street

(d) *Numbered items such as page numbers, chapter numbers, figure numbers, table numbers, chart numbers, serial numbers, and telephone numbers:*

Correct: Page 10
Chapter 10
Chapter X
Figure 8
Fig. 8
Table X
Table 10
Chart 10

Correct: Chart X
Service Serial No. 01845283
Policy No. V9109815
Policy # V9109815
Claim No. 13189756
Telephone 757-W
Telephone CA-7175
Model No. 3223

(e) *Decimals:*

Correct: 10.25
3.1414
.3535

(f) *Dimensions:*

Correct: 8½ × 11
8½ by 11 in.

Correct: 2 × 4 in.
2 by 4 in.

* All numerical street names under ten should be spelled out in accordance with general rule of ten.

(g) *Time:*

Correct:	7 P.M.	**Correct:**	7:35 P.M.
	7 a.m.		7:35 p.m.
	seven o'clock		seven in the morning

(h) *Percentages:*

Correct:	35%	**Correct:**	6%
	99.99%		6 percent
	0.09%		six percent
			("isolated" figure only)

(i) *Fractions:*

Correct:	1/32	one-half	110 1/5
	3/64	two-thirds	or
	25/64	one-fourth	
	25/100 or 0.25	three-fourths	110.2

PAGINATION

All pages of a report should be numbered except the fly leaf, if used, and the title page. The plan followed for numbering pages differs according to the type of report. The following practices are generally observed:

(1) *For Letter Reports.* The first page of a letter report is counted as page one, but no number appears on the page. Additional pages are numbered in the same manner as a business letter:

Either

Mrs. S. J. Brounson 2 December 10, 1955

Or

Mrs. S. J. Brounson
December 10, 1955
Page 2

Sometimes the subject of the report is used instead of the name of the person for whom the report is written.

(2) *For Memorandum Reports.* The first page of a memorandum report, although it is counted as page one, contains no number. Successive pages are numbered:

Either

The Loading of Trucks 2 December 10, 1955

Or

The Loading of Trucks
December 10, 1955
Page 2

The numbering of the pages also includes identification of the report by subject and date. Sometimes a memorandum number is also used:

Memorandum #56
The Loading of Trucks 2 December 10, 1955

(3) *For Short and Long, Formal Reports.* The elements are broken down and arranged according to prefatory material, report and supplemental or reference material.

Pages of prefatory sections are numbered with small Roman numerals (ii, iii, iv and so on) centered at the bottom of the page. Pages of the report text sections are numbered with Arabic numbers (2, 3, 4 and so on to the end of the report) placed at the top right-hand corner of the page, serving as a right marginal guide. Pages of the supplemental material are numbered with Arabic numerals, a continuation of the numbering of the report text. If the report text ends on page 21, for example, the first page of the supplemental material is page 22.

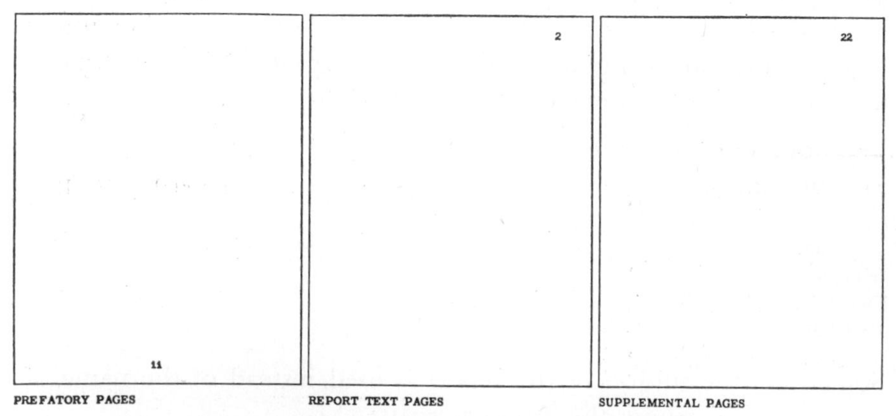

Numbering the pages of a business report.

On special layout pages, such as title fly, title page, division title pages, first page of the report text or on any special page carrying extra white space at the top for display, the page number is centered at the bottom of the page or omitted. It is *always* omitted, however, on the title page and on blank pages used for part divisions.

The page number may stand alone — no period after it, no dashes or parentheses around it.

(4) *For Other Report Types.* Bulletins, since they generally follow a similar format, are numbered in the same way as the memorandum report. Pamphlets, booklets and other similar reports follow the numbering plan of short, formal reports, except that they often do not contain prefatory material, so that only Arabic numbers are used.

PAPER

Standard-size typing paper, 8½″ by 11″, is used for most reports. Some business files are designed, however, for the 8½″ by 13″ size, and accordingly companies sometimes have their reports done on the legal-size paper.

A good-quality white bond paper that will stand handling and neat erasures should be used. Onion skin or lighter weight paper may be used for carbon copies; but when the copies are to be circulated and used, it is better for them to be on the same quality of paper as the original. The thin paper is better used for only routine filing record purposes.

QUOTATIONS

Quotations of fewer than four lines are incorporated in the report text and enclosed in double quotation marks. When they consist of four or more lines, they are indented from both margins and single spaced; no quotation marks are used. When several paragraphs are quoted, double spacing is used between paragraphs.

Quotations used in footnotes are likewise set off from the text of the note, but they are enclosed in quotation marks.

When portions of a quotation are omitted, ellipses (. . .) should be used to designate the omission. If a complete paragraph of prose or a full line of poetry is omitted a row of dots (. . . . . .) is typed all the way across the quotation.

Direct quotations should always be reproduced exactly — content, capitalization, spelling and punctuation the same as in the original material. The Latin *sic,* enclosed in brackets, may be interpolated within the body of the direct quotation to indicate that the error quoted is a part of the quoted material, not the author's own. The report writer's remarks may also be interpolated within the body of the direct quotation and set off by brackets. Parentheses are not used in either case.

To set off a quotation within a quotation, single quotation marks should be used.

In most cases frequent and long quotations are not justified in reports. In some instances they may be placed in a footnote or in the appendix. Many times it is preferable to summarize or paraphrase instead of quoting directly. Quoting should be done with discretion – where the statement is relatively concise and particularly apt, or where the idea is not a generally accepted fact.

REPRODUCTION

Except for certain confidential reports, it is advisable always to make a minimum of three to five copies of a report. The number of copies necessary for adequate use of the report and the cost of reproduction determine the method of duplication to be followed.

When ten or fewer copies are desired, carbon copies are typed. Making ten copies will necessitate the use of onion skin paper for the copies and bond paper for the original. Even then two typings may be needed for clear results. Of course, for only two or three copies bond paper may be used entirely. A black ribbon and black carbon are usually used for the clearest possible type.

For ten to a hundred copies, a ditto or mimeograph machine is used. The kind of paper most appropriate to the method of duplication must be selected. A master copy is typed for the ditto machine and a stencil for the mimeograph.

When a hundred or more copies are desirable the multilith is often used. Multilith plates (duplimats) are typed and copies run off on the multilith machine. The plates are more expensive than the stencils used in mimeographing.

If several hundred copies are to be distributed, the report would warrant printing. Typed carbon copies on bond paper are prepared for the printer and instructions set up for printing.

SPACING

Reports may be single or double spaced, depending upon the length and type of report and its purpose or use.

(*1*) Reports that consist of fewer than three pages are usually single spaced; those longer are double spaced.
(*2*) Letter reports, memoranda and bulletins are generally single spaced.
(*3*) Routine, intra-office reports are usually single spaced.
(*4*) Complete, formal reports are double spaced.

Since double spacing is easier to read, the longer the report the more necessary it is to consider the reader's time and effort in reading the report.

In single-spaced reports double spacing is used between paragraphs. In double-spaced reports the beginning of each paragraph is indented five to ten spaces, and double spacing is used between paragraphs. Occasionally the paragraphs are blocked and triple spacing used between paragraphs.

SUBJECT HEADINGS

The text material of a report is divided into sections and subsections.

Subject headings are used to indicate the content of the material of each section and the degree of relationship between the different sections. Headings should be descriptive in content and parallel in construction. A detailed table of contents is composed of the subject headings throughout the report. A general table of contents lists only the major headings. The following instructions on typing and spacing different degrees of subject headings are often followed:

FIRST-DEGREE HEADING

When it is necessary to have headings of five different degrees of importance, one generally accepted sequence is shown here. Note that the main heading above is centered and that it is written all in caps. It may be underscored or not.

Second-Degree Heading

The second degree heading is written in caps and lower case. It is underscored only if the main heading has been.

Third-Degree Heading

The text starts two spaces below this heading, at a standard identation. Note that there are three spaces between this heading and the last line of the preceding text.

Fourth-Degree Heading. This heading is followed by a period, dash or by a colon. The text begins on the same line as the heading.

The Fifth-Degree Heading is made by underscoring the first word or words of the sentence. This means arranging the sentence so that the key word or words are at the sentence beginning. Note that each of the key words underlined starts with a capital letter.

When only one degree of subordination is needed a center heading and a heading beginning flush with the margin – or a center heading and a heading beginning at the margin indentation – are commonly used. The subject headings may be numbered and lettered as in outlining, or the numbers and letters may be omitted. Subject headings may be underscored as suggested here or left free of underscoring, or a combination of the two may be worked out, as long as consistency is observed throughout the report.

A great deal of flexibility in the selection and use of subject headings is often desirable. The following types of headings,* suitable for typewritten reports, allow flexibility and yet permit a certain amount of standardization for consistency:

A. Centered on type page
   1. CAPITALS, CENTERED AND UNDERLINED
   2. CAPITALS, CENTERED AND NOT UNDERLINED
   3. Capitals and Lower Case, Centered and Underlined
   4. Capitals and Lower Case, Centered and Not Underlined

B. Side, flush with left edge of type page
   5. CAPITALS, SIDE HEAD AND UNDERLINED
   6. CAPITALS, SIDE HEAD AND NOT UNDERLINED
   7. Capitals and Lower Case, Side Head and Underlined
   8. Capitals and Lower Case, Side Head and Not Underlined
   9. Lower case, side head and underlined

C. Paragraph, or run-in on first line of paragraph
   10. CAPITALS, PARAGRAPH HEAD AND UNDERLINED
   11. Capitals and Lower Case, Paragraph Head and Underlined
   12. Lower case, paragraph head and underlined

* Frank Kerekes and Robley Winfrey, *Report Preparation,* The Iowa State College Press, Ames, Iowa, 1951, p. 87.

An important factor to consider in the selection of a heading schedule is the number of separate headings needed to indicate the relationship of the various sections. One of the following schedules usually will be found satisfactory:

Number of Different Types of Heads Needed	HEAD SCHEDULE (Numbers refer to foregoing list.)		
	First Choice	*Second Choice*	*Third Choice*
2	2, 6	2, 8	2, 7, or 1, 6
3	2, 6, 11	2, 7, 11	1, 6, 11
4	2, 4, 6, 11	2, 6, 7, 11	1, 3, 7, 11
5	2, 4, 6, 7, 11	2, 4, 6, 8, 11	1, 3, 5, 7, 11
6	2, 4, 6, 7, 10, 12	2, 4, 6, 8, 10, 12	1, 3, 5, 7, 10, 12

SYLLABICATION

To divide words at the ends of lines in order to keep the right margin as even as possible, and thus to produce a neatly typed page, the following suggestions should be helpful:

(*1*) Divide words only according to their syllabic division.
(*2*) Divide hyphenated words at the hyphen and nowhere else.
(*3*) Do not divide words of one syllable.
(*4*) Do not divide words of only four or five letters: *e. g., many.*
(*5*) Keep prefixes and suffixes intact, *e.g.: pre-, con-, ex-, -cial, -sion* and *-tion.*
(*6*) Avoid divisions leaving one letter of the word to a line: *e.g., o-ver, a-mong.*
(*7*) Avoid divisions leaving syllables of two letters, such as, *-ed, -en, -ly, etc.*
(*8*) Do not divide the last word in a paragraph or on a page.
(*9*) Do not divide initials, names of persons, numbers, abbreviations and titles.
(*10*) When in doubt, always consult the dictionary.

UNDERLINING

There are two major uses of underlining in reports.

(*1*) Titles and words that are usually printed in italics are underlined in typed reports:

Titles of books, works of art, music
Titles of periodicals
Footnote reference abbreviations
Foreign words and phrases

(2) Material may be underlined for emphasis in the text of the report:

Subject headings and subheads
Words and phrases containing important facts or figures

A single, solid line may be used in underlining or a broken line under each individual word:

Kate L. Turabian, A Manual for Writers of Dissertations

Or:

Kate L. Turabian, A Manual for Writers of Dissertations

Index